Canadian
Business English

Third Edition

Canadian
Business English

Mary Ellen Guffey
Los Angeles Pierce College

Patricia Burke
Humber College

THOMSON

NELSON

Australia   Canada   Mexico   Singapore   Spain   United Kingdom   United States

THOMSON

NELSON

Canadian Business English
Third Edition
By Mary Ellen Guffey and Patricia Burke

Editorial Director and Publisher:
Evelyn Veitch

Acquisitions Editor:
Anne Williams

Marketing Manager:
Cara Yarzab

Developmental Editor:
Rebecca Rea

Production Editor:
Julie van Veen

Copy Editor/Proofreader:
Valerie Adams

Production Coordinator:
Hedy Sellers

Interior Design Modifications:
Katherine Strain

Creative Director:
Angela Cluer

Cover Image:
New Division/MeikleJohn/FPG/
Getty Images

Cover Design:
Katherine Strain

Compositor:
Nelson Gonzalez

Printer:
Webcom

National Library of Canada Cataloguing in Publication Data

Guffey, Mary Ellen
   Canadian business English / Mary Ellen Guffey, Patricia Burke. — 3rd ed.

Includes index.

ISBN 0-17-616944-X

1. English language—Business English. I. Burke, Patricia, 1942– II. Title.

PE1115.G83 2002   808'.066651
C2002-902699-7

Contents

Preface

Canadian Business English, Third Edition, is the Canadian version of Mary Ellen Guffey's well-known and successful *Business English* text. The bold and innovative approach taken by Dr. Guffey in *Business English* continues to appeal to instructors and students in the United States and Canada. For over a decade, *Canadian Business English* has helped thousands of Canadian students improve their language skills. This edition of *Canadian Business English* continues to serve the Canadian student in reaching excellence in language skills and incorporates changes that more accurately reflect the Canadian landscape and the new technologies and challenges facing students in the business community.

Revisions That Expand Job Skills

Although *Canadian Business English,* Third Edition, largely retains the content and sequencing of previous editions, it puts new emphasis on employment skills such as editing, proofreading, and writing skills. We also examined every sentence to be sure that we demonstrate awareness of the massive effects of technology in the field of business communication. Here are some of the most significant changes in the third edition.

Writer's Workshops
To give students more practice in developing work-related writing skills, we've added six workshops that feature composition tips and techniques. These workshops begin with proofreading skills and progress through the writing of sentences, paragraphs, e-mail messages, memos, letters, and short reports. Frequent skill checks allow students to apply writing principles immediately. And each workshop presents an optional writing assignment. Instructors have been asking how to combine grammar and writing, and now it's possible. Our appendices have been reduced as material once covered in several appendices is covered within the Writer's Workshops.

Editor's Challenge Feature
A cumulative editing exercise in every chapter enables students to continuously review grammar and punctuation guidelines. Documents to be edited include e-mail messages, memos, letters, and short reports. These realistic documents familiarize students with the forms of business writing they are likely to see on the job.

Learning Web Ways
New to this edition are short exercises that help students improve their Internet skills. Students will learn about browsers, URLs, hotlinks, and many exciting tips for using the Web effectively.

Hotlinks
Also new to this edition are references to World Wide Web sites of interest to business English students. These "hotlinks" show students that the Internet can be useful for their personal and professional benefit.

Tried and True Textbook Features

Many unique features ensure that students will be successful with *Canadian Business English* in the classroom.

Pretest

Preceding Chapter 1 is a pretest designed to help students assess their business English strengths and weaknesses. Answer keys for this test and for all chapter exercises are provided in the Instructor's Manual.

Three-Level Approach

Beginning with Chapter 4, the language concepts appear in levels. These levels progress from fundamental frequently used concepts in Level I to more complex concepts in Level III. Each level has its own trial exercises as well as numerous relevant student reinforcement drills.

The three-level approach has three distinct advantages. First, the overall organization of the complex subject of English is immediately recognizable. Second, the three-level approach facilitates comprehension and promotes student confidence by providing small, easily mastered learning segments. Third, this strategy provides convenient blocks of material that allow individual instructors to tailor the content of the course to fit student abilities, institutional goals, and time constraints.

Hotline Queries

One of the most popular features of *Canadian Business English* has been its questions and answers from grammar hotline services. These authentic questions—and the answers to them—illustrate everyday communication problems encountered in the work world. In easy-to-read question-and-answer format, important distinctions in English grammar, usage, style, and vocabulary are explained.

Pretests and Posttests

Each chapter includes a brief pretest to preview concepts and to pique the interest of students. Chapters also provide a posttest to enable students to evaluate their achievement.

Self-Check Exercises and Unit Reviews

The first student exercise in each level of each chapter is self-checked. Students are thereby able to determine immediately whether they comprehend the concepts just presented. At the end of each unit, a self-checked review exercise enables students to test their mastery of the unit.

Learning Objectives

Concisely stated learning objectives introduce each chapter. These overtly stated goals summarize the concepts to be presented and facilitate learning by stimulating a student mind-set favourable to the learning process.

Spelling and Vocabulary

For students who desire them and for instructors who can find time to include them, optional spelling and vocabulary development materials are provided in separate appendices.

Writing Component

Sentence-writing exercises conclude each chapter. These skill-building opportunities encourage students to apply chapter principles in forming complete sentences. Optional editing and composition unit tests are available in the Instructor's Manual, which also includes ideas for incorporating this writing program in the business English course.

Self-Help Exercises

Because business English students need many opportunities to try out their learning, they appreciate additional self-paced exercises. Supplementary exercises for all levels of all chapters and their answers are provided in the back of the text. These self-checked exercises may be reproduced and distributed for self-paced reinforcement.

Marginal Annotations

The interesting marginal annotations continue to provide stimulus to our readers.

Study Tip

Memory devices and learning suggestions appear as study tips. They help you understand and retain the many language principles you will be reviewing.

Career Tip

These tips suggest applications and practical career advice that relate language concepts you are learning to your needs on the job.

Spot the Blooper

To provide humorous relief from the sometimes heavy load of grammar and mechanics, these bloopers demonstrate common language errors.

Did You Know?

These inquisitive tidbits relate interesting trivia to *Canadian Business English* concepts.

Notable Quotable

Thought-provoking quotations provide moments of reflection as well as enhance the total learning experience.

Hot Link

New! Recommended Web sites help you learn more about the chapter.

Unparalleled Supplements and Instructor Support

Canadian Business English includes a number of supplements to help students learn and instructors teach. Nelson provides the best support for business communication in Canada.

Web site for Students & Instructors. http://www.businessenglish3e.nelson.com
New to this edition is a Web site that provides chapter-specific quizzes for student review. Additional resources for students include: Editor's Challenges, Web Page Creation Tutorials, Skill Builders, Media and Study Resources, Career Tips, and

Grammar Review modules. A password-protected Instructor's Site includes download-able Microsoft® PowerPoint® slides and the Instructor's Manual. Instructors should request a password from their local sales representative.

Instructor's Manual. (017622405X). Written by the authors, this valuable resource includes solutions, discussion of the Writer's Workshop features, and other features to assist instructors in making the most of their classroom time.

Test Bank. (0176224068). The Test Bank provides Unit Tests and Chapter Tests. Each Chapter Test includes at least fifty objective questions and an answer key.

Computerized Test Bank. (0176224076). The Computerized Test Bank provides the same questions and answers as the paper-based test bank, but within an easy-to-use test creation program.

Microsoft® PowerPoint® Slides. (0176224084). The PowerPoint® slides are new to this edition. They feature important concepts in the text and are provided for class-room use.

Westwords Web site. http://www.westwords.com/instructor.html Dr. Mary Ellen Guffey maintains her own Web site for instructors of *Business English* and *Business Communication*. Instructors can sign up for the monthly Guffey Report to be delivered electronically at this Web site.

Writer's Online Workshop, 2e, (WOW). (0-324-01385-X). Available for sale with the text, this Internet-based program is designed to help users accurately assess their current skill level and refine their understanding of *Business English* and *Business Communication*. Users start by taking a self-assessment to aid in diagnosing their current skills. The results direct users to specific lessons for further review. Ask your Nelson representative for more details or a demonstration.

Acknowledgments

During my twenty-five years of teaching English at Humber College, colleagues and students have given me the experience necessary to appreciate and adapt Mary Ellen Guffey's excellent text. Many thanks go to all those colleagues and students.

Special thanks go again to two friends who are also colleagues at Humber – Joan Pilz and Janice Cermak – for their advice and encouragement during the preparation of this edition of *Canadian Business English*. I am also indebted to a newer colleague, Vaska Tumir, for her invaluable work on the new Hotlink and Learning Web Ways sections of the text. Numerous people at Nelson have worked on the Canadian editions of this text, and working with them has always been a pleasure. This time Rebecca Rea, Natalie Barrington, Valerie Adams, and Julie van Veen in particular should be acknowledged for being helpful, considerate, and patient.

Thanks must also go to the reviewers for their thoughtful comments and suggestions: Shirley Guthrie, Camosun College; Carol Evans, Saskatchewan Institute of Applied Science and Technology; Gloria Millsap, Northern Lights College; Joanne Roberston, Durham College; Madeleine J. Whitfield, Algonquin College; Ausra M. Karka, Humber College; Alan Ruthowski, Northern Alberta Institute of Technology; Ruth Johnson, Fanshawe College; Leslie Manion, Algonquin College; Patricia Pearson, College of the Rockies; Gloria Cott, Northern Alberta Institute of Technology; and Fred Tan, Southern Alberta Institute of Technology.

Patricia Burke

PRETEST

In the following sentences, errors in grammar, punctuation, capitalization, or number expression may appear. For each sentence underline any inappropriate form(s). Then write a corrected form in the space provided. *Clue:* one sentence at each level is correct.

Example: The inheritance will be given to my brother and <u>myself</u>
on our twenty-first birthdays.

me _____

LEVEL I

1. Mr. Kubryn paid into the system for thirty years, then he retired and began to draw benefits.

_____

2. The seminar in Saskatoon, Saskatchewan in the spring sounds as if it will be worthwhile.

_____

3. The announcement from our Human Resources Department surprised the secretaries as much as I.

_____

4. Jim and I certainly appreciate you answering the telephone when he and I are away from the office.

_____

5. A set of guidelines were developed for him and the others.

_____

6. Every classified employee, as well as every management and certified employee, is eligible for sales discounts.

_____

7. For you Mrs. Alison, we have a one-year subscription to your favourite magazine.

_____

8. Under the circumstances, we can give you only 90 days time in which to sell the house and its contents.

_____

9. We normally hire only experienced operators; but on occasion we consider well-trained individuals who lack experience.

_____

10. During the fall Lisa took courses in history, french, and accounting.

_____

11. All our customers names and addresses have been transferred to our computer database.

12. Either Mr. Harris or his assistant will be working at the shop on the next two Sunday's.

13. Of the 500 letters mailed, Ellen Turner's secretary reported that only five were returned.

14. If you want a three-week vacation, you must speak to the Manager immediately.

15. The warehouse has been moved from Wellington Street to Seneca Street.

16. Chapter 15 which is entitled "Credit Buying," is one of the best chapters in *Today's Consumer*.

17. Before her trip to the East last summer, my mother purchased a Kodak Camera.

18. We need at least one hundred eighty-cent postage stamps.

19. Your account is now 90 days overdue, therefore, we are submitting it to an agency for collection.

20. I feel badly about your missing the deadline, but the application has been lying on your desk for fifteen days.

21. The award will be made to whomever has the best record.

22. All letter styles must comply to those shown in the company style manual.

23. Iris Food Products is larger than any food processing plant on the West Coast.

24. The number of employees interested in attending the seminar are surprising.

25. The school's alumni are certainly different than its currently enrolled students.

26. She is one of those efficient, competent managers who is able to give sincere praise for work done well.

27. Because she looks like her sister, Mary is often taken to be her.

28. If I was him, I would call the Harrises' lawyer at once.

29. Three employees were given merit raises, namely, Carol Chang, Tom Nelson, and Toni Simpson.

30. Surely it was he who left the package on the boss's desk.

Laying a Foundation

Reference Skills

OBJECTIVES   When you have completed the materials in this chapter, you will be able to do the following:

- *Describe three types of dictionaries.*

- *Use a dictionary confidently to determine spelling, meaning, pronunciation, syllabication, accent, word usage, and word history.*

- *Select a dictionary to suit your needs.*

- *Anticipate what information is included in dictionaries and what information is not.*

- *Understand the value of reference manuals.*

- *Use an electronic dictionary with confidence.*

PRETEST

Each chapter begins with a brief pretest. Answer the questions in the pretest to assess your prior knowledge of the chapter content and also to give yourself a preview of what you will learn. Compare your answers with those at the bottom of the page. When you complete the chapter, take the posttest to measure your improvement.

Write *T* (true) or *F* (false) after the following statements.

1. College students need a current unabridged dictionary for daily use.   _____

2. Dictionary guide words help readers pronounce words correctly.   _____

3. The usage label *archaic* means that a word is very old.   _____

4. All dictionaries present word definitions in the same order.   _____

5. A reader should not expect to find the spelling of the plural form of *branch* in most dictionaries.   _____

1. F 2. F 3. T 4. F 5. T

This course in business English is the study of language fundamentals. These basics include grammar, usage, punctuation, capitalization, and number style. Because business people must express their ideas clearly and correctly, such language basics are critical. In today's workplace, you can expect to be doing more communicating than ever before. You will be participating in meetings, writing reports, and sending many e-mail messages. Suddenly, business English skills are becoming very important. Business people who never expected to be doing much writing on the job are finding that the Internet is forcing everyone to exchange written messages. As a result, business people are increasingly aware of their communication skills. Misspelled words, incorrect grammar, sloppy punctuation—all these faults stand out glaringly when printed. Not only are people writing more, but their messages are travelling farther and being seen by larger audiences than ever before.

Because of the growing emphasis on exchanging information, business English is increasingly relevant. As a business person, you will want to feel confident about your writing skills. This textbook and this course can help you sharpen your skills and greatly increase the confidence you have in expressing your ideas. Improving your communication skills is the first step toward success in your education, your career, and your life.

When Jennifer S. enrolled in business English, she did not plan to become an expert in the subject. When she finished the course, she didn't think of herself as an expert—although she had done well enough in the class. However, when she started to work, she discovered that many of her fellow workers considered her an English expert. Most of them had never had any specific training in grammar—or they had studied it long ago, and their skills were very rusty. Jennifer found that even her boss asked her questions like "What are they doing now about letter salutations?" or "Where do you think we should put that apostrophe?" Everyone seemed to think that because she had just finished school, she would know all the answers. Jennifer didn't know all the answers, but she knew where to find them.

One of the goals of your education is to know where to find the answers, as well as how to interpret the information you find. Experts do not know *all* the answers. Lawyers refer to casebooks. Doctors consult their medical libraries. And you, a student of the language, must develop skill and confidence in using reference materials. You will become a business English expert not only by learning from this textbook but also by learning where to find additional information when you need it.

Using references should become second nature to you. You'll use dictionaries and on-line resources to verify word spellings and meanings, punctuation style, and usage. You can find information quickly and efficiently by having your own personal library of reference materials. At the minimum a current desk or college dictionary and a good reference manual are needed. Another helpful reference book is a thesaurus, which is a collection of *synonyms* (words with similar meanings) and *antonyms* (words with opposite meanings). Many helpful resources are now available digitally, whether on-line or in a software program such as MS Word.

▶ Print Dictionaries

Business people today make use of both print dictionaries and electronic dictionaries. First, you will learn about print dictionaries, including how to select one and how to use it. Then, you will learn about using an electronic dictionary, such as the one that comes with your word processing software.

Types

Dictionaries can be grouped into three categories: pocket, desk (college-level), and unabridged. In choosing one for yourself, consider your needs. A *pocket* dictionary is handy and efficient. However, since it usually has no more than 75,000 entries, it may prove inadequate for college reference homework.

A *desk* or *college-level* dictionary may contain as many as 200,000 entries plus extra features. For college work you should own a current desk dictionary. The following list shows some of the best-known desk dictionaries, including three Canadian dictionaries. Spelling, definitions, and usage in this textbook are based on *The Canadian Oxford Dictionary* (1998).

Did You Know?
The English language has about three times as many words as any other language on earth. English is estimated to include at least 450,000 words. German has 185,000, Russian 130,000, and French 100,000.

Name	Approximate Number of Definitions
Gage Canadian Dictionary	140,000
ITP Nelson Canadian Dictionary	200,000
Merriam-Webster's Collegiate Dictionary	200,000
The Canadian Oxford Dictionary	200,000
The Concise Oxford Dictionary	140,000

An *unabridged* dictionary is a complete dictionary. (Abridged dictionaries, such as pocket and desk dictionaries, are shortened or condensed.) Because unabridged dictionaries contain nearly all English words, they are large, heavy volumes. Schools, libraries, newspapers, and business offices that are concerned with editing or publishing use unabridged dictionaries. One of the best-known unabridged dictionaries is *Merriam-Webster's New International Dictionary*, which has over 450,000 entries. Another famous unabridged dictionary is the *Oxford English Dictionary*. This 20-volume set shows the historical development of all English words; it is often used by professional writers, scholars of the language, and academics. CD-ROM versions are now available for easy computer searching.

Study Tip
To *abridge* means to "shorten," as a bridge shortens the distance between two points. An "unabridged" book has not been shortened.

Copyright Date

If the copyright date of your current dictionary shows that the dictionary was published ten or more years ago, consider investing in a more recent edition. English is a responsive, dynamic language that admits new words and recognizes changes in meanings, spellings, and usage of familiar words. These changes are reflected in an up-to-date dictionary.

Features

In selecting a dictionary, check the features it offers in addition to its word definitions. Many editions contain biographical and geographical data, abbreviations, standard measurements, signs, symbols, foreign words and phrases, lists of colleges and universities, given names, and information about the language. Non-native users of English will find especially helpful features in dictionaries such as the *Oxford Advanced Learner's Dictionary*.

Dictionary Entry

The following example from *The Canadian Oxford Dictionary** illustrates some of the points we will discuss here to help you use your dictionary more effectively.

---

* From *The Canadian Oxford Dictionary* edited by Katherine Barber. Copyright © Oxford University Press Canada 1998. Reprinted by permission of Oxford University Press Canada.

Dictionary Use

Introduction. Before using your dictionary, familiarize yourself with the instructions located in the pages just before the beginning of the vocabulary entries. Pay particular attention to the order of definitions. Some dictionaries show the most common definitions first. Other dictionaries develop meanings historically; that is, the first known meaning of the word is shown first.

Guide Words. In boldface type at the top of each dictionary page are two words that indicate the first and last entries on the page. When searching for a word, look *only* at these guide words until you locate the desired page.

Pronunciation. Special symbols (diacritical marks) are used to help you pronounce words correctly. A detailed explanation of pronunciation symbols is found in the front of a dictionary; a summary of these symbols may appear at the bottom of each set of pages. If two pronunciations are possible, the preferred one is usually shown first.

Accent. Many dictionaries show accents with a raised stress mark preceding the accented syllable, as shown for the syllable *kwɒl* in our example. Other dictionaries use a raised stress mark immediately *following* the accented syllable (*kwɒl'ə fai*). Secondary stress may be shown with a lowered stress mark, as illustrated for the syllable *fai* in our example, or it may be shown with a stress mark in lighter print (*kwɒl'ə fai'*).

Etymology. College-level dictionaries provide in square brackets [ ] or parentheses ( ) the brief history or etymology of the word. For example, the word *qualify* originated in Latin. Keys to etymological abbreviations may be found in the introductory notes in your dictionary. Do not confuse the etymological definition shown in brackets with the actual word definition(s).

Part of Speech. Following the phonetic pronunciation of an entry word is an italicized or boldfaced label indicating what part of speech the entry word represents. The most common labels are the following (sometimes followed by periods):

Notable Quotable

"Language is the dress of thought. Every time you talk, your mind is on parade."
—Samuel Johnson, creator of the first English dictionary

Career Tip

Don't be ashamed to use a dictionary on the job. Such use signifies diligence and eagerness to improve, qualities that employers seek.

Hotlink

You can explore some curious etymologies in The Word Lady's Fascinating Word Histories, a feature on the Canadian Oxford Dictionary Web site **<http://www.oup.com/ca/genref/dictionaries/word/>**.

adj	(adjective)	*prep*	(preposition)
adv	(adverb)	*pron*	(pronoun)
conj	(conjunction)	*v* or *vb*	(verb)
interj	(interjection)	*vt* or *tr. v.*	(transitive verb)
n	(noun)	*vi* or *int. v.*	(intransitive verb)

Spelling, pronunciation, and meaning may differ for a given word when that word functions as different parts of speech. Therefore, check its grammatical label carefully. If the parts of speech seem foreign to you at this time, do not despair. Chapter 2 and successive chapters will help you learn more about the parts of speech.

Labels. Not all words listed in dictionaries are appropriate for use in business or other writing. Usage or restrictive labels advise readers about the use of certain words. In the dictionary entry for *qualify*, one meaning is labelled *Grammar*, indicating that this meaning is restricted to a specific context. The following list defines some example usage labels. See the guide to your dictionary for more details.

Label	**Example**
archaic: from a previous period, now seldom used	*quittance* (meaning *release*)
dialect, Brit., US, Scot, Irish, etc.: used in certain regions	*gossoon* (Irish for *boy*)
informal or *colloquial:* used in casual writing or conversation	*hidey-hole* (meaning *hiding place*)
offensive: insulting, whether intentionally or not	*mongolism* (meaning *Down's syndrome*)
slang: most informal but may be used sparingly for effect, mainly in speech	*boonies* (meaning *rural area*)

If no usage label appears, a word is considered standard; that is, it is acceptable for all uses. However, it should be noted that many lexicographers, those who make dictionaries, have substantially reduced the number of usage labels in current editions.

Inflected Forms. When nouns, verbs, adverbs, or adjectives change form grammatically, they are said to be *inflected*, as when *child* becomes *children*. Because of limited space, dictionaries usually show only irregular inflected forms. Thus, nouns with irregular or unusual plurals (*wife, wives*) will be shown. Verbs with irregular tenses or difficult spelling (*gratified, gratifying*) will be shown. Adverbs or adjectives with irregular comparatives or superlatives (*good, better, best*) will also be shown. But regular noun plurals, verb tenses, and comparatives generally will *not* be shown in dictionaries. Succeeding chapters will elucidate regular and irregular parts of speech.

Syllabication. Most dictionaries show syllable breaks with a centred dot (*or·gan·ize*, for example). Be careful to interpret such a dot correctly when looking up a compound word. If a compound word is shown with a centred dot, it is one word, as in *work·out* (workout). If a compound word is shown with a hyphen, it is a hyphenated compound, as in *well-meaning*. If two words appear without a centred dot or a hyphen, they should be written separately, as in the verb *work up*. If you find no entry for a word or phrase in a current college-level dictionary, you may usually assume that the words are written separately.

Synonyms and Antonyms. *Synonyms,* words having similar meanings, are often provided after word definitions. For example, a synonym for *elucidate* is *explain*. Synonyms are helpful as word substitutes. *Antonyms,* words having opposite meanings, appear less frequently in dictionaries; when included, they usually follow synonyms. One antonym for *elucidate* is *confuse*. The best place to find synonyms and antonyms is a thesaurus.

Spot the Blooper

In a Chinese fortune cookie: "You will gain admiration from your pears."

Career Tip

Business people are judged by the words they use. Knowing the part of speech for a word helps you use it correctly. For example, if you discover that a word is a verb, you won't try to use it to describe a noun.

Hotlink

Oxford English
Dictionaries
**<http://www.askoxford.
com/>** maintains an
entertaining Web site with
Better Writing Tip of the
Week, Word of the Week,
and Question & Answer
features.

Plugging in to Electronic and On-line Dictionaries

An increasing number of electronic resources are available both on the Internet and on CD-ROMs. As shown in Figure 1.1, various kinds of dictionaries can be used at Web sites. By accessing Merriam-Webster Online, for example, you can search for word definitions at no cost. The site for OneLook Dictionaries provides over 700 different dictionaries in various fields. And all of these are searchable electronically. This means you can find words quickly and easily. You can also look for unusual words in a wide range of areas without owning a specialized dictionary and without travelling to a library. Electronic dictionaries are especially useful because, unlike print dictionaries, they can be updated immediately when new words enter the language.

Some people, however, don't want to be bothered with firing up a computer and using a Web browser to access on-line dictionaries. But they do want access to a large database of words, and they prefer the ease of electronic searching. For these people, a CD-ROM dictionary, such as the Microsoft Encarta World English Dictionary or the Random House Compact Unabridged Dictionary, is the answer. By the way, many new electronic dictionaries not only provide definitions but also offer *pronunciations*. Of course, your computer must be equipped with a sound card.

Using Electronic Dictionary Programs

Most high-end word processing programs today come with a dictionary/thesaurus feature that helps you locate misspelled words as well as search for synonyms and antonyms.

Figure 1.1
Notable Electronic and On-Line Dictionaries

- **Merriam-Webster Online <http://www.m-w.com>.** Indicates the pronunciations, etymologies, and authoritative definitions of a vast number of words. Site also provides essays on the history of English and the processes involved in the making of dictionaries. Word of the Day feature defines an infrequently used word.

- **OneLook Dictionaries <http://www.onelook.com>.** Features an index of over 428,000 words contained in more than 746 different dictionaries. Site accesses computer/Internet, science, medical, technological, business, sports, religion, and general dictionaries.

- **Management and Technology Dictionary <http://www.euro.net/innovation/Management_Base/Mantec. Dictionary.html>.** Claims to be the largest Internet dictionary on management and technology.

- **Online Dictionary of Social Sciences <http://datadump.icaap.org/cgi-bin/glossary/SocialDict/>.** Produced by Athabasca University. Covers the disciplines of sociology, criminology, political science, and women's studies. The entries are illustrated with Canadian examples.

- **Microsoft Encarta World English Dictionary (CD-ROM).** Features more than 3 million words with contributions from 250 lexicographers working in ten countries. Purports to be the world's first English dictionary. Also available in print version that is updated on the Web.

- **Random House Compact Unabridged Dictionary (CD-ROM).** Comprehensive resource with definitions for over 315,000 entries. Includes over 2,000 line drawings and offers spoken pronunciation of 120,000 words.

- **Oxford English Dictionary, 2nd ed. (CD-ROM).** Claims to be the most authoritative English dictionary. Traces use of each word through the centuries. Provides easy access to more than 2.5 million illustrative quotations. Continually updated Web version available by subscription **<www.oed.com>.**

For links to dozens of on-line dictionaries and other electronic reference tools, visit the Guffey Web site **<http://meguffey.com/reftools.html>** and this text's Web site **<http://www.businessenglish3e.nelson.com>** (click on the Study Resources link).

Locating Misspelled Words. An electronic dictionary (also called a *spell checker*) compares your typed words with those in the computer's memory. MS Word uses a wavy red line to underline misspelled words caught "on the fly" as you key. If you immediately recognize the error, you can quickly key in the correction. If you see the red wavy line and don't know what's wrong, you can click *Tools* and *Spelling and Grammar*. This opens a dialogue box. The box generally shows a variety of options to solve your spelling problem. If one of the suggested spellings appears helpful, you can click it and the misspelled word is replaced. If none of the suggestions is useful, you can type in the correct version in the "Not in Dictionary" box.

Although some writers dismiss dictionary spell checkers as an annoyance, most of us are only too happy to have our typos and misspelled words detected. The real problem is that spell checkers can't always distinguish between similar words, such as *too* and *two* and many other confusions. That's why you're wise to print out every message and proofread it word by word.

Searching for Synonyms and Antonyms. Electronic dictionary programs can also help you find alternative word choices. Let's say you are writing a message and find yourself repeating the same word. With MS Word you can highlight the overused word and click on *Tools, Language,* and *Thesaurus*. A number of synonyms appear in a dialogue box. If none of the suggested words seems right, you can change the search term by using a closely related word from the *Replace with Synonym* column. From the new *Meanings* list, you can also change the word or phrase to help you find the most precise word for your meaning.

You can use an electronic thesaurus feature to look up words and phrases even if you haven't selected any words in your document. Just type in the word and click the *Tools, Language,* and *Thesaurus* options. A good on-line thesaurus can be a terrific aid to writers who want to increase their vocabularies and are seeking precise language.

▶ Reference Manuals

Reference Manual Versus Dictionary

In addition to one or more dictionaries, all writers and office workers should have a good reference manual or handbook readily available.* In it you can find helpful information not available in dictionaries. Most reference manuals provide information such as the following.

1. Punctuation. Detailed explanations of punctuation rules are presented logically. A well-written manual will also provide ample illustrations of punctuation usage so that the reader can readily find solutions to punctuation dilemmas.

2. Hyphenation. Most dictionaries provide syllable breaks. Words cannot, however, be divided at all syllable breaks. A reference manual will supply rules for, and examples of, word division. Moreover, a good reference manual will explain when compound adjectives should be hyphenated.

3. Capitalization. Complete rules with precise examples illustrating capitalization style will be shown.

---

* For example, William A. Sabin et al., The Gregg Reference Manual, *Sixth Canadian Edition (Toronto: McGraw-Hill Ryerson, 2003).*

Hotlink

Statistics Canada offers an on-line thesaurus for economic terms and keywords. You can consult it at **<http://www.statcan.ca/english/thesaurus>**.

Hotlink

The World Wide Web is the home of many reference tools, including various guides to grammar and usage. The Reference Desk **<http://www.refdesk.com/factdict.html>** has a compilation of links you may find useful in college and beyond.

Notable Quotable

"Luck is a matter of preparation meeting opportunity."
—Oprah Winfrey

4. Numbers. Deciding whether to write a number as a figure or as a word can be very confusing. A reference manual will provide both instruction and numerous examples illustrating number and word styles.

Other topics covered in reference manuals are confusing words (such as *effect* and *affect*), abbreviations, contractions, literary and artistic titles, forms of address, and letter and report formats. In addition, some manuals contain sections devoted to English grammar, office procedures, and computers.

Reference Manual Versus Textbook

You may be wondering how a reference manual differs from a business English textbook such as the one you are now reading. Although their content is similar, the primary difference is one of purpose. A textbook is developed *pedagogically* (that is, for teaching) so that the student understands and learns concepts. A reference manual is organized *functionally* so that the reader finds accurate information efficiently. A well-written reference manual is complete, coherent, and concise.

Most of the language and style questions that perplex business people and students could be answered quickly by a trained person using a reliable dictionary and a well-written reference manual.

Thesaurus

A thesaurus can be useful when you are composing your own documents. In book form or in a word processing program, a thesaurus can help you avoid overrepetition of vocabulary items by listing related words that could be used as substitutes. It can also help you remember a word that may have slipped your mind. If you do use a thesaurus, be careful not to use an unfamiliar synonym or antonym unless your dictionary indicates that the word is appropriate for your sentence.

Now complete the reinforcement exercises on the following pages.

CHAPTER 1   Reinforcement Exercises

Note: At the beginning of every set of reinforcement exercises, a self-check exercise is provided so that you will know immediately if you understand the concepts presented in the chapter. Do not look at the answers until you have completed the exercise. Then compare your responses with the answers shown at the bottom of the page. If you have more than three incorrect responses, reread the chapter before continuing with the other reinforcement exercises.

A. **(Self-check)** Write *T* (true) or *F* (false) after the following statements.

1. Students and office workers would find an unabridged dictionary handy to carry with them.   _____

2. Guide words help a dictionary user to pronounce a word.   _____

3. Internet dictionaries are generally more up to date than print dictionaries.   _____

4. Internet dictionaries may be fast and current, but they are also expensive to use.   _____

5. All dictionaries show accented syllables with a raised stress mark preceding a syllable.   _____

6. Dictionaries usually show noun plurals only if they are irregular.   _____

7. Synonyms are words that are spelled alike or sound alike.   _____

8. A reference manual is a small dictionary.   _____

9. Rules for hyphenating compound adjectives may be found in a reference manual.   _____

10. Some dictionaries show definitions in historical order.   _____

Check your answers at the bottom of the page.

Use a *current* desk, college-level, or electronic dictionary to complete the following exercises. If you do not have a dictionary, use one at a library.

B. Select the letter that provides the best definition or synonym for each word shown.

1. cacophony (n)   (a) poor handwriting, (b) harsh sounds, (c) rhythmic beat, (d) enormous wealth   _____

2. entomology (n)   (a) study of words, (b) study of fossils, (c) study of insects, (d) love of outdoors   _____

3. jeopardy (n)   (a) game show, (b) adornment, (c) immunity, (d) danger   _____

1. F 2. F 3. T 4. F 5. F 6. T 7. F 8. F 9. T 10. T

4. obtuse (adj)   (a) dull, (b) old, (c) fixed, (d) stubborn   _____

5. peripatetic (adj)   (a) itinerant, (b) mutineer, (c) pacifist, (d) informer   _____

6. warrant (n)   (a) caution, (b) rabbits, (c) authorization, (d) program   _____

C. Write the correct form of the following words. Use a current dictionary to determine whether they should be written as one or two words or should be hyphenated.

Example: print out (n)   _____printout_____

1. daughter in law   _____

2. double check (v)   _____

3. in as much as   _____

4. off spring (n)   _____

5. old fashioned   _____

6. time clock   _____

D. For each of the following words, write the syllable that receives the primary accent. Then give a brief definition or synonym of the word.

Word	Syllable	Definition or Synonym
Example: judicious	_di_	_prudent, exhibiting sound judgment_
1. advertisement	_____	_____
2. comparable	_____	_____
3. desert (n)	_____	_____
4. desert (v)	_____	_____
5. formidable	_____	_____
6. indefatigable	_____	_____

E. If your dictionary shows usage labels for the following words, write them in the spaces provided. If no label appears for a word, which of the following labels would you consider giving it if you were a lexicographer? Put your initials next to the labels you suggest.

LABELS: archaic   Canadian   dialect   informal or colloquial   slang

Example: goo _____informal_____

1. cheapskate _____

2. hadst _____

3. ice road _____

4. petrol _____

5. raver _____

6. seat sale _____

7. spud (meaning "potato") _____

8. top-notch _____

F. Select the letter that most accurately completes the sentence.

1. A proposal to construct a shopping centre received *approbation* from city officials; therefore, the centre will probably be
(a) rejected   (b) delayed   (c) constructed   (d) modified   _____

2. The abbreviation *e.g.* stands for
(a) for example   (b) extra good   (c) that is   (d) eyeglasses   _____

3. If you have a *bibulous* uncle, he probably engages in too much
(a) sleeping   (b) drinking   (c) talking   (d) gambling   _____

4. To stage a *boycott*, individuals might follow which of the following actions?
(a) withhold their services   (b) refuse to buy a product   (c) reduce their production   (d) refuse to cross picket lines   _____

5. The word *eclectic* originated in which language?
(a) Latin   (b) Greek   (c) French   (d) Old English   _____

6. Condominiums that provide more than one form of *egress* must have more than one
(a) parking space   (b) level   (c) exit   (d) mortgage   _____

7. If you *encrypt* an e-mail message, you are
(a) preserving it   (b) encoding (scrambling) it   (c) erasing it   (d) decoding (unscrambling) it   _____

8. An office desk and chair that were *ergonomically* designed would
(a) reduce fatigue and discomfort   (b) improve office decor   (c) save money   (d) eliminate depreciation   _____

9. The abbreviation *i.e.* stands for
(a) for example   (b) for instance   (c) in earnest   (d) that is   _____

10. What professional would most likely hold the *D.D.S.* degree?
(a) dentist   (b) licensed broker   (c) banker   (d) surgeon   _____

11. The word *magazine* is derived from French, Italian, and Arabic terms meaning
(a) ammunition   (b) a storehouse   (c) a periodical   (d) a firearm compartment   _____

12. *Nepotism* is derived from French and Italian words suggesting
(a) pain   (b) nephew   (c) employment   (d) parent   _____

13. An individual who is *quixotic* is
(a) idealistic   (b) radical   (c) aggressive   (d) patient   _____

14. A member of the SIU most likely works
(a) for the government   (b) in an insurance agency   (c) on the water   (d) in a school   _____

15. Which of the following is written correctly?

   (a) unChristian   (b) un-christian   (c) un-Christian   (d) unchristian   _____

G. Answer true (*T*) or false (*F*).

1. Pocket dictionaries are handy but may be insufficient for all one's needs.   _____

2. If two pronunciations of a word are possible, most dictionaries show the most frequently used pronunciation first.   _____

3. When searching for a word in a dictionary, look only at the guide words until you locate the desired page.   _____

4. The abbreviations *v, vb, vi,* and *vt* may all indicate a verb.   _____

5. Rules for capitalization would more likely be found in a dictionary than in a reference manual.   _____

H. Optional Composition. Your instructor may ask you to complete this exercise on a separate sheet. Use a computer or type, if possible. Write eight complete sentences using the following words: *unabridged dictionary, abridged dictionary, synonym, antonym, hyphenate, archaic, dialect,* and *colloquial.*

Editor's Challenge

The following e-mail message contains 15 misspelled or misused words, some of which you looked up in earlier exercises. Underline any error, and write a correction above it. *Note:* The Editor's Challenge documents that you see in this book are double-spaced so that you can write in corrections. Actual business documents would be single-spaced.

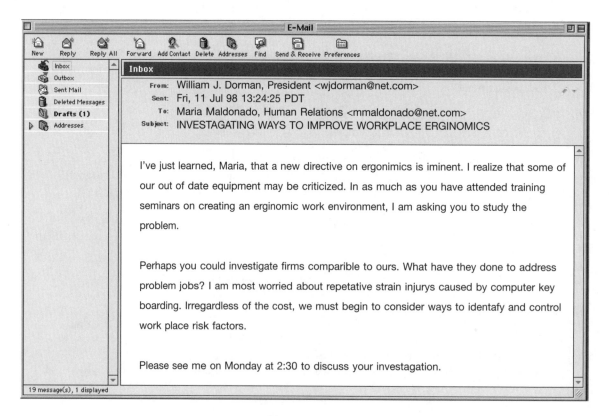

From: William J. Dorman, President <wjdorman@net.com>
Sent: Fri, 11 Jul 98 13:24:25 PDT
To: Maria Maldonado, Human Relations <mmaldonado@net.com>
Subject: INVESTAGATING WAYS TO IMPROVE WORKPLACE ERGINOMICS

I've just learned, Maria, that a new directive on ergonimics is iminent. I realize that some of our out of date equipment may be criticized. In as much as you have attended training seminars on creating an erginomic work environment, I am asking you to study the problem.

Perhaps you could investigate firms comparible to ours. What have they done to address problem jobs? I am most worried about repetative strain injurys caused by computer key boarding. Irregardless of the cost, we must begin to consider ways to identafy and control work place risk factors.

Please see me on Monday at 2:30 to discuss your investagation.

Write *T* (true) or *F* (false) after the following statements. Compare your answers with those at the bottom of the page.

1. The best dictionary for a college student's assignments is a pocket dictionary. _____

2. When searching for a word in a dictionary, look only at the guide words until you locate the desired word. _____

3. The etymology of a word is usually contained within square brackets or parentheses. _____

4. The usage label *colloquial* means that the word may be used in certain regions only. _____

5. A dictionary user could expect to find the spelling of the past tense of an irregular verb such as *build*. _____

learning.web.ways

To make sure you enter the work world with good Internet skills, *Canadian Business English* provides a short Web exercise in each chapter. If your instructor assigns this exercise, you will need access to a computer with an Internet connection. Additionally, your computer must have a Web browser, such as Microsoft Explorer or Netscape. These programs enable you to see and use Web pages.

All Web pages have addresses called URLs (Uniform Resource Locators). URLs must be typed exactly as they are shown, including periods (.), hyphens (-), underscores (_), slashes (/), tildes (~), and upper- or lower-case letters. URLs are often enclosed in angle brackets < >. You do not need to include the angle brackets when typing a URL.

The following exercise introduces you to an electronic dictionary. A major advantage of an on-line dictionary is that it presents the latest information. For example, you will look up two terms that are so new they are not currently listed in the print version of *Merriam-Webster's Collegiate Dictionary*.

Goal: To gain confidence in using an electronic dictionary.

1. With your Web browser on the screen, key the following URL in the location box: **<http://www.m-w.com>.** (Don't include the angle brackets.) Press **Enter**.

2. Look over the **Merriam-Webster Online** home page. Move up and down the page by using the scroll bar at the right.

3. Scroll to the top, and move your cursor to the **Collegiate Dictionary** box.

1. F 2. T 3. T 4. F 5. T

4. Key the word **spam**. Click **Look it up**.

5. Scroll down to see the definition for **spam—noun**.

6. Print a copy of the page by clicking on **File** (upper left corner of your browser). Click **Print** and **OK**. Save all printouts to turn in.

7. Click **Back** (upper left corner of browser) to return to the search page.

8. In the **Collegiate Dictionary** box, delete **spam**. Key the word **firewall** and click **Look it up**. Read the definition and print a copy.

9. Click **Back**. Using either the **Dictionary** or **Thesaurus** feature, look up one word from Exercise F. Print the definition or synonym.

10. Click **Word of the Day** (left navigation panel). Read about the word. Print a copy.

11. End your session by clicking the **X** box (upper right corner of browser). Turn in all printed copies.

Parts of Speech

OBJECTIVES   When you have completed the materials in this chapter, you will be able to do the following:

- *Define the eight parts of speech.*

- *Recognize how parts of speech function in sentences.*

- *Compose sentences showing words playing more than one grammatical role.*

PRETEST

Study the following sentence, and identify selected parts of speech. Underline the best answer. Compare your answers with those at the bottom of the page.

Ann and I carefully completed our tax forms before April 30.

1. *and*	(a) preposition	(b) conjunction	(c) verb	(d) adverb
2. *carefully*	(a) preposition	(b) conjunction	(c) verb	(d) adverb
3. *completed*	(a) preposition	(b) conjunction	(c) verb	(d) adverb
4. *tax*	(a) adjective	(b) pronoun	(c) noun	(d) adverb
5. *before*	(a) preposition	(b) conjunction	(c) noun	(d) adverb

---

As you learned in Chapter 1, business English is the study of the fundamentals of English grammar, current usage, and appropriate style. Such a study logically begins with the eight parts of speech, the building blocks of our language. This chapter provides a brief overview of the parts of speech; the following chapters will deal with these topics more thoroughly.

---

1. (b) conj 2. (d) adverb 3. (c) verb 4. (a) adj 5. (a) prep

▶ The Eight Parts of Speech

Learning the eight parts of speech helps you develop the working vocabulary necessary to discuss and study the language. You especially need to recognize the parts of speech in the context of sentences. That's because many words function in more than one role. Only by analyzing the sentence at hand can you see how a given word functions.

Nouns

In elementary school you probably learned that *nouns* are the names given to persons, places, and things. In addition, though, nouns name qualities, concepts, and activities.

Persons:	Maria, Mr. Hartman, president, Scott
Places:	Charlottetown, Canada, college, park
Things:	computer, stationery, motorcycle, chair
Qualities:	dependability, honesty, initiative, warmth
Concepts:	knowledge, freedom, friendship, happiness
Activities:	skiing, keyboarding, management, eating

Nouns are important words in our language. Sentences revolve around nouns since these words function both as subjects and as objects of verbs. To determine if a word is really a noun, try using it with the verb *is* or *are*. Notice that all the nouns listed here would make sense if used this way: *Maria is, Charlottetown is, honesty is,* and so on. In Chapter 4 (pp. 49–55) you will learn about four classes of nouns and about rules for making nouns plural.

Pronouns

As substitutes for nouns, *pronouns* are used in our language for variety and efficiency. Compare these two versions of the same sentence:

Without pronouns:	Elizabeth gave the book to John so that John could use the book to study.
With pronouns:	Elizabeth gave the book to John so that he could use it to study.

In sentences pronouns may function as subjects (for example, *I, we, they*) or as objects of verbs (*me, us, them*). They may show possession (*mine, ours, his*), and they may act as connectors (*that, which, who*). Only a few examples are given here. More examples, along with functions and classifications of pronouns, will be presented in Chapters 6 and 7 (pp. 83–105).

Verbs

Verbs do two things: (a) they show the action of a sentence, or (b) they join or link to the subject of the sentence words that describe it. Some action verbs are *runs, studies, works,* and *fixes*. Verbs that join descriptive words to the subject are called "linking" verbs. Some linking verbs are *am, is, are, was, were, be, being,* and *been*. Other linking verbs express the senses: *feels, appears, tastes, sounds, seems, looks,* and *smells*.

Verbs will be treated more fully in Chapters 8 through 11. At this point it is important that you be able to recognize verbs so that you can determine whether sentences are complete. All sentences have at least one verb; many sentences have more than one verb. Verbs may appear singly or in phrases.

Study Tip

The words *a, an,* and *the* are sometimes called "noun markers" because they identify or "mark" nouns.

Hotlink

For a brief overview of parts of speech, consult the University of Ottawa's Writing Centre materials at **<http://www. uottawa.ca/academic/ arts/writcent/ hypergrammar/ partsp.html>**.

Study Tip

To test whether a word is truly a verb, try using it with a noun or pronoun, such as *George runs, she seems, it is. He food* doesn't make sense because *food* is not a verb.

Honeywell recently *designed* that massive computer system. (Action verb)

It *is* a computer that *stores, processes,* and *retrieves* data. (Linking and action verbs)

I *feel* bad because Karen *worked* so late last night. (Linking and action verbs)

Our company *will be installing* a new computer system soon. (Verb phrase)

Adjectives

Words that describe nouns or pronouns are called *adjectives.* They often answer the questions *what kind? how many?* or *which one?* The adjectives in the following sentences are italicized. Observe that the adjectives all answer questions about the nouns that they describe.

Small, independent businesses are becoming *numerous.* (What kind of businesses?)

Fourteen franchises were granted in *four* provinces. (How many franchises? How many provinces?)

That chain of hotels started as *a small* operation. (Which chain? What kind of operation?)

He is *energetic* and *forceful,* while she is *personable* and *deliberate.* (What pronouns do these adjectives describe?)

Adjectives usually precede nouns and pronouns. They may, however, follow the words they describe, especially when used with linking verbs, as shown in the first and last examples above.

Here are a few more examples of words often used as adjectives:

successful	sensitive	effective	new
terrific	bright	small	tall
helpless	long	wet	bad

Three words—*a, an,* and *the*—form a special group of adjectives called *articles.*

Adverbs

Words that modify (describe or limit) verbs, adjectives, or other adverbs are *adverbs.* Adverbs often answer the questions *when? how? where?* or *to what extent?*

Today we must begin work. (Must begin when?)

Jones proceeded *rapidly* with the orders. (Proceeded how?)

He seemed *exceedingly* happy. (How happy?)

Did you see the schedule *there?* (Where?)

The prosecutor did not question him *further.* (Questioned him to what extent?)

Here are additional examples of common adverbs:

now	evenly	commercially	too
very	only	really	quickly
rather	carefully	greatly	sincerely

Many, but not all, words ending in *ly* are adverbs. Some exceptions are *friendly, costly,* and *ugly,* all of which are adjectives.

Study Tip

To remember more easily the definition of the word *adverb,* think of its two syllables: *ad* (its first syllable) suggests that you will be adding to or amplifying the meaning of a *verb* (its second syllable). Hence adverbs often modify verbs—but adverbs can also modify adjectives and other adverbs.

Prepositions

Prepositions join nouns and pronouns to other words in a sentence. As the word itself suggests (*pre* meaning "before"), a preposition is a word in a position *before* its object (a noun or pronoun). Prepositions are used in phrases to show a relationship between the object of the preposition and another word in the sentence. In the following sentence notice how the preposition changes the relation of the object (*Mr. Lee*) to the verb (*talked*):

> Marina often talked *with* Mr. Lee.
> Marina often talked *about* Mr. Lee.
> Marina often talked *to* Mr. Lee.

The most frequently used prepositions are *to, by, for, at, from, with,* and *of.* A more extensive list of prepositions can be found in Chapter 13. Learn to recognize objects of prepositions so that you won't confuse them with sentence subjects.

Conjunctions

Words that connect other words or groups of words are *conjunctions*. The most common conjunctions are *and, or, but,* and *nor.* These are called *coordinating conjunctions* because they join equal (coordinate) parts of sentences. Other kinds of conjunctions will be presented in Chapter 15. Study the examples of coordinating conjunctions shown here:

> Koshi, Bill, *or* Amber is going to get the job. (Joins equal words.)
> Word processing systems reduce work for our employees *and* for management.
>   (Joins equal groups of words.)

Interjections

Words expressing strong feelings are *interjections*. Interjections standing alone are followed by exclamation marks. When woven into a sentence, they are usually followed by commas.

> *Wow!* Did you see the total of our bill?
> *Gosh,* I hope I have my credit card!

▶ Summary

The sentence below illustrates all eight parts of speech.

Interjection Adverb Preposition Conjunction
Pronoun Verb Noun Adjective Noun

Oh, I certainly will send for literature and free samples!

You need to know the functions of these eight parts of speech so that you will be able to understand the rest of this textbook and profit from your study of business English. The explanation of the parts of speech has so far been kept simple. This chapter is meant to serve as an introduction to later, more fully developed chapters. At this stage you should not expect to be able to identify the functions of *all* words in *all* sentences.

A word of caution: English is a wonderfully flexible language. As we noted earlier, many words in our language serve as more than one part of speech. Notice how flexible the word *mail* is in the sentences below:

Our *mail* is late today. (Noun—serves as subject of sentence.)

The knight's suit of *mail* protected him. (Noun—serves as object of preposition *of.*)

Mail the letter today. (Verb—serves as action word in sentence.)

Your *mail* slot is full. (Adjective—used here to describe *slot,* a noun which is the subject of sentence.)

HOTLINE QUERIES

Business people are very concerned about appropriate English usage, grammar, and style. This concern is evident in the number and kinds of questions called in to grammar hotline services.

Among the callers are business supervisors, managers, executives, secretaries, clerks, and word processing specialists. Writers, teachers, librarians, students, and other community members also request answers to language questions.

Some of the questions asked and appropriate answers to them will be presented in the following chapters. In this way you, as a student of the language, will understand the kinds of everyday communication problems encountered in the work world.

The original questions in our Hotline Queries came from the Los Angeles Pierce College Business English Hotline, which is no longer in service. More recently, questions were selected from grammar hotline services across the United States. Some grammar hotlines provide e-mail addresses to which you can send inquires. In Canada, Grant MacEwan Community College in Edmonton, Alberta, runs Grammar Hotline, which has the e-mail address: drew@admin.gmcc.ab.ca. The hotline is open Monday through Friday only; address your queries to Lois Drew.

Question: Should an e-mail message begin with a salutation or some kind of greeting?

Answer: When e-mail messages are sent to company insiders, a salutation may be omitted. However, when e-mail messages travel to outsiders, omitting a salutation seems curt and unfriendly. Because the message is more like a letter, a salutation is appropriate (such as *Dear Courtney, Hi Courtney, Greetings,* or just *Courtney*). Including a salutation is also a visual cue to where the message begins. Some writers prefer to incorporate the name of the recipient in the first sentence (*Thanks, Courtney, for responding so quickly*).

Question: I saw this sentence recently in the newspaper: *At the movie premiere the crowd scanned the limousines for glitterati.* Is *glitterati* a real word?

Answer: A recent arrival to our vocabulary, *glitterati* means "celebrities or beautiful people." New words are generally considered legitimate when their use is clear and when they are necessary (that is, when no other words say exactly what they do). If educated individuals begin to use such words, the words then appear in dictionaries, and *glitterati* has made it.

Question: Which word should I use in this sentence? *Our department will* disburse *or* disperse *the funds shortly.*

Answer: Use *disburse. Disperse* means "to scatter" or "to distribute" (*Information will be dispersed to all divisions*). *Disburse* means "to pay out." Perhaps this memory device will help you keep them straight: associate the *b* in *disburse* with *bank* (*Banks disburse money*).

Question: How should I address a person who signed a letter *J. R. Henderson?*

Answer: Use *Dear J. R. Henderson.*

Question: What's the difference between *toward* and *towards?*

Answer: None. They are interchangeable in use. However, it is more efficient to use the shorter word *toward.*

Question: Is *every day* one word or two in this case? *We encounter these problems every day.*

Answer: In your sentence it is two words. When it means "ordinary," it is one word (*She wore everyday clothes*). If you can insert the word *single* between *every* and *day* without altering your meaning, you should be using two words.

Question: What is the name of a group of initials that form a word? Is it an abbreviation?

Answer: A word formed from the initial letters of an expression is called an acronym (pronounced *ACK ro nim*). Examples: *snafu,* from **s**ituation **n**ormal, **a**ll **f**ouled **u**p, and *DOS,* from **d**isk **o**perating **s**ystem. Acronyms are pronounced as single words and are different from abbreviations. Expressions like *RCMP* and *dept.* are abbreviations, not acronyms.

CHAPTER 2   Reinforcement Exercises

A. (**Self-check**) Complete these statements.

1. Used for variety and efficiency, pronouns substitute for
   (a) interjections   (b) nouns   (c) verbs   (d) conjunctions   _____

2. The part of speech that answers the question *what kind* is a/an
   (a) adverb   (b) adjective   (c) interjection   (d) conjunction   _____

3. Names for persons, places, things, qualities, concepts, and activities are
   (a) verbs   (b) adjectives   (c) nouns   (d) pronouns   _____

4. Words that modify verbs, adjectives, and adverbs are
   (a) adverbs   (b) adjectives   (c) pronouns   (d) conjunctions   _____

5. *I, we, you*, and *he* are examples of
   (a) nouns   (b) pronouns   (c) verbs   (d) adverbs   _____

6. Action words in sentences are
   (a) nouns   (b) pronouns   (c) adjectives   (d) verbs   _____

7. *Beautifully, frankly*, and *smoothly* are examples of
   (a) adjectives   (b) verbs   (c) interjections   (d) adverbs   _____

8. Words that express strong feeling are
   (a) conjunctions   (b) adverbs   (c) pronouns   (d) interjections   _____

9. *And, or, nor*, and *but* are
   (a) conjunctions   (b) verbs   (c) interjections   (d) adverbs   _____

10. Words that join noun or pronoun objects to other words in sentences are
    (a) adverbs   (b) prepositions   (c) interjections   (d) adjectives   _____

Check your answers.

B. In each of the following groups of sentences, one word is used as an adjective, as a noun, and as a verb. For each sentence indicate the part of speech for the italicized word.

Example: Much *work* must be done.   _____noun_____

    Can you *work* overtime?   _____verb_____

    We need two *work* orders.   _____adjective_____

1. In what *time* zone do you live?   _____

2. Do you have the *time*?   _____

1. b   2. b   3. c   4. a   5. b   6. d   7. d   8. d   9. a   10. b

3. The coach will *time* the runners. _____

4. Our *stock* of canned goods is low. _____

5. The *stock* clerk works tonight. _____

6. He will *stock* the shelves. _____

7. I like my *keyboarding* class. _____

8. *Keyboarding* is my best subject. _____

9. I am *keyboarding* my résumé. _____

Write complete sentences using the word *guard* as a noun, as an adjective, and as a verb.

10. (noun) _____

11. (adjective) _____

12. (verb) _____

C. The underlined words in the following sentences are either prepositions or conjunctions. Write *C* for conjunction or *P* for preposition.

1. Technical skills are important <u>for</u>   *for*   _____

entry-level positions, <u>but</u> communication skills   *but*   _____

are necessary for promotion <u>to</u> management.   *to*   _____

2. Writing good letters <u>and</u> e-mail messages   *and*   _____

<u>to</u> customers creates goodwill   *to*   _____

<u>for</u> business organizations.   *for*   _____

3. Neither large <u>nor</u> small service businesses   *nor*   _____

maintain much merchandise <u>in</u> inventory because   *in*   _____

selling goods <u>from</u> stock is not their function.   *from*   _____

D. Read the following sentences, and taking into account the function of each word within each sentence, identify the part of speech of each word shown. Use a dictionary if necessary.

Hurriedly she parked the small sports car and quickly raced to class.

Hurriedly	_____	small	_____	quickly	_____
she	_____	sports	_____	raced	_____
parked	_____	car	_____	to	_____
the	_____	and	_____	class	_____

Six students qualified, but only one young woman came to the session.

Six	_____	only	_____	came	_____
students	_____	one	_____	to	_____
qualified	_____	young	_____	the	_____
but	_____	woman	_____	session	_____

E. Selected verbs in the following sentences have been italicized. Use check marks to indicate whether these verbs are linking or action verbs.

	Linking Verb	Action Verb
Example: We *are* the chief suppliers of camera film.	✓	_____
1. The task of management *is* never an easy one.	_____	_____
2. Our company *produces* components for computers.	_____	_____
3. The human resources manager *selected* four outstanding applicants.	_____	_____
4. Sheila *felt* bad that too much month was left at the end of her money.	_____	_____
5. We *borrowed* three-fourths of the necessary capital.	_____	_____
6. The manager and the personnel director *studied* the job descriptions carefully.	_____	_____
7. The first equipment proposal *was* quite adequate for our needs.	_____	_____
8. Please *deliver* the computers and printers before April 4.	_____	_____

G. Optional Composition. Your instructor may ask you to complete this exercise on a separate sheet. Write eight sentences that illustrate the parts of speech: noun, pronoun, verb, adjective, adverb, conjunction, preposition, and interjection. Identify each part of speech by labelling it at the beginning of the sentence and underlining it within the sentence. If possible, use a computer or type this exercise.

Example: Noun: I hope to improve my basic communication skills.

Editor's Challenge

To develop your vocabulary skills, supply a single word for each blank in the following sentences. The word you supply should represent the part of speech shown.

Atlantic Industries
Interoffice Memo

TO: Allison Hever

FROM: Tran Nguyen

DATE: June 3, 200x

SUBJECT: JOB-SEARCH ADVICE

I'm sorry to learn that you have completed your internship with us and that you will be leaving, Allison. Since you (verb) _____ advice in finding a job, I'd like to share with you a few pointers that I've learned.

My experience suggests that serious candidates will devote as much (noun) _____ to job hunting as they do (preposition) _____ working at a full-time job. If possible, hand deliver your résumé (conjunction) _____ your cover letter to the (noun) _____ in charge of hiring.

Be sure that your (adjective) _____ letter (verb) _____ the requirements of the position advertised. If you mail your résumé, it's a(n) (adjective) _____ idea to follow up with a telephone call in a few days. A(n) (adverb) _____ high number of résumés are never received, are lost, or are thrown out.

You'll find that an interviewer often asks why (pronoun) _____ want this particular job. In addition to answering (noun) _____ , you should be prepared to ask (adjective) _____ questions of your own. Try to remember that interviews are (adjective) _____ learning experiences, whether (conjunction) _____ not you get the job.

I hope this (noun) _____ is helpful to you, and I wish you well in your (adjective) _____ search.

Identify selected parts of speech in the following sentence by underlining the correct choice. Compare your answers with those at the bottom of the page.

Our manager carefully explained the use of the new computer.

1. *manager*   (a) noun   (b) pronoun   (c) preposition   (d) conjunction
2. *carefully*   (a) verb   (b) adverb   (c) preposition   (d) conjunction
3. *explained*   (a) adverb   (b) verb   (c) preposition   (d) conjunction
4. *of*   (a) noun   (b) pronoun   (c) preposition   (d) conjunction
5. *new*   (a) verb   (b) adverb   (c) adjective   (d) preposition

learning.web.ways

Many colleges and universities offer on-line writing labs (OWLs). These Web sites provide helpful resources for students and business people. You can read on-line or download handouts providing help with punctuation, spelling, sentence construction, parts of speech, and writing in the job search.

Goal: To learn to use an on-line writing lab.

1. With your Web browser on the screen, key the following URL in the location box: **<http://webster.commnet.edu/grammar/index.htm>**. Press **Enter**.

2. Look at the **Capital Community College Guide to Grammar and Writing**.

3. Scroll down to **Peripherals and PowerPoints**.

4. Select **PowerPoint Presentations**.

5. From the list of materials, click on the **Parts of Speech** presentation. Be patient while it loads because it's huge!

6. View the presentation.

7. Click back twice to return to the **Guide to Grammar and Writing** page.

8. From the **Ask Grammar, Quizzes, Search Devices** section, select **170+ Interactive Quizzes**.

9. Click on **Recognizing Nouns** and do the quiz.

10. Print the whole page, with the correct answers included.

11. End your session by clicking the **X** box in the upper right corner of your browser. Turn in your printout.

1. a   2. b   3. b   4. c   5. c

Sentences: Elements, Patterns, Types

3

OBJECTIVES When you have completed the materials in this chapter, you will be able to do the following:

- *Recognize subjects and predicates.*

- *Convert fragments into complete sentences.*

- *Recognize basic sentence faults such as comma splices and run-on sentences.*

- *Complete sentences in three basic sentence patterns.*

- *Punctuate statements, commands, questions, and exclamations.*

PRETEST

Write the correct letter after each of the numbered groups of words below to identify it.

a = correctly punctuated sentence   c = comma splice
b = fragment   d = run-on sentence

1. John, completing the training course in less than four weeks. _____

2. John works 30 hours this week, Martha works 32. _____

3. Across the street are a copy store and a convenience store. _____

4. Some employees use the company van however others rely on their own cars. _____

5. Although some employees start at 6 a.m., which explains the empty parking lot. _____

1.b 2.c 3.a 4.d 5.b

Sentences are groups of words arranged to express complete thoughts. In this chapter you'll review the basic elements of every sentence. In addition, you'll learn to recognize sentence patterns and types. This knowledge will help you use and punctuate sentences correctly. This chapter also introduces proofreading marks, which are helpful in revising messages.

▶ Sentence Elements

Subjects and Predicates

Sentences are composed of two essential elements: subjects and predicates. The *subject* of a sentence is the person or thing being talked about; the *predicate* tells what the subject is, what the subject is doing, or what is being done to the subject. Study the following sentence:

The new <u>manager</u> of the office   <u>received</u> our co-operation.

complete subject   complete predicate

The *complete subject* of the preceding sentence includes the subject (in this case a noun) plus all the words that describe or limit the subject (its modifiers). The *complete predicate* includes the verb plus its modifiers.

The heart of the complete subject is the simple subject (*manager*), and the heart of the predicate is the simple predicate, or verb (*received*). The following sentences are divided into complete subjects and complete predicates. The simple subjects are underlined once, and the verbs (simple predicates) are underlined twice.

Complete Subjects	Complete Predicates
All <u>branches</u> of the company	<u>are linked</u> by computer.
Our largest department <u>store</u>	<u>will be having</u> a sale.
An Alberta pilot <u>program</u>	<u>will be launched</u> next month.
Chain store <u>executives</u>	<u>conduct</u> traffic counts.

Notice in the previous sentences that the verbs may consist of one word or several. In a verb phrase the principal verb is the final one; the other verbs are *helping* or *auxiliary* verbs. For example, in the verb phrase *will be having*, *having* is the principal verb and *will* and *be* are the helping verbs. The most frequently used helping verbs are *am, is, are, was, were, been, be, have, has, had, must, ought, might, can, could, would, should, will, do, does,* and *did.*

Sentence Sense

In addition to a subject and a predicate, a group of words must possess one additional element to qualify as a sentence: *the group of words must make sense.* Observe that two of the groups of words that follow express complete thoughts and make sense; the third does not.

<u>Bradley</u> <u>built</u> his business through personal contacts. (Subject plus predicate making sense = sentence.)

Career Tip

You may be worth an additional $5,000 to your employer (and to yourself) if you have writing skills, says one communications expert. Because companies can no longer afford expensive on-site training, employees with already developed skills are much more valuable to employers.

Study Tip

Many linking verbs also serve as helping verbs. Note that a verb phrase is *linking* only when the final verb is a linking verb, such as in the phrase *might have <u>been</u>.*

Efficient <u>service</u> <u>ensured</u> return business. (Subject plus predicate making sense = sentence.)

When <u>Bradley</u> <u>started</u> his own business (Subject plus predicate but NOT making sense = no sentence.)

In the third case a reader or listener senses that the idea expressed is incomplete. We do not have a sentence; instead, we have a fragment.

▶ Sentence Faults

Three typical sentence faults are fragments, comma splices, and run-on sentences. Good writers eliminate these sentence faults by applying the following advice.

Fragments

Fragments are most often groups of words that are broken off from nearby sentences. They cannot function as complete sentences. Avoid fragments by making certain that each sentence contains a subject and a verb and makes sense by itself. In the following examples the fragments are italicized. Notice how they can be revised to make complete sentences.

Fragment:	We're looking for a potential manager. *An individual who can accept responsibility and supervise other employees.*
Revision:	We're looking for a potential manager who can accept responsibility and supervise other employees.
Fragment:	My research report in business communication took a long time to prepare. *And then turned out badly.*
Revision:	My research report in business communication took a long time to prepare and then turned out badly.
Fragment:	The vending machine dispenses microwavable popcorn. *Which carries a warning to remove the plastic outerwrap before heating.*
Revision:	The vending machine dispenses microwavable popcorn, which carries a warning to remove the plastic outerwrap before heating.

Run-on Sentences

Another basic sentence fault is the *run-on* (or fused) *sentence*, which joins two or more complete thoughts without punctuation. Notice how the run-on sentences below can be corrected by dividing the two thoughts into separate sentences.

Run-on Sentence:	The work ethic in Canada is not dead it is deeply ingrained in most people.
Revision:	The work ethic in Canada is not dead. It is deeply ingrained in most people.
Run-on Sentence:	Gift certificates for courses are available prices range from $40 to $159.
Revision:	Gift certificates for courses are available. Prices range from $40 to $159.

Hotlink

For more examples of sentence faults and sentence patterns, visit the Purdue University Online Writing Lab **<http://owl.english. purdue.edu>.** Click on Instructional Handouts, Sentence Construction.

Spot the Blooper

From a newspaper article: "He is recovering from a near-fatal accident that sent him into a comma."

Run-on Sentence:	Send an e-mail message to all committee members tell them our next meeting is planned for Friday.
Revision:	Send an e-mail message to all committee members. Tell them our next meeting is planned for Friday.

Comma Splices

A *comma splice* results when two sentences are incorrectly joined or spliced together with a comma. The sentences below show how comma splices could be revised into acceptable sentences.

Comma Splice:	Let us help you develop your on-line résumé, visit us at Resume.org.
Revision:	Let us help you develop your on-line résumé. Visit us at Resume.org.
Comma Splice:	You must fill one more purchase order, then your work is finished.
Revision:	You must fill one more purchase order. Then your work is finished.
Comma Splice:	Many applicants responded to our advertisement, however only one had the proper training.
Revision:	Many applicants responded to our advertisement; however, only one had the proper training. (Semicolons will be discussed in Chapters 14 and 17.)

▶ Sentence Patterns

Three basic word patterns are used to express thoughts in English sentences.

Pattern No. 1: Subject–Verb

In the most basic sentence pattern, the subject is followed by its verb. No additional words are needed for the sentence to make sense and be complete.

Subject	**Verb**
We	worked.
Everyone	is studying.
She	might have called.
All the employees	should have been informed.

Pattern No. 2: Subject–Action Verb–Object

In this kind of sentence, the subject is followed by an action verb and its direct object. The object usually answers the question *What?* or *Whom?*

Subject	**Action Verb**	**Object**
Most students	brought	supplies.
The manager	praised	the employees.
Mrs. Chartrand	supervised	them.
All proceeds	support	volunteers.

Hotlink

The Capital Community College grammar materials are among the best on the Web. Don't miss Sentences (basic parts), found at **<http://webster. commnet.edu/ grammar/powerpoint. htm>**.

This basic sentence pattern may also employ an indirect object that usually answers the question *to whom?*

Subject	Action Verb	Indirect Object	Direct Object
Our company	offers	employees	excellent benefits.
Tiffany	gave	him	the book.
We	lent	the neighbour	our car.
Wendy	bought	her assistant	a gift.

Pattern No. 3: Subject–Linking Verb–Complement

In the third kind of sentence, the subject is followed by a linking verb and its complement. A *complement* is a noun, pronoun, or adjective that renames or describes the subject. A complement *completes* the meaning of the subject.

Subject	Linking Verb	Complement	
The author	was	Ms. Arnold.	*(Noun complements)*
Our customers	are	friends.	
Your supervisor	is	she.	*(Pronoun complements)*
The callers	might have been	they.	
These data	are	accurate.	*(Adjective complements)*
His report	is	excellent.	

The sentences shown here have been kept simple so that their patterns can be recognized easily. Although most speakers and writers expand these basic patterns with additional phrases and clauses, the basic sentence structure remains the same. Despite its length the following sentence follows the basic subject–action verb–object order:

> Many large *companies,* as well as small companies with sizable real estate holdings, *employ* specialized risk *managers* to handle their insurance problems. (The simple subject is *companies,* the action verb is *employ,* and the object is *managers.*)

Inverted Order

In some sentences the elements appear in inverted order, with the verb preceding the subject.

> Sitting in front is Doreen.
> Last came the school choir.

In questions the verb or a helping verb usually precedes the subject.

> What is the shipment number?
> Have the bills been sent?

Career Tip

In business writing you'll most often use Patterns 1, 2, and 3 because readers want to know the subject first. For variety and emphasis, however, you can use introductory elements and inverted order.

Hotlink

The University of Victoria has produced an extensive Writer's Guide available at **<http://web. uvic.ca/wguide/ Pages/sentencesTOC. html>**. Check out Some Things to Avoid.

Spot the Blooper

The menu of a restaurant in Columbia, South Carolina, offers "A humongous baked potato, slightly hallowed and stuffed."

In sentences beginning with the adverbs *here* or *there*, the word order is also inverted.

> Here <u>are</u> the <u>applications</u>.
> There <u>is</u> a <u>demand</u> for accountants.

To locate the true subject in any inverted sentence, mentally rearrange the words. Place them in the normal subject–verb order.

> <u>Doreen</u> <u>is sitting</u> in front.
> The shipment <u>number</u> <u>is</u> what?
> The <u>applications</u> <u>are</u> here.

▶ Punctuating Four Sentence Types

The end punctuation used for a sentence depends on whether it is a statement, question, command, or exclamation.

Statements

Statements make assertions and end with periods.

> <u>Laws</u> <u>require</u> truth in advertising.
> <u>Manufacturers</u> today <u>must label</u> the contents of packages.

Questions

Direct questions are followed by question marks.

> How many e-mail messages <u>do</u> <u>you</u> <u>receive</u> in a day?
> What employee benefits <u>will</u> <u>you</u> <u>receive</u>?

Commands

Commands end with periods or, occasionally, with exclamation points. Although both statements and commands end with periods, the two sentence types differ in purpose and in form. We see or hear the subject of a statement but not the subject of a command. Note that the subject in all commands is understood to be *you*. The subject *you* is not normally stated in the command.

> <u>Shut</u> the door. ([<u>You</u>] <u>shut</u> the door.)
> <u>Insure</u> your home against fire loss. ([<u>You</u>] <u>insure</u> your home ....)

Exclamations

Showing surprise, disbelief, or strong feelings, exclamations may or may not be expressed as complete thoughts. Both subject and predicate may be implied.

> Oh! Static <u>electricity</u> <u>gave</u> me a shock!
> What a remarkable employee <u>she</u> <u>is</u>!
> How extraordinary [<u>that</u> <u>is</u>]!

Hotlink

For further help with fragments and run-ons, consult this Hit Parade of Errors created by the University of Toronto's Health Sciences' Writing Centre **<http://www. utoronto.ca/hswriting/ hitparade.htm>**.

Notable Quotable

"Cut out all those exclamation marks. An exclamation mark is like laughing at your own joke."
—F. Scott Fitzgerald

HOTLINE QUERIES

Question: This sentence doesn't sound right to me, but I can't decide how to improve it: *The reason I'm applying is because I enjoy electronics.*

Answer: The problem lies in this construction: *the reason … is because….* Only nouns or adjectives may act as complements following linking verbs. In your sentence an adverbial clause follows the linking verb *is* and sounds awkward. One way to improve the sentence is to substitute a noun clause beginning with *that: The reason I'm applying is that I enjoy electronics.* An even better way to improve the sentence would be to make it a direct statement: *I'm applying because I enjoy electronics.*

Question: My colleague says that this sentence is correct: *Jill will first print all the letters, then she will prepare the envelopes.* I think something is wrong, but I'm not sure what.

Answer: You're right. This sentence has two short independent clauses, and some writers attempt to join them with a comma. But this construction produces a comma splice. The adverb *then* cannot function as a conjunction, such as *and,* to join these two clauses. Start a new sentence, or use a semicolon between the clauses.

Question: My boss dictated a report with this sentence: *Saleswise, our staff is excellent.* Should I change it?

Answer: Never change wording without checking with the author. You might point out, however, that the practice of attaching *-wise* to nouns is frowned upon by many language experts. Such combinations as *budgetwise, taxwise,* and *productionwise* are considered commercial jargon. Suggest this revision: *On the basis of sales, our staff is excellent.*

Question: At the end of a letter, I wrote: *Thank you for attending to this matter immediately.* Should I hyphenate *thank you*?

Answer: Do not hyphenate *thank you* when using it as a verb (*thank you for writing*). Do hyphenate it when using it as an adjective (*I sent a thank-you note*) or as a noun (*I sent four thank-yous*). Since *thank you* is used as a verb in your sentence, do not hyphenate it. Notice that *thank you* is never written as a single word.

Question: A fellow worker insists on saying, *I could care less.* Seems to me that it should be *I couldn't care less.* Who is right?

Answer: You are right. The phrase *I couldn't care less* has been in the language a long time. It means, of course, "I have little concern about the matter." Recently, though, people have begun to use *I could care less* with the same meaning. Most careful listeners realize that the latter phrase says just the opposite of its intent. Although both phrases are clichés, stick with *I couldn't care less* if you want to be clear.

CHAPTER 3   Reinforcement Exercises

A. (**Self-check**) Indicate whether the following statements are true (*T*) or false (*F*).

1. The verbs *are, may,* and *have* are examples of auxiliary or helping verbs.   _____

2. A group of words with a subject and a predicate is automatically a complete sentence.   _____

3. The complete subject of a sentence includes a noun or pronoun and all its modifiers.   _____

4. Two sentences joined only by a comma create a *comma splice.*   _____

5. In questions the verb may appear before the subject.   _____

6. The complete predicate of a sentence tells what the subject is, what the subject is doing, or what is being done to the subject.   _____

7. Sentences that show strong feeling are usually concluded with question marks.   _____

8. The verb phrase *could have been* is considered to be a linking verb.   _____

9. Sentences that begin with *here* or *there* follow normal subject–verb order.   _____

10. Complements may follow either action verbs or linking verbs.   _____

Check your answers.

B. Study the examples shown below. Then fill in the words necessary to complete the three sentence patterns.

Pattern No. 1: Subject–Verb

Example: The boss _called_ .

1. The telephone _____ .

2. Our computer _____ .

3. Students _____ .

4. Salespeople _____ .

5. Senators _____ .

6. Secretaries _____ .

7. Our fax machine _____ .

8. Money _____ .

Pattern No. 2: Subject–Action Verb–Object

Example: Administrative assistants use _software_ .

9. Patrick answered the _____ .

10. The mail carrier delivered _____ .

11. Salespeople sold _____ .

12. Investors bought _____ .

13. The carpenter built a _____ .

14. Shares pay _____ .

15. Students threw a _____ .

16. Lawyers represent _____ .

1.T 2.F 3.T 4.T 5.T 6.T 7.F 8.F 9.T 10.F

Pattern No. 3: Subject–Linking Verb–Complement

Fill in <u>noun</u> or <u>pronoun</u> complements.

Example: The manager is____John____ .

17. The applicant was _____.

18. Tina is the new _____.

19. The caller could have been _____.

20. The president is _____.

Fill in <u>adjective</u> complements.

Example: The salary is ___good_____ .

21. My investment was _____.

22. New York is _____.

23. Movies once were _____.

24. The report could have been _____.

C. Underline the simple subject once and the verb (simple predicate) twice.

Example: <u>She</u> <u>is resigning</u> for personal reasons.

1. The manuscript will be delivered by April 2.

2. Prince George is home to the University of Northern British Columbia.

3. Canada remains the United States' largest export market.

4. On October 26 this special offer will end.

5. The company has fired Vera Stewart.

6. Dynasty Motorcar was looking for new financing.

7. Earnings sank in the second quarter.

8. The airline's president was highly unpopular with employees.

D. The following sentences do not follow normal word order. To help you locate subjects, invert these sentences so that the subject comes first. Then underline the simple subject once and the verb twice.

Example: Here are some of the materials we need.

<u>Some</u> of the materials we need <u>are</u> here. _____

1. There are two telephone numbers listed for that organization. _____

_____

2. Here is the agenda for the Tuesday board meeting. _____

_____

3. Where is the Gibson contract? _____

_____

4. Across from our office is the subway station. _____

_____

5. Who is the leader in on-line shopping? _____

_____

E. From the list below select the letter that accurately describes each of the following groups of words. If a group of words requires an end punctuation mark, add it.

a = fragment   c = command   e = exclamation

b = statement   d = question

Example: The resources of that country, although never fully developed _____*a*_____

1. School and work holidays should always be scheduled to fall on Mondays and Fridays _____

2. Do employers and workers contribute jointly to the retirement fund _____

3. If there is mutual agreement to all contract terms _____

4. Analyze the gross national product for the past ten years _____

5. Although Singapore flourishes as a centre of banking, shipbuilding, offshore-oil technology, refining, aircraft maintenance, electronics manufacturing, and international trade _____

6. What a splendid view we have from the observatory on the tenth floor _____

7. In Europe, where most countries are part of the European Community _____

8. Do you know if Tom Truong received the purchase order _____

F. Expand the following sentence fragments into complete sentences.

1. If I had just won a lottery prize of $50 million _____

_____

2. My economics professor, although I promised to make up the work I missed _____

_____

3. All the helicopters, including those flying to Prince Edward Island _____

_____

4. Although we have no openings for a person with your skills _____

_____

5. Since we plan to update all equipment in the office _____

G. Write the correct letter after each of the following groups of words to indicate whether it represents a fragment, a correctly punctuated sentence, a comma splice, or a run-on sentence.

a = correctly punctuated sentence   c = comma splice
b = fragment   d = run-on sentence

Example: Which can save you valuable time.   _____*b*_____

1. Anyone doing business in another country should learn what kinds of gifts are expected and when to give them. _____

2. Our corporate headquarters will be moved next year, then I expect to be transferred. _____

3. Although we have a powerful printer capable of producing high-quality graphics. _____

4. Amina wanted a practical spreadsheet program she just didn't know what to purchase. _____

5. Mornings seem to be better than afternoons for catching business executives in their offices. _____

6. Mr. Harrington arrived at the airport on time, however, his flight was overbooked. _____

7. Some banks may require in-depth personal investigations. _____

8. Particularly if you are a married woman and want to open a credit account in your own name. _____

9. We have tried to collect this account in a friendly manner, our efforts, however, have failed to secure your co-operation. _____

10. Some employers weigh education and grades heavily they look at transcripts carefully. _____

11. Research suggests that job stress is linked to mental problems stress is also associated with ulcers and heart disease. _____

12. Next Monday is Victoria Day, hence all branch offices will be closed. _____

For class discussion: In the preceding exercise, how could each of the incorrectly punctuated groups of words be made acceptable?

H. Optional Composition. Your instructor may ask you to complete this exercise on a separate sheet. Write seven sentences, one to illustrate each of the following forms: a statement, a question, a command, an exclamation, a sentence with a noun complement, a sentence with an adjective complement, and a sentence in inverted order. Identify each sentence.

Editor's Challenge

The following e-mail message contains errors in sentence structure, spelling, and proofreading. Make corrections. Your instructor may ask you to read about proofreading marks on page 44 and use those marks in noting your corrections.

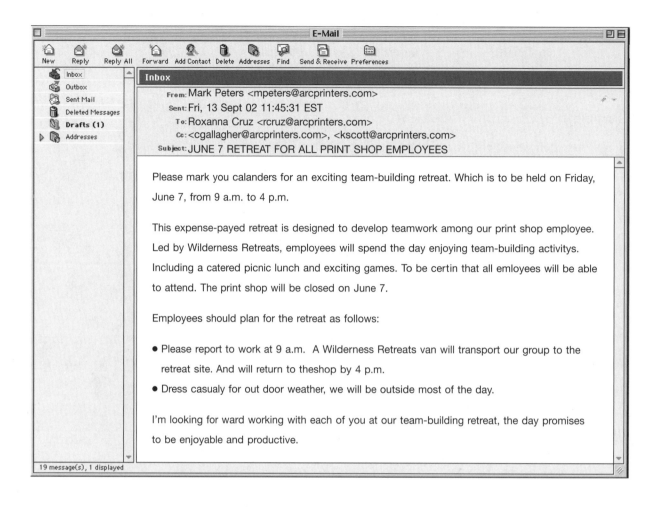

E-Mail

New | Reply | Reply All | Forward | Add Contact | Delete | Addresses | Find | Send & Receive | Preferences

Inbox
Outbox
Sent Mail
Deleted Messages
Drafts (1)
Addresses

Inbox

From: Mark Peters <mpeters@arcprinters.com>
Sent: Fri, 13 Sept 02 11:45:31 EST
To: Roxanna Cruz <rcruz@arcprinters.com>
Cc: <cgallagher@arcprinters.com>, <kscott@arcprinters.com>
Subject: JUNE 7 RETREAT FOR ALL PRINT SHOP EMPLOYEES

Please mark you calanders for an exciting team-building retreat. Which is to be held on Friday, June 7, from 9 a.m. to 4 p.m.

This expense-payed retreat is designed to develop teamwork among our print shop employee. Led by Wilderness Retreats, employees will spend the day enjoying team-building activitys. Including a catered picnic lunch and exciting games. To be certin that all emloyees will be able to attend. The print shop will be closed on June 7.

Employees should plan for the retreat as follows:

● Please report to work at 9 a.m. A Wilderness Retreats van will transport our group to the retreat site. And will return to theshop by 4 p.m.
● Dress casualy for out door weather, we will be outside most of the day.

I'm looking for ward working with each of you at our team-building retreat, the day promises to be enjoyable and productive.

19 message(s), 1 displayed

POSTTEST

Write the correct letter after each of the numbered items below.

a = correctly punctuated sentence   c = comma splice
b = fragment   d = run-on sentence

1. The computer was installed Monday the printer is expected shortly.   _____

2. Outside the front office is the receptionist's desk.   _____

3. Since the contract was mailed Monday but not received until late Friday.   _____

4. On Monday the mail is picked up early, on Friday it is not picked up until 3 p.m.   _____

5. Because Ahmed, who is one of our best employees, was ill last week   _____

1. d 2. a 3. b 4. c 5. b

learning.web.ways

A number of search tools—such as AltaVista, Yahoo!, and Google—are available at specialized Web sites devoted to searching. These tools help you find Web pages related to the search term you enter. However, search tools cannot index all the pages on the Web. Using a search tool is like using a telephone book that lists only a third of all the numbers available. Even though search tools don't survey everything that's available, they usually turn up more information than you want.

Goal: To become familiar with a search engine.

1. With your Web browser on the screen, key the following URL: **<http://www.altavista.com>**. Press **Enter**.

2. Look over the AltaVista home page. Ignore the advertisements and locate the **Find this** box.

3. In this box, key **"English grammar"** as your search term. Enclosing an expression in quotation marks ensures that the two words will be searched as a unit. Click **Search** or press **Enter**.

4. Wait a moment for AltaVista to locate Web pages with your search term. Then scroll down to **Web pages found**. Notice that nearly 40,000 Web pages were located.

5. To refine your search, scroll back to the **Find this** box and replace the search term with **"Business English grammar."**

6. Look over the listed pages. Click on one. Examine the page and print a copy (click on **File, Print,** and **OK**).

7. Return to the AltaVista home page. (It may be faster to key the URL in your browser **Location** box than to use the **Back** button.)

8. Choose another search item, such as **spam, netiquette,** or **intranets.** Select an interesting page. Examine it. Print one or two pages.

9. End your session by clicking the **X** in the upper right corner of your browser.

10. Turn in all printed copies.

UNIT 1 REVIEW Chapters 1–3 (Self-Check)

Begin your review by rereading Chapters 1 through 3. Then check your comprehension of those chapters by filling in the blanks in the exercises that follow. Compare your responses with those provided in the key at the end of the book.

Write *T* (true) or *F* (false) after the following statements.

1. All dictionaries use the same plan for showing the order of definitions.   _____

2. Usage labels such as *archaic* and *informal* warn dictionary users about appropriate usage.   _____

3. The etymology code helps you to pronounce a word correctly.   _____

4. Because the English language changes very little, the publication date of a dictionary is unimportant.   _____

5. Most dictionaries show noun plurals only if the plurals are irregular, such as the word *children.*   _____

6. A thesaurus is a collection of words and their definitions.   _____

7. Accent marks may appear before or after stressed syllables.   _____

8. The usage label *obsolete* means that a word is considered indecent or coarse.   _____

9. The terms *desk* and *college-level* refer to the same kind of dictionary.   _____

10. A summary of diacritical marks is often found at the bottom of dictionary pages.   _____

Read the following sentence carefully. Identify the parts of speech for the words as they are used in this sentence.

> *He looked quickly at the page and then scribbled two answers.*

11. *He*	(a) noun	(b) pronoun	(c) adj	(d) adverb	_____
12. *looked*	(a) conj	(b) prep	(c) verb	(d) adverb	_____
13. *quickly*	(a) conj	(b) prep	(c) adj	(d) adverb	_____
14. *at*	(a) conj	(b) prep	(c) adj	(d) adverb	_____
15. *page*	(a) noun	(b) pronoun	(c) conj	(d) adverb	_____
16. *and*	(a) noun	(b) pronoun	(c) conj	(d) prep	_____
17. *then*	(a) noun	(b) adverb	(c) conj	(d) prep	_____
18. *scribbled*	(a) verb	(b) adverb	(c) conj	(d) prep	_____
19. *two*	(a) verb	(b) adj	(c) adverb	(d) prep	_____
20. *answers*	(a) noun	(b) pronoun	(c) adj	(d) prep	_____

For each of the following statements, determine the word or phrase that correctly completes that statement and write its letter in the space provided.

21. In the sentence *Clean white paper is needed for this job,* the simple subject is
(a) Clean, (b) white, (c) paper, (d) job. _____

22. In the sentence *Here are the contracts,* the simple subject is (a) Here, (b) are, (c) contracts,
(d) you. _____

23. In the sentence *I feel bad,* the verb *feel* is considered a (a) linking verb, (b) helping verb,
(c) subject, (d) predicate. _____

24. The sentence *She sent many e-mail messages* represents what sentence pattern:
(a) subject–verb, (b) subject–action verb–object, (c) subject–linking verb–complement,
(d) subject–linking verb–object. _____

From the list below select the letter that describes each of the following groups of words.
a = command   b = complete sentence   c = fragment   d = comma splice   e = run-on sentence

25. I must call one more person, then I will be ready to evaluate his application. _____

26. Whenever Mr. Jackson calls to confirm the shipping date. _____

27. Turn on your computer when you arrive, and leave it on all day. _____

28. That company's products are excellent its service is somewhat slow, however. _____

29. Many employees are interested in the proposed in-service training. _____

30. Although you will be on vacation when your cheque is issued. _____

31. Complete the form, and send it with your cheque. _____

32. This computer and its sofware are very powerful, I'm not sure I need that much power. _____

33. The letter arrived today the package should be here next week. _____

34. Many companies today feature profit-sharing plans, but some employees are reluctant
to participate in them. _____

35. After you read the contract, sign and return it. _____

Hotline Review

Select the word or phrase that correctly completes each statement, and write its letter in the corresponding blank.

36. (a) Thankyou, (b) Thank-you, (c) Thank you for providing me with the application. _____

37. Informative literature and coupons will be (a) dispersed (b) disbursed at the beginning
of our promotion. _____

38. We can have deliveries (a) everyday, (b) every day, (c) every-day if we make
arrangements in advance. _____

39. The reason I am late is (a) because, (b) that my car stalled. _____

40. An e-mail message should (a) always, (b) never, (c) sometimes begin with a salutation. _____

Developing Proofreading Skills

As you complete a set of chapters (a unit), you will find a workshop exercise that introduces various techniques to help you improve your writing skills. This first workshop emphasizes proofreading skills. You will learn about proofreading marks, which are often used to edit printed material. Study the basic symbols shown here. See the inside front cover of your textbook for a more comprehensive list.

≡ Capitalize	ᵛ Insert apostrophe	⊙ Insert period
ℒ Delete	∧ Insert comma	/ Lower-case
∧ Insert	= Insert hyphen	⌒ Close up space

Example:

Proof reading marks are used by writers and editors too make corrections and revisions in

printed copy they use these standard Marks for clarity and consistency. If you are revis-

ing your own work Youll probably use these mark only occasional. In many jobs today,

however you will be working in a team environment Where writing tasks are shared.

Thats when its important to able to aply these well known marks correctly.

The preceding paragraph illustrates the use of proofreading marks. You'll also benefit from the following tips on how to look for errors.

- Be sure to check spelling. If you have composed at a computer, use its spell checker. But do not rely on it totally. It can't tell the difference between *it's* and *its* and many other confusing words.

- Look for grammar and punctuation errors. As you complete this book, you'll be more alert to problem areas, such as subject–verb agreement and comma placement.

- Double-check names and numbers. Compare all names and numbers with their sources because inaccuracies are not immediately visible. Especially verify the spelling of the names of individuals receiving the message. Most of us immediately dislike someone who misspells our name.

- For long or important documents, always print a copy (preferably double-spaced), set it aside for at least a day, and then proofread when you are fresh.

- Be prepared to find errors. One student confessed, "I can find other people's errors, but I can't seem to locate my own." Psychologically, we don't *expect* to find errors, and we don't *want* to find them. You can overcome this obstacle by anticipating errors and congratulating, not criticizing, yourself each time you find one.

Writing Application 1.1 After you read and edit the letter on the next page, your instructor may ask you to write a similar introductory personal business letter to her or him. On a separate sheet of paper, explain why you enrolled in this class, evaluate your present communication skills, name your major, describe the career you seek, and briefly tell about your current work (if you are employed) and your favourite activities. Your instructor may ask you to write a first draft quickly, print it, and then use proofreading marks to show corrections. Make a final copy. Double-space the rough draft; single-space the final copy. Turn in both copies. See Appendix C for a model personal business letter.

The following personal business letter contains intentional errors in typing, spelling, capitalization, and sentence punctuation. Use proofreading marks to edit this letter.

810 North Miller Road
Vancouver, BC V6B 4H3
September 8, 200x

Professor Margaret M. Sullivan
Department of Busness Administration
Schoolcraft College
Vancouver, BC V6B 5H6

Dear Professor Sulivan:

I enrolled this class to help me improve the way I use language I know that comunication skills are important, and I'm afraid that my present skills are below average. They're not good enough for me to get the kind of job I want I also enrolled in this class because its required in my major.

Accounting is my major I chose this major because I like working with figures. And because I know that many good jobs are available in accounting. Although I thought that accountants worked totaly with figures. My advisor tells me that accountants also need to be able to explain their work to management, to fellow employees, and to clients. My language skills are not terrific, and I want to improve. When I finish my accounting program, Ihope to get a job in the entertainment industry as a Junior Accountant.

I have a parttime job at Pizza Bob's. Where I deliver pizzas to campus dormitories, or to apartments an homes. I like my job because I get to meet people and because it helps me pay for my car and it's insurance.

When I'm not studing or working, I like to surf the internet. My favourite places to visit are World wide web sites devoted to unusual hobbys and businesses. Right now I'm interested in "CyberSlice," a site showing the menus of participating pizzerias in a neighbourhood. May be I can get Pizza Bob to participate!

Sincerely,

Knowing
the Namers

Nouns

4

OBJECTIVES   When you have completed the materials in this chapter, you will be able to do the following:

LEVEL I
- *Recognize four kinds of nouns.*
- *Follow the basic rules for spelling plural nouns.*

LEVEL II
- *Spell troublesome plural nouns ending in* y, o, *and* f.
- *Form the plurals of compound nouns, numerals, letters, degrees, and abbreviations.*

LEVEL III
- *Recognize and use correctly foreign plural nouns and selected special nouns.*
- *Use plural personal titles appropriately.*

PRETEST

Underline any incorrectly spelled noun in the following sentences. Spell the word correctly in the space provided.

1. Three children put their books on the bottom shelfs.   _____

2. At the market she purchased some tomatoes and potatos.   _____

3. Several Crown attornies requested tax write-offs for books.   _____

4. Our two RNAs both asked for leave of absences in June.   _____

5. Based on all the criterion, several diagnoses were given.   _____

1. shelves   2. potatoes   3. attorneys   4. leaves of absence   5. criteria

This business English textbook treats the study of our language *selectively*. We will not consider *all* the rules and conventions of English. Instead, this book will focus on those aspects of the language that have proved troublesome. Therefore, in this chapter on nouns, the principal concern will be the forming and spelling of plural nouns—an area of confusion for many business writers.

Beginning with this chapter, concepts are presented in levels, progressing from basic, frequently used concepts at Level I to more complex and less frequently used concepts at Level III.

LEVEL I

As you will recall from Chapter 2 (p. 18), nouns name persons, places, things, qualities, concepts, and activities.

▶ Kinds of Nouns

As the "namers" in our language, nouns perform an important function. They often serve as sentence subjects. To help you understand nouns better, we divide them into two categories: concrete and abstract.

Concrete and Abstract Nouns

Concrete nouns name specific objects that you can actually see, hear, feel, taste, or smell. Abstract nouns name qualities and concepts. Because concrete nouns are precise, they are more forceful and effective in writing and talking than abstract nouns.

Concrete Nouns		Abstract Nouns	
jetliner	valley	freedom	happiness
stapler	jasmine	success	accuracy
lemonade	affidavit	memory	personality
dentist	coffee	truth	love

Common and Proper Nouns

Common nouns name *generalized* persons, places, and things. Proper nouns, on the other hand, name *specific* persons, places, and things. They are always capitalized. Rules for capitalization are presented in Chapter 19 (pp. 351–358).

Common Nouns		Proper Nouns	
document	dog	Charter of Rights	Labrador retriever*
organization	computer	and Freedoms	Dell computer*
student	telephone	United Nations	Nokia cellphone*
photocopier	company	Mark Montgomery	Bata Shoes
		Xerox machine*	

Career Tip

Successful job applicants fill their résumés with concrete expressions and quantifiable data rather than abstractions. Instead of *Worked as lab assistant,* try *Assisted over 300 students and 25 faculty members using MS Word in computer lab.*

---

* *Note that common nouns following proper nouns are not capitalized.*

▶ Basic Plurals

Singular nouns name *one* person, place, or thing. Plural nouns name *two* or more. At Level I you will learn basic rules for forming plurals. At Level II you will learn how to form the plurals of nouns that create spelling problems.

Regular nouns form the plural with the addition of *s* or *es.*

Add s *to most nouns:*

desk, desks	advantage, advantages	graphic, graphics
merchant, merchants	house, houses	Tom, Toms*
passenger, passengers	issue, issues	Johnson, Johnsons*

Add es *to nouns ending in* s, x, z, ch, *or* sh:

brush, brushes	business, businesses	quartz, quartzes
tax, taxes	wrench, wrenches	Sanchez, Sanchezes*

Irregular nouns form the plural by changing the spelling of the word.

man, men	foot, feet	mouse, mice
goose, geese	child, children	ox, oxen

As noted in Chapter 1, most dictionaries do *not* show plurals of *regular* nouns because of space restrictions. Thus, if you look up the plural of *ranch*, you probably will not find it. Dictionaries *do* show the plurals of nouns that might be confusing or difficult to spell.

Apostrophes (') are *not* used to form plural nouns. Reserve the apostrophe to show possession. (Chapter 5 discusses possessive nouns in detail.)

Wrong: Management *executive's* have excellent *salary's.*

Right: Management *executives* have excellent *salaries.*

Now complete the reinforcement exercises for Level I on pp. 57–58.

Spot the Blooper

Nabisco introduced a new product as *Teddy Graham Bearwich's.* Not long after, it quietly gave the box a new design and new name, *T. G. Bearwiches.*

Hotlink

Additional material on Irregular Plurals of Nouns can be found at this University of Victoria Web site **<http://web2.uvcs. uvic.ca/elc/studyzone/ 330/grammar/irrplu. htm>**.

▶ Troublesome Noun Plurals

LEVEL II

Your ability to spell certain troublesome nouns can be greatly improved by studying the following rules and examples.

1. *Common nouns ending in* y *form the plural in two ways.*

    a. When the *y* is preceded by a vowel (*a, e, i, o, u*), the plural is formed by the addition of *s* only.

valley, valleys	journey, journeys	buoy, buoys
turkey, turkeys	delay, delays	Garvey, Garveys

    b. When the *y* is preceded by a consonant (all letters other than vowels), the plural is formed by changing the *y* to *ies.*

country, countries	quality, qualities	city, cities
currency, currencies	company, companies	secretary, secretaries

Study Tip

In making surnames plural, never change the original spellings. Adding *s* or *es* is acceptable, but changing *Kennedy* to *Kennedies* changes the original spelling.

---

* *Proper nouns are made plural in the same way that common nouns are made plural except for proper nouns ending in* y. *See the explanation in 1.b. in Level II.*

(This rule does *not* apply to the plural forms of proper nouns: *Amy, Amys; February, Februarys; Kelly, Kellys*.)

2. *Nouns ending in f, fe,* or *ff* follow no standard rules in the formation of plurals, though most simply add *s* to the singular from. Study the examples shown here, and use a dictionary when in doubt.

Add _s_	**Change to _ves_**	**Both Forms Recognized***
brief, briefs	half, halves	dwarfs, dwarves
cliff, cliffs	knife, knives	scarves, scarfs
proof, proofs	leaf, leaves	wharves, wharfs
safe, safes	shelf, shelves	
sheriff, sheriffs	wife, wives	
tariff, tariffs	wolf, wolves	
Wolf, Wolfs		

Do not confuse plural nouns with verb forms ending in *s*. He *saves* (verb) his money in two *safes* (noun). Be especially aware of the following words:

Nouns	**Verbs**
belief, beliefs	believe, believes
leaf, leaves (foliage)	leave, leaves (to depart)
loaf, loaves (of bread)	loaf, loafs (to be idle)
proof, proofs	prove, proves

3. *Nouns ending in o* may be made plural by adding *s* or *es*.

    a. When the *o* is preceded by a vowel, the plural is formed by adding *s* only.

studio, studios	curio, curios	radio, radios
patio, patios	ratio, ratios	portfolio, portfolios

    b. When the *o* is preceded by a consonant, the plural is formed by adding *s* or *es*. Study the following examples, and again use your dictionary whenever in doubt.

Add _s_	**Add _es_**	**Both Forms Recognized***
auto, autos	echo, echoes	cargoes, cargos
avocado, avocados	embargo, embargoes	ghettos, ghettoes
dynamo,	hero, heroes	innuendoes, innuendos
dynamos	potato, potatoes	mangoes, mangos
memo, memos	tomato, tomatoes	mosquitoes, mosquitos
silo, silos	veto, vetoes	mottoes, mottos
typo, typos		

    c. Musical terms ending in *o* always form the plural with the addition of *s* only.

alto, altos	cello, cellos	piano, pianos
banjo, banjos	contralto, contraltos	solo, solos

Career Tip

Find a job you love, and you'll never have to work a day in your life.

---

* *More common form shown first.*

4. *Compound nouns* may be written as single (or solid) words, may be hyphenated, or may appear as separate words (open form).

   a. When written as single words, compound nouns form the plural by appropriate changes in the final element.

bookshelf, bookshelves	printout, printouts
footnote, footnotes	stepchild, stepchildren
payroll, payrolls	workman, workmen

   b. When written in hyphenated or open form, compound nouns form the plural by appropriate changes in the principal noun.

lookers-on	bills of lading
mayors-elect	boards of directors
mothers-in-law	leaves of absence
runners-up	paper clips

   c. If a hyphenated compound noun has no principal noun at all, the final element is made plural.

cure-alls	look-alikes	show-offs
go-betweens	no-shows	trade-ins
know-it-alls	run-ins	write-offs

5. *Numerals, alphabet letters, isolated words,* and *degrees* are made plural by adding *s, es,* or *'s.* The modern trend is to use the *'s* only when necessary for clarity (see *d* below).

   a. Numerals and upper-case letters (with the exception of *A, I, M,* and *U*) require only *s* in plural formation.

   > Price trends from the *1980s* continued through the *1990s.*
   > Her new calculator was not printing *7s* and *9s.*
   > Narinder received all *Bs* and *Cs* on his report card.

   b. Isolated words used as nouns are made plural with the addition of *s* or *es,* as needed for pronunciation.

   > The Speaker of the House took a count of *yeses* and *noes* on the bill.
   > Numerous *ands, ahs,* and *you knows* made his speech ineffective.
   > She considered all the *pros* and *cons* before signing the contract.

   c. Degrees are made plural with the addition of *s.*

   > Dr. Helstrum holds two *Ph.D.s* in related fields.
   > Graduates with *M.B.A.s* are being heavily recruited.

   d. For clarity isolated lower-case letters and the capital letters *A, I, M,* and *U* require *'s.*

   > Unless she writes more legibly, her *o's* may be mistaken for *a's.*
   > In preparing the notice for the marquee yesterday, we ran out of *A's* and *I's.*

6. *Abbreviations* are usually made plural by adding *s* to the singular form.

yr., yrs.	mgr., mgrs.	dept., depts.	wk., wks.
c.o.d., c.o.d.s	CAAT, CAATs	IOU, IOUs	bldg., bldgs.

Hotlink

Irregular Noun Plurals get further attention at **<http://www.iei.uiuc. edu/structure/ structure1/nounplurals. html>**, available from the University of Illinois.

Hotlink

The English Language Centre at the University of Victoria offers more help with troublesome plurals at **<http://web2.uvcs. uvic.ca/elc/studyzone/ 330/grammar/plural. htm>**.

The singular and plural forms of abbreviations or symbols for units of measurement are, however, usually identical (*always* identical in the case of metric units of measurement).

g	(gram or grams)		L	(litre or litres)
km	(kilometre or kilometres)		deg.	(degree or degrees)
cm	(centimetre or centimetres)		ft.	(foot or feet)

Complete the reinforcement exercises for Level II on pp. 59–60.

LEVEL III

▶ Special Plural Forms

Selected nouns borrowed from foreign languages and other special nouns require your attention because their plural forms can be confusing.

1. *Nouns borrowed from foreign languages* may retain a foreign plural. A few, however, also have an anglicized plural form, shown second below. Check your dictionary for the preferred or more frequently used form.

Singular	Plural
alga	algae
alumna (*feminine*)	alumnae (pronounced *a-LUM-nee*)
alumnus (*masculine*)	alumni (pronounced *a-LUM-neye*)
analysis	analyses
bacterium	bacteria
basis	bases
crisis	crises
criterion	criteria
curriculum	curricula
datum	data*
diagnosis	diagnoses
erratum	errata
formula	formulae or formulas
hypothesis	hypotheses
larva	larvae
memorandum	memoranda or memorandums
parenthesis	parentheses
phenomenon	phenomena
stimulus	stimuli
thesis	theses

Hotlink

Another list of special plural forms can be found at the EduFind.com Web site <**http:www.edufind. com/english/grammar/ NOUNS2.cfm**>.

2. *Personal titles* may have both formal and informal plural forms.

Singular	Formal Plural	Informal Plural
Miss	the Misses Smith	the Miss Smiths
Mr.	Messrs.† Kahn and Lee	Mr. Kahn and Mr. Lee
Mrs.	Mmes.†† Davis and Klein	Mrs. Davis and Mrs. Klein
Ms.	Mses.††† Freiden and Allen	Ms. Freiden and Ms. Allen

---

* *See discussion in Hotline Queries, p. 55.*
† *Pronounced MES-erz (abbreviation of* Messieurs*)*
†† *Pronounced May-DAM (abbreviation of* Mesdames*)*
††† *Pronounced MIZ-ez (Ms. is probably a blend of Mrs. and Miss.)*

3. *Special nouns,* many of which end in *s,* may normally be *only* singular *or* plural in meaning. Other special nouns may be considered *either* singular *or* plural in meaning.

Usually Singular	Usually Plural	May Be Singular or Plural
economics	clothes	corps
genetics	goods	deer
mathematics	pants	politics
measles	scissors	sheep
news	thanks	Vietnamese

Study Tip

Practise these special nouns by using them with the singular verb *is* or the plural verb *are.* Genetics *is* fascinating (singular). Scissors *are* useful (plural).

4. *Single-letter abbreviations* may be made plural by doubling the letter.

pp. (pages)   See pp. 18–21. (pages 18 through 21)
ff. (and following) See pp. 18 ff. (page 18 and following pages)

Complete the reinforcement exercises for Level III on pp. 61–63.

HOTLINE QUERIES

Question: It seems to me that the meaning of the word *impact* has changed. I thought it meant "an effect." But now I hear this use: *How does this policy impact on the Middle East?* What's happening to this word?

Answer: In our language nouns often become verbs (to *bridge* the gap, to *corner* a market, to *telephone* a friend). Whether a noun-turned-verb is assimilated into the language seems to depend on its utility, its efficiency, and the status of the individuals who use it. For example, transformation of the noun *impact* into a verb would appear to be unnecessary, since the word *affect* clearly suffices in most constructions (*how does this program affect the Middle East?*). Although we hear *impact* used frequently as a verb today, many language specialists find it offensive.

Question: Could you help me spell the plurals of *do* and *don't?*

Answer: In forming the plurals of isolated words, the trend today is to add *s* and no apostrophe. Thus we have *dos* and *don'ts.* Formerly, apostrophes were used to make isolated words plural. However, if no confusion results, make plurals by adding *s* only.

Question: One member of our staff consistently corrects our use of the word *data.* He says the word is plural. Is it never singular?

Answer: The word *data* is indeed plural; the singular form is *datum.* Through frequent usage, however, *data* has recently become a collective noun. Collective nouns may be singular or plural depending on whether they are considered as one unit or as separate units. For example, *These data are much different from those findings,* or *This data is conclusive.*

Question: I don't have a dictionary handy. Can you tell me which word I should use in this sentence: *A (stationary/stationery) circuit board will be installed.*

Answer: In your sentence use *stationary,* which means "not moving" or "permanent" (*the concrete columns are stationary*). *Stationery* means "writing paper" (*his stationery has his address printed on it*). You might be able to remember the word *stationery* by associating *envelopes* with the *e* in *stationery.*

Question: My mother is always correcting me when I say, *I hate when that happens.* What's wrong with this? I hear it on TV all the time.

Answer: Your mother wants you to speak standard English, the written and spoken language we need to use in order to make the best impression in contexts such as business and school. Hearing an expression on TV is no assurance that it's acceptable in all situations. The problem with an expression like *I hate when that happens* is that an adverbial phrase (*when that happens*) is used as the object of a verb (*hate*). Only nouns, noun clauses, or pronouns may act as objects of verbs. Correction: *I hate it when that happens,* or *I hate this to happen.*

Question: As a sportswriter, I need to know the plural of *hole-in-one.*

Answer: Make the principal word plural, *holes-in-one.*

Question: In e-mail messages is it acceptable to use abbreviations such as *IMHO (in my humble opinion), ROTFL (rolling on the floor laughing),* and *TIA (thanks in advance)*?

Answer: Among close friends who understand their meaning, such abbreviations are certainly acceptable. But in business messages, these abbreviations are too casual and too obscure. Many readers would have no idea what they mean. Smileys such as :-) are also too casual for business messages.

Question: In the sentence, *Please read our FAQs,* does the abbreviation need an apostrophe?

Answer: No. The abbreviation for *Frequently Asked Questions* is *FAQs,* as you wrote it. Avoid using an apostrophe for plural forms.

CHAPTER 4   **Reinforcement Exercises**

LEVEL I

Note: At the beginning of each level, a self-check exercise is provided so that you may immediately check your understanding of the concepts in that level. Do not look at the answers until you have finished the exercise. Then compare your responses with the answers shown at the bottom of the page. If more than three of your answers do not agree with those shown, reread the level before continuing with the other reinforcement exercises.

A. (**Self-check**) Write the plural forms of the singular nouns shown in parentheses.

Example: The (Finch) have purchased an office building on Lakeshore Boulevard.   _____Finches_____

1. Some (business) are formed as limited partnerships.   _____

2. Traps were set to catch the many (mouse) recently seen in the building.   _____

3. The toy manufacturer invited many (child) to test the new products.   _____

4. After four lengthy (speech), boredom overcame the audience.   _____

5. All (fax) in our office are printed on plain paper.   _____

6. The condition will not change unless Parliament passes a law with (tooth) in it.   _____

7. One administrative secretary may serve six (boss).   _____

8. The (Morris) are planning to move to Saskatchewan as soon as their deal is closed.   _____

9. How many (sandwich) did you say he ate?   _____

10. All the (loaf) of bread are wheat bread.   _____

Check your answers.

B. Correct any errors in the use of plural nouns in the following sentences by underlining the incorrect form and writing the correct form in the space provided. If the sentence is correct as it stands, write *C*.

Example: The advertising agency submitted several <u>sketch</u> of the design.   _____sketches_____

1. Several men and woman were being considered for the vacant position.   _____

2. Anderson was one of the writer's working on the screenplay.   _____

3. Rashon transmitted both fax to them yesterday.   _____

4. Bunchs of spectators gathered outside the stock exchange.   _____

1. businesses 2. mice 3. children 4. speeches 5. faxes 6. teeth 7. bosses 8. Morrises 9. sandwiches 10. loaves

5. Mrs. Hollingsworth secured the door with two latchs. _____

6. Because three Brian's are employed in that department, surnames are used. _____

7. Each employee received two free pass's to the exhibit. _____

8. Kelly Jackson used two different lens for her photography assignment. _____

9. Last year the losses of Datapro exceeded its profits. _____

10. Have the Welshs submitted this year's income tax return? _____

11. The reception room has four benchs and two upholstered chairs. _____

12. Mr. Burtness and his two stepchilds attended the reunion. _____

13. Sharing ownership in the venture are the Joneses and the Garveys. _____

14. Only two news dispatchs were released concerning the stock split. _____

15. Swans, ducks, and gooses live in the sanctuary during the winter. _____

C. Write plural forms for the nouns listed.

1. employee _____   **11.** hunch _____

2. watch _____   **12.** sketch _____

3. Lynch _____   **13.** Banks _____

4. franchise _____   **14.** Lohman _____

5. quartz _____   **15.** service _____

6. rich _____   **16.** gas _____

7. mile _____   **17.** area _____

8. Ahmad _____   **18.** absence _____

9. tax _____   **19.** pamphlet _____

10. Lorna _____   **20.** Peretz _____

LEVEL II

A. (**Self-check**) Provide the correct plural forms of the words shown in parentheses.

1. We have decided to close on (Sunday) during July and August. _____

2. Upper (shelf) contain less frequently used company files. _____

3. Small businesses can afford few administrative (luxury). _____

4. For the past three (January), the directors voted dividends. _____

5. Students had to show their (ID) before they were admitted. _____

6. Two (bill of lading) were missing from the shipment. _____

7. Deciduous trees drop their (leaf) in the autumn. _____

8. Our organization is prepared to deal in foreign (currency). _____

9. Few orchestras have seven (cello) in the string section. _____

10. The committee debated the (pro and con) of decentralization. _____

Check your answers.

B. Write the correct plural forms of the singular expressions shown in parentheses.

1. All that remained standing were two blackened (chimney). _____

2. The liquidity (ratio) of the two companies were compared. _____

3. A total of 212 (MP) responded to the survey. _____

4. President Farley wanted a manager with conservative (belief). _____

5. Both (Lisa) are outstanding customer service representatives. _____

6. More graduates with (M.B.A.) are available than ever before. _____

7. Do the (Wolf) subscribe to *Canadian Business*? _____

8. City Council awarded medals to the fire (hero). _____

9. After the lecture three (hanger-on) remained at the lectern. _____

10. A worldwide economic depression occurred in the early (1890). _____

11. Computer users must distinguish between zeros and (O). _____

12. We will tabulate all (yes and no) before releasing the vote. _____

1. Sundays 2. shelves 3. luxuries 4. Januarys 5. IDs 6. bills of lading 7. leaves 8. currencies 9. cellos 10. pros and cons

13. The two (board of directors) voted to begin merger negotiations. _____

14. The manager hired her two (daughter-in-law) as salesclerks. _____

15. At least two employees have taken (leave of absence) this month. _____

C. Write plural forms for the nouns listed. Use a dictionary if you are unsure of the spelling.

1. editor-in-chief _____

2. half _____

3. bill of sale _____

4. 1990 _____

5. subsidiary _____

6. TV _____

7. July _____

8. balance of trade _____

9. Shelley _____

10. safe _____

11. company _____

12. 7 _____

13. turkey _____

14. banjo _____

15. port of entry _____

16. cure-all _____

17. B.A. _____

18. C _____

19. No. _____

20. mayor-elect _____

21. if _____

22. disk jockey _____

23. RSVP _____

24. dept. _____

25. q _____

26. Ph.D. _____

27. Emory _____

28. don't _____

29. Fox _____

30. in and out _____

D. Write sentences using the plural forms of the nouns shown in parentheses.

1. (trade-in) _____

_____

2. (Oakley) _____

_____

3. (up and down) _____

_____

4. (RN)* _____

_____

5. (mm) _____

* Check your dictionary if you are not sure of the meanings of abbreviations.

A. (**Self-check**) Write the plural forms of the singular expressions in parentheses.

LEVEL III

1. Moving lights and other (stimulus) affect the human eye.   _____

2. Black holes are but one of the (phenomenon) of astronomy.   _____

3. Art collections illustrate varying (emphasis) of museum directors.   _____

4. Friends and (alumnus) of the University of Manitoba attended.   _____

5. Formal invitations were sent to (Mrs.) Wagner, Phillips, and Wang.   _____

6. You will find the index on (p.) 116–120.   _____

7. Experts presented conflicting (analysis) of the problem.   _____

8. Greg's family was troubled by numerous (crisis).   _____

9. The announcement reported that (Mr.) Spinello and Busch had formed a partnership.   _____

10. Our office manager ordered new stationery for (memorandum).   _____

Check your answers.

B. Write the plural form in the space provided.

1. Researchers collected substantial (datum) to support their hypothesis.   _____

2. The girls' school will honour its illustrious (alumna).   _____

3. References to LaserJet printers may be found on pp. 25 (and following pages). _____

4. Dr. Hersh revealed the two startling (hypothesis) in a press conference.   _____

5. All variant spellings are shown in sets of (parenthesis).   _____

6. Galileo's (hypothesis) about the solar system were rejected by his peers.   _____

7. Jack asked for information about two related (curriculum).   _____

8. Our catalogue shows real estate courses on (p.) 226–231.   _____

9. Her disorder has resulted in several different (diagnosis).   _____

10. Betty's master's and doctor's (thesis) are both in the library.   _____

1. stimuli 2. phenomena 3. emphases 4. alumni 5. Mmes. 6. pp. 7. analyses 8. crises 9. Messrs. 10. memoranda (memorandums).

C. Complete the sentences below, selecting the proper singular or plural verb to agree with the noun subject of each.

1. Genetics (is, are) a dynamic field of study. _____

2. Curricula (is, are) currently being developed in office technologies. _____

3. (Is, Are) the proceeds to be donated to charity? _____

4. Leo said the scissors (is, are) on the desk. _____

5. Economics (is, are) a field with career potential. _____

6. The statistics on crime (is, are) staggering. _____

7. Thanks (is, are) due to our committee chairs. _____

8. Several Vietnamese (is, are) enrolled in this class. _____

9. News of the company takeover (is, are) rocking the market. _____

10. Insect larvae (is, are) responsible for the damage. _____

D. Review of Levels I, II, and III. (Self-check) In the following sentences underline any errors in nouns or noun–verb agreement. For each sentence write a corrected form in the space provided. If a sentence is correct, write *C* in the space. Then check your answers at the bottom of the next page.

1. Proper tools and modern equipment make businesses run smoothly. _____

2. When you first join an electronic news group, you'll want to read the FAQ's (frequently asked questions) before posting any messages. _____

3. All responses to our telephone inquirys must be received by May 2. _____

4. Although many stimulus are being studied, scientists have not yet determined an exact cause of the bacterial mysteries. _____

5. Unless Revenue Canada proves that the Kellys owe federal taxs, no penalty can be assessed. _____

6. Both woman asked for leaves of absence during the week of June 7. _____

7. Tomatoes are grown to perfection in the interior vallies. _____

8. Our directory lists RN's and MD's separately. _____

9. Because economics are the primary concern, be sure your proposal outlines a careful budget for the entire project. _____

10. After numerous brushs with the law, Mark became a consultant to a security company. _____

11. The Lynch's named three beneficiaries in their insurance policies. _____

12. Attorneys and judges were advised to place their heaviest books on the lower shelfs. _____

13. Because of numerous glitches in our software, e-mail messages arrived in irregular batchs. _____

14. Despite the new flexible hours for Mondays through Thursdays, all employees must put in a full workday on Fridays. _____

15. The Morrises discussed all the in's and out's of the transaction before signing the contract. _____

E. Optional Composition. Your instructor may ask you to complete this exercise on a separate sheet. Write ten complete sentences using the plural forms of the following nouns: *phenomenon, datum, tooth, CEO, delay, belief, business, company, Mr. and Mrs. Lopez, father-in-law.*

Editor's Challenge

The following letter contains intentional errors in spelling, proofreading, noun plurals, and sentence structure. Use proofreading marks to correct them.

SHEARMAN BROTHERS
415 Yonge Street
Toronto, ON M5B 2E7

Phone: (416) 502-8694   *Fax: (416) 502-7619*   *Web: http://www.shearmanbros.com*

April 5, 200x

Ms. Judy Bender Bachman
The Daily News
11 Thornhill Drive
Dartmouth, NS B3B 1R9

Dear Ms. Bender:

Thanks for the oportunity to contribute to the article. That you are writting about fast-food promotions. As an analyst with Shearman Brothers, I specialize in the fast-food and beverage industrys.

You specifically wanted information about what sells fast food. Actually, competition among the fast food giants has always been as much about appearances as reality. Its a lot like a three-ring circus, with flashy new showstoppers needed to keep men, woman, and children coming back. Some promotions by companys have been fiascos. I assume, however, that you are most interested in sucessful stategies such as the following:

• **Giveaways**. Fast-food giants suchas McDonald's use movie tie-ins and toy promotions that appeal children, who then persuade their parents to come into the stores.

• **Advertising**. Companys spend million on ad campaigns promoting expressions that they hope will become part of everyone's speech, such as classics like "You deserve a break today."

• **Food**. Nothing else matters if the food doesn't taste good. McDonald's, for example, grows its own potatos and raises cattle to ensure that its french frys and sandwichs meet rigid specifications.

• **Price**. Cutting prices increases sale, but usually for a short time only. In the end, price-cutting erodes profites. Another strategy is the repackaging of popular items in "value" combinations. Which is an effort to boost sales.

• **Convenience.** People often go to a fastfood restaurant on impulse, the more restaurants that a company has, the more likely that it will make a sale.

I hope theseideas are helpful to you in prepareing your article. If you use any of this material, I must submit your article to our lawyers for approval. Call me when you would like to talk further about this article.

Sincerely,

Paul Lahijanian

Paul Lahijanian
Senior Analyst

Underline any incorrectly spelled nouns. Write the correct forms.

1. All the children were warned to be careful of the sharp knifes. _____

2. Three bunches of red tomatos look ripe enough to eat. _____

3. Grey wolves are reported to live in the two vallies. _____

4. In the 1980s many companys were searching for graduates with M.B.A.s. _____

5. After several business crisis, we hired two troubleshooters. _____

learning.web.ways

Many Web sites provide summaries of information about well-known companies. Some sites, such as Hoovers.com, allow you to see a capsule of information at no charge. For more extensive information, you must subscribe. You can find information such as a company's addresses (Web and land), the names of its current officers, its subsidiary locations, its products, and its competition. You can even find out its annual revenue and other financial information. In this short exercise you will search for information about the Hudson's Bay Company.

Goal: To learn to search for company data on the Web.

1. With your Web browser on the screen, key the following URL: **<http:// www.hoovers.com>**. Press **Enter**.

2. Look over the Hoover's Online home page. Ignore the advertising clutter and click **Search Help**. A window opens. Scroll down to learn about search parameters (characteristics or boundaries). For how many companies does Hoover's provide data? Close the box by clicking the **X** in the right corner of the window.

3. Run your cursor over **Site Search**. Click **Company**. In the **For** box, key **Hudson's Bay**. Click **Go**.

4. Wait for the search results. When the **Search Results** page is fully loaded, scroll down to find a listing for the Hudson's Bay Company. Click **Capsule** to see a summary of company information.

5. Read about the Hudson's Bay Company's main chain stores. Which of them has the largest number of outlets across Canada?

1. knives 2. tomatoes 3. valleys 4. companies 5. crises

6. Print one page from the capsule.

7. Use the **Back** button to return to the **Search** page.

8. Search a company of your choice. Print one page of its capsule.

9. If you ever get lost at a Web site or can't find what you want, look for the **Site Map**. It is usually found in a navigation bar at the top, bottom, or along the left side. Find the Hoover's **Site Map** at the top of the screen. Click to see its contents.

10. End your session by clicking the **X** in the upper right corner of your browser. Turn in all printed copies.

Possessive Nouns

OBJECTIVES   When you have completed the materials in this chapter, you will be able to do the following:

LEVEL I

- *Distinguish between possessive nouns and noun plurals.*
- *Follow five steps in using the apostrophe to show ownership.*

LEVEL II

- *Use apostrophe construction for animate nouns.*
- *Distinguish between descriptive nouns and possessive nouns.*
- *Make compound nouns, combined ownership nouns, organization names, and abbreviations possessive.*
- *Understand incomplete possessives.*
- *Avoid awkward possessives.*

LEVEL III

- *Understand the effect of pronunciation on possessive forms of words ending in* s.
- *Make proper nouns possessive.*

Underline any incorrect possessive forms. Write correct versions in the spaces provided.

1. All customers inquiries will be answered immediately. _____

2. Michael's output this month is greater than Jeffreys. _____

3. Both accounts were credited with two months interest. _____

4. Mr. Ross real talent lies in the electronics field. _____

5. The Horowitzs daughters are both married. _____

Thus far you have studied four kinds of nouns (concrete, abstract, common, and proper), and you have learned how to make nouns plural. In this chapter you will learn how to use the apostrophe to make nouns possessive.

LEVEL I

Hotlink

This animated Microsoft® PowerPoint® presentation by Capital Community College will help you master the use of the apostrophe **<http:// webster.commnet.edu/ grammar/ppt/ apostrophe.pps>**.

▶ Showing Possession With Apostrophes

Notice in the following phrases how possessive nouns show ownership, origin, authorship, or measurement:

> Jack's computer (ownership)
> Quebec's citizens (origin)
> Atwood's writings (authorship)
> three years' time (measurement)

In expressing possession, speakers and writers have a choice. They may show possession with an apostrophe construction, or they may use a prepositional phrase with no apostrophe:

> the computer of Jack
> the citizens of Quebec
> the writings of Atwood
> the time of three years

The use of a prepositional phrase to show ownership is more formal and tends to emphasize the ownership word (the object of the preposition). The use of the apostrophe construction to show ownership is more efficient and more natural, especially in conversation. In writing, however, placing the apostrophe can be perplexing. Here are five simple but effective steps that will help you write possessives correctly.

1. customers' 2. Jeffrey's 3. months' 4. Mr. Ross' or Ross's 5. Horowitzes'

Five Steps in Using the Apostrophe Correctly

1. *Look for possessive construction.* Usually two nouns appear together. The first noun shows ownership of (or special relationship to) the second noun.

> the man['s] book
> the children['s] games
> a year['s] time
> both doctors['] offices
> the musicians['] instruments

2. *Reverse the nouns.* Use the second noun to begin a prepositional phrase. The object of the preposition is the ownership word.

> book of the *man*
> games of the *children*
> time of a *year*
> offices of both *doctors*
> instruments of the *musicians*

3. *Examine the ownership word.* To determine the correct possessive construction, you must know whether the ownership word is singular or plural.

4. *If the ownership word is singular, add apostrophe and* s.

> the man's book
> a year's time

5. a. *If the ownership word is plural and ends in* s, *add only an apostrophe.*

> both doctors' offices
> the musicians' instruments

   b. *If the ownership word is plural but does not end in* s, *add an apostrophe and* s.

> the children's games
> men's health

A word of caution. Once students begin to study apostrophes, they sometimes use a shotgun approach on passages with words ending in *s*, indiscriminately peppering them with apostrophes. Do *not* use apostrophes for nouns that simply show more than one of something. In the sentence *These companies are opening new branches in the West,* no apostrophes are required. The words *companies* and *branches* are plural; they are not possessive. In addition, be careful to avoid changing the spelling of singular nouns when making them possessive. For example, the *secretary's* desk (meaning the desk of one secretary) is *not* spelled *secretaries'*.

Pay particular attention to the following possessive constructions. Perhaps the explanations and hints in parentheses will help you understand and remember these expressions.

> a day's work (the work of one single day)
> three days' work (the work of three days)
> a dollar's worth (the worth of one single dollar)
> your money's worth (the worth of your money)
> today's weather (there can be only one *today*)
> tomorrow's work (there can be only one *tomorrow*)
> the shareholders' meeting (we usually assume that a meeting involves
>   more than one person)

Spot the Blooper

From Lois and Selma DeBakey's collection of bad medical writing: "The receptionist called the patients names." (How does the omitted apostrophe alter the meaning?)

Study Tip

Whenever you have any doubt about using an apostrophe, always put the expression into an "of" phrase. You'll immediately recognize the ownership word and see whether it ends in an *s*.

Hotlink

Another perspective on possessives and an online exercise with immediate feedback come from the University of Calgary's English Grammar Guide, available at **<http://www.ucalgary.ca/UofC/eduweb/grammar/>**. Click on Punctuation, and scroll down for the Apostrophe link.

The guides for possessive construction presented thus far cover the majority of possessives found in business writing.

Complete the reinforcement exercises for Level I on pp. 74–75.

LEVEL II

▶ Problem Possessive Constructions

You can greatly improve your skill in using apostrophes by understanding the following special cases.

1. *Animate versus inanimate nouns.* As a matter of style, some careful writers prefer to reserve the apostrophe construction for people and animals. For other nouns they use prepositional phrases or simple adjectives.

   > roof of the car, or car roof (better than *car's roof*)
   > colour of the desk, or the desk colour (better than *desk's colour*)
   > heat of the motor, or motor heat (better than *motor's heat*)

2. *Descriptive versus possessive nouns.* When nouns are used as adjectives to provide description or identification only, the possessive form is *not* used. Writers have most problems with descriptive nouns ending in *s*, such as *Claims* Department. No apostrophe is needed, just as none is necessary in *Personnel* Department.

   > Sales Department (*not* Sales' Department)
   > the electronics industry (*not* electronics' industry)
   > earnings record (*not* earnings' record)

3. *Compound nouns.* Make compound nouns possessive by adding an apostrophe or an *'s* to the final element of the compound.

   > his father-in-law's property
   > onlookers' interest
   > notary public's seal

4. *Incomplete possessives.* When the second noun in a possessive noun construction is unstated, the first noun is nevertheless treated as possessive.

   > You'll find bond paper at the stationer's [store].
   > Let's meet at Patrick's [home] after the game.
   > This year's sales are higher than last year's [sales].

5. *Separate or combined ownership.* When two nouns express separate ownership, make both possessive. When two nouns express combined ownership, make only the second one possessive.

Separate Ownership	**Combined Ownership**
landlords' and tenants' rights	the husband and wife's business
Mike's and Sam's stereos	my aunt and uncle's house

Study Tip

To identify descriptive nouns, ask if ownership is involved. Does *Department* belong to *Sales*? Is *industry* possessed by *electronics*? When the answer is no, omit the apostrophe.

Study Tip

Look at the object owned (*rights, business*, etc.). If that object is singular, ownership is usually combined.

6. *Names of organizations.* Organizations with possessives in their names may or may not use apostrophes. Follow the style used by the individual organization. (Consult the organization's stationery or a directory listing.)

      Metro Tenants Legal Services   Harvey's Restaurants
      Ontario Secondary School Teachers' Federation   Sears

7. *Abbreviations.* Make abbreviations possessive by following the same guidelines as for animate nouns.

      CMA's ruling   the Ph.D.'s credentials
      CBC's coverage   Ticketmaster Canada Inc.'s sales

Study Tip

To avoid an awkward possessive, use an *of* phrase starting with the object owned, such as *the advice of my sister's lawyer.*

8. *Awkward possessives.* When the addition of an apostrophe results in an awkward construction, show ownership by using a prepositional phrase.

Awkward	**Improved**
my brothers-in-law's opinions	opinions of my brothers-in-law
your neighbour's doctor's telephone number	telephone number of your neighbour's doctor
my professor, Dr. Aller's, office	office of my professor, Dr. Aller

Complete the reinforcement exercises for Level II on pp. 76–77.

▶ Additional Guideline

LEVEL III

You have learned to follow five steps in identifying possessive constructions and in placing the apostrophe correctly. The guides presented thus far cover most possessive constructions. Determining the possessive form of a few proper nouns, however, may require a refinement of Step 4.

Let us briefly review the five-step plan for placing the apostrophe in noun possessives, adding a refinement to the fourth step.

1. Look for possessive construction. (Usually, though not always, two nouns appear together.)

2. Reverse the nouns.

3. Examine the ownership word.

4. If the ownership word is singular, add an apostrophe and *s. However, if the ownership word is a name ending in an s sound, you may choose to add only an apostrophe* (see next page).

5. a. If the ownership word is plural and ends in *s*, add only an apostrophe.
    b. If the ownership word is plural but does not end in *s*, add an apostrophe and *s*.

Hotlink

North Carolina State University's Online Writing Lab has an excellent Web page that addresses advanced-level questions on apostrophes at **<http://www2.ncsu.edu/ncsu/grammar/Apostro3.html>**.

Spot the Blooper

Announcement pasted on top of each Domino's pizza box: "We accept all competitors coupons."

Study Tip

The word *the* preceding a name is a clue that the name is being used in a plural sense. For example, *the Rosses* means the entire Ross family.

▶ Making Singular Proper Nouns Possessive

Of all possessive forms, individuals' names—especially those ending in *s* sounds—are the most puzzling to students, and understandably so. Even experts don't always agree on the possessive form for singular proper nouns.

Traditionalists, as represented in *The Chicago Manual of Style* and *The Modern Language Association Style Manual,* prefer adding *'s* to troublesome *singular proper* nouns that end in *s* sounds. On the other hand, writers of more popular literature, as represented in *The Associated Press Stylebook and Libel Manual,* prefer the simpler style of adding just an apostrophe to singular proper nouns. You may apply either style, but be consistent. Please note in the examples below that the style choice applies *only* to singular names ending in *s* sounds. Plural names are always made possessive with the addition of an apostrophe only. Study the examples shown.

Singular Name	Singular Possessive— Traditional	Singular Possessive— Popular	Plural Possessive
Mrs. Jones	Mrs. Jones's	Mrs. Jones'	the Joneses'
Mr. Morris	Mr. Morris's	Mr. Morris'	the Morrises'
Mrs. Lopez	Mrs. Lopez's	Mrs. Lopez'	the Lopezes'
Mr. Horowitz	Mr. Horowitz's	Mr. Horowitz'	the Horowitzes'

Complete the reinforcement exercises for Level III on pp. 78–79.

HOTLINE QUERIES

Question: Where should the apostrophe go in *employee's handbook*?

Answer: This is tricky because the writer of that phrase must decide whether he or she considers the handbook from one employee's point of view or from all employees' points of view. Depending upon the writer's intention, the apostrophe could be justified for either position. The trend today seems to favour the singular construction (*employee's handbook,* one handbook per employee).

Question: I'm addressing a letter to the Canadian Nurses Association. What salutation shall I use? One person in our office suggested *Gentlewomen.* Is this being used?

Answer: I recommend that you use *Ladies and Gentlemen* since both male and female nurses are members of the association. In fact, this salutation is appropriate for any organization in which men and women may be represented in management. I would not use *Gentlewomen* because it sounds artificial. Businesses and individuals can avoid sexism in language without using stilted constructions. Salutations such as *Dear Sir* and *Gentlemen* are no longer used. Today we are more sensitive to women as employees, managers, and executives. The use of awkward terms like *Gentlewomen* or *Gentlepersons,* however, is an overreaction and should be avoided. Probably the best approach is to address specific people. Find the name of an individual to whom you can write.

Question: Should *undercapitalized* be hyphenated? I can't find it in my dictionary.

Answer: The prefixes *under* and *over* are not followed by hyphens.

Question: My boss has dictated, *I respectfully call <u>you</u> and your client's attention to ...* What's wrong with this? How can I make *you* possessive?

Answer: The best way to handle this awkward wording is to avoid using the possessive form. Use a prepositional phrase instead (*I respectfully call to the attention of you and your client ...*).

Question: Here at the Cancer Society we have a bureau of speakers. Where should the apostrophe go when we use the possessive form of the word *speakers*?

Answer: *Speakers' bureau.*

Question: As the holiday season approaches, I'm wondering whether it's *Season's Greetings* or *Seasons' Greetings.*

Answer: If you are referring to one season, it's *Season's Greetings.*

Question: I have a problem with the following sentence from a legal document: *The plaintiff was in fact fired ostensibly for violating Denny's alcoholic beverage service policy.* How do I make possessive a proper name that is already possessive?

Answer: As you suspected, you can't add another apostrophe. In the interests of clarity, I would consider the name descriptive, thus avoiding an additional *'s.* You would write *Denny's alcoholic beverage service policy.* By the same reasoning, you would not add another apostrophe to anything possessed by *McDonald's.*

CHAPTER 5   **Reinforcement Exercises**

A. **(Self-check)** Rewrite the following phrases without apostrophes. Use a prepositional phrase.

LEVEL I

<u>Revision</u>

Example: the trainee's hours   *hours of the trainee* _____

1. the defendant's pleas   _____

2. this customer's fax   _____

3. three men's suggestions   _____

4. our company's policy   _____

5. your money's worth   _____

6. a beginner's luck   _____

7. two years' time   _____

8. all drivers' engines   _____

9. the children's books   _____

10. six months' interest   _____

Check your answers.

B.   Using apostrophes, change the following prepositional phrases into possessive constructions. Ownership words are underlined.

Example: compensation of <u>women</u>   *women's compensation* _____

1. records of my <u>accountant</u>   _____

2. rights of <u>patients</u>   _____

3. permit for a <u>seller</u>   _____

4. interest for six <u>months</u>   _____

5. addresses of <u>customers</u>   _____

6. shares of this <u>company</u>   _____

1. pleas of the defendant 2. fax of this customer 3. suggestions of three men 4. policy of our company 5. worth of your money 6. luck of a beginner 7. time of two years 8. engines of all drivers 9. books of the children 10. interest of six months

7. prices of <u>competitors</u>   _____

8. duties of the <u>secretary</u>   _____

9. delay of a <u>month</u>   _____

10. meeting of <u>shareholders</u>   _____

C. Underline the errors in possessive construction in the following sentences. Write the correct form at the right. If the sentence is correct as it stands, write *C*.

Example: Some <u>students</u> cars were ticketed.   _____students'_____

1. Search engines can find only a fraction of the Web's vast contents.   _____

2. Customers expect a dollars worth of value for a dollar spent.   _____

3. In just one days e-mail, the manager receives as many as 250 messages.   _____

4. Both clerks salaries will be reviewed next quarter.   _____

5. A number of changes have occurred in the composition of the Board of Trustees. _____

6. Most students difficulties lie in recognizing possessives.   _____

7. Many management firms will tailor their services and charges to a clients needs. _____

8. Several bakeries in our neighbourhood provide excellent products.   _____

9. Three months interest will be due in four days.   _____

10. Success depends on a companies capacity to deliver.   _____

11. The four astronomers theories created international news.   _____

12. A customers credit card may be used quite safely on the Internet.   _____

13. Some companies are cutting expenses by requiring employees, customers, and vendors to communicate by e-mail. _____

14. An inventors patent protects his or her invention for seventeen years.   _____

15. At each buyers expense, high-quality speakers may be substituted.   _____

16. You have exactly four days in which to find new fire and liability insurance policies for the buildings. _____

17. All taxpayers returns are checked by computer.   _____

18. Many of Disneys animated films are now made in Vancouver, North America's second-largest film production centre. _____

19. Davids salary is higher than that of the other clerks because he has greater responsibilities. _____

20. Camille could not find her name on the voters list.   _____

A. **(Self-check)** For each of the following sentences, underline any possessive construction that could be improved. Write an improved form in the space provided. If the sentence is acceptable as it stands, write *C*.

LEVEL II

Examples: <u>Our office's roof</u> is leaking.

The meeting Friday is at <u>Ellens.</u>

<u>The roof of our office</u>

<u>Ellen's</u>

1. This pencil's point is dull. _____

2. The Jones' brothers both play hockey. _____

3. Lisa's and Bill's new home is close to the city. _____

4. This company's product line is superior to that companys. _____

5. The first runner-ups trophy will also be awarded tonight. _____

6. Sales of shares were stimulated by the CRTC's ruling. _____

7. She was elected by members of the Ontario Secondary School Teacher's Federation. _____

8. Our editor-in-chiefs suggestions are always followed. _____

9. Most ladies and mens raincoats are reduced in price. _____

10. Is your sister-in-laws job downtown? _____

Check your answers at the bottom of the page.

B. For each of the following sentences, underline any possessive construction that could be improved. Write an improved form in the space provided. If the sentence is acceptable as it stands, write *C*.

1. What is that sticky substance on the computer's keys? _____

2. The King and Queen's limousine approached slowly. _____

3. Web graphics must be designed with the audience's browsers in mind. _____

4. Many manufacturer's representatives displayed equipment. _____

5. All beneficiaries names must be submitted when policies are issued. _____

6. NATOs member countries include Canada and France. _____

7. Duplicate forms were sent to the Claims' Department. _____

1. The point of this pencil or This pencil point 2. Jones 3. Lisa 4. company's 5. runner-up's 6. C 7. Teachers' 8. editor-in-chief's 9. ladies', men's 10. sister-in-law's

8. This month's production figures are lower than last months. _____

9. Numerous employees personnel folders will be reviewed. _____

10. Several new roses were described in news releases. _____

11. Both the husband's and wife's signatures must be secured before the sale is valid. _____

12. Most of this companys customers are concentrated nearby. _____

13. At least a dozen buyers and sellers finances were scrutinized. _____

14. The last power failure happened on New Years' Eve. _____

15. Your totals for the last three columns are certainly different from Carols. _____

16. Because of the gravity of the offence, the Crown attorneys staff is investigating. _____

17. Lyon & Co.s annual sale is scheduled to begin in three days. _____

18. Frank's and Pam's new car has a two-year warranty. _____

19. Although I'm interested in the electronics' field, I have not settled on a definite career. _____

20. Were you at Theresas Saturday night? _____

C. Rewrite these sentences to remedy awkward or incorrect possessives. (*Hint:* Start your sentence with the word that is owned.)

Example: My brother's friend's car is available. _____ *The car of my brother's friend is available.* _____

1. His company's accountant's suggestions are wise.

_____

_____

2. Brent Harris, my dentist's, practice is flourishing.

_____

_____

3. Were both your sisters-in-law's cars ticketed on the same day?

_____

_____

4. The engineer's secretary's computer held all the necessary equations.

_____

_____

5. My friend's brothers' motorcycles were always parked in the driveway.

_____

_____

A. (**Self-check**) Select the acceptable possessive form.

LEVEL III

1. Miss (a) Betz' or Betz's, (b) Betzes' vacation is scheduled for April. _____

2. We can't locate (a) Guses', (b) Gus' or Gus's employee record. _____

3. Is that a realtor's sign on the (a) Harrises's, (b) Harrises' home? _____

4. Only one (a) waitress's, (b) waitresses' service was criticized. _____

5. Cheryl took Dr. (a) Fox' or Fox's, (b) Foxes' prescription to a pharmacy. _____

6. All (a) creditor's, (b) creditors' claims will be honoured. _____

7. Have you seen Annie (a) Leibovitz' or Leibovitz's, (b) Leibovitzes' photographs? _____

8. Please verify Mrs. (a) Lopezes', (b) Lopez's or Lopez' hours. _____

9. Have you noticed that the (a) Horowitzes, (b) Horowitzes' have a new car? _____

10. Are you using a computer to schedule your (a) bosses', (b) boss's appointments? (One boss) _____

Check your answers.

B. Fill in the singular possessive forms for the two styles shown below.

Name	Traditional Style	Popular Style
Example: [Mr. Jones] suit	Mr. Jones's suit	Mr. Jones' suit
1. [Ms. Burns] purse	_____	_____
2. [Mr. Harris] desk	_____	_____
3. [Dr. Cortez] office	_____	_____
4. [Miss Mertz] letter	_____	_____
5. [Lois] computer	_____	_____

1.a 2.b 3.b 4.a 5.a 6.b 7.a 8.b 9.a 10.b

C. **Review of Levels I, II, and III.** Each of the following sentences has one error in the use of a possessive. Write the corrected form in the space provided.

1. I believe that Russ letter is on the top of the pile. _____

2. His landlord said that four months rent was due. _____

3. Mrs. Otis paycheque did not reflect the deduction. _____

4. We were all invited to the party at the Thomas. _____

5. Despite a weeks delay the package finally arrived. _____

6. Mr. Gross investments were carefully selected. _____

7. All city council representatives were invited to the homeowners meeting. _____

8. Our records show that Mr. Murray account has an error. _____

9. In seven years time the loan will be repaid in full. _____

10. One witnesses testimony was questioned. _____

11. The Moskowitz two sons are enrolled in a British Columbia college. _____

12. Do you feel that you got your moneys worth? _____

13. After three days practice all trainees qualified. _____

14. Today's weather is much better than yesterday. _____

15. We were told to report to Mr. Norris office. _____

D. **Optional Composition.** Your instructor may ask you to complete this exercise on a separate sheet. Write ten original sentences that illustrate the possessive forms of the following words: *Tiffany, two years, driver, Jason and Ann, waitress, one month, customers, company, editor-in-chief, the Cosbys*. Underline the possessive form in each sentence.

Editor's Challenge

The following personal business letter has errors in sentence structure, plural nouns, and possessive nouns. Use standard proofreading marks (see the inside front cover) to show your corrections.

2320 Centennial Road
Oshawa, ON L1G 8K7
February 9, 200x

Mr. Jonathon Benson
Benson Brothers Management Services
368 Glenlake Ave.
Toronto, ON M9B 2B4

Dear Mr. Bensen:

SUBJECT: MANAGING APARTMENT COMPLEX IN DON MILLS

Please send me more information about your companys managment service for apartment owners' I especially would like answers to the following questions.

What are your fees to manage an apartment complex with six unit, Do you take care of renting the units when they become vacant? What percentage of all renters payments do you keep?

Will you enforce a list of do's and don't's that the owner provides? Do you require the last months rent in advance, do you maintain lawyers to handle legal problems?

Its now my responsibility to care for my father-in-laws six-unit apartment complex in Don Mills, your firms management services' may be exactly what I need. Since I do not live near the apartment complex. Please respond to my questions before March 1. So that I may evaluate the pro's and con's of your services.

Sincerely,

Laura W. Stephens

Laura W. Stephens

Underline any incorrect possessive forms. Write correct versions.

1. New dividends were announced at the share-holders meeting. _____

2. This month's sales figures were better than last months. _____

3. In just two years time, your profits will likely double. _____

4. Mrs. Holtz secretary located all the accounts receivable. _____

5. The three witnesses testimonies required seven court days. _____

learning.web.ways

Your boss is irritated by unwanted e-mail messages, such as "Earn Big Money Working at Home!" She asks you to use the Web to find a way to stop this misuse of her computer. You decide to use a well-known search engine, Google.

Goal: To learn to refine search terms.

1. With your Web browser on the screen, key the following URL in the location box: **<http://www.google.com>**. Press **Enter**.

2. Look at the Google opening page. Try to ignore the clutter and banner advertisements (the price we pay for free search engines). Locate the **Find** box.

3. Key the following search term: **e-mail**. Press **Enter** or click **Search**. Wait for Google to complete its search.

4. Note how many results were obtained. You will see that over 7,870,000 pages include the word *e-mail*. Look over the site titles presented. See any relevant sites?

5. To reduce the number of "hits," you must refine your search term. Locate the **Find** box again, and key a new search term: **"unwanted e-mail."** Enclose the phrase in quotation marks.

6. Check the number of hits. This refined search term still brings over 11,000 hits.

7. Go back to the **Find** box, and insert a new search term. Include quotation marks: **"unwanted e-mail/spam."** This time Google will find only those sites that include "unwanted e-mail/spam" as a unit.

1. shareholders' 2. last month's 3. years' 4. Holtz' or Holtz's 5. witnesses'

8. You will now have 300-odd results. Click on one of the pages that looks most promising. Find an answer to this question: What can an e-mail user do about unwanted messages (spam)?

9. If you have no success with Google, try another search engine such as **<www.altavista.com>**.

10. Find and print one or two pages with advice on how to deal with unwanted e-mail.

11. End your session by clicking the **X** in the upper right corner of your browser. Turn in all printed copies.

Personal Pronouns

OBJECTIVES   When you have completed the materials in this chapter, you will be able to do the following:

LEVEL I
- *Use personal pronouns correctly as subjects and objects.*
- *Distinguish between personal possessive pronouns (such as* its*) and contractions (such as* it's*).*

LEVEL II
- *Choose the correct pronoun in compound constructions, comparatives, and appositives.*
- *Use reflexive pronouns correctly.*

LEVEL III
- *Use nominative case pronouns with subject complements.*
- *Select the correct pronouns for use with the infinitive* to be*.*

PRETEST

Underline the correct pronouns.

1. The contract was signed by Mr. Lee and (I, me, myself) last week.
2. (Us, We) employees receive additional benefits in September.
3. Only one of the job applicants can keyboard as fast as (her, she).
4. Are you sure it was (he, him) who called me yesterday morning?
5. Good workers like you and (he, him) are difficult to locate.

As you will remember from Chapter 2 (p. 18), pronouns are words that substitute for nouns and other pronouns. They enable us to speak and write without awkward repetition. Grammatically, pronouns may be divided into seven types (personal, relative, interrogative, demonstrative, indefinite, reflexive, and reciprocal). Rather than consider all seven pronoun types, this textbook will be concerned only with those pronouns that cause difficulty in use.

1. me 2. We 3. she 4. he 5. him

▶ Personal Pronouns

Personal pronouns indicate the person speaking, the person spoken to, or the person or object spoken of. Notice in the following table that the personal pronouns change their form (or *case*) depending upon who is speaking (called the *person*), how many are speaking (the *number*), and the sex (or *gender*) of the speaker. For example, the third person feminine objective singular case is *her*. Most personal pronoun errors by speakers and writers involve faulty usage of case forms. Study this table to avoid errors in personal pronoun use, and be sure that you understand how these pronouns function in sentences.

	Nominative Case*		Objective Case		Possessive Case	
	Singular	**Plural**	**Singular**	**Plural**	**Singular**	**Plural**
First person (person speaking)	I	we	me	us	my, mine	our, ours
Second person (person spoken to)	you	you	you	you	your, yours	your, yours
Third person (person or thing spoken of)	he, she, it	they	him, her, it	them	his, her, hers, its	their, theirs

Basic Use of the Nominative Case

Nominative case pronouns are used primarily as the subjects of verbs. Every verb or verb phrase, regardless of its position in a sentence, has a subject. If that subject is a pronoun, it must be in the nominative case.

> *I* thought *he* had left the office.
> *They* asked if *we* had valid passports.

Basic Use of the Objective Case

Objective case pronouns are used most commonly in two ways:

1. **Object of a Verb.** When pronouns act as direct or indirect objects of verbs, they must be in the objective case.

   > Give *them* a building map. (indirect object)
   > Bob asked *her* for help. (direct object)

2. **Object of a Preposition.** The objective case is used for pronouns that are objects of prepositions.

   > Supplies were sent to *them*.
   > An excellent report was given by *him*.
   > Just between *you* and *me*, profits are slipping.

   When the words *between, but, like*, and *except* are used as prepositions, errors in pronoun case are likely to occur. To avoid such errors, isolate the prepositional phrase,

---

* *Some authorities prefer the term* subjective case.

and then use an objective case pronoun as the object of the preposition. Example: *Every employee [but Tom and him] completed the form.*

Basic Use of the Possessive Case

Possessive pronouns show ownership. Unlike possessive nouns, possessive pronouns require no apostrophes. Study these five possessive pronouns: *hers, yours, ours, theirs, its.* Notice the absence of apostrophes. Do not confuse possessive pronouns with contractions. Contractions are shortened (contracted) forms of subjects and verbs, such as *it's* (for *it is* or *it has*), *there's* (for *there is* or *there has*), *they're* (for *they are*), and *you're* (for *you are*). In contractions the apostrophes indicate omitted letters.

Possessive Pronouns	**Contractions**
Theirs is the first car in line.	*There's* no stationery left.
The cat is cleaning *its* fur.	*It's* a dangerous situation.
Your presentation was excellent.	*You're* the next speaker.
Their anniversary is tomorrow.	*They're* going to have a party.

Complete the reinforcement exercises for Level I on pp. 90–91.

Study Tip

Never use *it's* unless you can substitute *it is* or *it has;* if you cannot, use the pronoun *its.*

▶ Problems in Using Personal Pronouns

Image label: LEVEL II

Compound Subjects and Objects

When a pronoun appears in combination with a noun or another pronoun, special attention must be given to case selection. Use this technique to help you choose the correct pronoun case: Ignore the extra noun or pronoun and its related conjunction, and consider separately the pronoun in question to determine what the case should be.

> Laura asked [you and] *me* for advice. (Ignore *you and.*)
> [Larry and] *he* enrolled in the class. (Ignore *Larry and.*)
> Will you permit [Tony and] *them* to join you? (Ignore *Tony and.*)

Notice in the first sentence, for example, that when *you and* is removed, it is much easier to recognize that the pronoun *me* must be selected because it functions as the object of the verb.

Hotlink

This Summary of Personal Pronouns **<http:// grammar.englishclub. com/pronouns- personal.htm>** will give you a quick, at-a-glance overview of their main forms and functions.

Comparatives

In statements of comparison, words are often implied but not actually stated. To determine pronoun case in only partially complete comparative statements introduced by *than* or *as,* always mentally finish the comparative by adding the implied missing words.

> Each month Jon saves as much as *they.* (Jon saves as much as *they* [not *them*] save.)
> Lisa spells better than *he.* (… better than *he* [not *him*] spells.)
> Tardiness annoys Mr. Britton as much as *me.* (… as much as it annoys *me* [not *I*].)

Spot the Blooper

Television commercial for Continental Insurance Co.: "Nobody does it better than us."

Appositives

Appositives explain or rename previously mentioned nouns or pronouns. A pronoun in apposition takes the same case as that of the noun or pronoun with which it is in apposition. In order to determine more easily what pronoun case to use for a pronoun in combination with an appositive, temporarily ignore the appositive.

> *We* [consumers] are protected by laws. (Ignore *consumers*.)
> Precautions were taken by *us* [neighbours]. (Ignore *neighbours*.)

Reflexive (or Compound Personal) Pronouns

Reflexive pronouns that end in *-self* or *-selves* emphasize or reflect on their antecedents (the nouns or pronouns previously mentioned).

> The president *himself* presented the award. (Emphasizes *president*.)
> The matter should resolve *itself*. (Refers to *matter*.)

Errors result when reflexive pronouns are used instead of personal pronouns. If no previously mentioned noun or pronoun is stated in the sentence, use a personal pronoun instead of a reflexive pronoun.

> Bring the proposed agenda to either Bradley or *me*. (Not *myself*.)
> Mr. Stewart and *I* analyzed the numerous possibilities. (Not *myself*.)

Complete the reinforcement exercises for Level II on pp. 92–93.

Spot the Blooper

From the side of a General Mills Cinnamon Toast Crunch cereal box: "What gives Cinnamon Crunch it's totally intense taste?"

LEVEL III

▶ Advanced Uses of Nominative Case Pronouns

Although the following applications appear infrequently, careful speakers and writers try to understand why certain pronoun forms are used.

Subject Complement

As we saw earlier in this chapter, nominative case pronouns usually function as subjects of verbs. Less frequently, nominative case pronouns also perform as subject complements. A pronoun that follows a linking verb and renames the subject must be in the nominative case. Be especially alert to the linking verb forms *am, is, are, was, were, be, being,* and *been.*

> It *was I* who placed the order.
> I'm sure it *is she* who usually answers the telephone.
> If you *were I,* what would you do?

When a verb of several words appears in a phrase, look at the final element of the verb phrase. If it is a linking verb, use a nominative pronoun.

> It *might have been they* who made the bid.
> The driver *could have been he.*
> If the teacher *had been she,* my grade might have been higher.

In conversation it is common to say, *It is me,* or more likely, *It's me.* Careful speakers and writers, though, normally use nominative case pronouns after linking verbs. If the resulting constructions sound too "formal," revise your sentences appropriately. For example, instead of *It is I who placed the order,* use *I placed the order.*

Study Tip

Whenever a pronoun follows a linking verb, that pronoun will always be in the nominative case.

Infinitive *To Be* Without a Subject

Infinitives are the present forms of verbs preceded by *to;* for example, *to sit, to run,* and *to walk.* Nominative pronouns are used following the infinitive *to be* when the infinitive has no subject. In this instance the infinitive joins a complement (not an object) to the subject.

> Her twin sister was often taken to be *she.* (The infinitive *to be* has no subject; *she* is the complement of the subject *sister.*)
>
> Darrell was mistakenly thought to be *I.* (The infinitive *to be* has no subject; *I* is the complement of the subject *Darrell.*)
>
> Why would Jennifer want to be *she?* (The infinitive *to be* has no subject; *she* is the complement of the subject *Jennifer.*)

Infinitive *To Be* With a Subject

When the infinitive *to be* has a subject, any pronoun following it will function as an object. Therefore, the pronoun following the infinitive will take the objective case.

> The teacher believed Meaghan to be *her.* (The subject of the infinitive *to be* is *Meaghan;* therefore, the pronoun functions as an object. Try it another way: *The teacher believed her to be Meaghan.* You would not say, *The teacher believed she to be Meaghan.*)
>
> John expected the callers to be *us.* (The subject of the infinitive *to be* is *callers;* therefore, the pronoun functions as an object.)
>
> Colonel Dunn judged the winner to be *him.* (The subject of the infinitive *to be* is *winner;* therefore, use the objective case pronoun *him.*)

Whenever you have selected a pronoun for the infinitive *to be* and you want to test its correctness, try reversing the pronoun and its antecedent. For example, *We thought the winner to be her* (We *thought her* [not *she*] *to be the winner*) or *Cheryl was often taken to be she* (*She* [not *her*] *was often taken to be Cheryl).*

Summary of Pronoun Cases

The following table summarizes the uses of nominative and objective case pronouns.

Nominative Case

Subject of the verb:	*They* are sky divers.
Subject complement:	That is *he.*
Infinitive *to be* without a subject:	Ed pretended to be *he.*

Objective Case

Direct or indirect object of a verb:	We interviewed *her.*
	Give *him* another chance.
Object of a preposition:	Send the order to *him.*
Infinitive *to be* with subject:	We thought the guests to be *them.*

▶ Types of Pronouns

For those of you interested in a total view, here is a summary of the seven types of pronouns, with sentences illustrating each type. This list is presented only for your interest, not for potential testing.

Hotlink

For more advanced work on pronouns—and helpful review/quiz material—look at Chapter 13 of this on-line grammar "book" prepared by Capital Community College **<http://ccc.commnet. edu/sensen/>**.

Study Tip

This memory device may help you to remember the correct pronoun form to use with the infinitive *to be*: No subject, then nominative. That is, if the infinitive *to be* has no subject, supply a nominative pronoun. For example, *I was thought to be* she.

Spot the Blooper

From *The Province* [North Vancouver, BC]: "Dr. Ivan Rebeyka sees the day when surgeons like he will repair tiny hearts in the womb."

1. **Personal pronouns** replace nouns or other pronouns.

Nominative case:	I, we, you, he, she, it, they
Objective case:	me, us, you, him, her, it, them
Possessive case:	my, mine, our, ours, your, yours, his, her, hers, its, their, theirs

   Dr. Benton said *she* put *her* signature on *it* yesterday.

2. **Relative pronouns** join subordinate clauses to antecedents. Examples: who, whose, whom, which, that, whoever, whomever, whichever, whatever.

   He is the candidate *whom* we all admire.

3. **Interrogative pronouns** replace nouns in a question. Examples: who, whose, whom, which, what.

   Who is sitting here?

4. **Demonstrative pronouns** designate specific persons or things. Examples: this, these, that, those.

   This must be the work request we need.

5. **Indefinite pronouns** replace nouns: everyone, anyone, someone, each, everybody, anybody, somebody, one, none, some, most, all.

   Everybody needs adequate nourishment.

6. **Reflexive pronouns (compound personal)** emphasize or reflect back on antecedents. Examples: myself, yourself, himself, herself, itself, oneself, ourselves, yourselves, themselves.

   The president *himself* answered that letter.

7. **Reciprocal pronouns** indicate mutual relationship. Examples: each other, one another.

   The three chief executive officers consulted *one another* before making the announcement.

Complete the reinforcement exercises for Level III on pp. 94–96.

HOTLINE QUERIES

Question: On the radio I recently heard a talk-show host say, *My producer and myself...* A little later the same host said, *Send any inquiries to the station or myself at this address.* This sounded half right and half wrong, but I would have trouble explaining the problem. Can you help?

Answer: The problem is a common one: use of a reflexive pronoun (*myself*) when it has no preceding noun on which to reflect. Correction: *My producer and I* and *Send inquiries to the station or me.* Reflexive pronouns like *myself* should be used only with obvious antecedents, such as *I, myself, will take the calls.* Individuals in the

---

media often misuse reflexive pronouns, perhaps to avoid sounding egocentric with overuse of *I* and *me*.

Question: I have a question about the use of *etc.* in this sentence: *We are installing better lighting, acoustical tile, sound barriers, and etc.* Should I use two periods at the end of the sentence, and does a comma precede *etc.*?

Answer: Although the use of *etc.* (meaning "and so forth") is generally avoided, do not, if it is to be used, include the redundant word *and*. When *etc.* is found at the end of a sentence, one comma should precede it. When *etc.* appears in the middle of a sentence, two commas should set it off. For example, *Better lighting, acoustical tile, sound barriers, etc., are being installed. Never* use two periods at the end of a sentence, even if the sentence ends with an abbreviation, such as *etc.*

Question: We're having a disagreement in our office about the word *healthy*. Is it correct to write *Exercise is healthy*?

Answer: Strictly speaking, *healthy* means "having or possessing good health." For example, *The rosy-cheeked schoolchildren look healthy.* The word *healthful* means "giving health; good for the health." Your sentence should read: *Exercise is healthful.*

Question: Should a hyphen be used in the word *dissimilar*?

Answer: No. Prefixes such as *dis* and *un* do not require hyphens. Even when the final consonant of a prefix is repeated in the initial letter of the root word, no hyphens are used: *disspirited, misspell, unnamed.*

Question: I thought I knew the difference between *to* and *too*, but could you provide me with a quick review?

Answer: *To* may serve as a preposition (*I'm going to the store*), and it may also serve as part of an infinitive construction (*to sign his name*). The adverb *too* may be used to mean "also" (*Andrea will attend too*). In addition, the word *too* may be used to indicate "to an excessive extent" (*the letter is too long*).

Question: I have a lot of trouble with the word *extension*, as in the terms *extension* cord and telephone *extension.* Is the word ever spelled *extention*?

Answer: You are not alone in having trouble with *extension*. No, it is never spelled with the familiar suffix *tion*. Perhaps you could remember it better if you associate the word *tension* with *extension.*

Question: My son is studying a foreign language; and he asked me, a teacher of business English, why we capitalize the personal pronoun *I* in English when we don't capitalize other pronouns.

Answer: That's a fascinating topic, and a little research on the Web revealed that linguists ponder the same question. In a linguistic journal, some relevant theories were discussed. One linguist thought that perhaps the lower-case *i* was too easily confused with the number *1* or with similar looking *i*'s, *u*'s, and *v*'s in medieval handwriting. Another attributed the word's capital letter to our egocentric nature. Another suggested that since the pronoun *I* usually appeared as the first word in a sentence, it was capitalized for that reason. In earlier centuries before the language was standardized, most nouns and pronouns were capitalized haphazardly. One linguist thought that a better question to ask would be why all of the other pronouns lose their capital letters and *I* retains its.

CHAPTER 6   Reinforcement Exercises

A. (**Self-check**) Select the correct form.

LEVEL I

1. We are sure that (he, him) graduated from Queen's University.   _____

2. All the students except (she, her) use e-mail regularly.   _____

3. Send the letter to (they, them) at their Florida address.   _____

4. (They, Them), as well as some other employees, volunteered for the project.   _____

5. It seems strange that someone like (he, him) could be given the assignment.   _____

6. Please discuss it with Michael Scott and (she, her) before proceeding.   _____

7. Purchases made by (she, her) were billed incorrectly.   _____

8. Are you sure (there's, theirs) time to complete the form?   _____

9. Miriam said that (its, it's) your turn next.   _____

10. Don is certain that nobody but (he, him) can open the lock.   _____

Check your answers.

B. In the spaces provided, list five personal pronouns that can be used as subjects of verbs and five that can be used as objects of verbs or objects of prepositions.

As Subjects		As Objects
1. _____	1.	_____
2. _____	2.	_____
3. _____	3.	_____
4. _____	4.	_____
5. _____	5.	_____

C. In this set of sentences, all the omitted pronouns serve as subjects of verbs. Write the correct pronoun for each sentence.

1. The project director and (she, her) worked on the program budget.   _____

2. I know that James Naylor and (he, him) will be purchasing the franchise as a joint venture.   _____

1. he 2. her 3. them 4. They 5. him 6. her 7. her 8. there's 9. it's 10. him

3. After the series of interviews, only (she, her) was asked to submit additional recommendations. _____

4. When the product was introduced, other salespeople and (they, them) attended four training sessions. _____

5. We are pleased to learn that (he, him) will be transferred to our division. _____

In the next set of sentences, all the omitted pronouns serve as objects of verbs or as objects of prepositions. (Selected prepositions have been underlined to help you recognize them.) Write the correct pronoun for each sentence.

6. Mr. Jacobson asked if the terms of the agreement were satisfactory <u>to</u> (we, us). _____

7. Capital for the enterprise was subscribed <u>by</u> (he, him). _____

8. Send Mrs. Jordan and (I, me) your latest prices for Model T-S40. _____

9. Everyone <u>but</u> (they, them) invested in growth stocks. _____

10. When you finish with it, please give the video <u>to</u> (we, us). _____

D. In the spaces provided, write *a, b,* or *c* to indicate how the italicized pronouns function in these sentences.

   a = subject of a verb   b = object of a verb   c = object of a preposition

Example: Please ask *her* for the fax number. _____*b*_____

1. Ms. Larsen asked *me* for the assignment. _____

2. Cheryl and *she* were late for their counselling appointments. _____

3. When Mike completed the difficult task, the supervisor praised *him*. _____

4. The secret agreement between Hana Harper and *him* was not revealed. _____

5. *They* made an offer to purchase the two-hectare property. _____

E. Select the correct pronoun.

1. Please have (he, him) notarize this document. _____

2. Our sales team can take pride in (it's, its) sales record. _____

3. Nobody but (he, him) has been authorized to use the premises. _____

4. Are you sure that this apartment is (there's, theirs, their's)? _____

5. Between you and (I, me), who will be our next company president? _____

6. We have already sent the parts to (they, them) for inspection. _____

7. (It's, Its) roof may collapse under the weight of the wet snow. _____

8. As Mr. Hadley and (she, her) discussed the matter, new information came to light. _____

LEVEL II

A. (Self-check) Select the correct pronoun, and write it in the space provided.

1. A profit-sharing plan was offered to (we, us) employees in place of cost-of-living raises. _____

2. No one made more profit in that transaction than (he, him). _____

3. His counsellor and (he, him) worked out a schedule of classes. _____

4. Both girls, Alicia and (she, her), will be able to work this weekend. _____

5. (Us, We) delegates stayed at the Hotel Dupar during the convention. _____

6. Catherine Ferguson and (myself, I, me) received new job classifications. _____

7. Proposals submitted by (her and me, she and I) were considered. _____

8. No one but my friend and (myself, I, me) spoke up during the discussion. _____

9. Separate planes were taken by the business manager and (he, him). _____

10. The tragedy shocked Dr. Callihan as much as (myself, I, me). _____

Check your answers.

B. Select the correct pronoun, and write it in the space provided.

1. Her friend and (she, her) ordered double-dip Dutch chocolate ice cream cones. _____

2. Carrie is much taller than (she, her). _____

3. A lawyer is in charge of (we, us) trainees. _____

4. No other employees are quite like Steve and (he, him). _____

5. Idle gossip disturbs Mrs. Bronski as much as (I, me). _____

6. He has no one but (him, himself) to blame. _____

7. It's interesting that (us, we) accountants were audited this year. _____

8. The production manager told a reporter and (he, him) that computerization had virtually eliminated the need for paperwork. _____

9. The co-pilots, Turner and (he, him), requested permission to land. _____

10. A serious disagreement between the management and (he, him) caused his dismissal. _____

11. Mr. Jefferson and (I, me, myself) will make the announcement very soon. _____

12. No one knows that problem better than (I, me). _____

13. News of the merger upset President Davis as much as (I, me). _____

14. All employees but Mr. Herzog and (I, me, myself) agreed to the economy measures. _____

15. Several of (we, us) salespeople surpassed our monthly selling goals. _____

16. Do you think Melanie can complete the work more quickly than (he, him)? _____

17. Campaign literature was sent to (we, us) homeowners prior to the elections. _____

18. The signatures on the letter appear to have been written by you and (she, her). _____

19. The authors typed the manuscripts (themself, themselves). _____

20. Everyone except two drivers and (he, him) has checked in with the dispatcher. _____

C. Write complete sentences that begin with the words shown. Supply a pronoun where indicated.

Example: Mr. Paulson and (pronoun) _Mr. Paulson and he agreed to market their invention._

1. My friend and (pronoun)_____

_____

_____

2. The two students, Don and (pronoun), _____

_____

_____

3. Just between you and (pronoun), _____

_____

_____

4. Except for Mr. Sanders and (pronoun), _____

_____

_____

5. The manager expected Yumiko and (pronoun) _____

_____

_____

6. Ours _____

_____

_____

A. (**Self-check**) Select the correct pronoun, and write it in the space provided.

LEVEL III

1. Was it (they, them) who sent the gift?   _____

2. If you were (she, her), would you have sent that e-mail?   _____

3. Ramco asked my partner and (I, me) to design a logo.   _____

4. If I were (he, him), I would withdraw my endorsement.   _____

5. Gilbert said that it was (he, him) who used the printer last.   _____

6. Sherilyn Hennigar is often taken to be (her, she).   _____

7. It might have been (she, her) who called in the alarm.   _____

8. The audience didn't discover that Marcelle was (she, her) until after the performance.   _____

9. They thought Marcelle to be (she, her).   _____

10. I was asked to contact you and (they, them) immediately.   _____

Check your answers.

B. Select the correct pronoun.

1. When Frank answered the telephone, he said, "This is (he, him)."   _____

2. If you were (I, me), would you take an internship?   _____

3. The librarian showed Paul and (I, me) how to use the on-line catalogue.   _____

4. Nearly everyone mistook the statuesque blonde to be (her, she).   _____

5. Surely it was (they, them) who left the package last night.   _____

6. An attempt was made to reach (he and she, him and her) in Geneva.   _____

7. We are unsure whether the supervisor will be (he, him).   _____

8. I'm sure that it was (she, her) who called this morning.   _____

9. The lifeguard credited with the rescue was thought to be (he, him).   _____

10. If the newly elected council member had been (he, him), our worst fears might have been realized. _____

11. Dr. Alisha Meza judged the winner to be (her, she).   _____

_____

1. they 2. she 3. me 4. he 5. he 6. she 7. she 8. she 9. her 10. them

12. The committee invited Professor Basil and (he, him) to speak at the conference. _____

13. Adam and Tanisha were certain it was not (they, them) who created the shortage. _____

14. The intruder was taken to be (he, him). _____

15. When Lakshmi opened the door, she expected to see you and (he, him). _____

16. It must have been (they, them) who reported the missing funds. _____

17. We hope to include Russ McGovern and (she, her) in our next series of interviews. _____

18. If the caller is (he, him), please get his telephone number. _____

19. The office staff expected the new manager to be (she, her). _____

20. Are you certain it was (she, her) who called this morning? _____

C. Review of Levels I, II, and III. Select the correct pronoun.

1. The personnel director and (he, him) discussed job enrichment programs that would benefit our employees. _____

2. If the task had been given to anyone but (she, her) to do, I would have less apprehension. _____

3. Do you know (whose, who's) working on the final version of the Jet Com proposal? _____

4. A convincing sales talk was given by (she, her) when she met with their chief executive officer. _____

5. One of our principal concerns about the motor is (it's, its) tendency to overheat. _____

6. The wage discussions between Mr. O'Donnell and (they, them) appear to be progressing smoothly. _____

7. I'm not sure whether this ruler is (yours, your's) or mine. _____

8. We believe that no one is more familiar with the situation than (he, him). _____

9. (We, Us) investors, of course, expect to make at least a minimal profit. _____

10. No one could have been more surprised at the announcement than (we, us). _____

11. Jensen assumed it was (they, them) who made the initial report. _____

12. It's strange that Martin is sometimes taken to be (he, him). _____

13. The insurance salespeople, Mr. Stalls and (her, she), made several appointments for evening interviews. _____

14. Everyone except the broker and (I, me) claimed a share of the commission. _____

15. The inventor credited with the idea was thought to be (he, him). _____

D. Review of Chapter 5 (Possessive Nouns) and Chapter 6 (Personal Pronouns). Underline any errors in possessive nouns or personal pronouns in the following sentences. For each sentence write a corrected form in the space provided. Be alert! Some sentences have more than one correction. If a sentence is correct, write *C* in the space.

1. Many small business owners', like Deborah and I, must equip offices in our homes. _____

2. On the way to the airport, Stacy and me passed a white stretch limousine that was stalled at the side of the road with it's hood up. _____

3. The governor invited Hillary and I to dinner, but Hillaries invitation was never delivered. _____

4. Although I'm sure it was him who sent the e-mail announcement, the CEO doesn't seem to remember it at all. _____

5. Our companys Web site describing our new graphic's design capabilities stimulated many calls. _____

6. Just between you and me, I think all passengers luggage except our's will be opened and inspected. _____

7. If chocolate could teach, Marta and me would now be extremely well educated. _____

8. Since the envelope was addressed to Mark and I, he and I should receive the free gift. _____

9. Theirs just one problem: neither Craig nor me have credit cards. _____

10. All our customers names and addresses are stored in Mr. Betz database. _____

11. Neither Mr. Persaud nor I could believe that Jeff was taken to be him. _____

12. Although Tonya and me agreed to pay two months rent in advance, the landlord would not rent to us. _____

13. No one can navigate the Internet better than me. _____

14. All of we sales associates began to receive faxes announcing First Federal's grand opening. _____

15. After reviewing our insurance policy and the companys explanation, my wife and I are certain their is a mistake in the reimbursement amount. _____

16. Some people think vacations are a necessary evil, but we in management believe that recharging one's batteries away from the office really works wonders. _____

17. No matter how rich a gardens soil may be, seeds must be sown and nutrients added to produce a harvest. _____

18. If you were me, would you step into the managers shoes at this time? _____

19. Please send all RSVP's to Jamilah or I before December 1. _____

20. Although Anne protested, I'm convinced it was her who sent the gift to Robert and I. _____

E. Optional Composition. Your instructor may ask you to complete this exercise on a separate sheet. Write four original sentences that illustrate pronouns with the following functions: subject of verb, object of verb, object of preposition, and complement of subject. Label each pronoun and its function. In addition, write sentences using these words: *there, theirs, there's, its, it's,* and *yours.*

Editor's Challenge

The following memo has intentional errors related to principles you have studied thus far. Use proofreading marks to make corrections. Your instructor may ask you to print the revised memo on your computer printer or to handwrite it on a separate sheet. Leave side margins of about 1 1/4 inches and a top margin of at least 1 inch. Double-space if your instructor directs.

DATE: July 25, 200x

TO: Anita Musto, Vice-President

FROM: Rick Juarez, Research Analyst

SUBJECT: ANALYSIS OF PEPSI XL

Here is a summary of the research project assigned to David Quimby and I regarding Pepsi XL this is the reduced-sugar cola drink being introduced by our companies No. 1 competitor.

In just under a years time, Pepsi-Cola developed this new drink. Containing a mix of 50 per cent sugar (high-fructose corn syrup) and 50 per cent artificial sweetener (aspartame). Apparently, Pepsi-Colas plan is to spend over $8 million to introduce the drink and to assess consumers reactions to it. It will be tested on the shelfs of grocerys, mass merchants, and convenience stores in five citys in Florida.

The companys spokesperson said, "The 'X' stands for excelent taste and the 'L' for less sugar." Aimed at young adult's who don't like the taste of aspartame but who want to control calories, the new cola is a hybrid sugar and diet drink. Our studys show that similar drinks tried in the U.S. in the 1980's were unsuccessful. On the other hand, a 50-calorie low-sugar cola introduced in Canada two year ago was well received, and a 40-calorie soda is now marketed sucessfully by Coca-Cola in Japan.

However, neither Mr. Quimby nor myself believe that theres any reason for this countrys consumers to be interested in a midcalorie cola. In fact, all of we analysts in the lab were surprised at Wall Streets favourable response to Pepsis announcement of it's new drink Pepsi-Colas stock value rose slightly.

If the decision were up to Mr. Quimby or I, him and I would take a wait-and-see attitude. Toward the interduction of our own low-sugar drink.

learning.web.ways

When you are working on your own computer, you will want to *bookmark* or save the URLs of your favourite Web pages.

Goal: To learn to bookmark favourite pages.

1. With your Web browser on the screen, key the following URL in the location box and press **Enter**: **<http://www.buscomm.nelson.com>**.

2. Because you will be returning to this page, bookmark it by clicking **Bookmark** in the upper section of your browser. Click **ADD Bookmark** (or whatever your browser says). Check the list to see whether the page was added. Close this box.

3. Return to the location box and key this URL: **<http://www.refdesk.com>**.

4. This page claims to be the "single best source for facts on the Net." What kind of information is available? Bookmark this page.

5. Click on several of the links under "Facts of the Day" or "Reference Resources." Print one page that interests you, or take notes if you cannot print.

6. Return to Nelson's Business Communication Web site by clicking **Bookmark** and the appropriate link.

7. End your session, and turn in all printed copies or notes.

1. I 2. us 3. she 4. they 5. me

Pronouns and Antecedents

OBJECTIVES   When you have completed the materials in this chapter, you will be able to do the following:

LEVEL I
- *Make personal pronouns agree with their antecedents in number and gender.*
- *Understand the traditional use of common gender and be able to use its alternatives with sensitivity.*

LEVEL II
- *Make personal pronouns agree with subjects joined by* or *or* nor.
- *Make personal pronouns agree with indefinite pronouns, collective nouns, and organization names.*

LEVEL III
- *Understand the functions of* who *and* whom.
- *Follow a three-step plan in selecting* who *or* whom.

PRETEST

Underline the correct word.

1. Every one of the girls was surprised by (her, their) mark.
2. Before voting, the committee took a poll of (its, their) members.
3. Either of the departments may send (its, their) manager to the meeting.
4. (Who, Whom) would you recommend for the supervisory position?
5. Send the brochures to (whoever, whomever) requested them first.

1. her 2. its 3. its 4. whom 5. whoever

Pronouns enable us to communicate efficiently. They provide short forms that save us from the boredom of repetitious nouns. But they can also get us in trouble if the nouns to which they refer—their *antecedents*—are unclear. This chapter shows you how to avoid pronoun–antecedent problems. It also presents solutions to a major problem for sensitive communicators today—how to handle the *his/her* dilemma.

LEVEL I

❝❞

Notable Quotable

"Over 60 percent of all management problems result from faulty communications."
—Peter Drucker

Hotlink

Vague or missing pronoun references can wreck a sentence! This University of Ottawa one-page guide on pronoun reference **<http://www. uottawa.ca/academic/ arts/writcent/ hypergrammar/ pronref.html>** will help you out.

Did You Know?

English is the first language in history of which the majority of speakers are non-native. Of the 750 million people who use English regularly, only 300 million are native speakers. It is the universal language of scholarship, science, and trade.

▶ Fundamentals of Pronoun–Antecedent Agreement

When pronouns substitute for nouns, the pronouns must agree with their antecedents in number (either singular or plural) and gender (either masculine, feminine, or neuter). Here are suggestions for using pronouns effectively.

Making Pronoun References Clear

Do not use a pronoun if your listener or reader might not be able to identify the noun it represents.

Unclear:	Nathalie told Lisa that *she* should verify the balance.
Clear:	Nathalie told Lisa to verify the balance.
Unclear:	Kevin's boss said that *he* deserved a raise.
Clear:	Kevin's boss said that Kevin deserved a raise.
Unclear:	*They* consider 60 per cent a passing grade at this college.
Clear:	This college considers 60 per cent a passing grade.
Or:	A passing grade at this college is 60 per cent.
Unclear:	In that restaurant *they* do not allow *you* to smoke.
Clear:	The restaurant management does not allow its patrons to smoke.
Or:	Smoking is not allowed in that restaurant.

Making Pronouns Agree With Their Antecedents in Number

Pronouns must agree in number with the nouns they represent. For example, if a pronoun replaces a singular noun, that pronoun must be singular.

> *Michelangelo* felt that *he* was a failure. (Singular antecedent and pronoun)
> Great *artists* often doubt *their* success. (Plural antecedent and pronoun)

If a pronoun refers to two nouns joined by *and*, the pronoun must be plural.

> The *president* and the *shareholders* discussed *their* differences. (Plural antecedent and pronoun)
> *Warren* and *Jerome* asked that suggestions be sent to *them*. (Plural antecedent and pronoun)

Pronoun–antecedent agreement can be complicated when words or phrases come between the pronoun and the word to which it refers. Disregard phrases such as those introduced by *as well as, in addition to,* and *together with*. Find the true antecedent, and make the pronoun agree with it.

> The *general*, together with the chiefs of staff, is considering *his* strategy carefully. (Singular antecedent and pronoun)
> The *chiefs* of staff, along with the general, have submitted *their* plans. (Plural antecedent and pronoun)
> A female *member* of the group of protesting students demanded that *she* be treated equally. (Singular antecedent and pronoun)

Making Pronouns Agree With Their Antecedents in Gender

Pronouns exhibit one of three genders: masculine (male), feminine (female), or neuter (neither masculine nor feminine). Pronouns must agree with their antecedents in gender.

> John read *his* assignment. (Masculine gender)
> Nancy studied *her* notes. (Feminine gender)
> The idea had *its* limits. (Neuter gender)

Choosing Alternatives to Common-Gender Pronouns. The English language has no all-purpose singular pronoun that can represent or refer to nouns of unclear gender. For this reason, using masculine, or common-gender, pronouns to refer to nouns that might be either masculine or feminine had become an accepted practice. For example, in the sentence "A student has *his* rights," the pronoun *his* referred to the word *student,* which might name either a female or male person.

Communicators today, however, avoid masculine pronouns (*he, his*) when referring to indefinite nouns that could be masculine or feminine. Critics call these pronouns "sexist" because they exclude women. To solve the problem, sensitive communicators rewrite those sentences requiring such pronouns. Although many alternatives exist, here are three common options:

Common gender:	An employee has *his* job to do.
Alternative No. 1:	Employees have *their* jobs to do.
Alternative No. 2:	An employee has *a* job to do.
Alternative No. 3:	An employee has *his* or *her* job to do.
Wrong:	An employee has *their* job to do.

In Alternative No. 1 the subject has been made plural to avoid the need for a singular common-gender pronoun. In Alternative No. 2 the pronoun is omitted, and an article is substituted for it, although at the cost of making the original meaning less emphatic. In Alternative No. 3 both masculine and feminine references (*his* or *her*) are used. Because the latter construction is wordy and clumsy, frequent use of it should be avoided. Substituting the plural pronoun *their* is incorrect since it does not agree with its singular antecedent, *employee.*

Some language experts continue to defend the use of common-gender pronouns. They insist that common-gender pronouns have always referred to both men and women and that everyone using them has always been clear about their meaning. Writers who are sensitive and alert to modern trends, however, generally avoid sexist language. Whatever you do, though, do not attempt to solve the problem by using a plural pronoun to refer to a singular antecedent: *An employee has their job to do* is wrong.

Now complete the reinforcement exercises for Level I on pp. 107–109.

Career Tip

Business people strive to avoid "sexist" and biased language. For example, use parallel terms (instead of *men and ladies,* say *men and women*). Use neutral titles (*salesperson* instead of *salesman*). Avoid implied gender (instead of *managers and their wives,* say *managers and their spouses*).

Spot the Blooper

Television commercial for *Encyclopedia Britannica:* "Every parent has a wish list for their child."

▶ Problems With Pronoun–Antecedent Agreement

Antecedents Joined by *or* or *nor*

When antecedents are joined by *or* or *nor,* the pronoun should agree with the antecedent closer to it.

LEVEL II

Either Alice or *Vicki* left *her* coat in the office.
Neither the manager nor the *employees* objected to *their* salary cuts.

You may be wondering why antecedents joined by *and* are treated differently from antecedents joined by *or* or *nor*. The conjunction *and* joins one plus one to make two antecedents; hence a plural pronoun is used. The conjunctions *or* or *nor* require a choice between Antecedent No. 1 and Antecedent No. 2. Always match the pronoun to the closer antecedent.

Indefinite Pronouns as Antecedents

Pronouns such as *anyone, something,* and *anybody* are called *indefinite* because they refer to no specific person or object. Some indefinite pronouns are always singular; others are always plural.

Always Singular		**Always Plural**
anybody	everything	both
anyone	neither	few
anything	nobody	many
each	no one	several
either	nothing	
everybody	somebody	
everyone	someone	

When indefinite pronouns function as antecedents of pronouns, make certain that the pronoun agrees with its antecedent. Do not let prepositional phrases obscure the true antecedent.

> *Somebody* in the men's league left *his* lights on.
> *Each* of the corporations had *its* own home office.
> *Few* of the vendors missed the opportunity to demonstrate *their* equipment.
> *Several* of our branches communicate *their* documents electronically.

The words *either* and *neither* can be confusing. When these words stand alone and function as pronoun subjects, they are always considered singular. When they are joined with *or* or *nor* to form the conjunctions *either/or* and *neither/nor*, however, they may connect plural subjects. These plural subjects may act as antecedents to plural pronouns.

> Has *either* of the women made *her* selection? (*Either* is a pronoun and functions as the subject of the sentence.)
> *Either* the woman *or* her friends left *their* packages. (*Either/or* is used as a conjunction joining the two subjects, *woman* and *friends*. The pronoun *their* agrees with its plural antecedent, *friends*.)

Collective Nouns as Antecedents

Words such as *jury, faculty, committee, union, team,* and *group* are called *collective* nouns because they refer to a collection of people, animals, or objects. Such words may be either singular or plural depending on the mode of operation of the collection to which they refer. When a collective noun operates as a unit, it is singular. When the elements of a collective noun operate separately, the collective noun is plural.

> Our *staff* reaffirmed *its* position on bargaining. (*Staff* operating as one unit.)

The management *team* of Rosen and Ross Ltd. is planning *its* strategy. (*Team* operating as one unit.)

The *jury* were divided in *their* opinions. (*Jury* operating as individuals.)

However, if a collective noun is to be used in a plural sense, the sentence can often be made to sound less awkward by the addition of a plural noun (*The jury members were divided in their opinions*).

Company and Organization Names as Antecedents

Company and organization names are generally considered singular. Unless the actions of the organization are attributed to individual representatives of that organization, pronouns referring to organizations should be singular.

Sears is having *its* biggest annual sale ever.

The United Nations, in addition to other organizations, is expanding *its* campaign to fight hunger.

Maclean Hunter Limited can trace *its* roots back to the nineteenth century.

The Antecedents *each*, *every*, and *many a*

If the limiting adjectives *each*, *every*, or *many a* describe either noun or both nouns in a compound antecedent, that antecedent is considered singular.

Every player and coach on the men's team has *his* assigned duties.

Many a daughter and mother will receive *her* award at the banquet.

Complete the reinforcement exercises for Level II on pp. 110–111.

▶ Advanced Pronoun Use

LEVEL III

The Problem of *who* and *whom*

The use of *who* and *whom* presents a continuing dilemma for speakers and writers. In conversation the correct choice of *who* or *whom* is often especially difficult because of the mental gymnastics necessary to locate subjects and objects. In writing, however, an author has ample time to analyze a sentence carefully and make a correct choice—if the author understands the traditional functions of *who* and *whom*. *Who* is the nominative case form. Like other nominative case pronouns, *who* may function as the subject of a verb or as the subject complement of a noun following a linking verb. *Whom* is the objective case form. It may function as the object of a verb or as the object of a preposition.*

Who do you think will be chosen to direct the play? (*Who* is the subject of *will be chosen*.)

Jerry asked *who* your friend is. (*Who* is the complement of *friend*.)

Whom should we hire? (*Whom* is the object of *should hire*.)

She is the one to *whom* I spoke. (*Whom* is the object of *to*.)

---

* Whom *may also function as the subject or object of an infinitive. Since little confusion results from these constructions, they will not be discussed.*

How to Choose Between *who* and *whom*

The choice between *who* and *whom* becomes easier if the sentence in question is approached according to the following procedure:

1. Isolate the *who/whom* clause.

2. Invert the clause, if necessary, to restore normal subject–verb–object order.

3. Substitute the nominative pronoun *he* (or *she* or *they*) for *who*. Substitute the objective pronoun *him* (or *her* or *them*) for *whom*. If the sentence sounds correct with *him*, replace *him* with *whom*. If the sentence sounds correct with *he*, replace *he* with *who*.

Study the following sentences, and notice how the choice of *who* or *whom* is made:

Here are the records of those (who/whom) we have selected.

Isolate:	_____ we have selected
Invert:	we have selected _____
Substitute:	we have selected ___him___
Equate:	we have selected ___whom___
Complete:	Here are the records of those *whom* we have selected.

Do you know (who/whom) his doctor is?

Isolate:	_____ his doctor is
Invert:	his doctor is _____ (*or* _____ is his doctor)
Substitute:	his doctor is ___he___ (*or* ___he___ is his doctor)
Equate:	his doctor is ___who___ (*or* ___who___ is his doctor)
Complete:	Do you know *who* his doctor is?

In choosing *who* or *whom*, ignore parenthetical expressions such as *I hope, we think, I believe,* and *you know.*

Edward is the candidate (who/whom) we believe is best.

Isolate:	_____ we believe is best
Ignore:	_____ [we believe] is best
Substitute:	___he___ is best
Equate:	___who___ is best
Complete:	Edward is the candidate *who* we believe is best.

Examples:

Whom do you think we should call? (Invert: do you think we should call her/*whom*)

The person to *whom* the article referred was Mr. Stein. (Invert: the article referred to him/*whom*)

Do you know *who* the manager is? (Invert: the manager is she/*who*)

Whom would you like to see appointed to that position? (Invert: you would like to see him/*whom* appointed to that position)

The Use of *whoever* and *whomever*

Whoever, of course, is nominative and *whomever* is objective. The selection of the correct form in clauses is sometimes complicated. These clauses may act as objects of prepositions, objects of verbs, or subjects of verbs. Within the clauses, however, you must determine how *whoever* or *whomever* is functioning in order to choose the correct form (either subject or object). Study the following examples and explanations:

> Give the surplus to *whoever needs it.* (The clause *whoever needs it* is the object of the preposition *to*; but, within the clause itself, *whoever* acts as the subject of *needs* and is therefore in the nominative case.)
>
> Special provision will be made for *whoever* meets the conditions. (The clause *whoever meets the conditions* is the object of the preposition *for.* Within the clause, *whoever* acts as the subject of *meets* and is therefore in the nominative case.)
>
> We will accept the name of *whomever they nominate.* (The clause *whomever they nominate* is the object of the preposition *of.* Within the clause, *whomever* is the object of *they nominate* and is therefore in the objective case.)

Complete the reinforcement exercises for Level III and the review exercises on pp. 112–115.

Hotlink

Another tip for dealing with *who* and *whom* (and a review exercise to help you master their use) can be found at **<http://www.grammarbook.com/grammar/whoVwhom.html>**.

HOTLINE QUERIES

Question: My friend insists that the combination *all right* is shown in her dictionary as one word. I say that it's two words. Who's right?

Answer: *All right* is the only acceptable spelling. The listing *alright* is shown in many dictionaries to guide readers to the acceptable spelling, *all right.* Do not use *alright.* By the way, some individuals can better remember that *all right* is two words by associating it with *all wrong.*

Question: I don't seem to be able to hear the difference between *than* and *then.* Can you explain it to me?

Answer: The conjunction *than* is used to make comparisons (*your watch is more accurate than mine*). The adverb *then* means "at that time" (*we must complete this task; then we will take our break*) or "as a consequence" (*if all the angles of the triangle are equal, then it must be equilateral as well*).

Question: Why does the sign above my grocery market's quick-check stand say *Ten or less items*? Shouldn't it read *Ten or fewer items*?

Answer: Right you are! *Fewer* refers to numbers, as in *fewer items. Less* refers to amounts or quantities, as in *less food.* Perhaps the markets prefer *less* because it has fewer letters.

Question: If I have no interest in something, am I *disinterested*?

Answer: No. If you lack interest, you are *uninterested.* The word *disinterested* means "unbiased" or "impartial" (*disinterested judges are necessary for the cause of justice*).

Question: Everyone says "consensus of opinion." Yet I understand that there is some objection to this expression.

Answer: Yes, the expression is widely used. However, since *consensus* means "collective opinion," adding *opinion* results in a redundancy.

Question: I'm disgusted and infuriated at a New York University advertisement I just saw in our newspaper. It says, *It's not just <u>who</u> you know....* Why would a leading institution of learning use such poor grammar?

Answer: Because it sounds familiar. But familiarity doesn't make it correct. You're right in recognizing that the proper form is *whom* (isolate the clause *you know him* or *whom*). The complete adage—or more appropriately, cliché—correctly stated is, *It's not what you know but <u>whom</u> you know.*

CHAPTER 7   Reinforcement Exercises

A. (**Self-check**) Select the correct word(s) to complete the following sentences.

1. When a student completes the course, (his, her, his or her, their) grade is recorded immediately.

   _____

2. In addition to other family members, each winner was sent tickets for (his, her, its, his or her, their) personal use.

   _____

3. The visiting scientist and our resident engineer had (his, her, his or her, their) problems finding the control centre.

   _____

4. No veterinarian's assistant will be assigned to that task until (he is, she is, he or she is, they are) trained.

   _____

5. One of the members of the boys' choir lost (his, his or her, their) robe.

   _____

6. After a contractor signs, (he is, she is, he or she is, they are) responsible for fulfilling the terms of the contract.

   _____

7. One of the women asked how many sick days (she, he or she, they) had accumulated.

   _____

8. All flight attendants must have (her, his, his or her, their) uniforms cleaned regularly.

   _____

9. Miss Simon, after consulting the production staff and others, made (her, his or her, their) pricing decision.

   _____

10. Any employee of this college must automatically retire when (he reaches, it reaches, he or she reaches, they reach) the age of sixty-five.

    _____

Check your answers.

B. Select the correct word(s) to complete the following sentences.

1. Workers in the four plants asked that (his, his or her, their) working conditions be improved.

   _____

2. An office manager, as well as the other members of management, must do (his, her, his or her, their) best to promote good employee relations.

   _____

3. A judge often feels that (he, she, he or she, they) should review the charges for the jury.   _____

4. Both Dr. Alonzo and Dr. Reese have given (his, her, his or her, their) approval.   _____

5. Lisa Lee, one of the clerks in the front office, asked that (her, their) vacation be changed.   _____

6. In that mall (you, shoppers) aren't allowed to smoke.   _____

1. his or her 2. his or her 3. their 4. he or she is 5. his 6. he or she is 7. she 8. their 9. her 10. he or she reaches

7. Unless careful, an employee might not get all the retirement benefits to which (he is, she is, he or she is, they are) entitled.

_____

8. Mr. Tomkins and Mr. Ramos were not eager to have (his, their) complaints discussed in public.

_____

9. If the insured party causes an accident, (he, she, it, he or she, they) will be charged an additional fee in future premiums.

_____

10. The human resources manager advised each candidate of (his, her, his or her, their) opportunities for advancement within the organization.

_____

11. The firm will use the funds to reduce (his or her, its, their) debt.

_____

12. (They, Analysts) say that Air Canada's financial outlook is excellent.

_____

C. Rewrite the following sentences to avoid the use of common-gender pronouns. Show three versions of each sentence.

1. Every homeowner must have his home insured in order to get a mortgage.

   a. _____

   b. _____

   c. _____

2. Be sure that each new employee has received his orientation packet.

   a. _____

   b. _____

   c. _____

3. A patient who doesn't accurately report his history to the doctor runs the risk of misdiagnosis.

   a. _____

   b. _____

   c. _____

D. Rewrite these sentences to make the pronoun references clear.

1. The article reported that Comcard had acquired Datacard and that it had sold its foreign subsidiaries.

_____

_____

_____

2. They make you wear shoes and shirts in that restaurant.

_____

_____

3. Because Mr. Redman was replaced by Mr. Vaccaro, his parking space was changed.

_____

_____

_____

4. Speer was Hitler's companion until the final days of the war when he turned against him.

_____

_____

_____

5. Mrs. Hartmann talked with Courtney about her telecommuting request, but she needed more information.

_____

_____

_____

A. (**Self-check**) Select the correct word(s) to complete the following sentences.

LEVEL II

1. Someone left (his, her, his or her, their) keys on the counter. _____

2. Apparently, neither the memorandum nor the letters had (its, their) contents proofread very carefully. _____

3. Gold, Steinmetz & Burns Inc. held an open house in honour of (its, their) anniversary. _____

4. Someone on the girls' team lost one of (her, their) shoes. _____

5. Each man, woman, and child in the club made (his, her, his or her, their) own contribution to the food drive. _____

6. Either Mrs. Wall or Mrs. Snyder will offer (her, their) home for the meeting. _____

7. Nobody in the boisterous crowd could hear (his, her, his or her, their) name when it was called. _____

8. The International Olympic Committee indicated (its, his or her, their) concern about possibly misleading advertisements. _____

9. Neither of the men had signed (his, their) contract. _____

10. The Coast Guard has five regional offices, but (its, his or her, their) headquarters is in Ottawa. _____

Check your answers.

B. Select the appropriate pronoun(s) to complete the following sentences.

1. Every worker and supervisor was notified when (his, her, his or her, their) yearly physical examination was due. _____

2. Dun and Bradstreet bases (its, their) financial ratings on accounting reports. _____

3. As directed, the committee submitted (its, their) annual report. _____

4. Not one of the creditors would allow (his, her, his or her, their) claims to be decreased. _____

5. Did someone say that (his, her, his or her, their) test copy was illegible? _____

6. The CRTC can use (its, their) power to increase the amount of Canadian content in the media. _____

7. Every one of the drawers had (its, their) contents dumped. _____

8. The inspection team will have (its, their) decision on your desk Monday. _____

1. his or her 2. their 3. its 4. her 5. his or her 6. her 7. his or her 8. its 9. his 10. its

9. Neither the glamour nor the excitement of the job had lost (its, their) appeal. _____

10. Any new subscriber may cancel (his, her, his or her, their) subscription within the first ten days. _____

11. The union members elected (its, their) officers by mailed ballot. _____

12. Has everybody on the girls' team had (her, its, their) picture taken? _____

13. Either of the companies may move (its, their) headquarters to Calgary. _____

14. Every renter and homeowner should exercise (his, her, his or her, their) right to vote. _____

15. If anyone needs assistance, Mr. Torres will help (him, her, him or her, them). _____

16. Our staff agreed that (its, their) stand must be unified. _____

17. *Consumer Reports* announced a plan to change (its, their) method of distribution. _____

18. Each of the supermarkets featured (its, their) advertisements on Thursday. _____

19. Every one of the girls was pleased with (her, their) internship program. _____

20. Neither the father nor his sons wanted (his, their) shares to be sold. _____

A. (**Self-check**) Select the correct word, and write it in the space provided.

LEVEL III

1. I know perfectly well (who, whom) you are. _____

2. Are you the individual (who, whom) submitted an application? _____

3. The contract will be awarded to (whoever, whomever) submits the lowest bid. _____

4. (Who, Whom) do you think we should interview for the newsletter? _____

5. She is the investment counsellor of (who, whom) I spoke. _____

6. When I return the call, for (who, whom) should I ask? _____

7. (Who, Whom) did you say would drop by? _____

8. Will you recommend a lawyer (who, whom) can handle this case? _____

9. To (who, whom) were these messages sent? _____

10. The prize will be given to (whoever, whomever) the judges select. _____

Check your answers.

B. Select the correct word, and write it in the space provided.

1. Do you know (who, whom) the telephone caller is? _____

2. He is a graphics designer (who, whom) we believe developed their prize-winning Web site. _____

3. The position will be filled by (whoever, whomever) the manager hires. _____

4. Mr. Brooks said that Mrs. Harris, (who, whom) starts next Monday, is an excellent accountant. _____

5. (Who, Whom) have you asked to research promotion of our products on the Internet? _____

6. For (who, whom) does the bell toll? _____

7. I have a pizza for (whoever, whomever) placed the telephone order. _____

8. The economics expert to (who, whom) the professor referred was Milton Friedman. _____

9. Mr. Stewart is the one (who, whom) we think should be made supervisor. _____

10. Rob Evans is the player against (who, whom) offensive interference was called. _____

1. who 2. who 3. whoever 4. Whom 5. whom 6. whom 7. Who 8. who 9. whom 10. whomever

11. You'll never guess (who, whom) we saw in town. _____

12. Do you know (who, whom) will be taking your place? _____

13. Dr. Song will see (whoever, whomever) is next in line. _____

14. I wonder (who, whom) the speaker is talking about. _____

15. In making introductions, who should be introduced to (who, whom)? _____

16. Mrs. Silver asked us (who, whom) we think should train Kelly. _____

17. Please direct my inquiry to (whoever, whomever) is in charge of quality control. _____

18. Tom Garcia is the graduate (who, whom) applied first. _____

19. (Who, Whom) shall I say is calling? _____

20. Mr. Rodman, (who, whom) we thought should be appointed, was not among the final candidates. _____

21. For (who, whom) is this book being ordered? _____

22. Please send us the name of (whoever, whomever) you suggest for the opening. _____

C. Review of Levels I, II, and III. Underline any errors, and write a correction in the space provided. Write *C* if the sentence is correct.

1. Our president told each member of their voting rights. _____

2. Whomever is in charge of finances should receive the bill. _____

3. Someone on the girls' team left their running shoes at home. _____

4. Have you decided whom the winner is? _____

5. Every man, woman, and child in the country is expected to make their contribution. _____

6. Patricia Best, whom we think will be at the meeting, is a magazine editor. _____

7. The Fitness Committee held their meeting at 2 p.m. _____

8. To whom should I speak about my claim? _____

9. Neither the professor nor the student knew their rights. _____

10. We will hire whomever the committee recommends. _____

11. Either of the possible lottery winners must present his winning ticket by the end of the month. _____

12. Whom is sending all these e-mail messages? _____

13. Any taxpayer may ask to have his property reassessed. _____

14. None of us could believe whom the new manager is. _____

15. Each of the fitness centres promoted their own programs. _____

D. Cumulative Review. (Self-check) These sentences review Chapters 1 through 7. Underline any errors. Then write corrected forms in the spaces provided. Be alert! Some sentences contain more than one correction. If a sentence is correct, write *C* in the space. Then check your answers below.

1. Federal Express conducted an extensive survey of there employees. _____

2. In a progressive company a CEO is able to act on his believes. _____

3. Itinerarys of all employees travel plans must be sent to Rick or myself before any reservations are made. _____

4. The manager just assumed it was them because of there numerous earlier calls. _____

5. How many faxes do you and her normally receive in a day? _____

6. Advocates for both tenants and landlords rights brought their arguments to the city councils weekly meeting. _____

7. Because us renters demanded our rights', a mayors committee was appointed to study the matter further. _____

8. Two attornies were necessary to handle my father's-in-laws business transactions. _____

9. A business owner often feels that he must seek advice. _____

10. Kim said that her childrens needs always came before her companys demands on her time. _____

11. If you were him, would you disregard five years experience and switch careers? _____

12. Before going over your bosses head, be sure to ask her permission. _____

13. In total sales Lisa is more productive than him. Which explains why she will receive the promotion. _____

14. In some companys its standard practice to distribute a months pay at Christmas as a bonus. _____

15. Just between you and I, whom do you think will be named CEO? _____

16. The branch offices faxes look better than ours. _____

17. Todays companies will generally send employment applications to whomever requests them. _____

18. Neither of the men had their driver's licence with them. _____

19. Jeff James, whom was interviewed by Mr. Woo and I, is our best candidate. _____

20. Nearly all libraries offer computerized indexes and databases to whoever needs it. _____

Check your answers.

---

1. its employees 2. his or her beliefs 3. Itineraries employees' 4. it was they because of their 5. faxes you and she 6. tenants' landlords' council's 7. we renters rights' mayor's 8. attorneys father-in-law's 9. he or she 10. children's company's month's 11. you were he years' 12. boss's than he, which 14. companies it's month's 15. you and me, who 16. office's faxes 17. Today's whoever 18. his driver's licence with him 19. who Mr. Woo and me 20. needs them.

E. **Optional Composition.** Your instructor may ask you to complete this exercise on a separate sheet. Write seven original sentences with the following words that function as subjects: *either, everyone, many, somebody, staff, committee,* and *McDonald's*. In each of the sentences, the verb should be either *is* or *are*. You may add phrases for clarity, such as *Either of the two choices....* In addition, write sentences showing *who* as the subject of a verb, *whom* as the object of a preposition, and *whoever* as the subject of a clause. Label each sentence.

Editor's Challenge

The following business letter contains errors reflecting the concepts you have studied in Chapters 1–7. Use standard proofreading marks (see the inside front cover) to show your corrections.

❖ BENSON BROTHERS MANAGEMENT SERVICES ❖

368 Glenlake Ave.
Toronto, ON M9B 2B4

(416) 358-2249   E-mail: bensonbros@world.com   Web: www.bensonbros.com

February 9, 200x

Ms. Laura W. Stephens
2320 Centennial Road
Oshawa, ON L1G 8K7

Dear Ms. Stephens:

My partner and myself are certain that our rental management service can help you care for you're fathers-in-law apartment complex in Don Mills, here are answers to you're questions.

To manage a clients rental units, we charge 10 per cent of all fees' collected, we will advertise whenever a unit becomes vacant. We charge an additional 10 per cent on the first years rent whenever we fill a vacant unit. Whether we charge the last months rent in advance is between you and I. Our firms two lawyers are available to assist you and I. If necessary.

During the 1990's we expanded, our's is now the only firm to offer maintenance and cleaning services to their customers.

Ms. Stephens, we now manage over 75 rental propertys in the Toronto area. We are available to whomever needs rental assistance. Either for private residences or for multiple unit. One client wrote to us saying, "You've managed my units much better than I, and you're firm has made life much easier for my husband and I." We are convinced that we can ease the burden of your responsibilitys also, please call my partner or I at 416-358-2249 to arrange an appointment this week.

Sincerely yours,

Jonathon Benson

Jonathon Benson

Underline the correct word.

1. Did anyone on the boys' team leave (his, their) shoes in the gym?

2. The entire faculty sent (its, their) support to the president.

3. Neither of the companies could identify (its, their) equipment.

4. (Who, Whom) would you like to see as the next department manager?

5. Give the prize to (whoever, whomever) earned the most points.

learning.web.ways

As you become more familiar with the Web, you may begin to think that the Web is the perfect place for all research. Wrong! The Web does not include all useful data, and what it does contain is not always accurate. The following exercise helps you learn to think more critically about what you find on the Web.

Goal: To learn to evaluate Web site credibility.

1. Open your Web browser, and type this URL in the location box: **<http:www.ecf.utoronto.ca/~writing/resources.htm>**.

2. This Web site, maintained by the University of Toronto's Engineering Writing Centre, has a series of links to Web pages that will help you learn how to search the Internet and evaluate the material you find on it.

3. Click on **How to Do Research on the Internet**. Then click on **Things to Know**.

4. Follow the link to the **Recommended Search Strategies** page. Read the **Five-Step Search Strategy We Recommend**.

5. Scroll down the page and read **Search Strategies We DO NOT Recommend**; then click on **evaluations**.

6. Scroll down to the section **These pages are designed to provide you with four things**, and click on **questions**.

7. Make a list of five or more questions you might ask in deciding whether a Web site is reliable.

8. Click **BACK** once, and try some of the **exercises** about evaluating the Internet.

9. End your session by clicking the **X** in the upper right corner. Turn in your list of questions.

1. his 2. its 3. its 4. Whom 5. whoever

UNIT 2 REVIEW   Chapters 4–7 (Self-Check)

Begin your review by rereading Chapters 4 through 7. Then test your comprehension of those chapters by filling in the blanks in the exercises that follow. Compare your responses with the key at the end of the book.

LEVEL I

1. I understand that the (a) Lutzes, (b) Lutz, (c) Lutz's are opening a copy service on Fifth Street in Lethbridge.   _____

2. Every political campaign is filled with wordy (a) speechs, (b) speeches, (c) speech's.   _____

3. Each summer I search the farmers' market for the best (a) peachs, (b) peaches.   _____

4. After just two (a) years, (b) year's, (c) years' time, investors are promised a 25 per cent return.   _____

5. We are giving careful consideration to that (a) company's, (b) companies', (c) companys' shares.   _____

6. Many of our (a) students', (b) students, (c) student's have difficulty with possessive constructions.   _____

7. The committee completed (a) it's, (b) its work last week.   _____

8. Just between you and (a) me, (b) I, what do you think?   _____

9. All employees except Paul and (a) he, (b) him agreed to the reorganization.   _____

10. Ask both of the designers when (a) she, (b) he, (c) he or she, (d) they can give us estimates.   _____

11. When a customer makes a complaint, (a) he, (b) she, (c) he or she, (d) they must be treated courteously.   _____

LEVEL II

12. Parking is not allowed in the back (a) alleys, (b) allies, (c) alleys', (d) alley's.   _____

13. Adrienne Hale consulted her three (a) sister-in-laws, (b) sister-in-law's, (c) sisters-in-law before making her decision.   _____

14. The (a) pro's and con's, (b) pros and cons of merging the two departments were discussed heatedly.   _____

15. (a) Steve and Leslie's, (b) Steve's and Leslie's new home is in Clarenville.   _____

16. I certainly hope that today's weather is better than (a) yesterdays, (b) yesterday's, (c) yesterday.   _____

17. Brad hoped to find a job in the (a) electronics, (b) electronic's, (c) electronics' industry.   _____

18. Insincerity irritates Mr. Sanchez as much as (a) I, (b) me, (c) myself.   _____

19. The president and (a) I, (b) me, (c) myself will answer all questions.   _____

20. Neither the mother nor her children wanted (a) her, (b) their savings accounts to
be changed.   _____

21. Every clerk and every secretary elected to exercise (a) his, (b) her, (c) his or her,
(d) their voting rights.   _____

22. Marsten, Davis, and Jackson Inc. plans to move (a) it's, (b) its, (c) their offices to
a new location.   _____

LEVEL III

23. Following several financial (a) crisis, (b) crises, (c) crisises, the corporation was
forced to declare bankruptcy.   _____

24. Because of its excellent work, thanks (a) is, (b) are in order for our organizing committee.   _____

25. We read an announcement that the (a) Harris', (b) Harris's, (c) Harrises, (d) Harrises'
son won a scholarship.   _____

26. I'm certain that my (a) bosses, (b) boss's, (c) bosses' signature will be forthcoming.   _____

27. Revenue Canada is checking Mr. (a) Smitts's, (b) Smitts', (c) Smittses' return.   _____

28. The employee credited with the suggestion was thought to be (a) he, (b) him.   _____

29. If I were (a) her, (b) she, I would decline the offer.   _____

30. To (a) who, (b) whom did you send your application?   _____

31. (a) Who, (b) Whom has been asked to head the commission?   _____

32. Give the extra supplies to (a) whoever, (b) whomever needs them.   _____

33. (a) Who, (b) Whom would you prefer to see in that job?   _____

34. You'll never guess (a) who, (b) whom I saw today.   _____

35. It could have been (a) her, (b) she who called you.   _____

Hotline Review

36. Professor Breuer said it was (a) to, (b) too early to sign up for these classes.   _____

37. Check your (a) owner's, (b) owners' warranty carefully.   _____

38. Daily exercise is recommended because it is (a) healthful, (b) healthy.   _____

39. (a) Less, (b) Fewer people came to the event than were expected.   _____

40. If it's (a) alright, (b) all right, (c) allright with you, I'll call the technician.   _____

Techniques for Effective Sentences

The basic unit in writing is the sentence. Sentences come in a variety of sizes, shapes, and structures. As business communicators, we are most interested in functional sentences that say what we want to say correctly and concisely. In this workshop you'll concentrate on two important elements: writing complete sentences and writing concise sentences.

Writing Complete Sentences

To be complete, a sentence must have a subject and a predicate and it must make sense. As you learned in Chapter 3, incomplete sentences are fragments. Let's consider four common fragment errors you'll want to avoid.

1. The fragment contains a subject and a predicate, but it begins with a subordinate word (such as *because, as, although, since,* or *if*) and fails to introduce a complete clause. You can correct this problem by joining the fragment to a relevant main clause.

    Fragment: Because world markets and economies are becoming increasingly intermixed.

    Revision: Because world markets and economies are becoming increasingly intermixed, Canadians will be doing more business with people from other cultures.

    Fragment: Although North Americans tend to come to the point directly.

    Revision: Although North Americans tend to come to the point directly, people from some other cultures prefer indirectness.

2. The fragment does not contain a subject and a predicate, but a nearby sentence completes its meaning.

    Fragment: In the spring of every year in Las Vegas. That's when computer vendors stage a huge show.

    Revision: In the spring of every year in Las Vegas, computer vendors stage a huge show.

3. The fragment starts with a relative pronoun such as *which, that,* or *who.* Join the fragment to a main clause to form a complete sentence.

    Fragment: Which is a precious item to North Americans and other Westerners.

    Revision: Concise business letters save time, which is a precious item to North Americans and other Westerners.

4. The fragment starts with a noun followed by a *who, that,* or *which* clause. Add a predicate to form a complete sentence.

    Fragment: The visiting Asian executive who was struggling to express his idea in English.

    Revision: The visiting Asian executive who was struggling to express his idea in English appreciated the patience of his listener.

Skill Check 2.1 Eliminating Sentence Fragments

Each of the following consists of a fragment and a sentence, not necessarily in that order. Use proofreading marks to eliminate the fragment.

   Example: Speak in short sentences and use common words. If you want to be understood abroad.

1. Although you should not raise your voice. You should speak slowly and enunciate clearly.

2. A glazed expression or wandering eyes. These alert a speaker that the listener is lost.

3. In speaking with foreign business people, be careful to avoid jargon. Which is special terminology that may confuse listeners.

4. Kevin Chambers, who is an international specialist and consultant. He said that much of the world wants to like us.

5. Graciously accept the blame for not making your meaning clear. If a misunderstanding results.

Skill Check 2.2 Completing Sentences

Expand the following fragments into complete sentences. Add your own ideas. Be ready to explain why each fragment is incomplete and what you did to remedy the problem.

Example: Unless you keep notes of conversations with clients.

Revision: Unless you keep notes of conversations with clients, you are not likely to remember the details of a telephone conversation that you had with a client several months ago.

1. The business person who engages a translator for important contracts _____

   _____

2. Assuming that a nod, a yes, or a smile indicates agreement _____

   _____

3. If you learn greetings and a few phrases in the language of the country where you are visiting _____

   _____

4. Although global business transactions are often conducted in English _____

   _____

5. Which is why English speakers sometimes put words in the mouths of foreign friends struggling to express an idea _____

   _____

Avoiding Run-on (Fused) Sentences and Comma Splices

Also in Chapter 3 you learned to recognize run-on sentences and comma splices. Remember that locating subjects and verbs may help in identifying and correcting run-ons and comma splices.

A run-on sentence consists of two or more complete thoughts without punctuation to separate them. A comma splice consists of two or more complete thoughts with only a comma between them. The simplest way to avoid these errors is to separate complete thoughts.

Run-on sentence: Profit for the second quarter rose to $24.1 million sales rose to $151.9 million.

Revision: Profit for the second quarter rose to $24.1 million. Sales rose to 151.9 million.

Comma splice:	Analysts expected a decline of 2.3 per cent in sales, the decline was actually 5 per cent.
Revision:	Analysts <u>expected</u> a decline of 2.3 per cent in sales. The <u>decline</u> <u>was</u> actually 5 per cent.

Note that other methods of correcting run-ons or comma splices can be used.

Analysts expected a decline of 2.3 per cent in sales, but the decline was actually 5 per cent. (Coordinating conjunctions are discussed in Chapter 14.)

Analysts expected a decline of 2.3 per cent in sales; the decline was actually 5 per cent. (Semicolons are discussed in Chapter 17.)

Skill Check 2.3 Correcting Comma Splices and Run-on Sentences

Use proofreading marks to correct any comma splices or run-ons in the following items.

1. Internet companies now provide listings of available vacation homes these services reduce the risks of long-distance renting.

2. The Ontario government will probably build a new highway in the Niagara Region, the location of the new road has not been announced.

3. Although Singapore Airlines announced that it was the first airline to offer in-flight Web browsing, it had to admit that the service was initially quite limited.

4. The tour operator offers motor coach tours throughout Europe participants choose from a variety of itineraries, activities, and accommodations.

5. Quebec City was founded by Champlain in 1608, its historic district was named a UNESCO World Heritage Site in 1985.

6. After September 11, 2001, tourism fell sharply in the U.S. capital, and within two months an estimated 17,000 Washington residents had lost jobs related to the tourist industry.

7. *Mrs. Miniver* is the title of a British bestseller from 1939 it is also the title of an extremely popular American movie from 1942.

8. Munich is Germany's Silicon Valley, it is a cultural centre as well.

9. Nicholas checked his e-mail then he checked his voice mail.

10. The Japanese delicacy *fugu,* or blowfish, is known for its exhorbitant price, furthermore, it is well known for being extremely poisonous.

11. One minute he was there the next minute he was gone.

12. Thailand offers many adventures, more than 80,000 Canadians visited the country in 2000.

Writing Concise Sentences

Business people value concise, economical writing. Wordy communication wastes the reader's time and sometimes causes confusion. You can make your sentences more concise by avoiding opening fillers, revising wordy phrases, and eliminating redundant words.

Avoiding Opening Fillers

Openers such as *there is, it is,* and *this is to inform you that* fill in sentences but generally add no meaning. These fillers reveal writers spinning their wheels until deciding where the sentence is going. Train yourself to question these constructions. About 75 per cent can be eliminated, almost always resulting in more concise sentences.

Wordy: *There are* three students who volunteered to help.
Revised: Three students volunteered to help.

Wordy: *This is to inform you that* our offices will be closed on Monday.
Revised: Our offices will be closed on Monday.

Revising Wordy Phrases

Some of our most common and comfortable phrases are actually full of "word fat." When examined carefully, these phrases can be pared down considerably.

Wordy Phrases	Concise Substitutes
at the present time	now
at this point in time	now
due to the fact that	because
for the purpose of	to
in all probability	probably
in connection with	for
in spite of the fact that	even though
in the amount of	for
in the event that	if
in the near future	soon
in the neighbourhood of	about
in view of the fact that	since
with regard to	about

Notice how you can revise wordy sentences to make them more concise:

Wordy: *Due to the fact that* fire damaged our distribution centre, we must delay some shipments.
Revised: *Because* fire damaged our distribution centre, we must delay some shipments.

Wordy: The cost for the entire system is *in the neighbourhood of* $18,000.
Revised: The cost for the entire system is *about* $18,000.

Eliminating Redundant Words

Words that are needlessly repetitive are said to be "redundant." Business writers must be alert to eliminating redundant words and phrases, such as the following:

advance warning	exactly identical	perfectly clear
alter or change	few in number	personal opinion
assemble together	free and clear	positively certain
basic fundamentals	grateful thanks	proposed plan
collect together	great majority	refer back
consensus of opinion	integral part	today's modern world
contributing factor	midway between	true facts
each and every	new changes	very unique
end result	past history	visible to the eye

Wordy: We studied the *past* history of *each and every* potential donor.
Revised: We studied the history of every potential donor.

Wordy: Please collect *together* all the *true* facts before proceeding.
Revised: Please collect all the facts before proceeding.

Skill Check 2.4 Writing Concise Sentences

In the space provided, rewrite the following sentences to make them more concise.

1. There is a free booklet that shows all the new changes in employee benefits.

_____

_____

2. In view of the fact that health care benefits are being drastically altered, this is to inform you that an orientation meeting will be scheduled in the near future.

_____

_____

3. A great majority of students will in all probability support the proposed satellite parking plan.

_____

_____

4. In the event that McDonald's offers new menu items for the purpose of increasing sales, experts think that there is every reason to believe that the effort will be successful.

_____

_____

5. There will be a special showing of the orientation training film scheduled at 10 a.m. due to the fact that there were so few in number who were able to attend the first showing.

_____

_____

6. This is to give you advance warning that we plan to alter or change the procedures for submitting travel expenses in the very near future.

_____

_____

Skill Check 2.5 Proofreading a Memo

In the following memo we have deliberately introduced sentence fragments and wordy writing. Use proofreading marks to make all sentences complete and concise.

Writing Application 2.1 After you edit the following memo, your instructor may ask you to respond to it. In a memo on a separate sheet, assume that you have received this memo. Show your appreciation to Jason Corzo for his advice. Explain that you are both excited and worried about your new assignment. Use your imagination to tell why. Describe how you expect to prepare for the new assignment. You might say that you plan to start learning the language, to read about the culture, and to talk with colleagues who have worked in Japan. Put this in your own words, and elaborate.

Becktelman Worldwide Contractors

Interoffice Memo

TO: Marcia Murphy
FROM: Jason Corzo
DATE: August 20, 200x
SUBJECT: CONGRATULATIONS ON YOUR ASSIGNMENT TO JAPAN

Your assignment to Kansai, Japan, as office manager of our International Business Relations Department. That's cause for celebration! This is to inform you that although I'm a little late in responding to your request, I do have some experiences and advice that may interest you.

When I was on assignment in connection with our firm in Japan. My job was to help us break into the construction business. I found it very difficult to locate a Japanese construction firm. That would act as a subcontractor for us. In time I did find a company, and eventually we began to win contracts. In spite of the fact that the process was slow and frustrating.

Despite the slow pace of qualifying for and winning contracts. I am optimistic with regard to expanding our business in Asian countries. In my personal opinion, an important contributing factor in our successful entrance into Pacific Rim markets is how willing we are to play the game according to Asian rules. In the event that we are willing to work from the inside and show our long-term commitment. I am positively certain that we can succeed in gaining a great majority of Asia's construction business in the near future.

On a personal level, Marcia, there are a few things that really helped me in communicating with the Japanese. I learned to smile a lot due to the fact that a smile is perfectly clear to everyone. I also learned to listen without interrupting, and I learned to accept blame each and every time a communication misunderstanding occurred.

Due to the fact that you are in all probability midway between assignments. This message may take a while to catch up with you. Regardless, I congratulate you on this promotion, Marcia. It is the consensus of opinion in our office that you will be very successful in managing our Kansai office in Japan.

Showing the Action

Verbs: Kinds, Voices, Moods

OBJECTIVES   When you have completed the materials in this chapter, you will be able to do the following:

LEVEL I
- *Distinguish between transitive and intransitive verbs.*
- *Identify at least eight linking verbs.*

LEVEL II
- *Recognize active- and passive-voice verbs.*
- *Convert sentences written in the passive voice to sentences in the active voice.*

LEVEL III
- *Recognize sentence constructions requiring the subjunctive verb mood.*
- *Use subjunctive forms correctly.*

PRETEST

Underline the appropriate answers.

1. In the sentence *Maria listened to the instructions,* the verb *listened* is (a) transitive, (b) intransitive, (c) linking.

2. In the sentence *Written instructions were provided,* the verb phrase *were provided* is in the (a) active voice, (b) passive voice, (c) subjunctive mood, (d) intransitive mood.

3. In the sentence *Barbara Benesch taught the class,* the verb *taught* is in the (a) active voice, (b) passive voice, (c) subjunctive mood, (d) intransitive mood.

4. Jackie acts as if she (a) was, (b) were the professor.

5. Della Jones moved that a vote (a) is, (b) be taken.

1. b   2. b   3. a   4. b   5. b

Verbs express an action, an occurrence, or a state of being. In relation to subjects, verbs tell what the subject is doing or what is being done to the subject. Verbs may also link to the subject words that describe the subject or identify it.

The verb is the most complex part of speech. A complete treatment of its forms and uses would require at least a volume. Our discussion of verbs will focus mainly on practical applications and will be limited to four chapters.

In our discussion of sentences in Chapter 3, you became familiar with three basic sentence patterns: subject–verb, subject–action verb–object, and subject–linking verb–complement. Sentence patterns are determined by their verbs. You have already learned to identify action and linking verbs. Let's now consider how these verbs actually function.

First we'll deal with action verbs. They express their action either transitively or intransitively. When action verbs are transitive, they may create subject–action verb–object sentence patterns. When action verbs are intransitive, they may create subject–verb sentence patterns.

LEVEL I

Hotlink

For a quick on-line overview of verbs, visit the University of Ottawa site **<http://www.uottawa. ca/academic/arts/ writcent/ hypergrammar/ useverb.html>**.

▶ Kinds of Verbs

Transitive Verbs

A verb expressing an action directed toward a person or thing is said to be *transitive*. An action verb used transitively needs, in addition to its subject, a noun or pronoun to complete its meaning. This noun or pronoun functions as the direct object of the transitive verb. Notice in the following sentences that the verbs direct action toward objects (shown in italics).

> The <u>directors</u> <u>demanded</u> improved *profits*.
> Yesterday the <u>president</u> <u>called</u> *him*.
> <u>We</u> <u>sold</u> the *shares* at a profit.

Objects usually answer the questions *what?* or *whom?* In the first example, the directors demanded *what?* The object is *profits*. In the second example, the president called *whom?* The object is *him*.

Intransitive Verbs

An action verb that does not require an object to complete its action is said to be *intransitive*.

> <u>Ralph</u> <u>worked</u> in the Human Resources Department last summer.
> <u>E-commerce</u> <u>grows</u> rapidly because of the Internet.
> <u>Tanya</u> <u>listened</u> carefully to the directions.

Notice that the verbs in these sentences do not express actions directed toward persons or things. Prepositional phrases (*in the Human Resources Department, because of the Internet, to the directors*) and adverbs (*rapidly, carefully*) do not receive the action expressed by the verbs, nor do they answer the questions *what?* or *whom?* Therefore, prepositional phrases and adverbs do not function as objects of verbs.

Linking Verbs

You will recall that linking verbs *link* to the subject words that rename or describe the subject. A noun, pronoun, or adjective that renames or describes the subject is called a *complement* because it *completes* the meaning of the subject.

> Angie <u>is</u> the *manager*. (*Manager* is a noun complement that completes the meaning of the sentence by renaming *Angie*, the subject.)
>
> Her <u>salary</u> <u>is</u> *excellent*. (*Excellent* is an adjective complement that completes the meaning of *salary*.)
>
> The <u>caller</u> <u>was</u> *he*. (*He* is a pronoun complement that completes the meaning of *caller*.)

Notice in the preceding sentences that the noun, pronoun, or adjective complements following the linking verbs do not receive action from the verbs; instead, the complements *complete* the meaning of the subject.

You are already familiar with those linking verbs that are derived from the *to be* verb form: *am, is, are, was, were, be, being, been*. Other words that often serve as linking verbs are *feel, appear, taste, seem, sound, look,* and *smell*. Notice that many of these words describe sense experience. Verbs expressing sense experience may be followed by complements just as the *to be* linking verbs often are.

> They <u>feel</u> *bad* about the sale of the company. (*Bad* is an adjective complement following the linking verb *feel*. An adjective—not the adverb *badly*—is needed here to describe the senses.)
>
> Settlement of the strike <u>appears</u> *imminent*. (*Imminent* is an adjective complement following the linking verb *appears*.)

The use of adjectives following such verbs is discussed more completely in Chapter 12.

The function of a verb in a sentence determines its classification. The action verb *filed,* for example, is intransitive when it has no object (*Ralph filed*). The same verb is transitive when an object follows (*Ralph filed a letter*). The verb *felt* is linking when it is used to connect a complement describing the subject (*Maria felt marvellous*). The same verb is transitive when it directs action to an object (*Maria felt the wet desk*). To distinguish between classifications, study carefully the constructions in which the verbs appear.

To review briefly:

1. Action Verbs—two kinds:

    a. Transitive: need objects to complete their meaning.

    b. Intransitive: do not need objects to complete their meaning.

2. Linking Verbs: form a link to words that rename or describe the subject.

Complete the reinforcement exercises for Level I on pp. 135–137.

▶ Verb Voices

A verb expressing an action directed toward a person or thing is said to be transitive. Transitive verbs fall into two categories depending upon the receiver of the action of the verbs.

Study Tip

Here's a mnemonic (memory) device to help you remember the verbs of the senses. Call them the FATS verbs, an acronym (word formed of initials) made from the first letters of *feel, appear, taste,* and *seem*.

LEVEL II

Active Voice

When the verb expresses an action directed by the subject toward the object of the verb, the verb is said to be in the *active voice.*

> <u>Alison</u> <u>answered</u> the telephone. (Action directed to the object, *telephone*.)
> Our <u>department</u> <u>uses</u> Excel. (Action directed to the object, *Excel*.)

Verbs in the active voice are direct and forceful; they clearly identify the doer of the action. For these reasons, writing that frequently uses the active voice is vigorous and effective. Writers of business communications strive to use the active voice; in fact, it is called the *voice of business.*

Passive Voice

When the action of the verb is directed toward the subject, the verb is said to be in the *passive voice.* Compare the two groups of sentences below:

Passive Voice	**Active Voice**
<u>Computers</u> <u>are used</u> daily.	<u>We</u> <u>use</u> computers daily.
The <u>machines</u> <u>are being sold</u> by Mr. Chavez.	<u>Mr. Chavez</u> <u>is selling</u> the machines.
Three <u>errors</u> <u>were made</u> in the report.	The <u>accountant</u> <u>made</u> three errors in the report.
The <u>order</u> <u>was submitted</u> after the deadline.	<u>You</u> <u>submitted</u> the order after the deadline.

Because the passive voice can be used to avoid mentioning the performer of the action, the passive voice is sometimes called the *voice of tact.* Notice how much more tactful the passive versions of the last two examples are. Although directness in business writing is generally preferable, in certain instances the passive voice is used when indirectness is desired.

Complete the reinforcement exercises for Level II on pp. 138–140.

LEVEL III

▶ Verb Moods

Three verb moods are available to enable a speaker or writer to express an attitude toward a subject: (1) the *indicative mood* is used to express a fact; (2) the *imperative mood* is used to express a command; (3) the *subjunctive mood* is used to express a doubt, a conjecture, or a suggestion. The subjunctive mood usually causes speakers and writers difficulty and therefore demands special attention.

Subjunctive Mood

Although the subjunctive mood is seldom used today, it is, however, still employed by careful individuals in the following constructions.

1. ***If* and *wish* clauses.** When a statement that is doubtful or contrary to fact is introduced by *if, as if, as though,* or *wish,* the subjunctive form *were* is substituted for the indicative form *was.*

    > If Lori *were* here, we could proceed. (Lori is *not* here.)
    > She acts as if she *were* the boss. (She is *not* the boss.)

He spends money as though he *were* a millionaire. (He is *not* a millionaire.)
George wishes he *were* able to type. (George is *not* able to type.)

But if the statement could possibly be true, use the indicative form.

If Chris *was* in the audience, I missed him. (Chris might have been in the audience.)

2. **That clauses.** When a *that* clause follows a verb expressing a command, recommendation, request, suggestion, or requirement, the subjunctive verb form *be* is used (not *am, is,* or *are*).

    The doctor recommended that everyone *be* inoculated.
    Our manager ordered that all reports *be* proofread twice.

3. **Motions.** When a motion is stated, a subjunctive verb form should be used in the following *that* clause.

    Sheldon moved that a vote *be* taken.
    It has been seconded that the meeting *be* adjourned.

Caution: In a sentence without *that* clauses, do not mix subjunctive and indicative verbs.

    Right: If she *were skilled,* she *would receive* job offers. (Both verbs subjunctive)
    Right: If she *is skilled,* she *will receive* job offers. (Both verbs indicative)
    Wrong: If she *were skilled,* she *will receive* job offers. (One subjunctive verb and one indicative verb)

Complete the reinforcement exercises for Level III on pp. 141–142.

" "

Notable Quotable

"One should aim not at being possible to understand but at being impossible to misunderstand."
—Quintilian

Hotlink

Grammar Slammer illustrates subjunctive mood verbs at **<http://www. englishplus.com/ grammar/00000031. htm>**.

HOTLINE QUERIES

Question: Which is better: *The truck carried canisters of highly <u>flammable</u> or <u>inflammable</u> liquid?*

Answer: Actually, both *flammable* and *inflammable* mean "easily set on fire." Either would be correct in your sentence. However, *flammable* is preferred because its meaning is less likely to be confused. Since the prefix *in* often means "not," the word *inflammable* could be misunderstood. Therefore, use *flammable* in technical matters, particularly if you wish to suggest a warning. You may use *inflammable* or its derivatives for non-technical descriptions, such as *Her words were <u>inflammatory</u>.*

Question: I have a sentence that begins *Beside(s) providing financial aid ....* Is there any real difference between *beside* and *besides*?

Answer: Yes, indeed! *Beside* is a preposition meaning "by the side of" (*come sit <u>beside</u> me*). *Besides* is an adverb meaning "in addition to" (*<u>besides</u> paper we must order ribbons*). In your sentence use *besides*.

Question: I have looked and looked, but I cannot find this word in a dictionary. I'll pronounce it phonetically for you: *per-rog-a-tive*. I know it exists. What am I doing wrong?

Answer: You, like many other people, are mispronouncing it. The word is <u>pre-rog-a-tive</u>, meaning "a right or privilege" (*it is your <u>prerogative</u> to join a union*).

Question: I received a magazine advertisement recently that promised me a *free gift* and a *15 per cent off discount* if I subscribed. What's wrong with this wording?

Answer: You have a double winner here in the category of redundancies. The word *gift* suggests *free*; therefore, to say *free gift* is like saying *I'm studying English English*. It would be better to say *special gift*. In the same way, *15 per cent off discount* repeats itself. Omit *off*.

Question: When do you use *may*, and when do you use *can*?

Answer: Traditionally, the verb *may* is used in asking or granting permission (*yes, you may use that desk*). *Can* is used to suggest ability (*you can succeed in business*). In informal writing, however, authorities today generally agree that *can* may be substituted for *may*.

Question: On my computer I'm using a program that checks the writer's style. My problem is that it flags every passive voice verb and tells me to consider using active voice verbs. Are passive voice verbs totally forbidden in business writing?

Answer: Of course not! Computer style checkers capitalize on language areas that can be detected mechanically, and a passive voice verb is easily identified by a computer. Although active voice verbs are considered more forceful, passive voice verbs have a genuine function in business writing. Because they hide the subject and diffuse attention, passive verbs are useful in sensitive messages where indirect language can develop an impersonal, inconspicuous tone. For example, when a lower-level employee must write a persuasive and somewhat negative message to a manager, passive voice verbs are quite useful.

Question: What's the correct verb in this sentence? *Tim recognized that, if his company (was or were) to prosper, it would require considerable capital.*

Answer: The verb should be *were* because the clause in which it functions is not true. Statements contrary to fact that are introduced by words like *if* and *wish* require subjunctive mood verbs.

CHAPTER 8   Reinforcement Exercises

A. (**Self-check**) In the spaces provided, indicate whether the italicized verbs are transitive (*T*), intransitive (*I*), or linking (*L*).

> ## LEVEL I

Example: Elvira *is* the supervisor in that department.   _____L_____

1. Despite medication, Ann *feels* worse.   _____

2. Canada *exports* products to numerous foreign countries.   _____

3. After dinner the delegates *returned* to their rooms.   _____

4. Mr. Rose *is* the one on whom we all depend.   _____

5. Rachel *expects* Ms. Partington to return to the office soon.   _____

6. It *was* he who devised the current work schedule.   _____

7. The production manager *called* over four hours ago.   _____

8. Shari Adams *feels* certain that the calendar date is clear.   _____

9. Well-written business letters *get* results.   _____

10. We *sent* a replacement order to you as soon as we received your letter.   _____

Check your answers.

B. Each of the following sentences contains a verb that is either transitive or intransitive. If the verb is intransitive, underline it and write *I* in the space provided. If the verb is transitive, underline it, write *T* in the space provided, and also write its direct object.

Examples: After her presentation the salesperson <u>left</u>.   _____I_____

   Workers <u>brought</u> their lunches.   __T (lunches)__

1. Insurance agents certify claims.   _____

2. Traffic stopped.   _____

3. Fedex maintains a busy Web site for its customers.   _____

4. Our suppliers raised their prices.   _____

5. Storm clouds gathered.   _____

6. Over the years our assets increased.   _____

7. Mr. Bateson sends many e-mail messages.   _____

1. L 2. T 3. I 4. L 5. T 6. L 7. I 8. L 9. T 10. T

8. The telephone rang. _____

9. Gregory answered it. _____

10. Many employees take the subway to work. _____

Linking verbs are followed by complements that identify, rename, or describe the subjects. The most common linking verbs are the forms of *to be* (*am, is, are, was,* etc.) and the verbs of the senses (*feel, appear, taste, smell,* etc.). The following sentences all contain linking verbs. For each sentence underline the linking verb or verb phrase and write its complement in the space provided.

Examples: Joanna <u>feels</u> good about her project.   *good*

Our current director <u>is</u> Ms. Abzug.   *Ms. Abzug*

11. Employees are happy about pay increases. _____

12. Our trip was long and tiring. _____

13. The flowers on her desk smell fragrant. _____

14. Over the telephone his voice sounds resonant. _____

15. It was she who called you earlier. _____

16. Mr. Flores was the committee representative last year. _____

17. This sweater feels warm and comfortable today. _____

18. The manager of that department might be Mr. Dorsey. _____

19. That table will be fine. _____

20. It seems unusually cold in here today. _____

C. In the following sentences selected verbs have been italicized. For each sentence indicate whether the italicized verb is transitive (*T*), intransitive (*I*), or linking (*L*). In addition, if the verb is transitive, write its object. If the verb is linking, write its complement.

Examples: The new employee *is* Janet Oso.   *L (Janet Oso)*

Our computer *prints* the mailing list.   *T (list)*

1. My top assistant on the project *is* Margaret McHenry. _____

2. Traffic *moves* from the suburbs along three major arteries. _____

3. General Motors *offered* a warranty on certain engine parts. _____

4. It *is* he who is responsible for processing all equipment requests. _____

5. Please *lay* the keys on the desk when you finish with them. _____

6. Her report *appears* accurate, but some data must be verified. _____

7. Mitchell *feels* marvellous about his recent promotion. _____

8. Producers *move* goods to market to meet seasonal demands. _____

9. It *must have been* they who made the anonymous gift. _____

10. The economy *appears* bright after the recent drop in interest rates. _____

11. Mr. Borman *is* the person whom you should call. _____

12. Despite vigorous consumer protests, the government *ended* the service. _____

13. Please *raise* the window before you leave. _____

14. Your report *is lying* over there. _____

15. All of us *feel* bad about her transfer. _____

A. (**Self-check**) Transitive verbs in the following sentences have been italicized. For each sentence write *active* or *passive* to indicate the voice of the italicized verb.

Example: Two important omissions in the report *were found* by the committee.   _____*passive*_____

1. The Internet activity of all employees *is monitored* by our company.   _____

2. The copy machine *produces* sharp, clean copies when it is operating properly.   _____

3. Computer and transcription skills *were required* by some companies advertising for secretaries.   _____

4. Some companies *required* only keyboarding skills.   _____

5. Our insurance company *is* now *offering* a new method of premium payment on life insurance.   _____

6. The new plan *was devised* to make premium payment completely automatic.   _____

7. Jennifer *sent* e-mail messages to all employees.   _____

8. E-mail messages *were sent* to all employees.   _____

9. Funds for the youth campaign *were collected* from private donors.   _____

10. Private donors *made* contributions to the campaign because they believed in the merit of the project.   _____

Check your answers.

B. In the spaces provided, write *active* or *passive* to indicate the voice of the italicized verbs in the following sentences.

1. Elsa Davis *prepared* the certified cheque.   _____

2. The certified cheque *was prepared* by Elsa Davis.   _____

3. Intranets and wireless devices *are being used* in many companies.   _____

4. You *withdrew* the funds in question on May 29.   _____

5. From his gross income, Harrison *deducts* medical expenses and contributions.   _____

6. Arthur Haig *was told* to visit the Human Resources Department.   _____

7. Contract arbitration *will be conducted* by the union and the manufacturer.   _____

1. passive 2. active 3. passive 4. active 5. active 6. passive 7. active 8. passive 9. passive 10. active

C. Careful writers strive to use the active voice in business communications. This is an important skill for you to develop. To give you practice in developing this skill, rewrite the following sentences, changing their passive-voice verbs to active voice. Normally you can change a verb from passive to active voice by making the doer of the action—usually contained in a *by* phrase—the subject of the sentence.

Example: *Passive:* Production costs must be reduced *by manufacturers.*
  Active: Manufacturers must reduce production costs.

1. Pollution was greatly reduced by Chrysler Canada when the company built its new plant. (*Hint: Who* greatly reduced pollution? Start your sentence with that name.)

_____

_____

_____

2. Funds for the multi-purpose shopping complex were contributed by federal, provincial, and private groups.

_____

_____

_____

3. Massive short-term financing is used by Nike to pay off its production costs during its slow season.

_____

_____

_____

D. Some sentences with passive-voice verbs do not identify the doer of the action. Before these sentences can be converted, a subject must be provided.

Example: *Passive:* New subscribers will be offered a bonus.
       (By whom?—by *Maclean's*)
  Active: *Maclean's* will offer new subscribers a bonus.

In each of the following sentences, first answer the question *by whom?* Then rewrite the sentence, beginning with your answer as the subject.

1. Our office was recently reorganized to increase efficiency and production.

(By whom?) _____

_____

_____

2. Net income before taxes must be calculated carefully when you fill out your tax return.

(By whom?) _____

_____

_____

3. Only a few of the many errors and changes were detected during the first proofreading.

(By whom?) _____

_____

_____

LEVEL III

A. (**Self-check**) Select the correct word, and write it in the space provided.

1. If Mr. Cortez (was, were) our manager, he would not have approved these work rules. _____

2. Do we have a motion that the meeting (is, be) adjourned? _____

3. If I (was, were) you, I'd get a new alarm clock. _____

4. Did your instructor suggest that you (be, are) excused from class? _____

5. If Mr. McHenry (was, were) at the opening session, he did not announce himself. _____

6. The supervisor suggested that everyone (is, be) informed of the availability of the training seminar. _____

7. If you were in my place, I'm sure you (will, would) agree. _____

8. Sandi Woodruff recommended that additional chairs (are, be) set up for the afternoon session. _____

9. He acts as if he (was, were) the only employee who had to work overtime. _____

10. It is extremely important that all applications (are, be) completed by the 15th of the month. _____

Check your answers.

B. Underscore verbs that are incorrectly used in the following sentences. Write the correct forms in the spaces provided. Write *C* if correct.

1. Mr. Harris wished that Vicki was happier about her work. _____

2. I move that Natalie is appointed acting president for the remainder of this year. _____

3. President Atkins asked that all salaried workers be made eligible for health care benefits. _____

4. If a better employee benefit program was available, recruiting would be easier. _____

5. A shareholder moved that dividends are declared immediately. _____

6. If he were in my place, he will be more understanding. _____

7. I wish the server was working so that I could read my mail. _____

8. Lianne McGinley advised that antiglare shields are installed. _____

1. were 2. be 3. were 4. be 5. was 6. be 7. would 8. be 9. were 10. be

9. Henri said he wished that you were able to accompany him. _____

10. If Sam were in the office that day, I did not see him. _____

C. Choose the correct verb forms, and complete the following sentences.

1. I wish that I (was, were)_____

2. If my boss (was, were)_____

3. If you (was, were) in my position, _____

D. Optional Composition. Your instructor may ask you to complete this exercise on a separate sheet. Write six sentences to illustrate the following: a transitive verb, an intransitive verb, a linking verb, an active voice verb, a passive voice verb, and a verb in the subjunctive mood. Label each sentence.

Editor's Challenge

The following e-mail message contains intentional errors in spelling, proofreading, and grammar principles you have studied thus far. Use proofreading marks to correct them.

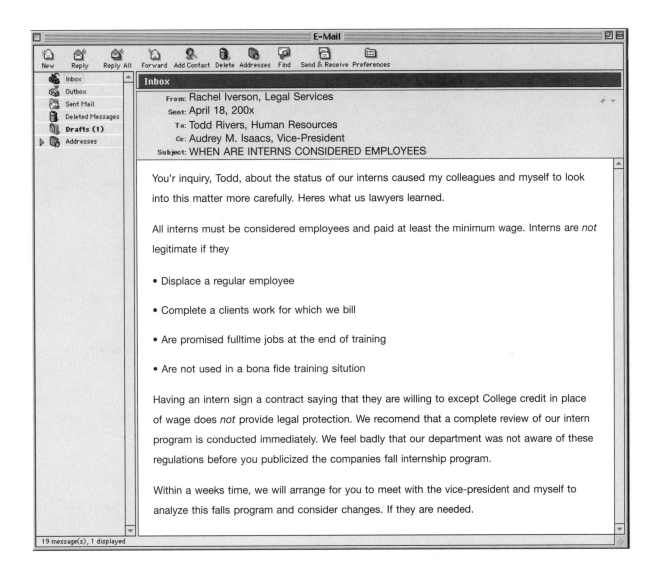

Inbox

From: Rachel Iverson, Legal Services
Sent: April 18, 200x
To: Todd Rivers, Human Resources
Cc: Audrey M. Isaacs, Vice-President
Subject: WHEN ARE INTERNS CONSIDERED EMPLOYEES

You'r inquiry, Todd, about the status of our interns caused my colleagues and myself to look into this matter more carefully. Heres what us lawyers learned.

All interns must be considered employees and paid at least the minimum wage. Interns are *not* legitimate if they

• Displace a regular employee

• Complete a clients work for which we bill

• Are promised fulltime jobs at the end of training

• Are not used in a bona fide training situtaion

Having an intern sign a contract saying that they are willing to except College credit in place of wage does *not* provide legal protection. We recomend that a complete review of our intern program is conducted immediately. We feel badly that our department was not aware of these regulations before you publicized the companies fall internship program.

Within a weeks time, we will arrange for you to meet with the vice-president and myself to analyze this falls program and consider changes. If they are needed.

19 message(s), 1 displayed

Underline the appropriate answers. Compare your answers with those at the bottom of the page.

1. In the sentence *Billie Scott wrote the memo,* the verb *wrote* is (a) transitive, (b) intransitive, (c) subjunctive, (d) passive.

2. In the sentence *Lucy Williams hired four employees,* the verb *hired* is in the (a) active voice, (b) passive voice, (c) subjunctive mood, (d) intransitive mood.

3. In the sentence *Angela Clouse was given the award,* the verb phrase *was given* is in the (a) active voice, (b) passive voice, (c) subjunctive mood, (d) intransitive mood.

4. If Clara Smith (a) was, (b) were the instructor, the class would be full.

5. Professor St. Clair recommended that students (a) be, (b) are admitted free.

learning.web.ways

Colleges and universities now routinely provide grammar help in writing centres or writing labs. You should check the hours when the writing centre is open so that you can make an appointment with a tutor. You also want to check if your college offers a grammar hotline service, since you'd like to telephone or e-mail a language specialist with a question.

Goal: To learn about the writing centre at your college.

1. With your Web browser on the screen, enter the URL of your college. (Do you have it bookmarked?)

2. Find the **Search** box, and enter "Writing Centre" as your search term. Remember to include the quotation marks.

3. Find the Web page that belongs to your college's writing centre (or lab), and print out the timetable that shows its hours of operation.

4. Jot down the contact telephone number you will need to call in order to make an appointment with a tutor.

5. Go back to the college home page, and do another search, this time for "grammar hotline."

6. Note the name, telephone number, and/or e-mail address. If your college doesn't offer this service, consider using Grant MacEwan Community College's Grammar Hotline given on p. 21 of this textbook.

7. End your session, and submit your printed page and listing.

1. a 2. a 3. b 4. b 5. a

Verb Tenses and Parts

9

OBJECTIVES

When you have completed the materials in this chapter, you will be able to do the following:

LEVEL I
- *Write verbs in the present, past, and future tenses correctly.*

LEVEL II
- *Recognize and use present and past participles.*
- *Write the correct forms of 60 irregular verbs.*
- *Use correct forms of three pairs of frequently misused verbs.*

LEVEL III
- *Supply correct verb forms in the progressive and perfect tenses.*

PRETEST

Underline the correct verb.

1. Anthony and she (came, come) over last night to use my computer.

2. After they had (gone, went), I was able to do my own homework.

3. When last seen, the papers were (laying, lying) near the desk.

4. The value of our shares has been steadily (raising, rising) all day.

5. The condominium project has (set, sat) there untouched for a year.

English verbs change form (inflection) to indicate number (singular or plural), person (first, second, or third), voice (active or passive), and tense (time). In contrast to verbs in languages like French and German, English verbs are today no longer heavily inflected; that is, our verbs do not change form extensively to indicate number or person. To indicate precise time, however, English employs three rather complex sets of tenses: primary tenses, perfect tenses, and progressive tenses. Level I will focus on the primary tenses. Level II will consider participles and irregular verbs. Level III will treat the progressive and perfect tenses.

1. came 2. gone 3. lying 4. rising 5. sat

NEL 145

Hotlink

If you are an ESL (English as a Second Language) student, you'll find lots of helpful material on verbs at **<http://www.ruthvilmi.net/hut/LangHelp/Grammar/>**.

▶ Primary Tenses

Present Tense

Verbs in the present tense express current or habitual action and facts that are true at all times. Present tense verbs may also be used in constructions showing future action.

> We *order* office supplies every month. (Current or habitual action)
> Water *boils* at 100°C. (Fact)
> He *flies* to St. John's tomorrow. (Future action)

Past Tense

Verbs in the past tense show action that has been completed. Regular verbs form the past tense with the addition of *d* or *ed*.

> Mr. Pasternak *needed* the forms yesterday.
> Our vendor *provided* toner cartridges.
> She *used* to have a cellphone.

Future Tense

Verbs in the future tense show actions that are expected to occur at a later time. Traditionally, the helper verbs *shall* and *will* have been joined with principal verbs to express future tense. In business writing today, however, the verb *will* is generally used as the helper to express future tense. Some writers continue to use *shall* in appropriate first-person constructions (*I/we shall attend the meeting*).

> Andy *will need* office supplies next week.
> You *will receive* your order on Thursday.

Summary of the Primary Tenses

The following table summarizes the various forms employed to express the primary tenses:

Notable Quotable

"For good or ill, your conversation is your advertisement. Every time you open your mouth, you let me look into your mind."
—Bruce Barton

	Present Tense		Past Tense		Future Tense	
	Singular	**Plural**	**Singular**	**Plural**	**Singular**	**Plural**
First person:	I need	we need	I needed	we needed	I will need	we will need
Second person:	you need	you need	you needed	you needed	you will need	you will need
Third person:	he, she, it needs	they need	he, she, it needed	they needed	he, she, it will need	they will need

Problems With Primary Tenses

Most adult speakers of our language have few problems using present, past, and future tense verbs. A few considerations, however, merit mention.

1. A dictionary should be used to verify spelling of verbs that change form. One must be particularly careful in spelling *y*-ending verbs (*hurry, hurries, hurried*) and verbs for which the final consonant is doubled (*occurred, expelled*). (Guidelines 4 and 5 in Appendix A discuss these changes.)

2. Present tense verbs may be used to express "timeless" facts, even if these verbs occur in sentences with other past tense verbs.

> What did you say his duties *are*? (To indicate he continues to perform these duties)
> We were often told that a penny saved *is* a penny earned. (To emphasize that this is a general truth)
> What did you say the caller's name *is*? (To indicate the name hasn't changed)

3. Third-person singular verbs require an *-s* ending (*he needs*). Although you might drop the *-s* or *-es* in speaking, be sure to include it in writing.

> This equipment *breaks* down too often. (Not *break*)
> Matt *drives* a pickup truck. (Not *drive*)

Hotlink

If you still feel unsure about the forms and tenses of English verbs, this University of Toronto chart of forms **<http://prod.library. utoronto.ca/utel/ language/Grammar9. htm>** will help you sort them out.

▶ Helping (Auxiliary) Verbs

A verb that combines with a main verb to convey information about tense, mood, or voice functions as a helping or auxiliary verb. The most common helping verbs are forms of *be (am, is, are, was, were, being, been)*, forms of *do (does, did, done)*, and forms of *have (has, had)*. As you will recall, the verb *be* and all its forms also function as linking verbs.

> Our manager *is* a funny guy. (The linking verb *is* joins the complement *guy* to the subject.)
> Our manger *is using* his computer. (The helping verb *is* combines with the main verb *using* to form a verb phrase whose object is *computer*.)
> Our manager *has hired* a new assistant. (The helping verb *has* combines with the main verb *hired* to form a verb phrase.)

Complete the reinforcement exercises for Level I on pp. 155–156.

Study Tip

In the present tense singular third person, verbs require an *s* ending (*he needs*); plural third person verbs do *not* (*they need*).

▶ Present and Past Participles

LEVEL II

To be able to use all the tenses of verbs correctly, you must understand the four principal parts of verbs: present, past, present participle, and past participle. You have already studied the present and past forms. Now, let's consider the participles.

Present Participle

The present participle of a regular verb is formed by adding *ing* to the present form of the verb. When used in a sentence as part of a verb phrase, the present participle is always preceded by some form of the helping verb *to be (am, is, are, was, were, be, been)*.

> Betty *is changing* jobs.
> You *are doing* a fine job.

Past Participle

The past participle of a regular verb is usually formed by adding a *d* or a *t* sound to the present form of the verb. Like present participles, past participles may function as parts of verb phrases, preceded by one or more helping verbs.

Ryan *has checked* his homework.
The homework *has been checked* by Ryan.
Ms. Melchiori *should have built* the factory earlier.
New roads to the building *should have been built*.

▶ Irregular Verbs

Up to this point, we have considered only regular verbs. Regular verbs form the past tense by the addition of a *d* or a *t* sound to the present tense form. Many verbs, however, form the past tense and the past participle irregularly. (More specifically, irregular verbs commonly form the past tense by a variation in the root vowel and the past participle by the addition of an *en* sound.) A list of the more frequently used irregular verbs follows. Learn the forms of these verbs by practising in patterns such as the following:

Present tense:	Today I ____drive____ .
Past tense:	Yesterday I ____drove____ .
Past participle:	In the past I have ____driven____ .

Frequently Used Irregular Verbs

Present	**Past**	**Past Participle**
arise	arose	arisen
be (am, is, are)	was, were	been
bear (to carry)	bore	borne
become	became	become
begin	began	begun
bite	bit	bitten
blow	blew	blown
break	broke	broken
bring	brought	brought
build	built	built
choose	chose	chosen
come	came	come
do	did	done
draw	drew	drawn
drink	drank	drunk
drive	drove	driven
eat	ate	eaten
fall	fell	fallen
fly	flew	flown
forbid	forbade	forbidden
forget	forgot	forgotten *or* forgot
forgive	forgave	forgiven
freeze	froze	frozen
get	got	gotten *or* got
give	gave	given
go	went	gone
grow	grew	grown
hang (to suspend)	hung	hung

Present	Past	Past Participle
hang (to execute)	hanged	hanged
hide	hid	hidden *or* hid
know	knew	known
lay (to place)	laid	laid
leave	left	left
lie (to rest)	lay	lain
lie (to tell a falsehood)	lied	lied
pay	paid	paid
prove	proved	proved *or* proven
raise (to lift)	raised	raised
ride	rode	ridden
ring	rang	rung
rise (to move up)	rose	risen
run	ran	run
see	saw	seen
set (to place)	set	set
shake	shook	shaken
shrink	shrank	shrunk
sing	sang	sung
sink	sank	sunk
sit (to rest)	sat	sat
speak	spoke	spoken
spring	sprang	sprung
steal	stole	stolen
strike	struck	struck *or* stricken
swear	swore	sworn
swim	swam	swum
take	took	taken
tear	tore	torn
throw	threw	thrown
wear	wore	worn
write	wrote	written

Spot the Blooper

From *The Times-Union* [Albany, NY]: "Jane Fonda's Beverly Hills hairdresser sweared the thick blond braid she's been sporting ... is her real hair."

▶ Three Pairs of Frequently Misused Irregular Verbs

The key to the correct use of the following pairs of verbs lies in developing the ability to recognize the tense forms of each and to distinguish transitive verbs and constructions from intransitive ones.*

Lie–Lay

These two verbs are confusing because the past tense of *lie* is spelled exactly the same way the present tense of *lay* is spelled. Memorize these verb forms.

Study Tip

Whenever you use *lay* in the sense of "placing" something, you must provide a receiver (object) of the action: *Please lay the book down.* If nothing receives action, you probably want the verb *lie,* which means "resting."

	Present	Present Participle	Past	Past Participle
Intransitive:	lie (to rest)	lying	lay	lain
Transitive:	lay (to place)	laying	laid	laid

---

* *Transitive and intransitive verbs are explained in Chapter 8, Level I.*

The verb *lie* is intransitive; in other words, it requires no direct object to complete its meaning.

> Today I *lie* down. (Note that *down* is not a direct object.)
> "*Lie* down," he told his dog. (Commands are given in the present tense.)
> Yesterday I *lay* down for a nap. (Past tense)
> The papers are *lying* on the desk. (Present participle)
> They have *lain* there for some time. (Past participle)

The verb *lay* is transitive and must have a direct object to complete its meaning.

> A bricklayer *lays* bricks. (*Bricks* is the direct object.)
> *Lay* the bricks over there. (Command in the present tense)
> The mason is *laying* bricks. (Present participle)
> He *laid* the bricks in a row. (Past tense)
> He has *laid* bricks all his life. (Past participle)

Sit–Set

Less troublesome than *lie–lay*, the combination of *sit–set* is nevertheless perplexing because the sound of the verbs is similar. The intransitive verb *sit* (past tense, *sat*; past participle, *sat*) means "to rest" and requires no direct object.

> Do you *sit* here often? (Note that *here* is not an object.)
> Are you *sitting* here tomorrow? (Present participle)

The transitive verb *set* (past tense, *set*; past participle, *set*) means "to place" and must have a direct object.

> Letty usually *sets* her books there. (*Books* is the direct object.)
> She is *setting* her books here today. (Present participle)

Rise–Raise

The intransitive verb *rise* (past tense, *rose*; past participle, *risen*) means "to go up" or "to ascend" and requires no direct object.

> The sun *rises* every morning in the east. (*Every morning* is an adverbial
>   phrase, not an object.)
> Our elevator is *rising* to the seventh floor. (Present participle)
> The bread dough *rose* nicely. (Past tense)
> Prices have *risen* substantially. (Past participle)

Study Tip

To help you remember that these verbs are intransitive, look at the second letter of each:
> lie
> sit
> rise
Associate *i* with *i*ntransitive.

The transitive verb *raise* (past tense, *raised*; past participle, *raised*) means "to lift up" or "to elevate" and must have a direct object.

> Please *raise* the window. (*Window* is the direct object.)
> Apple Canada Inc. may *raise* prices next month. (*Prices* is the direct object.)

Complete the reinforcement exercises for Level II on pp. 157–159.

▶ Progressive and Perfect Tenses

LEVEL III

So far in this chapter, you have studied the primary tenses and irregular verbs. The remainder of this chapter focuses on two additional sets of verb tenses: the perfect tenses and the progressive (or continuous) tenses. Most native speakers and writers of English have little difficulty with these verb forms (although the names of these forms may be unfamiliar) because they have frequently heard them used correctly. This largely descriptive section is thus directed at individuals who are not native speakers and at those who are eager to study the entire range of verb tenses.

Progressive Tenses

Present Progressive Tense

	First Person	Second Person	Third Person
Active:	I am hearing we are hearing	you are hearing	he, she, it is hearing they are hearing
Passive:	I am being heard we are being heard	you are being heard	he, she, it is being heard they are being heard

Past Progressive Tense

	First Person	Second Person	Third Person
Active:	I was hearing we were hearing	you were hearing	he, she, it was hearing they were hearing
Passive:	I was being heard we were being heard	you were being heard	he, she, it was being heard they were being heard

Future Progressive Tense

	First Person	Second Person	Third Person
Active:	I will be hearing we will be hearing	you will be hearing	he, she, it will be hearing they will be hearing
Passive:	I will be being heard we will be being heard	you will be being heard	he, she, it will be being heard they will be being heard

Examples:

> We *are exporting* grain to numerous countries. (Present progressive tense expresses action in progress.)
>
> Many textile companies *were sending* delegates to the government conference. (Past progressive tense indicates action in the past.)
>
> They *will be receiving* the announcement shortly. (Future progressive indicates action in the future.)

Hotlink

For a different perspective on verbs and more examples, take a look at "An On-Line English Grammar" **<http://www.edufind.com/english/grammar/toc.cfm>**. Scroll down to the Verbs and Verb Tenses section.

Hotlink

If you'd like a really exhaustive reference site with "all about verbs," visit and bookmark this Capital Community College Web page **<http://webster.commnet.edu/grammar/verbs.htm>**.

Perfect Tenses

Present Perfect Tense

	First Person	Second Person	Third Person
Active:	I have heard we have heard	you have heard	he, she, it has heard they have heard
Passive:	I have been heard we have been heard	you have been heard	he, she, it has been heard they have been heard

Past Perfect Tense

	First Person	Second Person	Third Person
Active:	I had heard we had heard	you had heard	he, she, it had heard they had heard
Passive:	I had been heard we had been heard	you had been heard	he, she, it had been heard they had been heard

Future Perfect Tense

	First Person	Second Person	Third Person
Active:	I will have heard we will have heard	you will have heard	he, she, it will have heard they will have heard
Passive:	I will have been heard	you will have been heard	he, she, it will have been heard they will have been heard

Examples:

He *has* just *heard* the news. (Present perfect tense expresses action just completed or *perfected*.)

The cheque *had cleared* the bank before I cancelled payment. (Past perfect tense shows an action finished before another action in the past.)

The polls *will have been* closed two hours when the results are telecast. (Future perfect tense indicates action that will be completed before another future action.)

Summary of Verb Tenses

Primary Tenses	Progressive Tenses	Perfect Tenses
Present	Present progressive	Present perfect
Past	Past progressive	Past perfect
Future	Future progressive	Future perfect

Complete the reinforcement exercises for Level III and reviews on pp. 160–162.

Notable Quotable

"The only place success comes before work is in the dictionary."
—Donald Kendall, former chair, PepsiCo

HOTLINE QUERIES

Question: We have a new electronic mail system, and one of its functions is "messaging" people. When folks say, *I'll message you,* it really grates on my nerves. Is this correct?

Answer: "Messaging" is certainly a hot term with the explosion of e-mail. As to its correctness, I think we've caught language in the act of evolving. What's happened here is the reinstitution of a noun (*message*) as a verb. Converting nouns into verbs is common in English (he *cornered* the market, we *tabled* the motion, I *pencilled* it in on my calendar, the farmer *trucked* the vegetables to market). Actually, *message* was sometimes used as a verb a century ago (in 1896 *the bill was messaged over from the house*). However, its recent use has been almost exclusively as a noun. Today it is increasingly being used again as a verb. New uses of words usually become legitimate when the words fill a need and are immediately accepted. Some word uses, though, appear to be mere fads, like *The homeless child could not <u>language</u> her fears.* Forcing the noun *language* to function as a verb is unnecessary since a good word already exists for the purpose: *express.* But other "nouns-made-verbs" have been in use long enough to sound reasonable: I *faxed* the document, he *videotaped* the program, she *keyed* the report.

Question: I'm embarrassed to ask this because I should know the answer—but I don't. Is there an apostrophe in this: *its relevance to our program?*

Answer: No. Use an apostrophe only for the contraction *it's,* meaning *it is* (*it's a good plan*) or *it has* (*it's been a long time*). The possessive pronoun *its,* as used in your example, has no apostrophe (*the car had its oil changed*).

Question: How do you spell *Moosonee?* I looked in the dictionary, but it isn't there.

Answer: *Moosonee* and other names are not in all dictionaries. Some dictionaries include proper nouns in the main entries; others have separate sections with biographical and geographical entries. You might also look up place names in a postal code directory or a telephone book if you have no other reference book handy.

Question: I thought I knew the difference between *principal* and *principle,* but now I'm not so sure. In a report I'm typing I find this: *The principal findings of the market research are negative.* I thought *principal* always meant your "pal," the school principal.

Answer: You're partly right and partly wrong. *Principal* may be used as a noun meaning "chief" or "head person." In addition, it may be used as an adjective to mean "chief" or "main." This is the meaning most people forget, and this is the meaning of the word in your sentence. The word *principle* means a "law" or "rule." Perhaps it is easiest to remember *principl<u>e</u>* = *rul<u>e</u>.* All other uses require *principal*: the *principal* of the school, the *principal* of the loan, the *principal* reason.

Question: Even when I use a dictionary, I can't tell the difference between *affect* and *effect.* What should the word be in this sentence? *Changes in personnel (affected/effected) our production this month.*

Answer: No words generate more confusion than do *affect/effect.* In your sentence use *affected.* Let's see if we can resolve the *affect/effect* dilemma. *Affect* is a verb meaning "to influence" (*smoking affects health; government policies* *affect citizens*). *Affect* may also mean "to pretend or imitate" (*he affected a British accent*). *Effect* can be a noun or a verb. As a noun, it means "result" (*the effect of the law is slight*). As a verb (and here's the troublesome part), *effect* means "to produce a result" (*small cars effect gasoline savings; GM effected a new pricing policy*).

Question: I'm editing a screenplay for a studio, and I know something is grammatically wrong with this sentence: *The old man left the room hurriedly after discovering a body laying near the window.*

Answer: As you probably suspected, the verb *laying* should be *lying*. *Lay* means "to place" and requires an object (*he is laying the report on your desk now*). *Lie* means "to rest" and requires no object (*the document is lying on your desk*).

Question: I learned that the verb *set* is transitive and requires an object. If that's true, how can we say that the sun *sets* in the west?

Answer: Good question! The verb *set* is generally transitive, but it does have some standardized intransitive uses, such as the one you mention. Here's another: *Glue sets quickly.* I doubt that anyone would be likely to substitute *sit* in either of these unusual cases. While we're on the subject, the verb *sit* also has some exceptions. Although generally intransitive, *sit* has a few transitive uses: *Sit yourself down* and *The waiter sat us at Table 1.*

CHAPTER 9   Reinforcement Exercises

A. (**Self-check**) Select the correct verb. Use your dictionary to verify spelling if necessary.   **LEVEL I**

1. Workers (applyed, applied) two coats of paint.   _____

2. What did you say your friend's name (is, was)?   _____

3. The machine (jamed, jammed) when conflicting instructions were entered.   _____

4. Mr. Milne said that the distance between Calgary and Edmonton (is, was) 300 kilometres.   _____

5. We (hurryed, hurried) through the rehearsals.   _____

6. Shirley's maiden name (is, was) Eiseman.   _____

7. He was (refered, referred) to an orthopedic surgeon.   _____

8. They (studyed, studied) past midnight.   _____

9. The chair announced yesterday that all professors (are, were) now required to teach five classes.   _____

10. He (write, writes) about a dozen e-mails a day.   _____

Check your answers.

B. In the following sentences, provide three tenses for each verb.

Example: I (arrive) at the office at 7:45 a.m.

> Past ___arrived___   Present _____arrive_____   Future _____will arrive_____

1. The nation's tax system (need) to stimulate investment.

   Past _____   Present _____   Future _____

2. Our administrative assistant (copy) the contracts for clients.

   Past _____   Present _____   Future _____

3. Lori (hurry) to catch the bus.

   Past _____   Present _____   Future _____

4. You (apply) the same standards in judging your own success.

   Past _____   Present _____   Future _____

1. applied 2. is 3. jammed 4. is 5. hurried 6. is 7. referred 8. studied 9. are 10. writes

5. Professor Darlene Williams (cover) the same material.

Past _____ Present _____ Future _____

6. Monsanto (label) its plastic soft-drink bottle.

Past _____ Present _____ Future _____

7. Donald (plan) to major in business management.

Past _____ Present _____ Future _____

8. Corporations (use) their profits for investing in new equipment.

Past _____ Present _____ Future _____

9. The Prime Minister (announce) the appointments today.

Past _____ Present _____ Future _____

10. Questionnaires (sample) customers' reactions to our new product.

Past _____ Present _____ Future _____

C. Compose sentences using the verbs shown.

1. (Past tense of *bury*) _____

_____

_____

2. (Present tense of *try*) _____

_____

_____

3. (Future tense of *study*) _____

_____

_____

4. (Past tense of *cancel*) _____

_____

_____

5. (Present tense of *learn*) _____

_____

_____

A. (**Self-check**) Write the correct verb form. Do not add a helper verb.

LEVEL II

Example: He wished he had (eat) before he left. _____eaten_____

1. Several of his friends (come) over yesterday. _____

2. Have you (see) the film before? _____

3. That helicopter has (fly) over the intersection twice. _____

4. Yesterday Lon (swim) the length of the pool. _____

5. Our e-mail manual was (write) by Mrs. Shapiro. _____

6. This morning's mild earthquake (shake) the dishes in the cabinet. _____

7. Over the past year Dr. Crowley (give) freely of his time. _____

8. Have you (speak) with the supervisor yet? _____

9. I wish Scott had (know) about the scholarship earlier. _____

10. All employees should have (go) to the software demonstration. _____

Check your answers.

B. Underline any verb errors you find in the following sentences. Write the correct forms in the spaces provided. Do not add helper verbs. Write *C* if the sentence is correct as it stands.

Example: Janet said she <u>seen</u> the accident. _____saw_____

1. Because of advances in technology, the world has shrank. _____

2. Maureen set a record when she swam the Channel. _____

3. The office staff must chose a new letterhead stationery. _____

4. Fibreglass was blown into the ceiling for insulation. _____

5. Omar and Ross have went to the lecture in Massey Hall. _____

6. Her friend asked if she had ate dinner yet. _____

7. His car was stole over the weekend. _____

8. Coach Meyer has worn the same lucky shirt to three games. _____

9. The water bill was not payed last month. _____

10. Is that the dog that has bit two passersby? _____

1. came 2. seen 3. flown 4. swam 5. written 6. shook 7. gave 8. spoken 9. known 10. gone

11. Mark brang his bike to the mall. _____

12. The telephone has rang only twice in the past hour. _____

13. In lieu of the month's vacation to Tahiti, Mrs. Ferguson choose a foreign sports sedan. _____

14. Prices on the stock exchange sunk to a new low. _____

15. The first pitch of the season was thrown out by the Prime Minister. _____

C. *Lie–lay.* Write the correct forms of the verb.

	Present	Present Participle	Past	Past Participle
lie (to rest):	_____	_____	_____
lay (to place):	_____	_____	_____

Select the correct verb.

1. Mr. Gilson told his dog to (lay, lie) down. _____

2. She (layed, laid) the papers on Mrs. Maracle's desk. _____

3. The papers had been (lying, laying) there for some time. _____

4. In fact, they had (laid, lain) there over a week. _____

5. Every day at 2 p.m., Arnold (lies, lays) down to rest. _____

6. Yesterday, however, he (lay, laid) down at 3 p.m. _____

7. Her clothes were (laid, lain) out on the bed. _____

8. Fred was (laying, lying) in the sun without sunscreen. _____

D. *Sit–set; rise–raise.* Write the correct forms of the verb.

	Present	Present Participle	Past	Past Participle
sit (to rest):	_____	_____	_____
set (to place):	_____	_____	_____
rise (to go up):	_____	_____	_____
raise (to lift):	_____	_____	_____

Select the correct verb.

1. Please (raise, rise) the windows to let in fresh air. _____

2. We'll never finish if Roland (sits, sets) there all day. _____

3. Working computers (raise, rise) the temperature in a room. _____

4. The temperature (raises, rises) rapidly in a room filled with people busy working at computers. _____

5. Managers are (sitting, setting) goals for the production and sales staffs. _____

6. The value of gold (raises, rises) or falls in relation to the dollar. _____

7. Miss Tibari (raised, rose) the question of retroactive benefits. _____

8. Julie and Tom Kokales always (sit, set) near the door. _____

9. The employee parking lot (sits, sets) some distance away. _____

10. Consumer prices have (raised, risen) faster than consumer income. _____

E. Compose original sentences using the verb forms shown.

1. choose _____

2. blown _____

3. shrank _____

4. laid _____

5. rose _____

A. **(Self-check)** Verbs in the following sentences have been italicized. In the space provided, indicate the tense of each of these verbs. Indicate also if any verbs are in the passive voice. Refer to the text to guide you.

LEVEL III

Example: Your credit cards *had been recovered* by the time you reported the loss.   _past perfect, passive_

1. You *will have heard* the news before we have heard it.   _____

2. Those orders *are being sent* to your Oshawa branch.   _____

3. Mr. Adams' case *will have been heard* in six weeks.   _____

4. I cannot believe what I *am hearing*.   _____

5. Charles *had been told* to report at once.   _____

6. We *have* just *seen* your product advertised on television.   _____

7. The manager's suggestions for reduced paper use *have been followed* by all employees.   _____

8. You *will be seeing* many changes in our Web site shortly.   _____

9. The Birches *have lived* in that neighbourhood for years.   _____

10. We *are* now *experiencing* the effects of the last cutback.   _____

Check your answers.

B. Write the proper verb forms according to the specifications in parentheses.

Example: They (drive) all night before they found a motel. (Past perfect)   _had driven_

1. Before the office announcement was made, we (hear) rumours about layoffs. (Past perfect)   _____

2. When the fire alarm sounded, Miss Waters (help) Olga. (Past progressive)   _____

3. By next April, Rayco (open) four branch outlets. (Future perfect)   _____

4. I'm sure they (tell) us about their trip when they return. (Future progressive)   _____

5. Plans (develop) to reduce administrative costs. (Present progressive, passive)   _____

6. Our department (think) about installing more modern information processing equipment. (Present progressive)   _____

7. We are certain they (receive) our proposal by now. (Present perfect)   _____

9. present perfect 10. present progressive

5. past perfect, passive 6. present perfect 7. present perfect, passive 8. future progressive

1. future perfect 2. present progressive, passive 3. future perfect, passive 4. present progressive

8. By 5 p.m. the contract (finish) and faxed to our client. (Past perfect, passive) _____

9. Before next Monday he (paint) all the exterior and trim on the house. (Future perfect) _____

10. Is it true that you (live) in the same house all your life? (Present perfect) _____

11. Until last night our basketball team (win) every game by at least five points. (Past perfect) _____

12. The company spokesperson says that the computer purchase (cancel) because of "the difficult economic environment." (Present perfect, passive) _____

13. Geac (sell) two money-losing divisions recently. (Present perfect) _____

14. Ford (offer) no-interest financing on its vehicles since the beginning of the month. (Present perfect progressive) _____

15. The CEO said that the corporation (lose) money in six divisions. (Past progressive) _____

C. Cumulative Review. These sentences review Chapters 1 through 9. Underline any errors. Then write corrected forms in the spaces provided. Some sentences require more than one correction. If a sentence is correct, write *C* in the space.

1. Fees for visits to a doctors office have rose steadily over the decade. _____

2. Although some policys allow you to chose any doctor, the plan selected for us office workers offers less freedom. _____

3. Steve and me could have forgave her if she had softened her tone. _____

4. Brets dirt bike looks as if it has been drove through a mud puddle. _____

5. We advise every job candidate to submit their résumé in scannable form. _____

6. During it's first month of operation, the recycling program has broke records for reducing waste. _____

7. Everyone except Yasmin and I was impressed by the months recycling profits. _____

8. Many larger facilitys can generally recycle at no net cost because there haulers are taking away less trash. _____

9. Has anyone on the womens team submitted their doctor's release form yet? _____

10. Mr. Sanchez contract, which is laying on the desk, must be delivered immediately. _____

11. The vice-president has swore that no one would work harder than him to meet the deadline. _____

12. Not one of the job candidates who we interviewed has wrote a thank-you letter. _____

13. Although I told James dog to lay down, it jumped up and knocked me over. _____

14. Because it has took two hours to complete the test, I will be late. _____

15. Next Monday is Labour Day, hence we won't need the ride you offered to Beth and I.

_____

16. The product had sank so low in the eyes of consumers' that it was removed from store shelfs.

_____

17. Our research shows that the average part-time employee will have stole over $300 worth of merchandise in a years time.

_____

18. You may set the printer on this desk until a better location is found. _____

19. Cheryl said she seen you and him at Omars party.

_____

20. Because to many computers were running, the rooms temperature had raised to 27°C.

_____

D. Optional Composition. Your instructor may ask you to complete this exercise on a separate sheet. Write ten original sentences, one for each of the following verb forms: *given, chose, begun, lying (resting), raise, seen, comes, drunk, spoke,* and *driven.*

Editor's Challenge

The following memo contains errors reflecting the concepts you have studied thus far. Use standard proofreading marks to show your corrections.

DATE: January 21, 200x

TO: All Employees

FROM: Vice-President, Human Resources

SUBJECT: CHANGE IN FLOATING HOLIDAY POLICY

The senior executive staff has approve a change in the companys floating holiday plan. Employees in the past vote on a single date to be took by all workers as there floating holiday, now, however, each employee will be allowed to chose the date that they wish to use as a floating holiday.

To reserve your floating holiday. Please notify your supervisor or I. Approval will be base on your units staffing needs. If a supervisor or myself receive several requests for the same date, employment seniority will govern.

A question has arose about how to record these holidays. I have spoke to Payroll, and they say you should use the Attendance Bonus code on your time card. This method will be used until Payroll has went over all employees records and modified it.

We wish it was possible for everyone to have their holiday exactly when desired, but we must urge you to be flexible. Because your supervisor has all ready began a schedule of employees floating holidays. It's not too early for you to submit your request.

Underline the correct verb. Compare your answers with those at the bottom of the page.

1. After we (saw, seen) the advertisement, we bought the machine.

2. Your telephone has (rung, rang) only twice while you were gone.

3. The contracts have (laid, lain) on your desk for over a week.

4. Soil temperatures will slowly (raise, rise) during the spring.

5. Mr. Freeman has (worn, wore) the same suit every day this week.

 # learning.web.ways

Assume you're on the job and a new employee needs a little instruction in the use of e-mail. You decide to use the Web to provide a quick tutorial.

Goal: To learn to use an e-mail tutorial.

1. With your Web browser on the screen, key the following URL: **<http://www.fvrl.bc.ca/learn/tutorial/e-mail.html>**.

2. Read the five sections on this page.

3. How does e-mail save natural resources?

4. How are multiple addresses entered in the "**Cc**" field?

5. This site provides a quick on-line tutorial for introducing e-mail, but it suffers from some writing lapses. Can you find two comma splices?

6. Print two pages from this site, underline the answers to our questions, submit your printouts, and end your session.

1. saw. 2. rung 3. lain 4. rise 5. worn

Verb and Subject Agreement

OBJECTIVES   When you have completed the materials in this chapter, you will be able to do the following:

LEVEL I
- *Locate the subjects of verbs despite intervening elements and inverted sentence structure.*
- *Make verbs agree with true subjects.*
- *Make verbs agree with subjects joined by* and.

LEVEL II
- *Make verbs agree with subjects joined by* or *or* nor.
- *Select the correct verbs to agree with indefinite pronouns and collective nouns.*

LEVEL III
- *Make verbs agree with quantities, fractions, portions, clauses, and* the number/a number.
- *Achieve subject–verb agreement within* who *clauses.*

PRETEST

Underline the correct verb.

1. One of our plans for reducing costs (require, requires) considerable capital.

2. The manager, along with the administrative assistant and the accountant, (was, were) invited to the conference.

3. Neither the wholesaler nor his clients (is, are) satisfied with the level of service.

4. Behind this building (lies, lie) the parking lot and swimming pool.

5. The number of e-mail users (is, are) increasing daily.

1. requires 2. was 3. are 4. lie 5. is

Subjects must agree with verbs in number and person. Beginning a sentence with *He don't* damages a speaker's credibility and limits a communicator's effectiveness.

If an error is made in subject–verb agreement, it can generally be attributed to one of three lapses: (1) failure to locate the subject, (2) failure to recognize the number (singular or plural) of the subject after locating it, or (3) failure to recognize the number of the verb. Suggestions for locating the true subject and determining the number of the subject and its verb follow.

LEVEL I

Hotlink

For an interactive exercise that will help you locate sentence subjects, visit the University of Ottawa's Hypergrammar Web page **<http://www. uottawa.ca/academic/ arts/writcent/ hypergrammar/rvsubj. html>**.

▶ Locating Subjects

All verbs have subjects. Locating these subjects can be difficult, particularly when (a) a prepositional phrase comes between the verb and its subject, (b) an intervening element separates the subject and verb, (c) sentences begin with *there* or *here*, and (d) sentences are inverted.

Prepositional Phrases

Subjects of verbs are not found in prepositional phrases.* Therefore, you must learn to ignore such phrases in identifying subjects of verbs. Some of the most common prepositions are *of, to, in, from, for, with, at,* and *by.* Notice that the italicized prepositional phrases in these sentences do not contain the subjects of the verbs:

> Only <u>one</u> *of the company executives* has insurance. (The verb *has* agrees with its subject *one*, not with *executives*, the object of the preposition.)
> We wonder if the <u>invoice</u> *for the two shipments* is lost. (The verb *is* agrees with its subject *invoice*.)
> The <u>range</u> *of tasks and skill requirements* allows for upward growth potential. (The verb *allows* agrees with the subject *range*.)

Some of the less easily recognized prepositions are *except, but, like,* and *between.* In the following sentences, distinguish the subjects from the italicized prepositional phrases:

> All <u>employees</u> *but Tom* are to report early. (The verb *are* agrees with its subject *employees*.)

> <u>Everyone</u> *except the Harrises* is able to attend. (The verb *is* agrees with its subject *everyone*.)

Intervening Elements

Groups of words introduced by *as well as, in addition to, such as, including, together with,* and *other than* do *not* contain sentence subjects.

> The priceless <u>book</u>, *as well as other valuable documents,* was lost in the fire.

In this sentence the writer has elected to emphasize the subject *book* and to de-emphasize *other valuable documents*. The writer could have given equal weight to these elements by writing *The priceless book <u>and</u> other valuable documents were lost in the fire*. Notice that the number (singular or plural) of the verb changes when both *book* and

Spot the Blooper

From the Inmac computer catalogue: "WORD is full of new automatic features that really does simplify your workday."

---

* *Occasionally a prepositional phrase may help to determine whether an indefinite pronoun, portion, or fraction is singular or plural; but the object of the preposition does not function as the subject of a verb. These points are discussed later in this chapter on pages 168 and 170.*

documents are given equal emphasis. Here are additional examples involving intervening elements:

> Our <u>president</u>, *together with her entire staff of nine employees*, sends her greetings. (The singular subject *president* agrees with the singular verb *sends*.)
> Other <u>pianists</u>, *such as Pennario*, appear on the program. (The plural subject *pianists* agrees with the plural verb *appear*.)

The Adverbs *there* and *here*

In sentences beginning with *there* or *here*, look for the true subject *after* the verb. As adverbs, *here* and *there* cannot function as subjects.

> There <u>are</u> four <u>candidates</u> for the position. (The subject *candidates* follows the verb *are*.)
> Here <u>is</u> the fuel oil consumption <u>report</u>. (The subject *report* follows the verb *is*.)

Inverted Sentence Order*

Look for the subject after the verb in inverted sentences and in questions.

> <u>Attending</u> the conference <u>are</u> <u>salespeople</u> from four provinces. (The verb precedes the subject.)
> <u>Have</u> the product <u>specifications</u> <u>been submitted</u>? (The subject interrupts the verb phrase.)
> How important <u>are</u> <u>salary</u>, <u>benefits</u>, and job <u>security</u>? (The verb precedes the subjects.)

▶ Basic Rules for Verb–Subject Agreement

Once you have located the sentence subject, decide whether the subject is singular or plural and select a verb that agrees in number. The chart on p. 146 of Chapter 9 will remind you that the third person singular form of most present tense verbs requires an *s*.

Subjects Joined by *and*

When one subject is joined to another by the word *and*, the result is a compound subject; the subject is plural and requires a plural verb.

> <u>Carolyn</u> and her <u>brother</u> <u>work</u> at Baker's. (*Carolyn* and *brother* = they)
> The proposed <u>law</u> and its <u>amendment</u> <u>are</u> before the legislature. (*law* and *amendment* = they)

Company Names and Titles

Even though they may appear to be plural, company names and titles of publications are singular; therefore, they require singular verbs.

> <u>*Country Homes and Gardens*</u> <u>makes</u> an excellent magazine gift subscription. (one magazine = it)

---

* See also Chapter 3, pp. 33–34.

Career Tip

Skilful writers avoid starting sentences or clauses with the unnecessary expletive *there*. Usually sentences can be rewritten without it.

Hotlink

For another look at the basic rules of subject–verb agreement, consult the University of Victoria's Writer's Guide at **<http://web.uvic.ca/wguide/Pages/SentSVAgr.html>**.

Spot the Blooper

From *The St. John's* [Newfoundland] *Evening Telegram*: "It's important that we have in that position someone who's judgment, integrity, and incompetence is beyond question." (Did you spot three bloopers?)

Thai Airways connects with Air Canada in Los Angeles. (one company = it)
Richards, Batemen, and Richards is offering the bond issue. (one company = it)

Complete the reinforcement exercises for Level I on pp. 172–173.

LEVEL II

▶ **Special Rules for Verb–Subject Agreement**

Making sure your subjects agree with your verbs sometimes requires the application of special rules. This is especially true when dealing with subjects joined by *or* or *nor*, indefinite pronouns as subjects, and collective nouns as subjects.

Subjects Joined by *or* or *nor*

When two or more subjects are joined by *or* or *nor*, the verb should agree with the closer subject.

> Neither the supervisor nor the <u>clerks</u> <u>know</u> the order number.
> Either Leslie or <u>you</u> <u>are</u> in charge of ordering supplies.
> The manufacturer or the <u>distributors</u> <u>carry</u> spare parts.

Indefinite Pronouns as Subjects

As you may recall from Chapter 7 (p. 102), some indefinite pronouns are always singular, and some indefinite pronouns are always plural. In addition, some may be either singular or plural, depending on the words to which they refer.

Always Singular	Always Plural	Singular or Plural
anyone, anybody, anything,	both	all
each, either, every, everyone,	few	more
everybody, everything, many a,	many	most
neither, nobody, nothing, someone,	several	some
somebody, something		any
		none*

> *Either* of the two applicants *is* satisfactory.
> *Everybody* in the lottery *has* an equal chance.
> A *few* of the workers *are* applying for shares.
> *Neither* of the Web sites *is* particularly helpful.

Indefinite pronouns such as *all, more,* and *most* provide one of the few instances when prepositional phrases become important in determining agreement. Although the prepositional phrase does not contain the subject of the sentence, it may contain the noun to which the indefinite pronoun refers.

> *Most* of the letters *are* finished. (*Most* is plural because it refers to the plural noun *letters*.)
> *Most* of the work *is* completed. (*Most* is singular because it refers to the singular noun *work*.)

---

* *See discussion in Hotline Queries on p. 171.*

Study Tip

Unlike subjects joined by *and,* subjects joined by *or* or *nor* require a choice between Subject No. 1 and Subject No. 2.

Hotlink

More guidance on special subject–verb agreement rules can be found at the University of Wisconsin–Madison Writing Center site **<http://www.wisc.edu/ writing/Handbook/ SubjectVerb.html>**.

If the indefinite pronouns *each, every*, or *many a* are used to describe two or more subjects joined by *and*, the subjects are considered separate. Therefore, the verb is singular.*

> Many a semicolon and colon *is* misused.
> Every man, woman, and child *is* affected by the tax cut.

The indefinite pronouns *anyone, everyone,* and *someone* should be spelled as two words when followed by *of* phrases.

> *Any one* of the offers is available.
> *Every one* of the candidates has a campaign committee.

Collective Nouns as Subjects

Words such as *faculty, committee,* and *council* may be singular or plural, depending on their mode of operation. Usually a collective noun operates as a single unit, so its verb should be singular. When the elements of a collective noun operate separately, the verb should be plural.

> Our <u>faculty</u> *has* approved the proposal. (*Faculty* is operating as a single unit.)
> The <u>council</u> *were* sharply divided over appropriations. *(Council* members
> were acting separately. While technically correct as it stands, the sentence
> would be less awkward if it read, "The council *member*s were sharply .... ")

Complete the reinforcement exercises for Level II on pp. 174–175.

▶ Additional Rules for Verb–Subject Agreement

LEVEL III

In some instances it is difficult to know whether a subject is singular or plural. Here are a few additional rules to guide you in selecting appropriate verbs for such subjects.

The Distinction Between *the number* and *a number*

When the word *number* is the subject of a sentence, its article (*the* or *a*) becomes significant. *The* is specific and therefore implies *singularity*; *a* is general and therefore implies *plurality*.

> *The number* of managers *is* declining. (Singular)
> *A number* of orders *were* lost. (Plural)

Quantities, Measures

When they refer to *total* amounts, quantities and measures are singular. If they refer to individual units that can be counted, quantities and measures are plural.

> Three years *is* the period of the loan. (Quantity as a total amount)
> Three years *are* needed to renovate the property totally. (Quantity as
> individual units)

Spot the Blooper

Radio ad: "A new block of tickets are now on sale for *The Phantom of the Opera*."

---

* *This use of a singular verb for two or more subjects joined by* and *is the only exception to the general rule presented in Level I.*

Fractions, Portions

Fractions and portions may be singular or plural depending on the nouns to which they refer.

> Two-thirds of the cassettes *are* satisfactory.
> Over half of the contract *was* ratified.
> A majority of employees *agree* with the proposal.
> A minimum of work *is* required to receive approval.
> A small percentage of the delegates *are* in favour of the plan.
> Part of the proposal *is* ambiguous.

Who Clauses

Verbs in *who* clauses must agree in number and person with the nouns to which *who* refers. In *who* clauses introduced by *one of*, the verb is usually plural because *who* refers to a plural antecedent. In *who* clauses introduced by *the <u>only</u> one of*, the verb is singular because *who* refers to *one*.

> Mrs. Stephens is *one of* those managers who always <u>support</u> the employees.
> John is *one of* those people who <u>are</u> late sleepers.
> Margaret is *the only one of* the girls who <u>is</u> prepared.

Verbs must agree in person with the nouns or pronouns to which *who* refers.

> It is <u>you</u> who <u>are</u> responsible for security.
> Could it be <u>I</u> who <u>am</u> to blame?

Study Tip

To determine the correct verb in *one of those who* clauses that do <u>not</u> include the word *only*, begin reading with the word *of*: *Of those people who <u>are</u> late sleepers, John is one.*

Phrases and Clauses as Subjects

Use a singular verb when the subject of a sentence is an entire phrase or clause.

> *To learn about the stock market* <u>is</u> fascinating.
> *That verbs must agree with subjects* <u>is</u> accepted.

Subject Complements

In Chapter 8 you learned that linking verbs are followed by complements. Although a complement may differ from the subject in number, the linking verb should always agree with the subject.

> The best <u>part</u> of the show <u>is</u> the *singing and dancing*. (The singular subject *part* agrees with the singular verb *is* despite the plural complement *singing and dancing*.)
> The <u>reason</u> for his bankruptcy <u>is</u> poor *investments*.

To avoid awkwardness, you may wish to reconstruct such sentences so that the plural element is first: *Poor investments are the reason for the bankruptcy.*

Complete the reinforcement exercises for Level III on pp. 176–177.

Hotlink

For extra help on special and additional rules for subject–verb agreement, don't miss Martine Johnson's advice and explanations on this University of Toronto Web page **<http://www.utoronto.ca/writing/l2agr.html>**.

HOTLINE QUERIES

Question: My uncle insists that *none* is singular. My English book says that it can be plural. Who's right?

Answer: Times are changing. Thirty years ago *none* was almost always used in a singular sense. Today, through usage, *none* may be singular or plural depending on what you wish to emphasize. For example, you may write *None are more willing than we.* On the other hand, you may say *None of the students is failing,* to emphasize *not even one.*

Question: When do you use *all together,* and when do you use *altogether*?

Answer: *All together* means "collectively" or "all the members of a group" (*we must work all together to reach our goal*). *Altogether* means "entirely" (*he was altogether satisfied*).

Question: Please help me with this sentence that I'm transcribing for a medical laboratory: *A copy of our analysis, along with our interpretation of its results, (has or have) been sent to you.*

Answer: The subject of your sentence is *copy;* thus the verb must be *has.* Don't let interrupting elements obscure the real sentence subject.

Question: After looking in the dictionary, I'm beginning to wonder about this: *We have alot of work yet to do.* I can't find the word *alot* in the dictionary, but it must be there. Everyone uses it.

Answer: The two-word phrase *a lot* is frequently used in conversation or in very informal writing (*the copier makes a lot of copies*). *Alot* as one word does not exist. Don't confuse it with *allot* meaning "to distribute" (*the company will allot to each department its share of supplies*).

Question: I'm totally confused by job titles for women today. What do I call a woman who is a *fireman,* a *policeman,* a *chairman,* or a *spokesman*? And what about the word *mankind*?

Answer: As more and more women enter non-traditional careers, some previous designations are being replaced by neutral, inclusive titles. Here are some substitutes:

actor	for actress
firefighter	for fireman
mail carrier	for mailman
police officer	for policeman
flight attendant	for steward or stewardess
reporter or journalist	for newsman

Words like *chairman, spokesman,* and *mankind* have traditionally been used to refer to both men and women. Today, however, sensitive writers strive to use language that cannot be considered sexist. Possible substitutes are *chair, spokesperson,* and *humanity.*

Question: I'm never sure how to handle words that are used to represent quantities and proportions in sentences. For example, what verb is correct in this sentence: *A large proportion of voters (was or were) against the measure?*

Answer: Words that represent fractional amounts (such as *proportion, fraction, minimum,* and *majority*) may be singular or plural, depending on the words they represent. In your sentence *proportion* represents *voters,* which is plural. Therefore, use the plural verb *were.*

CHAPTER 10   Reinforcement Exercises

A. (**Self-check**) Select the correct word to complete each sentence below. Write it in the space provided.

1. Everyone except Jan and two other workers (is, are) parking in the company lot. _____

2. The copy machine in our department, along with those on the second and third floors, (need, needs) servicing. _____

3. Here (is, are) one of the reasons we are establishing a Web site. _____

4. (Has, Have) the title page and bibliography been completed yet? _____

5. No one but Nina and her cousins (has, have) seen the ranch. _____

6. The computer and the monitor, along with the printer, (was, were) less expensive than we had expected. _____

7. Addressing the graduating class (is, are) members of the class of '80. _____

8. We understand that British Airways (is, are) interviewing flight attendants. _____

9. A set of guidelines to standardize input and output (was, were) developed. _____

10. *Workplace Communications Strategies* by Eleanor M. Yueda (appear, appears) to be our departmental selection. _____

Check your answers.

B. For each of the following sentences, cross out any phrases that separate the verb from its subject. Underline the subject. Then choose the correct verb, and write it in the space provided.

Examples: The <u>supervisor</u>, ~~together with two of his assistants~~, (is, are) here.   *is*

           Our <u>catalogue</u> ~~of gift ideas~~ (is, are) being sent to you.   *is*

1. Our company's full range of products and services (is, are) available through our local dealers. _____

2. A description of the property, along with several other legal documents, (was, were) filed with my lawyer. _____

3. Everyone except the mailing room and shipping department workers (is, are) being trained on the new computer. _____

4. The list of vendors providing leased machines (was, were) recently revised. _____

1. is 2. needs 3. is 4. Have 5. has 6. were 7. are 8. is 9. was 10. appears

5. All co-operatives except the Lemon Growing Exchange (has, have) been able to provide supplies at reduced prices.   _____

6. Although the economy is improving, only one of the major automobile manufacturers (is, are) showing profits.   _____

7. Outstanding salespeople like Mrs. Love (has, have) helped make our company a leader in the field.   _____

8. One of your duties, in addition to the tasks already described, (is, are) the budgeting of funds for both departments.   _____

C. Assume that the following phrases serve as sentence subjects. Underline the simple subject(s) in each item. Then indicate if the subject is singular or plural.

	Singular	Plural
Example: the <u>controller</u> and the <u>treasurer</u> of the county	_____	✓
1. a list of management objectives	_____	_____
2. the instructor, together with his students	_____	_____
3. other services such as HTML coding and graphics	_____	_____
4. the production cost and the markup of each item	_____	_____
5. one of the most interesting Web sites on the Internet	_____	_____
6. current emphasis on product safety and consumer protection	_____	_____
7. Madison, Lee & Cassidy, an executive placement service	_____	_____
8. the tone and the wording of the letter	_____	_____

D. Select the correct verb, and write it in the space provided.

1. Here (is, are) the full list of names and addresses.   _____

2. Seated next to the Alvarados (is, are) Joe Miranda.   _____

3. There (is, are) two things you must do immediately.   _____

4. How important (is, are) location, benefits, and salary?   _____

5. Our president, along with the general manager and three salespeople, (plan, plans) to attend the conference.   _____

6. Not one of our four customer service representatives (is, are) available.   _____

7. WestJet Airlines (is, are) featuring a low fare to San Diego.   _____

8. Lying on my desk (is, are) my itinerary and plane tickets.   _____

9. Kerr, McClellan, and Horn, a legal firm in Halifax, (specializes, specialize) in corporate law.   _____

10. Considerable time and money (was, were) spent on the final product.   _____

A. (**Self-check**) Write the correct form.

1. A task force of four men and five women (is, are) to be appointed. _____

2. Either Eric Leibeler or Lily Chow (has, have) the room key. _____

3. The inventory and the report (is, are) being prepared. _____

4. Each of the classifications (contains, contain) four parts. _____

5. The union members (has, have) to vote on the proposed contract. _____

6. Nothing but catalogues and bulletins (is, are) in this box. _____

7. Many a clerk and receptionist (has, have) complained about the switchboard. _____

8. (Everyone, Every one) of the wills can be produced on word processing equipment. _____

9. All that work (is, are) yet to be logged in. _____

10. Each clerk, administrative assistant, and word processing specialist (was, were) asked to complete a questionnaire. _____

Check your answers.

B. Write the correct form.

1. The National Council of Jewish Women (has, have) taken a firm position. _____

2. Neither Sergio Rossi nor Bonnie Hahn (is, are) afraid of hard work. _____

3. (Everyone, Every one) of the surgical reports required careful editing. _____

4. Several of the proposals (contain, contains) complex formulas. _____

5. Either the judge or the lawyers (has, have) asked for a recess. _____

6. The group of players, coaches, and fans (plan, plans) to charter a plane. _____

7. Either of the two companies (is, are) satisfactory. _____

8. Something about these insurance claims (appear, appears) questionable. _____

9. Neither the president nor the faculty members (favour, favours) a tuition increase. _____

10. Abstracts and affidavits (is, are) the principal work in this office. _____

1. is 2. has 3. are 4. contains 5. have 6. is 7. has 8. Every one 9. is 10. was

11. (Was, Were) any of the members of the organization present that afternoon?   _____

12. (Is, Are) either of the letters ready for signature?   _____

13. The jury (has, have) announced its verdict.   _____

14. Preservation of the ocean and its creatures (is, are) a major concern.   _____

15. Either of the photocopies (is, are) acceptable for our purpose.   _____

16. A map showing campgrounds and picnic areas (is, are) provided at the gas station.   _____

17. Either a book or an article (has, have) to be read as part of the assignment.   _____

18. Our program, along with the efforts of other civic-minded businesses, (is, are) aimed at urban renewal.   _____

19. Any one of the shareholders (has, have) the right to delegate his or her proxy.   _____

20. Some of the handwriting in the sales reports (is, are) illegible.   _____

C. Use your imagination to complete the sentences started below, after choosing the correct verb from the choices in parentheses.

1. The staff (is, are) _____

   _____

2. Our city council (has, have) _____

   _____

3. Not one of the plans (was, were) _____

   _____

4. Some of the jury members (believe, believes) _____

   _____

5. Somebody in the bus filled with students (was, were) _____

   _____

A. (Self-check) For each sentence write the correct verb in the space provided.

LEVEL III

1. The number of on-line job applicants (was, were) greater than expected. _____

2. Part of the loss of customers (is, are) the result of poor service. _____

3. Our company president is one of those executives who (is, are) able to delegate responsibility. _____

4. Fourteen metres of pipe (is, are) not enough for this job. _____

5. Didn't you know it is you who (is, are) to be honoured at the ceremony? _____

6. A number of problems (is, are) yet to be resolved. _____

7. She is the only one of the technicians who (operate, operates) all the equipment. _____

8. Whoever is named for the job (has, have) my approval. _____

9. About one-third of the records (is, are) stored on microfiche. _____

10. The hardest part of the job (is, are) the bending and lifting. _____

Check your answers.

B. Select the correct verb.

1. Thirty-five dollars (is, are) required as a deposit before one can rent a tandem bicycle. _____

2. Our latest advertisements featuring our spring clothing line (is, are) an example of the campaign. _____

3. Is it he who (is, are) the new account representative? _____

4. Carole is the only one of the lab assistants who (was, were) able to repair the malfunctioning machine. _____

5. Vacations for employees who are entitled to three or more weeks (is, are) the next item on the agenda. _____

6. Sixty days (is, are) the period of the loan. _____

7. At the rear of the building complex (is, are) the quality control lab and the science department. _____

8. Only a fraction of the conference delegates (was, were) unable to find accommodations in the Royal Manor. _____

1. was 2. is 3. are 4. is 5. are 6. are 7. operates 8. has 9. are 10. is

9. Serving on the student council (is, are) a representative from each of the twenty departments on campus. _____

10. Over 80 per cent of the individuals attending the lecture series (is, are) residents of nearby communities. _____

11. Michael is one of those people who always (get, gets) along well with fellow workers. _____

12. The reason for his wealth (is, are) wise investments in oil. _____

13. Neither the staff nor the students (think, thinks) that higher fees will solve the budget crisis. _____

14. Representing our office (is, are) several men and women with many years of experience. _____

15. Trimark Mutual Funds, with headquarters in Toronto, often (advertise, advertises) in *The Globe and Mail.* _____

16. One of the problems, in addition to those already mentioned, (seem, seems) to be resistance to change. _____

17. A chart showing all staff positions and responsibilities (was, were) prepared by the vice-president. _____

18. Neither the defendant nor the plaintiffs (was, were) satisfied with the judgment. _____

19. Ms. Ornstein is one of those investors who (study, studies) a firm's annual report very carefully. _____

20. In our company the number of highly successful salespeople (is, are) steadily increasing. _____

C. Optional Composition. Your instructor may ask you to complete this exercise on a separate sheet. Write ten original sentences using the following words as subjects of *present tense* verbs: *anyone, any one, everyone, every one, the number, a number, none, everything, council,* and *one of the managers.*

Editor's Challenge

The following letter proposal contains intentional errors in spelling, proofreading, and grammar principles you have studied thus far. Use standard proofreading marks to show your corrections.

Wright Research Consultants

385 Eglinton Ave. West
Toronto, ON M4T 2H9

Web: http://www.wrightresearch.com   Phone: (416) 220-9184   E-mail: rwright@wrightresearch.com

April 15, 200X

Mr. Morris Edelson
Consumer Credit Service
1021 Birchmount Road
Toronto, ON M1K 5G3

Dear Mr. Edelson:

At your request, my staff and myself is submitting the following proposal regarding a survey of university students credit habits in southern Ontario.

Problem

As you point out, credit purchase's among university students is burdening them with to much debt, more than half of full-time undergraduate students now has at least one major credit card. Although students account for less than 3 per cent of the domestic credit card business, a significant number of these students is having more trouble than other borrowers in repaying. Credit card use among students has rose dramatically in the past decade.

Background

We understand that your non-profit organizations principle goal is to open a credit counselling service aimed at university students in southern Ontario. Specifically, you want to investigate (1) credit card habit's among university students in general, (2) credit card habits among students in your area, and (3) the affectiveness of student counselling services in other university towns.

Proposed Plan

On the basis of our experience in conducting many local and national surveys. Wright Research propose to develop a short but thorough questionnaire probing the data you desire. We will submit the questionnaire for you approval, and we will consult with you regarding the exact sample and it's demographics. Data from the surveywill be analyze by our experienced team of experts. Using the latest computer systems and advanced statistical measures.

Staffing and Budget

Wright Research Consultants are a nationally recognized, experienced research consulting firm specializing in survey investigation. My staff and myself has assigned your survey to Dr. Rebecca Horne, whom is our director of research. Dr. Horne was trained at the University of Alberta and has successfully supervise our research program for the past nine years. Further information about her qualifications and our staffs training is provided in the attached brochure. Everyone of the members of our staff are experienced in survey research. Budget figures for this proposed survey is showed in the attach brochure.

Authorization

My staff and myself sincerely believe that our profesionally designed and administered survey are exactly what you need to enable you to make a decision about the establishment of a student credit-counselling service in southern Ontario. Wright Research can have the results for you by July 2. If you sign the enclosed duplicate copy of this letter and return them immediately to Dr. Horne or I with a retainer of $3,000. The prices in this offer is in affect only until September 1.

Sincerely,

Lawrence R. Wright

Lawrence R. Wright
President

Enclosures

Underline the correct verb.

1. At least one of our accountants (suggest, suggests) using a tax-deferred plan.

2. The cost of supplies, along with service and equipment costs, (is, are) a major problem.

3. Either the administrative assistant or the engineers (has, have) to find the original copy.

4. Appearing next on the program (was, were) Raye Staples and Connie Aragun.

5. A number of surprising events (is, are) occurring in the stock market.

learning.web.ways

"Netiquette" is network etiquette covering the dos and don'ts of on-line communication. To become familiar with some of the informal "rules of the road" in cyberspace, you will visit the "Business Netiquette International" site.

Goal: To learn about netiquette.

1. With your Web browser on the screen, enter the following URL: **<http://www.bspage.com/1netiq/Netiq.html>** (that's a number "1" preceding "netiq").

2. If this URL doesn't work, find the site by using a search engine **<www.google.com>** with the term **Business Netiquette International**.

3. Scroll through the Business Netiquette International site. Don't click any links.

4. What is the basic rule of etiquette in any circumstance?

5. When is it permissible to send attachments to e-mail messages?

6. Should you use first names in e-mail messages?

7. Print the first page of this site.

8. End your session, and submit your printed page and written answers.

1. suggests 2. is 3. have 4. were 5. are

Verbals

OBJECTIVES When you have completed the materials in this chapter, you will be able to do the following:

LEVEL I
- *Recognize gerunds and supply appropriate modifiers of gerunds.*
- *Identify and remedy split infinitives that result in awkward sentences.*

LEVEL II
- *Correctly punctuate introductory and other verbal phrases.*
- *Avoid writing awkward participial phrases.*

LEVEL III
- *Spot dangling verbal phrases and other misplaced modifiers.*
- *Rewrite sentences to avoid misplaced verbal phrases and modifiers.*

PRETEST

Write *a, b,* or *c* to describe the following sentences.

a = contains no errors
b = contains error in use of verbal form
c = contains error in punctuation of verbal form

1. Opening his book to the assigned chapter, the headings were read by Paul. _____

2. After considering the project carefully the vice-president gave his approval. _____

3. To register by mail, return the enclosed application form. _____

4. Expertly trained in accounting techniques, the interviewer hired Kelly for the position. _____

5. To be finished on time the report required many hours of extra effort by the staff. _____

1.b 2.c 3.a 4.b 5.c

As you learned earlier, English is a highly flexible language in which a given word may have more than one grammatical function. In this chapter you will study verbals. Derived from verbs, verbals are words that function as nouns, adjectives, or adverbs. Three kinds of verbals are gerunds (verbal nouns), infinitives, and participles (verbal adjectives).

▶ Gerunds

A verb form ending in *ing* and used as a noun is called a *gerund*.

> *Advertising* is necessary. (Gerund used as the subject)
> Dale enjoys *computing*. (Gerund used as direct object)

Using Gerunds Correctly

In using gerunds, follow this rule: Make any noun or pronoun modifying a gerund possessive, as Karen's *keyboarding* or her *computing*. Because we sometimes fail to recognize gerunds as nouns, we fail to make their modifiers possessive.

> *Wrong:*   The staff objects to Kevin *smoking*.
> *Right:*   The staff objects to Kevin's *smoking*.

The staff does not object to Kevin, as the first version states; it objects to his smoking. If we substitute a more easily recognized noun for *smoking*, the possessive form seems more natural: *The staff objects to Kevin's behaviour. Behaviour* is a noun, just as *smoking* is a noun; the noun or pronoun modifiers of both must be possessive.

> Mr. Drake resented *his* calling during lunch. (The gerund *calling* requires the possessive pronoun *his*, not the objective case pronoun *him*.)
> We appreciate *your* bringing this matter to our attention. (Not *you bringing*)

Not all verb forms ending in *ing* are, of course, gerunds. Some are participles acting either as elements in verb phrases or as adjectives.* Compare these three sentences:

> I saw Monica keyboarding. (The word *keyboarding* functions as an adjective describing Monica.)
> I admired Monica's keyboarding. (As the object of the verb, *keyboarding* acts as a gerund.)
> Monica is keyboarding. (Here, *keyboarding* is part of a verb phrase.)

Study Tip

To distinguish between *ing* forms used as nouns and those used as adjectives, try the *what?* question approach. In the sentence *I admired Monica's keyboarding,* say to yourself, "I admired *what?*" Answer: "I admired Monica's *keyboarding,* not Monica." Therefore, *keyboarding* is the object and functions as an *ing* noun.

▶ Infinitives

When the simple present form of a verb is preceded by *to*, the most basic verb form results: the *infinitive*. The sign of the infinitive is the word *to*.

> Try *to sign* the papers immediately.
> *To write* gracefully requires great skill.

---

* *Participles will be discussed in Level II of this chapter.*

Using Infinitives Correctly

In certain expressions infinitives may be misused. Observe the use of the word *to* in the following infinitive phrases. Do not substitute the conjunction *and* for the *to* of the infinitive.

> Try *to call* when you arrive. (Not *try and call*)
> Be sure *to put* your initials on the letter. (Not *be sure and put*)
> Check *to see* when your appointment is. (Not *check and see*)

When any word appears between *to* and the verb (*to* carefully *prepare*), an infinitive is said to be split. At one time split infinitives were considered great grammatical sins. Today most authorities agree that infinitives may be split if necessary for clarity and effect. Avoid, however, split infinitives that result in awkward sentences.

Awkward:	Mr. Stokes wanted *to*, if he could find time, *recheck* his figures.
Better:	If he could find time, Mr. Stokes wanted *to recheck* his figures.
Awkward:	Our company has *to*, when the real estate market returns to normal, *consider* purchasing an office building.
Better:	Our company has *to consider*, when the real estate market returns to normal, purchasing an office building.
Acceptable:	*To* wilfully *lie* under oath is perjury. (No awkwardness results from split infinitive.)
Acceptable:	Mrs. Higgins expects you *to* really *concentrate* when you proofread. (No awkwardness results from split infinitive.)

Complete the reinforcement exercises for Level I on pp. 188–190.

▶ Participles

In Chapter 9 you studied the present and past forms of participles functioning as parts of verb phrases. You will recall that in such constructions present and past participles always require helping verbs: *is typing, was seen, had broken.*

In this chapter we will be concerned with a second possible function of participles. Participles can function as adjectives. As adjectives, participles modify nouns or pronouns and do not require helping verbs. Here are sentences that illustrate the five forms of the participle.

Present participle, active:	*Helping William with the proposal,* we are staying late. (The participial phrase *Helping William with the proposal* modifies *we.*)
Present participle, passive:	William McCain, *being helped* by his colleagues, is completing the proposal. (*Being helped* is here a participle that describes *William McCain.*)
Past participle, passive:	Although *helped* by three others, William found it difficult to admit their assistance. (The participle *helped* functions as an adjective to describe *William.*)

Spot the Blooper

Headline from *The Urbana* [Ohio] *Daily Citizen:* "Volunteers Use Sandbags to Try and Save Water Plant."

Hotlink

Help with using gerunds is available on this University of Toronto Web page **<http://www.utoronto.ca/writing/l2ger.html>**.

LEVEL II

Hotlink

Should split infinitives be condemned? Check the Bartleby.com site for the opinion of the American Heritage® *Book of English Usage* **<http://www.bartleby.com/64/C001/059.html>**.

| *Perfect participle, active:* | *Having helped William* on many previous occasions, his colleagues were accustomed to his inability to thank them. (The participial phrase *Having helped William* describes *his colleagues*.) |
| *Perfect participle, passive:* | William, *having been helped on many big projects*, was deeply indebted to his colleagues. (The participle *having been helped* functions as an adjective to describe *William*.) |

Using Participles Correctly

Avoid using participial phrases that sound awkward, such as the following:

Awkward:	Pam's having been promoted to office manager was cause for celebration.
Better:	Pam's promotion to office manager was cause for celebration.
Awkward:	Being you have arrived early, may I leave now?
Better:	Since you have arrived early, may I leave now?

▶ Punctuating Verbal Forms

Determining whether verbal forms require commas often causes difficulty. Let's try to clear up this difficulty with explanations and examples.

Punctuating Introductory Verbal Forms

When verbal forms are used in introductory words or expressions, there's no question about punctuating them. A comma should be placed between an introductory verbal form and the main clause of a sentence.

Astonished, the lawyer turned to the jury. (Introductory verbal form)
To improve product distribution, Burke hired a traffic manager. (Introductory verbal phrase)
Receiving too many e-mail messages, Andy established filters. (Introductory verbal phrase)
Having completed forty-three years with the company, Betty Bond retired. (Introductory verbal phrase)

Not all verbal phrases that begin sentences, however, are considered introductory. If the verbal phrase represents the subject or part of the predicate of the sentence, *no* comma should separate it from the rest of the sentence.

Preparing a budget is Andy's responsibility. (Verbal phrase used as subject; no comma)
To change our budget at this time is almost impossible. (Verbal phrase used as subject; no comma)
Located in the other building is our Shipping Department. (Verbal phrase used as part of predicate; no comma)

Punctuating Non-Essential Verbal Phrases

Essential (restrictive) information is needed for the reader to understand the sentence. Verbal phrases often help identify the subject; these phrases require no commas. Non-essential (non-restrictive) information could be omitted without altering the basic meaning of the sentence; non-essential phrases are set off by commas.

Mrs. Lanier, *working late at the office*, was able to meet the deadline. (The verbal phrase *working late at the office* adds additional information, but it is not essential. The subject is fully identified by name. Use commas to set off the non-essential phrase.)

The woman *working late at the office* was able to meet the deadline. (In this sentence the verbal phrase *working late at the office* is essential; it is needed to identify the subject. *Which* woman was able to meet the deadline? The woman *working late at the office*. No commas separate this essential verbal phrase.)

Canada Trust, *opening a new branch in St. John's*, offered gifts to attract customers. (The verbal phrase is not essential because there is only one Canada Trust, and it has been identified. Commas enclose this non-essential verbal phrase.)

A company *opening a new branch in St. John's* offered gifts to attract customers. (This verbal phrase is essential to identify *which* company offered gifts. No commas are needed. *Note:* Even if you pause when you reach the end of the verbal phrase, don't be tempted to add a comma.)

Notice in the preceding sentences that whenever a non-essential verbal phrase interrupts the middle of a sentence, *two* commas set it off.

Complete the reinforcement exercises for Level II on pp. 191–193.

Study Tip

To help you understand the use of commas in dealing with non-essential information, think of a window shade. Use commas to lower the window shade and cover the words enclosed. If words in a verbal phrase are not essential to the meaning of a sentence, use a "comma window shade" to obscure them.

▶ Avoiding Misplaced Verbal Modifiers

LEVEL III

Used correctly, verbal modifiers and phrases add clarity and description to your writing. Let's consider the best way to position them within sentences.

Introductory Verbal Phrases

Introductory verbal phrases must be followed by words they can logically modify. Such phrases can create confusion or unintended humour when placed incorrectly in a sentence. Consider this sentence: *Sitting in the car, the mountains were breathtaking.* The introductory participial phrase in this sentence is said to *dangle* because it is not followed immediately by a word it can logically modify. The sentence could be improved by revising it to read: *Sitting in the car, we saw the breathtaking mountains.* (*We*, a word logically modified by the verbal phrase, has been placed directly after the phrase.) See how the following illogical sentences have been improved:

Illogical: Slipping on the ice, his back was injured.
Logical: Slipping on the ice, *he* injured his back.

Illogical: Turning on the fan, papers flew about the office.
Logical: Turning on the fan, *I* caused papers to fly about the office.

Illogical: After answering the telephone, the doorbell began to ring insistently.
Logical: After answering the telephone, *Jeremy* heard the doorbell ring insistently.

Illogical: Skilled with computers, the personnel director hired Kay.
Logical: Skilled with computers, *Kay* was hired by the personnel director.

Spot the Blooper

From *Country Collectibles*: "Sitting by a blazing fire, reading a good mystery novel, a dog can jump into your lap and beg for a few playful pats on the head."

Hotlink

Dangling modifiers get a page to themselves at **<http://www.ucalgary. ca/UofC/eduweb/ grammar/>**. Go to Sentence Elements, and then scroll down to the link for dangling modifiers.

But: To ensure academic success, study diligently. (In commands, the understood subject is *you*. Therefore, this verbal phrase is correctly followed by the word to which it refers: To ensure academic success, [you] study diligently.)

Study Tip

After reading an introductory verbal phrase, ask the question *who?* The answer to that question must immediately follow the introductory phrase. For example, *To find a good job, who?* Answer: To find a good job, *Derek* wrote to many companies.

Verbal Phrases in Other Positions

In other positions within sentences, verbal phrases must also be placed in logical relation to the words they modify—in other words, as close as possible to those words.

Illogical: The missing purchase orders were found by Mrs. Seldon's assistant lying in the top desk drawer.

Logical: Mrs. Seldon's assistant found the missing purchase orders lying in the top desk drawer.

Illogical: Mr. South returned the envelope and its contents, recognizing his error.

Logical: Mr. South, recognizing his error, returned the envelope and its contents.

Illogical: Emma met many women who were planning weddings while working at Sunnylea Bridal.

Logical: While working at Sunnylea Bridal, Emma met many women who were planning weddings.

Complete the reinforcement exercises for Level III on pp. 194–196.

HOTLINE QUERIES

Question: Are there two meanings for the word *discreet*?

Answer: You are probably confusing the two words *discreet* and *discrete*. *Discreet* means "showing good judgment" and "prudent" (*the witness gave a discreet answer, avoiding gossip and hearsay*). The word *discrete* means "separate" or "non-continuous" (*Alpha Inc. has installed discrete computers rather than a network computer system*). You might find it helpful to remember that the *e*'s are separate in *discrete*.

Question: Should I use *complimentary* or *complementary* to describe free tickets?

Answer: Use *complimentary,* which can mean "containing a compliment, favourable, or free" (*the dinner came with complimentary wine; he made a complimentary remark*). *Complementary* means "completing or making perfect" (*the complementary colours enhanced the room*). An easy way to remember *compliment* is by thinking "*I* like to receive a compl*i*ment."

Question: I confuse *i.e.* and *e.g.* What's the difference?

Answer: The abbreviation *i.e.* stands for the Latin *id est,* meaning "that is" (*the package exceeds the weight limit, i.e., 5 pounds*). The abbreviation *e.g.* stands for the Latin *exempli gratia,* meaning "for the sake of example" or "for example" (*the manufacturer may offer a purchase incentive, e.g., a rebate or discount plan*). Notice the use of commas before and after *i.e.* and *e.g.*

Question: We're having an argument in our office about abbreviations. Can *department* be abbreviated as *dep't*? How about *manufacturing* as *mf'g*? Where could we find a correct list of such abbreviations?

Answer: In informal writing or when space is limited, words may be contracted or abbreviated. If a conventional abbreviation for a word exists, use it instead of a contracted form. Abbreviations are simpler to write and easier to read. For example, use *dept.* instead of *dep't;* use *natl.* instead of *nat'l;* use *cont.* instead of *cont'd.* Other accepted abbreviations are *ins.* for *insurance; mfg.* for *manufacturing; mgr.* for *manager;* and *mdse.* for *merchandise.* Notice that all abbreviations end with periods. Some dictionaries show abbreviations within the main entries so that a reader must know how to spell the word in full in order to be able to locate the abbreviation. Reference manuals often have helpful lists of abbreviations.

Question: I'm not sure which word to use in this sentence: *They have used all (they're, their, there) resources in combatting the disease.*

Answer: Use *their,* which is the possessive form of *they.* The adverb *there* means "at that place or at that point" (*we have been there before*). *There* is also used as an expletive or filler preceding a linking verb (*there are numerous explanations*). *They're* is a contraction of *they are* (*they're coming this afternoon*).

Question: A sentence in a letter written by my boss reads, *We do not want an open invoice without there being justifiable reasons.* How should we spell *there*?

Answer: *There* is spelled correctly, but its use creates an awkward verbal form. If your boss agrees, revise the sentence to read, *We do not want an open invoice without justification.*

CHAPTER 11   **Reinforcement Exercises**

A. (**Self-check**) In the following sentences gerunds are italicized. Other *ing* words that are not italicized are not functioning as gerunds. Select appropriate modifiers.

LEVEL I

1. She is unhappy with (you, your) *handling* of the order.   _____

2. I saw (Mardi, Mardi's) loading the paper tray.   _____

3. (His, Him) *travelling* first class was questioned by the auditor.   _____

4. Did Gene tell you about (Gail, Gail's) *moving* to Yellowknife?   _____

5. The manager was upset about (Steve, Steve's) *leaving* early.   _____

6. The (clerk, clerk's) making the sale receives the commission.   _____

7. Renate suggested (you, your) *making* reservations early.   _____

8. I noticed Mrs. (Lee, Lee's) *handwriting* on the invoice.   _____

9. I appreciate (them, their) *answering* the telephone.   _____

10. The (salesperson, salesperson's) making the appointment is here.   _____

Check your answers.

B. Gerunds are again italicized. Choose the correct modifier.

1. Because of (you, your) *taking* responsibility, we are able to remain open.   _____

2. The (executive, executive's) submitting four disks forgot to sign his work request.   _____

3. The accuracy of this report depends on (him, his) *proofreading*.   _____

4. They said (you, your) *printing* of the brochures was excellent.   _____

5. The (firm, firm's) printing the forms went out of business.   _____

6. Our success depends on (you, your) *making* the best investments.   _____

7. The (customer, customer's) paying his bill complimented the service.   _____

8. We are incredulous at (them, their) *winning* the series.   _____

9. The (player, player's) winning the final game takes the prize.   _____

10. (Him, His) *being* on time for the appointment is very important.   _____

C. From each of the pairs of sentences shown, select the more acceptable version, and write its letter in the space provided.

1. (a) Emilio Aguilar was asked to, as soon as possible, develop a Web site.
   (b) Emilio Aguilar was asked to develop a Web site as soon as possible. _____

2. (a) Happily, Mrs. Nasrin began to open her birthday cards.
   (b) Mrs. Nasrin began to happily open her birthday cards. _____

3. (a) Be sure and say hello for me.
   (b) Be sure to say hello for me. _____

4. (a) We wondered about his ordering so few office supplies.
   (b) We wondered about him ordering so few office supplies. _____

5. (a) The secretary started to, as the deadline approached, check the names and addresses.
   (b) As the deadline approached, the secretary started to check the names and addresses. _____

6. (a) Try to find out when the meeting is scheduled.
   (b) Try and find out when the meeting is scheduled. _____

7. (a) I think their being present at the hearing is crucial.
   (b) I think them being present at the hearing is crucial. _____

8. (a) Please check to see if the contract is ready.
   (b) Please check and see if the contract is ready. _____

9. (a) You may wish to, if you have time, contact your broker.
   (b) You may wish to contact your broker if you have time. _____

10. (a) The travel counsellor recommended our travelling by train.
    (b) The travel counsellor recommended us travelling by train. _____

D. Rewrite the following sentences to remedy any gerund or infinitive faults.

1. We plan to, if all the papers have been signed, initiate proceedings tomorrow.

   _____

   _____

   _____

2. Be sure and call to, if you haven't changed your mind, make your plane reservations.

   _____

   _____

   _____

3. I hope that you will inform your two agents that I appreciate them listening to my complaints.

_____

_____

_____

4. When you are in Montreal, try and visit the art gallery.

_____

_____

_____

LEVEL II

A. (Self-check) Verbal phrases in the following sentences are shown in italics. All the sentences have been punctuated correctly. Study each sentence, and select the letter that explains the reason for including or omitting commas.

> a = Introductory verbal phrase, comma necessary
> b = Essential verbal phrase, no commas necessary
> c = Non-essential verbal phrase, commas necessary
> d = Verbal phrase used as a subject, no commas necessary

Examples: To *settle the matter* is extremely difficult. _____d_____

Mrs. Manning, *to settle the matter,* flipped a coin. _____c_____

1. *Preparing copies of her résumé,* Terri Mays used a laser printer. _____

2. The student *looking for a parking place* was late to class. _____

3. Terri Mays, *preparing copies of her résumé,* used a laser printer. _____

4. *Finding an earlier class* is very unlikely. _____

5. *Preparing copies of a résumé* is easy when one uses a laser printer. _____

6. *Consulting her astrologer,* Linda Blustein refused to set foot outside. _____

7. The person *consulting her astrologer* refused to set foot outside. _____

8. *Looking at the class schedule,* I see that I can take English. _____

9. Anyone *looking at a class schedule* can see what classes are available. _____

10. Professor Kathleen Allix, *looking at a class schedule,* announced a change in our class time. _____

Check your answers.

B. Selected verbal words and phrases have been italicized in the sentences below. Insert commas if needed. In the space provided at the right, write the number of commas that you insert for each sentence. If no commas are needed, write *0*.

Example: *To complete the job before the deadline* ⌄ we worked late. _____1_____

1. *To introduce a new product successfully* manufacturers often depend on advertising. _____

2. *Setting personal goals and objectives* is one important step in career planning. _____

3. *After studying the company's files* Mrs. Wohl recommended a more efficient records management system. _____

1.a 2.b 3.c 4.d 5.d 6.a 7.b 8.a 9.b 10.c

4. *Perplexed* the new owner of the retail outlet hired a financial expert for advice. _____

5. *Working in another office* are the legal secretaries who specialize in contracts. _____

6. *Sending frequent e-mail messages and writing reports* the manager could not get along without her computer. _____

7. *To improve the writing of government employees* consultants were hired. _____

8. *Startled* Jane Juralski dropped the letter folder. _____

9. *Beginning as a sole proprietor* H. J. Heinz eventually built a large corporation. _____

10. *Breaking down a job cycle into separate units of work* is the first task in a time-and-motion study. _____

C. Selected verbal phrases in the following sentences have been italicized. Insert commas if the phrases are non-essential. In the space provided, write the number of commas that you insert for each sentence. If you add no commas, write *0*.

1. Tommy Porter *sitting in the first seat of the third row* is next. _____

2. The student *sitting in the first seat of the third row* is next. _____

3. Sales Manager Everett *accessing her e-mail network daily* was able to stay in contact with her clients and her office while travelling. _____

4. You may be interested to know that any student *enrolled in the college* has full library privileges. _____

5. The latest company contract enables employees *participating in our profit-sharing plan* to benefit from the stock split. _____

6. Kim Odjig *striving to qualify for a promotion* enrolled in a Saturday course. _____

7. Anyone *striving to qualify for a promotion* should consider enrolling in college courses. _____

8. The clerk *keyboarding at her computer for as many as 14 hours a day* developed repetitive stress injury. _____

D. If necessary, insert commas to punctuate verbal forms in the following sentences. In the space provided, indicate the number of commas added.

1. To plan effectively management must have a realistic picture of production. _____

2. General Motors facing unexpected competition from foreign suppliers decided to close the small fabrication plant. _____

3. After considering the matter carefully we have decided to implement your suggestion. _____

4. Explaining the failure of the merger negotiations proved a difficult task for the business reporters. _____

5. Anyone possessing the necessary background may apply for the position. _____

6. Our CEO facing another year of intense pressure resigned his post. _____

7. Having reduced safety and health hazards in the past few years our division recently set a record for consecutive accident-free workdays. _____

8. Human Resources Director Higgins hoping to help employees improve their job skills organized an in-service training class. _____

9. All employees interested in improving their job skills are invited to attend the in-service programs. _____

10. To enrol in any of the programs employees must sign up immediately. _____

A. (**Self-check**) From each of the pairs of sentences that follow, select the sentence that is stated in the more logical manner. Write its letter in the space provided.

LEVEL III

1. (a) To locate precisely the right word, a thesaurus is often used.
    (b) To locate precisely the right word, one may often use a thesaurus.   _____

2. (a) Sealed in an airtight crock, the Joneses savoured the fine cheese.
    (b) Sealed in an airtight crock, the fine cheese was savoured by the Joneses.   _____

3. (a) To complete the accounting equation, one must add liabilities to equity.
    (b) To complete the accounting equation, it is necessary to add liabilities to equity.   _____

4. (a) Before starting the project, permission must be obtained.
    (b) Before starting the project, one must obtain permission.   _____

5. (a) In sorting the names and addresses, Monika discovered an error.
    (b) In sorting the names and addresses, an error was discovered by Monika.   _____

6. (a) To graduate early, carry more credits.
    (b) To graduate early, more credits must be carried.   _____

7. (a) After collecting author references on note cards, write the bibliography.
    (b) After collecting author references on note cards, the bibliography should be written.   _____

8. (a) Having completed twenty years of service, Charles Mercier was presented with a gold watch.
    (b) Having completed twenty years of service, a gold watch was presented to Charles Mercier.   _____

9. (a) After seeing the job advertisement, a letter was sent by Miss Bruner.
    (b) After seeing the job advertisement, Miss Bruner sent a letter.   _____

10. (a) To qualify for the certificate, perfect attendance must be maintained.
    (b) To qualify for the certificate, students must maintain perfect attendance.   _____

Check your answers.

B. Each of the following sentences has an illogical introductory verbal phrase. Rewrite each sentence using that introductory phrase so that it is followed by a word it can logically modify. Adding a subject may be necessary. Keep the introductory verbal phrase at the beginning of the sentence.

Example: Driving through the hills, the city came into view.

Driving through the hills, we saw the city come into view.

1.b 2.b 3.a 4.b 5.a 6.a 7.a 8.a 9.b 10.b

1. Answering the telephone on the first ring, goodwill is created by our staff.

_____

_____

_____

2. Comparing figures from four sources, the error in the balance sheet was finally discovered.

_____

_____

_____

3. To be binding, a consideration must support every contract.

_____

_____

_____

4. Repainted and completely reconditioned in every part, Laura was amazed at her old Volkswagen.

_____

_____

_____

5. Selected as Employee of the Year, the CEO presented an award to Cecile Chang.

_____

_____

_____

6. After breaking into the building, the police heard the alarm set off by the burglars.

_____

_____

_____

7. To be promoted, your performance appraisal must be excellent.

_____

_____

_____

The preceding sentences had misplaced introductory verbal phrases. The next sentences have misplaced verbal phrases in other sentence positions. Rewrite these sentences so that the verbal phrases are close to the words they can logically modify.

8. An autopsy revealed the cause of death to be strangulation performed by the coroner.

_____

_____

9. Noxious fumes made many office workers sick coming from the nearby auto paint shop.

_____

_____

10. Agnes Macphail became the first female parliamentarian in the British Empire elected to the House of Commons in 1921.

_____

_____

_____

11. The brochure states that the Ambassador Bridge is the world's longest international suspension bridge stretching between terminals in Windsor, Ontario, and Detroit, Michigan.

_____

_____

_____

C. Optional Composition. Your instructor may ask you to complete this exercise on a separate sheet. Write ten original sentences, two for each of the following verb forms: gerund, infinitive, present participle, past participle, and perfect participle. Label each sentence.

Editor's Challenge

The following letter contains errors in spelling, proofreading, and language principles covered thus far. Use standard proofreading marks to show your corrections.

Mr. Michael K. Topton
455 Zionsville Road
Corner Brook, NF A2H 4G1

Dear Mr. Topton:

At the suggestion of your former partner, Ms. Molly Harned. I am submiting this application for the position of legal secretery in your office. I understand that you are seeking an individual whom has communication, transcription, and microcomputer skills. Both my education and my experience, I believe, qualifies myself for this position.

Having finish two years' of schooling at Valley Community College. My skills include word processing, machine transcription, and business letter writing. To learn about working for a lawyer, a course in legal procedures was completed. Being that we studied personal injury, dissolution, and unlawful detainer procedures, I now have skill in these areas. Moreover, I have took a course in legal terminology.

In addition to my education, I have complete a six-month internship with two lawyers, Mr. Ronald W. Schultz and Ms. Robin Sawicki, in Halifax. Keyboarding legal documents and updating a client database in Mr. Schultz office has helped me learn about current computer software program.

Please study the enclosed résumé to review my complete educational and employment background. Ms. Harned said that you needed some one immediately, if I was hired for this position, I would be able to start in June. I must give at least two weeks notice to my present employer. If I meet your requirements, I would appreciate you calling me at 389-5910 to arrange a interview at a time convenent to you.

Sincerely,

Michelle A. Robinson

Enclosure

POSTTEST

Write *a*, *b*, or *c* to describe the following sentences.

a = contains no errors
b = contains error in use of verbal form
c = contains error in punctuation of verbal form

1. Deciding that his first letter was unclear, a second letter was written by Mr. Holmes. _____

2. To supervise effectively a manager must have excellent communication skills. _____

3. To collect health benefits, fill out the long application. _____

4. Improving health and dental benefits for all employees is our primary goal. _____

5. Having submitted an application, benefits should be forthcoming immediately. _____

 # learning.web.ways

You've been asked to make a presentation on personal finance and credit debt. You decide that you need a good Canadian (and perhaps humorous) quotation on money. Many Web sites provide free quotations.

Goal: To find a Canadian quotation.

1. With your Web browser on the screen, enter **<http://www. conservativeforum.org/quotesmast.asp>**.

2. In the search box, enter the term "money."

3. Read all the selections provided. Print the pages, and circle the quotation you like best.

4. Use Google.com **<http://www.google.com>**, and enter "Canadian quotations" in the search box.

5. Select a site and print a selection, circling the quotation you like best.

6. End your session, and submit your printed pages.

1.b 2.c 3.a 4.a 5.b

UNIT 3 REVIEW   Chapters 8–11 (Self-Check)

Begin your review by rereading Chapters 8 through 11. Then test your comprehension of those chapters by completing the exercises that follow. Compare your responses with those provided at the end of the book.

In the blank provided, write the letter of the word or phrase that correctly completes each of the following sentences.

LEVEL I

1. In the sentence *He seems responsible,* the verb *seems* is (a) transitive, (b) intransitive, (c) linking. _____

2. In the sentence *She is the president,* the word *president* is a(n) (a) object, (b) linking verb, (c) complement. _____

3. A keyboard with 106 characters (a) has, (b) have been developed for your computer. _____

4. The president, together with her entire staff of employees, (a) send, (b) sends greetings to you. _____

5. The president and her entire staff (a) send, (b) sends greetings to you. _____

6. Be sure (a) to write, (b) and write the name and address legibly. _____

7. We certainly appreciate (a) him, (b) his handling of the program. _____

8. Davis, Crowley, and Kovacs, Inc., (a) is, (b) are expecting an increase in profits this quarter. _____

9. The shipping statement for the equipment and supplies (a) was, (b) were delayed. _____

10. Is there any possibility of (a) your, (b) you coming early? _____

11. How effective (a) is, (b) are the company guidelines on Internet use? _____

Write the letter of the word or phrase that correctly completes each of the following sentences.

12. When converting a verb from the passive to the active voice, the writer must make the doer of the action the (a) subject, (b) object of the active voice verb. _____

13. In the sentence *Three form letters were typed by Mary,* the verb is in the (a) active, (b) passive voice. _____

14. Many letters and packages have (a) laid, (b) lain, (c) lay on that desk for the past week. _____

15. If you had (a) rang, (b) rung the bell, I'd have heard it. _____

16. The contract (a) laying, (b) lying on your desk must be signed. _____

17. Neither the computer nor the printers (a) is, (b) are working. _____

18. We think that (a) anyone, (b) any one of our representatives will serve you well. _____

Insert commas where necessary in the next group of sentences. Indicate the number of commas that you added. Write *0* for none.

19. We were very pleased to see that Rebecca working until 10 p.m. was able to complete the job. _____

20. Storing thousands of customer files became physically possible when we installed an electronic database. _____

21. Working until 10 p.m. Rebecca was able to complete the job. _____

In the blank provided, write the letter of the word or phrase that correctly completes each sentence.

22. The problem would be handled differently if I (a) was, (b) were in charge. _____

23. A motion was made that members (a) be, (b) are admitted free. _____

24. The number of employees participating in elective classes (a) is, (b) are steadily increasing. _____

25. It is you who (a) is, (b) are to do the judging tomorrow. _____

26. It looks as if three-fourths of the brochures (a) has, (b) have yet to be assembled. _____

27. She is one of those executives who always (a) tell, (b) tells the truth. _____

For each sentence below, indicate whether (a) the sentence is written correctly or (b) the sentence has a verbal phrase placed illogically. Rewrite illogical sentences.

28. To qualify for the retirement incentive, applications must be made by January 1. _____

_____

_____

29. Skilled at programming computers, the human resources manager hired Hans instantly. _____

_____

_____

30. Driving to the office, two accidents were seen by Debbie. _____

_____

_____

31. Although her mother was in it, thieves stole a suitcase containing jewellery and
clothing from the car of Mrs. Mercier. _____

_____

_____

Hotline Review

Select the word or phrase that correctly completes each statement, and write its letter in the corresponding blank.

32. Karen Kain was promoted to (a) principal, (b) principle dancer within one year of
joining The National Ballet of Canada.   _____

33. A great deal of research is being done on the (a) affects, (b) effects of food additives.   _____

34. Human resources staff members are required to be (a) discreet, (b) discrete when
dealing with employees' files.   _____

35. We attract many customers by offering a (a) free gift, (b) valuable gift with a minimum
purchase of $40.   _____

36. They are not (a) all together, (b) altogether happy with the results of the survey.   _____

Techniques for Effective Paragraphs

As you learned in Workshop 2, the basic unit in writing is the sentence. The next unit is the paragraph. Although no rule regulates the length of paragraphs, business writers recognize the value of short paragraphs. Paragraphs with fewer than eight printed lines look inviting and readable, whereas long, solid chunks of print appear formidable. In this workshop you will learn writing techniques for organizing sentences into readable, coherent, and clear paragraphs. The first very important technique involves topic sentences.

Organizing Paragraphs Around Topic Sentences

A well-organized paragraph has two important characteristics. First, it covers just one subject. For example, if you are writing about your booth at a computer show, you won't throw in a sentence about trouble with your taxes. Keep all the sentences in a paragraph related to one topic. Second, a well-organized paragraph begins with a topic sentence that summarizes what the paragraph is about. A topic sentence helps readers by preparing them for what follows.

Consider the following scenario. Let's say your company promotes an extensive schedule of team sports for employees after hours. One group enjoys weekend bicycling. You've been assigned the task of writing a memo to the members of this group stating that they must wear helmets when cycling. One paragraph of your memo covers statistics about cycling accidents and the incidence of brain injury for unhelmeted riders. Another paragraph discusses the protection offered by helmets:

> *Helmets protect the brain from injury.* They spread the force of a crash from the point of impact to a wider area. When an accident occurs, an unhelmeted head undergoes two collisions. The first occurs when the skull slams into the ground. The second occurs when the brain hits the inside of the skull. A helmet softens the second blow and acts as a shock absorber. Instead of crushing the brain, the impact crushes the foam core of the helmet, often preventing serious brain injury.

Notice how the preceding paragraph focuses on just one topic: how helmets protect the brain from injury. Every sentence relates to that topic. Notice, too, that the first sentence functions as a topic sentence, informing the reader of the subject of the paragraph.

The best way to write a good paragraph is to list all the ideas you may include. Here's a rough draft of the list of items for the preceding paragraph. Notice that the fourth item doesn't relate to the topic sentence. By listing the ideas to be included in a paragraph, you can immediately see what belongs—and what doesn't. Once the list is made, you can easily write the topic sentence.

Paragraph Idea List
1. Helmets spread force of impact.
2. Crashes cause two collisions, the first when skull hits ground and the second when brain hits skull.
3. Foam core of helmet absorbs impact.
4. ~~The federal government has issued biking regulations requiring helmets.~~

Topic Sentence: Helmets protect the brain from injury.

Skill Check 3.1 Organizing a Paragraph

In a memo to the college president, the athletic director is arguing for a new scoreboard in the gym. One paragraph will describe the old scoreboard and why it needs to be replaced. Study the following list of ideas for that paragraph.

1. The old scoreboard is a tired warhorse that was originally constructed in the 1970s.
2. It's now hard to find replacement parts for it when something breaks.
3. The old scoreboard is not energy efficient.
4. Coca-Cola has offered to buy a new sports scoreboard in return for exclusive rights to sell drinks on campus.
5. The old scoreboard should be replaced for many reasons.
6. It shows only scores for basketball games.
7. When we have track meets, we're without any functioning scoreboard.

    a. Which sentence should be the topic sentence?   _____

    b. Which sentence(s) should be developed in a different paragraph?   _____

    c. Which sentences should follow the topic sentence?   _____

Writing Coherent Paragraphs

Effective paragraphs are coherent; that is, they hold together. Coherence is a quality of good writing that doesn't happen accidentally. It is consciously achieved through effective organization and through skilful use of three devices. These writing devices are (a) repetition of key ideas or key words, (b) use of pronouns that refer clearly to their antecedents, and (c) use of transitional expressions.

Repetition of Key Ideas or Key Words. Repeating a key word or key thought from a preceding sentence helps guide a reader from one thought to the next. This redundancy is necessary to build cohesiveness into writing. Notice how the word *deal* is repeated in the second sentence.

> For the past six months, college administrators and Coca-Cola have been working on a *deal* in which the college would receive a new sports scoreboard. The *deal* would involve exclusive rights to sell non-alcoholic beverages on the 12,000-student campus.

Use of Pronouns That Refer Clearly to Their Antecedents. Pronouns such as *this, that, they, these, those,* and *it* help connect thoughts in sentences. But these pronouns are useful only when their antecedents are clear. Often it's better to make the pronoun into an adjective joined with its antecedent to ensure that the reference is absolutely clear. Notice how the pronoun *this* is clearer when it is joined to its antecedent *contract*.

Confusing:	The Coca-Cola offer requires an exclusive contract committing the college for ten years without any provision preventing a price increase. *This* could be very costly to students, staff, and faculty.
Improved:	The Coca-Cola offer requires an exclusive contract committing the college for ten years without any provision preventing a price increase. *This contract* could be very costly to students, staff, and faculty.

Avoid vague pronouns, such as *it* in the following example.

Confusing:	If your kitten will not drink cold milk, put *it* in the microwave for a few seconds.
Improved:	If your kitten will not drink cold milk, put *the cold milk* in the microwave for a few seconds.

Use of Transitional Expressions. One of the most effective ways to achieve paragraph coherence is through the use of transitional expressions. These expressions act as road signs. They indicate where the message is headed, and they help the reader anticipate what is coming. Some common transitional expressions follow:

also	hence	moreover
as a result	however	nevertheless
consequently	in addition	of course
for example	in this way	on the other hand
for this reason	instead	therefore
furthermore	meanwhile	thus

Other words that act as connectives are *first, second, finally, after, next, after all, specifically, likewise, as,* and *as if.*

The following paragraph achieves coherence through use of all three techniques. (1) The key idea of *surprising battle* in the first sentence is echoed in the second sentence with repetition of the word *battle* coupled with *unexpected,* a synonym for *surprising.* (2) The use of a pronoun, *This,* in the second sentence connects the second sentence to the first. (3) The transitional expressions *however* and *as a result* in following sentences continue to build coherence.

A *surprising battle* between two global cola giants was recently fought in Venezuela. *This battle* was unexpected because Venezuelans had always been loyal Pepsi drinkers. *However,* when the nation's leading bottler sold half of its interest to Coca-Cola, everything changed. *As a result,* Coca-Cola turned the Pepsi-drinking nation of Venezuela into Coke drinkers almost overnight.

Skill Check 3.2 Improving Paragraph Coherence

On a separate sheet of paper, use the information from Skill Check 1 to write a coherent paragraph about replacing the sports scoreboard. Remember that this paragraph is part of a memo from the athletic director to the college president. Include a topic sentence. Strive to illustrate all three techniques to achieve coherence.

Developing Parallel Construction

Paragraph clarity can be improved by using similar grammatical structures to express similar ideas. For example, if you are listing three ideas, do not use *ing* words for two of the ideas and a *to* verb with the third idea: *reading, eating, and studying* (not *to study*). Use adjectives with adjectives, verbs with verbs, phrases with phrases, and clauses with clauses. In the following list, use all verbs: the *machine sorted, stamped, and counted* (not *and had a counter*). For phrases, the wording for all parts of the list should be matched; *safety must be improved in the home, in the classroom, and on the job* (not *for office workers*).

Poor: Miss Tanaga is energetic, resourceful and she can be relied on.

Improved: Miss Tanaga is energetic, resourceful, and reliable. (Matches adjectives.)

Poor: The new shredder helped us save money, reduce pollution, and paper could be recycled.

Improved: The new shredder helped us save money, reduce pollution, and recycle paper. (Matches verb–noun construction.)

Skill Check 3.3 Improving Parallel Construction

Revise each of the following sentences to improve parallel construction.

1. Your job is to research, design, and the implementation of a diversity program.

_____

_____

2. Few managers are able to write letters accurately, concisely, and with efficiency.

_____

_____

3. The new software totals all balances, gives weekly reports, and statements are printed.

_____

_____

For further practice, see Chapter 21 (Exercise B on pp. 401–402.)

Writing Application 3.1 On a separate sheet revise the following paragraph. Add a topic sentence and improve the organization. Correct pronouns with unclear antecedents, wordiness, and misplaced verbal modifiers (which you learned about in Chapter 11). Add transitional expressions if appropriate.

> You may be interested in applying for a new position within the company. The Human Resources Department has a number of jobs available immediately. The positions are at a high level. Current employees may apply immediately for open positions in production, for some in marketing, and jobs in administrative support are also available. To make application, these positions require immediate action. Come to the Human Resources Department. We have a list showing the open positions, what the qualifications are, and job descriptions are shown. Many of the jobs are now open. That's why we are sending this now. To be hired, an interview must be scheduled within the next two weeks.

Writing Application 3.2 On a separate sheet revise the following poorly written paragraph. Add a topic sentence and improve the organization. Correct misplaced modifiers, pronouns with unclear antecedents, wordiness, and any other writing faults. Add transitional expressions if appropriate.

> As you probably already know, this company (Lasertronics) will be installing new computer software shortly. There will be a demonstration April 18, which is a Tuesday. We felt this was necessary because this new software is so different from our previous software. It will be from 9 to 12 a.m. in the morning. This will show employees how the software programs work. They will learn about the operating system, and this should be helpful to nearly everyone. There will be information about the new word processing program, which should be helpful to administrative assistants and product managers. For all you people who work with payroll, there will be information about the new database program. We can't show everything the software will do at this one demo, but for these three areas there will be some help at the Tuesday demo. Oh yes, Paula Roddy will be presenting the demonstration. She is the representative from Quantum Software.

Writing Application 3.3 Assume you work in the Human Resources Department of Imperial Trust. You must write an announcement describing a special program of classes for your employees. Use the following information to write a well-organized paragraph announcement. Explain that Imperial Trust will reimburse any employee the full cost of tuition and books if that employee attends classes. Describe the plan. Skyline Community College, in co-operation with Imperial Trust, will offer a group of courses for college credit at very convenient locations for our employees. Actually, the classes will be offered at your downtown and East Bay branches. Tell employees that they should call Jean Fujimoto at Ext. 660 if they are interested. You'd better mention the tuition: $80 for a semester course. Explain that we (Imperial Trust) are willing to pay these fees because we value education highly. However, make it clear that employees must receive a grade of *C* or higher before they are eligible for reimbursement of course and book fees. It might be a good idea to attach a list of the courses and the times that they will be offered. Include a deadline date for calling Jean.

Modifying and Connecting Words

Modifiers: Adjectives and Adverbs

12

OBJECTIVES

When you have completed the materials in this chapter, you will be able to do the following:

LEVEL I

- *Form the comparative and superlative degrees of regular and irregular adjectives and adverbs.*

- *Use the articles* a *and* an *correctly and avoid double negatives.*

LEVEL II

- *Use adjectives after linking verbs and use adverbs to modify verbs, adjectives, and other adverbs.*

- *Punctuate compound and successive independent adjectives correctly.*

LEVEL III

- *Compare degrees of absolute adjectives and make comparisons within a group.*

- *Place adverbs and adjectives close to the words they modify.*

PRETEST

Underline the correct word.

1. This is the (worse, worst) business report I've ever read.

2. It is (a, an) honour to be selected by the interviewing committee.

3. If you did (good, well) enough in the interview, you will be hired.

4. Our (six-year-old, six year old) lease must be renegotiated.

5. The (newly repaired, newly-repaired) copier seems to be working well.

1. worst 2. an 3. well 4. six-year-old 5. newly repaired

Both adjectives and adverbs act as modifiers; that is, they describe or limit other words. Since many of the forms and functions of adjectives and adverbs are similar and since faulty usage often results from the confusion of these two parts of speech, adjectives and adverbs will be treated together in this chapter.

LEVEL I

Hotlink

The Parts of Speech section of **<http://www.ucalgary.ca/UofC/eduweb/grammar/>** has an excellent page that will help you practise distinguishing between adjectives and adverbs.

Career Tip

Good writers avoid vague and overworked adverbs and adjectives (such as *interesting, good, nice, great, really,* and *bad*). Strive for precise words that say exactly what you mean.

Spot the Blooper

From an editorial in *U.S. News & World Report:* "Of two interpretations of conduct, they prefer the worst."

▶ Basic Functions of Adjectives and Adverbs

Adjectives describe or limit nouns and pronouns. As you have already learned, they often answer the questions *what kind? how many?* or *which one?* Adjectives in the following sentences are italicized.

> *Short* visits are *the best* visits.
> *Large government* grants were awarded to *the eight top* institutions.

Adverbs describe or limit verbs, adjectives, or other adverbs. They often answer the questions *when? how? where?* or *to what extent?*

> *Yesterday* our work went *slowly.*
> He answered *quite decisively.*

Comparative and Superlative Forms

Most adjectives and adverbs have three forms, or *degrees*: positive, comparative, and superlative. The examples below illustrate how the comparative and superlative degrees of regular adjectives and adverbs are formed.

	Positive	**Comparative**	**Superlative**
Adjective:	warm	warmer	warmest
Adverb:	warmly	more warmly	most warmly
Adjective:	careful	more careful	most careful
Adverb:	carefully	more carefully	most carefully

The positive degree of an adjective or an adverb is used in merely describing or in limiting another word. The comparative degree is used to compare two persons or things. The superlative degree is used in the comparison of three or more persons or things.

The comparative degree of short adjectives (nearly all one-syllable and most two-syllable adjectives ending in *y*) is usually formed by adding *r* or *er* (*warmer*). The superlative degree of short adjectives is usually formed by the addition of *st* or *est* (*warmest*). Long adjectives, and those difficult to pronounce, form the comparative and superlative degrees, as do adverbs, with the addition of *more* and *most* (*more careful, most careful*). The following sentences illustrate degrees of comparison for adjectives and adverbs.

Adjectives:	Sales are unusually *high.*	(Positive degree)
	Sales are *higher* than ever before.	(Comparative degree)
	Sales are the *highest* in years.	(Superlative degree)
Adverbs:	He drives *carefully.*	(Positive degree)
	He drives *more carefully* now.	(Comparative degree)
	He drives *most carefully* at night.	(Superlative degree)

Do *not* create a double comparative form by using *more* and the suffix *er* together (such as *more neater*) or by using *most* and the suffix *est* together (such as *most fastest*).

A few adjectives and adverbs form the comparative and the superlative degrees irregularly. Common irregular adjectives include *good* (*better, best*), *bad* (*worse, worst*), *little* (*less, least*), and *many* (*more, most*). Common irregular adverbs include *well* (*better, best*) and *much* (*more, most*).

Modifiers That Deserve Special Attention

Adjectives as Articles. The articles *a, an,* and *the* merit special attention. When describing a specific person or thing, use the definite article *the*, as in *the* film. When describing persons or things in general, use the indefinite articles *a* or *an*, as in *a film* (meaning *any* film). The choice of *a* or *an* is determined by the initial sound of the word modified. Use *a* before consonant sounds; use *an* before vowel sounds.

Before Vowel Sounds		Before Consonant Sounds	
an operator		a shop	
an executive		a plan	
an hour	*h* is not voiced;	a hook	*h* is voiced
an honour	vowel is heard	a hole	
an office	*o* sounds like a	a one-man show	*o* sounds like
an onion	vowel	a one-week trip	the consonant *w*
an understudy	*u* sounds like	a union	*u* sounds like
an umbrella	a vowel	a unit	the consonant *y*
an X-ray	*X* and *M* sound	a xylophone	*x* sounds like the
	like vowels ("ex"		consonant *z*;
an M.D.	and "em")	a meteor	*m* consonant sound is heard

Adverbs and Double Negatives. When a negative adverb (*no, not, scarcely, hardly, barely*) is used in the same sentence with a negative verb (*didn't, don't, won't*), a substandard construction called a *double negative* results. Such constructions are considered illogical. In the following examples, notice how eliminating one negative corrects the double negative.

Incorrect:	Calling her *won't* do *no* good.
Correct:	Calling her will do no good.
Correct:	Calling her won't do any good.
Incorrect:	We *couldn't hardly* believe the news report.
Correct:	We could hardly believe the news report.
Correct:	We couldn't believe the news report.
Incorrect:	Drivers *can't barely* see in the heavy fog.
Correct:	Drivers can barely see in the heavy fog.
Correct:	Drivers can't see in the heavy fog.

Study Tip

The sound, not the spelling, of a word governs the choice between *a* and *an*. When the letter *u* sounds like a *y*, it is treated as a consonant: a *utility*, a *used* car.

Hotlink

ESL students will find the Rensselaer Polytechnic Institute material on article usage **<http://www.rpi.edu/dept/llc/writecenter/web/esl.html>** particularly helpful.

Did You Know?

At one time in the history of the English language (going back farther than Chaucer), multiple negatives were used to emphasize an idea. (*Don't never say nothing wicked!*) But in the 18th century, grammarians adopted Latin logic and decreed that two negatives created a positive.

Hotlink

To learn more about the antiquity of the double negative, visit **<http://www.bartleby.com/185/45.html>**. Is a double negative bad grammar and vulgar?

The Adjectives *this/that* and *these/those*. The adjective *this* and its plural form *these* indicate something nearby. The adjective *that* and its plural form *those* indicate something at a distance. Be careful to use the singular forms of these words with singular nouns and the plural forms with plural nouns: *this shoe, that road, these accounts, those records*. Pay special attention to the nouns *kind, type,* and *sort*. Match singular adjectives to the singular forms of these nouns and plural adjectives to the plural forms.

Incorrect: Job candidates should be prepared for *these type questions*.
Correct: Job candidates should be prepared for this type of question.
Correct: Job candidates should be prepared for these types of questions.

Complete the reinforcement exercises for Level I on pp. 217–218.

LEVEL II

Career Tip

The misuse of *badly* for *bad* is one of the errors made most frequently by educated persons. Following the linking verb *feel*, use the adjective *bad*, not the adverb *badly*.

Spot the Blooper

From a full-page IBM advertisement: "Can you really buy a computer that makes someone feel differently about their job?" (Do you see two problems?)

▶ **Problems With Adjectives and Adverbs**

In the following discussion you will learn not to confuse adjectives with adverbs. You will also learn to express compound adjectives and independent adjectives.

Confusion of Adjectives and Adverbs

Because they are closely related, adjectives are sometimes confused with adverbs. Here are guidelines that will help you avoid common adjective–adverb errors.

1. Use adjectives to modify nouns and pronouns. Note particularly that adjectives (not adverbs) should follow linking verbs.

    This orange tastes *sweet*. (Not *sweetly*—adjective modifies the noun *orange*)
    I feel *bad* about the loss. (Not *badly*)
    He looks *good* in his uniform. (Not *well*)

2. Use adverbs to describe verbs, adjectives, or other adverbs.

    The engine runs *smoothly*. (Not *smooth*)
    It runs *more smoothly* than before. (Not *smoother*)
    Listen *carefully* to the directions. (Not *careful*)
    He listened *really well*. (Not *real good*)

Note that a few adverbs have two acceptable forms: *slow, slowly; deep, deeply; direct, directly; close, closely*. Check your dictionary for the uses of such forms.

    Drive *slowly*. (Or, less formally, *slow*)
    Pack the fruits *closely*. (Or, less formally, *close*)

Compound Adjectives

Writers may form their own adjectives by joining two or more words. When these words act as a single modifier preceding a noun, they are temporarily hyphenated. If these same words appear after a noun, they are generally not hyphenated.

Words Temporarily Hyphenated Before a Noun	Same Words Not Hyphenated After a Noun
never-say-die attitude	attitude of never say die
eight-storey building	building of eight storeys
a case-by-case analysis	analysis that is case by case
high-performance computer	computer that has high performance
income-related expenses	expenses that are related to income
four-year-old child	child who is four years old
out-of-warranty repair	repair that is out of warranty

Compound adjectives shown in your dictionary with hyphens are considered permanently hyphenated. Regardless of whether such a compound appears before or after a noun, it retains the hyphens. Use a current dictionary to determine what expressions are always hyphenated. Be sure that you find the dictionary entry that is marked *adjective*. Here are samples:

Permanent Hyphens Before Nouns	Permanent Hyphens After Nouns
old-fashioned attitude	attitude that is old-fashioned
short-term loan	loan that is short-term
well-behaved child	the child is well-behaved
well-rounded program	the program that is well-rounded
first-class service	service was first-class

Spot the Blooper

Headline in *The Milwaukee Sentinel*: "Police killing suspect to be tried as an adult." (What unintended meaning resulted from the omission of a hyphen?)

Don't confuse adverbs ending in *ly* with compound adjectives: *newly decorated* office and *highly regarded* architect would not be hyphenated.

In some cases hyphens are not used. When familiar compound nouns, written as separate words (e.g., *income tax*, *community college*), are used as adjectives, they are not hyphenated. Proper names used as adjectives are not hyphenated either. Here are some examples:

car insurance policy	real estate agent
charge account customer	St. Lawrence Seaway locks
home office staff	Royal Bank account
data processing centre	Wayne Gretzky poster

Independent Adjectives

Two or more successive adjectives that independently modify a noun are separated by commas. No comma is needed, however, when the first adjective modifies the combined idea of the second adjective and the noun.

Study Tip

To determine whether successive adjectives are independent, mentally insert the word *and* between them. If the insertion makes sense, the adjectives are probably independent and require a comma.

Two Adjectives Independently Modifying a Noun	First Adjective Modifying a Second Adjective Plus a Noun
confident, self-reliant individual	efficient administrative assistant
attractive, efficient car	blue sports car
short, provocative book	luxurious mobile home

Special Cases

The following adjectives and adverbs cause difficulty for many writers and speakers. With a little study, you can master their correct usage.

almost (adv.—nearly):	Almost (not *Most*) everybody wants to work.
most (adv.—greatest in amount):	*Most* people want to work.

farther (adv.—actual distance):	How much *farther* is the market?
further (adv.—additionally):	To argue the matter *further* is fruitless.
sure (adj.—certain):	He is *sure* of victory.
surely (adv.—undoubtedly):	He will *surely* be victorious.
later (adv.—after expected time):	The contract arrived *later* in the day.
latter (adj.—the second of two things):	Of the two options, I prefer the *latter*.
fewer (adj.—refers to numbers):	*Fewer* requests for tours were granted this year.
less (adj.—refers to amounts or quantities):	*Less* time remains than we anticipated.
real (adj.—actual, genuine):	The *real* power in the company lies with the treasurer.
really (adv.—actually, truly):	Jan wondered if she could *really* learn to operate the equipment in five hours.
good (adj.—desirable):	A number of *good* plans were submitted.
well { (adv.—satisfactorily) (adj.—healthy)	Robert did *well* on the test. Deborah feels quite *well* since the operation.

Complete the reinforcement exercises for Level II on pp. 219–221.

LEVEL III

❝❞

Notable Quotable

"The difference between the almost-right word and the right word is ... [like] the difference between the lightning bug and the lightning."
—Mark Twain

▶ Other Uses of Adjectives and Adverbs

In this section you will learn how to use absolute modifiers, how to make comparisons within a group, and how to place adjectives and adverbs appropriately in sentences.

Absolute Modifiers

Adjectives and adverbs that name perfect or complete (absolute) qualities cannot logically be compared. For example, to say that one ball is *more round* than another ball is illogical. Here are some absolute words that should not be used in comparisons:

round	dead	complete
perfect	true	right
unique	correct	straight
perpendicular	endless	unanimous

Authorities suggest, however, that some absolute adjectives may be compared by the use of the words *more nearly* or *most nearly*. Study the following sentences for various alternatives:

Illogical:	A truer statement has never been spoken.
Logical:	A more nearly true statement has never been spoken.
Illogical:	This rose is the most perfect flower in our garden.
Logical:	This rose is the most nearly perfect flower in our garden.

Illogical:	A straighter route through the Prairies is the Trans-Canada Highway.
Logical:	A more nearly straight route through the Prairies is the Trans-Canada Highway.

Comparisons Within a Group

When the word *than* is used to compare a person, place, or thing with other members of a group to which it belongs, be certain to include the words *other* or *else* in the comparison. This inclusion ensures that the meaning of the comparison is absolutely clear.

Illogical:	Calgary is larger than any city in Alberta. (This sentence suggests that Calgary is larger than itself or that it is not a city in Alberta.)
Logical:	Calgary is larger than any *other* city in Alberta.
Illogical:	Our team had more points than any league team. (Implies that our team does not belong to the league.)
Logical:	Our team had more points than any *other* league team.
Illogical:	Alex works harder than anyone in the office.
Logical:	Alex works harder than anyone *else* in the office.

Placing Adverbs and Adjectives

The position of an adverb or adjective can seriously affect the meaning of a sentence. Study these examples:

Only I can program this computer. (No one else can program it.)
I can *only* program this computer. (I can't do anything else to it.)
I can program *only* this computer. (I can't program any other computer.)

To avoid confusion, adverbs and adjectives should be placed close to the words they modify. In this regard, special attention should be given to the words *only, merely, first,* and *last.*

Confusing:	He *merely* said that all soldiers couldn't be generals.
Clear:	He said *merely* that all soldiers couldn't be generals.
Confusing:	Seats in the five *first* rows have been reserved.
Clear:	Seats in the *first* five rows have been reserved.

Complete the reinforcement exercises for Level III on pp. 222–223.

HOTLINE QUERIES

Question: One of my favourite words is *hopefully,* but I understand that it's often used improperly. How should it be used?

Answer: Language purists insist that the word *hopefully* be used to modify a verb (*we looked at the door hopefully, expecting Mr. Gross to return momentarily*). The word *hopefully* should not be used as a substitute for *I hope that* or *We hope that* in formal English. Instead of saying, *Hopefully, interest rates will decline,* one should say, *I hope that interest rates will decline.*

Question: Is it necessary to hyphenate a *25 per cent discount*?

Answer: No. Per cents are not treated in the same way that numbers appearing in compound adjectives are treated. Thus, you would not hyphenate a *15 per cent loan*, but you would hyphenate a *15-year loan*.

Question: Should hyphens be used in *a point-by-point analysis*?

Answer: Yes. When words are combined in order to create a single adjective preceding a noun, these words are temporarily hyphenated (*last-minute decision, two-semester course, step-by-step procedures*).

Question: In my writing I want to use *firstly* and *secondly.* Are they acceptable?

Answer: Both words are acceptable, but most good writers prefer *first* and *second* because they are more efficient and equally accurate.

Question: How many hyphens should I use in this sentence? *The three, four, and five year plans continue to be funded.*

Answer: Three hyphens are needed: *three-, four-,* and *five-year plans.* Hyphenate compound adjectives even when the parts of the compound are separated or suspended.

Question: Why can't I remember how to spell *already*? I want to use it in this sentence: *Your account has <u>already</u> been credited with your payment.*

Answer: You—and many others—have difficulty with *already* because two different words (and meanings) are expressed by essentially the same sounds. The adverb *already* means "previously" or "before this time," as in your sentence. The two-word combination *all ready* means "all prepared," as in *The club members are all ready to board the bus.* If you can logically insert the word *completely* between *all* and *ready,* you know the two-word combination is needed.

Question: I never know how to write *part time.* Is it always hyphenated?

Answer: The dictionary shows all of its uses to be hyphenated. *She was a part-time employee* (used as adjective). *He worked part-time* (used as adverb).

Question: Here are some expressions that caused us trouble in our business letters. We want to hyphenate all of the following. Right? *Well-produced play, awareness-generation film, decision-making tables, one-paragraph note, swearing-in ceremony, commonly-used book.*

Answer: All your hyphenated forms are correct except the last one. Don't use a hyphen with an *ly*-ending adverb.

Question: Why are these two expressions treated differently: *two-week vacation* and *two weeks' vacation*?

Answer: Although they express the same idea, they represent two different styles. If you omit the *s, two-week* is hyphenated because it is a compound adjective. If you add the *s,* as in *two weeks' vacation,* the expression becomes possessive and requires an apostrophe. Don't use both styles together (not *two-weeks' vacation*).

CHAPTER 12   Reinforcement Exercises

A. **(Self-check)** Write the correct forms in the spaces provided.

LEVEL I

1. This is undoubtedly the (worse, worst) coffee we have ever drunk. _____

2. It is certainly (worse, worst) than yesterday's coffee. _____

3. (This, These) sort of error could be prevented through more careful training. _____

4. I can't think of a (better, more better) plan. _____

5. We (can, can't) hardly work in this room without air conditioning. _____

6. Is Chris or Margaret the (better, best) person for the job? _____

7. Examine closely the blades on (this, these) pair of scissors. _____

8. Driving to the bank and back requires at least (a, an) hour's time. _____

9. Rainfall for this year (has, hasn't) been barely 22 centimetres. _____

10. The outcome of the race between Connors and Morelli will determine the (faster, fastest) driver. _____

Check your answers.

B. Write the correct form in the spaces provided.

1. (That sort, Those sorts) of businesses have been asked to restrict exports. _____

2. Bill Gates is the (more, most) powerful of the software manufacturers. _____

3. Audrey keeps (a, an) umbrella in her office at all times. _____

4. Ask the tailor if (this, these) pair of pants is ready. _____

5. After paying his taxes, Gunther complained that he (has, hasn't) barely a dollar left. _____

6. Health care and communications are two service industries growing at (a, an) unusually fast pace. _____

7. Of the four brothers and sisters, he is the (younger, youngest). _____

8. Which of these two colours is (better, best) for the hall? _____

9. Susan said she couldn't see (no, any) other way to install the program. _____

10. The company couldn't give (nothing, anything) to its favourite charity this year. _____

1. worst 2. worse 3. This 4. better 5. can 6. better 7. this 8. an 9. has 10. faster

C. Can you find 12 errors in this paragraph? Cross out the errors, and write the correct form above the line. *Hint:* eight errors involve adverbs and adjectives from Level I.

In Winnipeg a officer of a bank was involved in one of the worse embezzlement schemes in the banks history. Because of lax bank controls, the embezzler was able to withdraw hundreds of thousands of dollars in a unprecedented banking loss. To avoid detection by the banks computer fraud defences, the embezzler took advantage of his position as an bank officer. The scheme involved making debit and credit transactions in two offices, but the embezzler found the Winnipeg office was best for withdrawals. As the size of the theft grew, the bank officer couldn't hardly conceal it any longer. The bank discovered it's loss when the embezzler made a error in filling out a credit slip instead of a debit slip. Embarrassed bank officials have announced there intention to set up new operational controls to prevent these kind of fraudulent scheme in the future.

D. Supply the proper article (*a* or *an*) for the following words:

Example: ___an___ adjustment

1. _____ number	7. _____ warehouse	13. _____ insult
2. _____ honour	8. _____ agency	14. _____ X-ray
3. _____ inventory	9. _____ combination	15. _____ illegible letter
4. _____ pattern	10. _____ idea	16. _____ one-year lease
5. _____ hammock	11. _____ utility	17. _____ eight-year lease
6. _____ orange	12. _____ airplane	18. _____ oil embargo

E. In the space provided, write the correct comparative or superlative form of the adjective shown in parentheses.

Example: Of the three filing systems, which is (good)? ___*best*___

1. He was the (tall) player on the team. _____

2. This is the (good) illustration submitted thus far. _____

3. Please send me the (current) figures you can find. _____

4. The 20-pound stationery is (heavy) than the 16-pound paper. _____

5. It appears that this plan is (costly) than our previous insurance coverage. _____

6. Of all the employees Richard is the (little) talkative. _____

7. Ms. Hansen is (businesslike) than the office manager she replaced. _____

8. Have you ever met a (kind) individual than Mr. Stevenson? _____

9. This is the (bad) winter we've had in years. _____

10. Which is the (interesting) of the two novels? _____

NAME _____

A. (**Self-check**) Select the correct form, and write it in the space provided.

1. Brendan looked (calm, calmly) as the verdict was read. _____

2. The lighthouse is (farther, further) away than it first appeared. _____

3. Better service is ensured if a purchaser has (face-to-face, face to face) dealings with the manufacturer. _____

4. (Fewer, Less) homes have been constructed than ever before. _____

5. Unless data can be assembled (quicker, more quickly), we lose business to our competitors. _____

6. Mr. Burton (sure, surely) made his personal feelings apparent when he announced the policy change. _____

7. Because he forgot your birthday, Matthew felt (bad, badly). _____

8. Of probationary and permanent employees, only the (later, latter) are eligible for tuition reimbursement. _____

9. Some small businesses barely exist from (year-to-year, year to year). _____

10. Asked about her health, Aunt Edna said she felt (good, well). _____

Check your answers.

B. Write the correct words in the spaces provided.

1. For about a week our new copier worked just (perfect, perfectly). _____

2. Because of the construction decline, (fewer, less) housing is available. _____

3. Lee thought that she did (good, well) in her interview. _____

4. Honeydew melons taste (good, well) with lemon juice. _____

5. Our office manager will (sure, surely) call for repairs. _____

6. Since its tune-up, the engine runs (smoother, more smoothly). _____

7. Lavonda wasn't (real, really) sure she could attend. _____

8. I hope you won't take this comment (personal, personally). _____

9. Do these peaches taste (bitter, bitterly) to you? _____

10. Your new suit certainly fits you (good, well). _____

11. The new suit looks very (good, well) on you. _____

12. She wanted to debate the question (further, farther). _____

13. He completed the aptitude test (satisfactory, satisfactorily). _____

14. If you write (fewer, less) cheques, your service charges will decline. _____

15. Henry feels (sure, surely) that part-time salaries will improve. _____

16. (Most, Almost) everyone agreed that work is the price one pays for money. _____

17. Four specialists keyed the lengthy report (perfect, perfectly). _____

18. To reduce costs, they pressed for a settlement (quick, quickly). _____

19. Mr. Turner was (sure, surely) proud of his pilot's licence. _____

20. Recovering from his illness, Luis said he felt (good, well). _____

C. Select the correct group of words below. Write its letter in the space provided.

1. (a) coast to coast broadcast
(b) coast-to-coast broadcast _____

2. (a) well-documented report
(b) well documented report _____

3. (a) child who is ten-years-old
(b) child who is ten years old _____

4. (a) ten-year-old child
(b) ten year old child _____

5. (a) fully certified nurse
(b) fully-certified nurse _____

6. (a) pet that is well behaved
(b) pet that is well-behaved _____

7. (a) data-processing service
(b) data processing service _____

8. (a) arm-twisting tactics
(b) arm twisting tactics _____

9. (a) last-minute preparations
(b) last minute preparations _____

10. (a) widely-acclaimed cure
(b) widely acclaimed cure _____

11. (a) Red-River cart
(b) Red River cart _____

12. (a) tongue-tied child
(b) tongue tied child _____

Are any of the above in your dictionary?

D. Place commas where needed in the following groups of words.

1. red sports car

2. narrow winding path

3. concise courteous letter

4. snug cheerful apartment

5. imaginative daring designer

6. efficient clerical employee

E. Write sentences using the following words as compound adjectives. Be sure that the compound adjectives precede nouns.

Example: (on the spot) _We offer on-the-spot appraisals._

1. (three year old) _____

_____

2. (once in a lifetime) _____

_____

3. (month by month) _____

_____

4. (work related) _____

_____

5. (first time) _____

_____

LEVEL III

A. **(Self-check)** Underline any errors in the following sentences, and write their corrected forms in the spaces provided. If a sentence is correct as it is written, write *C*.

Example: Elwood is the <u>most unique</u> individual I know.   *most nearly unique*

1. Because he used a ruler, his line is more straight than mine.   _____

2. Professor Anita Fugi is the most conscientious teacher I've ever had.   _____

3. She is more conscientious than any teacher I've ever had.   _____

4. We were told to answer the ten last questions.   _____

5. Gomez has the most perfect sales routine in the business.   _____

6. Preston is only concerned with your welfare and happiness.   _____

7. He merely thought you wanted one page copied.   _____

8. Mountains in the West are more perpendicular than those in the East.   _____

9. Tourists often say that Quebec City is the most fascinating city in Canada.   _____

10. Toronto is more cosmopolitan than any city in Ontario.   _____

Check your answers.

B. Underline errors, and write corrected forms in the spaces provided. If correct, write *C*.

1. The *Times* story about the embezzlement is more accurate than the *Globe* article.   _____

2. For rapid sale, the 15 last homes were drastically reduced.   _____

3. I would rather sell property for Doris than for any broker in the area.   _____

4. Is this the most correct answer among all the applicants' tests?   _____

5. Bricklin only produced quality custom cars.   _____

6. Halifax is the largest city in Nova Scotia.   _____

7. Halifax is larger than any city in Nova Scotia.   _____

8. That encyclopedia is only sold by door-to-door salespeople.   _____

9. Kinko's offers the most complete office service in town.   _____

10. The two first applicants were extremely well-spoken.   _____

1. more nearly straight 2. C 3. any other teacher 4. last ten questions 5. most nearly perfect 6. with only 7. you merely wanted or wanted merely one 8. more nearly perpendicular 9. C 10. any other city

C. Review of Levels I, II, and III. For each sentence below, underline any error. Then write a corrected form in the space provided.

1. It took us over a hour to decipher a nearly unreadable handwritten memo. _____

2. Is Model Z3 or Model X10 best for our office needs? _____

3. Sandy said that she couldn't barely hear you when you called. _____

4. Because of excessive costs, designer Donna Karan made less trips to the Far East and Africa in search of "creative inspiration." _____

5. Hawkins interviewed a Canadian official and an European diplomat concerning the proposed two-year trade program. _____

6. If deliveries can't be made more quicker, we will change carriers. _____

7. In using our newly-installed voice mail system, be sure to leave clear, complete messages. _____

8. One applicant felt that he had done good on the skills test. _____

9. I like this job better than any job I've ever had. _____

10. We can better judge our inventory once we have conducted our end of the year stock count. _____

11. The designer attempted to create an attractive functional working environment. _____

12. We only try to file necessary paperwork. _____

13. Did you say that the two first rows had empty seats? _____

14. He passed my desk so quick I hardly saw him. _____

15. Dana made a point by point comparison of the machines. _____

D. Optional Composition. Your instructor may ask you to complete this exercise on a separate sheet. Write original sentences using the following adjectives: *state of the art, step by step, federally funded, fast moving,* and *fewer.* In addition, write sentences using the following words as adverbs: *well, farther, further, already,* and *only.*

Editor's Challenge

The following memo proposal contains intentional errors representing language principles covered thus far, spelling, and proofreading. Use standard proofreading marks to show your corrections.

Rawlinson Enterprises
Interoffice Memo

DATE: June 5, 200x

TO: Larry LaGrange, Vice-President, Operations

FROM: Elyse Ellerman, Manager, Accounting

SUBJECT: INSTALLATION OF UNDERCARPET WIRING

Proposal

Because the Accounting Department needs a flexible economical wiring system that can accommodate our ever changing electrical needs. That's why I propose that we install a flat undercarpet wiring system.

Present System

At this time the Accounting Department has an out of date system of floor wiring and power poles that limit us to surface wiring. This network of surface wiring appear to be totally overwhelmed by the demands we are now placing on them. The operation of 27 pieces of equipment in addition to 34 telephone lines require extensive electrical circuits and cabling. Moreover, our overhead lighting, which consist of fluorescent fixtures in a suspended egg-crate structure, contains excessive wiring above the ceiling. Technicians whom have came to our office have said that its the worse system theyve ever saw.

Advantages of Proposed System

Cabling for telephone, power, and data are now available in a flat form only 1 mm thick. This flat flexible cable can be install underneath existing carpeting. Thus preventing costly and disruptive renovation. Undercarpet wiring would mean less office power poles. Moreover, flat cables can be moved easy, giving we accountants greater flexibility when we need to add equipment. Installation of a undercarpet wiring system in the Accounting Department would also enable the company to evaluate the systems affectiveness before considering it for other departments.

Cost and Savings

Suppliers and consultants estimates that an undercarpet wiring system for the Accounting department would cost about $75,000. If we was to use conventional methods to install round wiring, we would have to renovate our entire department, costing over $300,000. Equally important, however, is the savings in terms of productivity and employee satisfaction. Which would decline if renovation was required.

Underline the correct word.

1. We seem to have (fewer, less) applications than ever before.

2. Please use (a, an) orange marking pen to highlight the report.

3. Mrs. Sherman said she felt (good, well) following her surgery.

4. Yusef completed a (page by page, page-by-page) check of the book.

5. The employees liked their (completely-redecorated, completely redecorated) office.

 # learning.web.ways

Your boss heard a news story on the way to work, and she asks you to verify it. Many newspapers have on-line editions that provide the latest news at no cost.

Goal: To use an on-line newpaper.

1. With your Web browser on the screen, go to **<http://www.globeandmail. com>**.

2. Make a list of the headlines for the top three news stories. Read one of the stories, and summarize it in one or two sentences.

3. To look at another newspaper, key this URL: **<http://www.buscomm. nelson.com>**.

4. Enter the textbook site, and click on **Research Tools**.

5. Then click on **Canadian and World Newspapers**. Select a newspaper that interests you.

6. As before, make a list of the headlines of the top three news stories. Read one of the stories, and summarize it in one or two sentences.

7. End your session, and submit your lists and summaries.

1. fewer 2. an 3. well 4. page-by-page 5. completely redecorated

Prepositions

13

OBJECTIVES   When you have completed the materials in this chapter, you will be able to do the following:

LEVEL I
- *Use objective case pronouns as objects of prepositions.*
- *Avoid using prepositions in place of verbs and adverbs.*

LEVEL II
- *Use nine troublesome prepositions correctly.*
- *Omit unnecessary prepositions and retain necessary ones.*
- *Construct formal sentences that avoid terminal prepositions.*

LEVEL III
- *Recognize words and constructions requiring specific prepositions (idioms).*

PRETEST

Underline the correct word.

1. Speed is important, but proofreading is necessary (to, too).
2. (As, Like) I said, all our documents must be accurate.
3. Do you plan (on taking, to take) a two-week vacation?
4. Management and workers alike agreed (to, with) the contract.
5. The printer should be placed (beside, besides) the computer.

1. too 2. As 3. to take 4. to 5. beside

Prepositions are connecting words that show the relationship of a noun or pronoun to another word in a sentence. This chapter reviews the use of objective case pronouns following prepositions. It also focuses on common problems that communicators have with troublesome prepositions. Finally, it presents many words in our language that require specific prepositions (idiomatic expressions) to sound "right."

LEVEL I

Career Tip

"You are the same today that you are going to be five years from now except for two things: the people with whom you associate and the books you read."
—Charles Jones

▶ Common Use of Prepositions

In this list of commonly used prepositions, notice that prepositions may consist of one word or several.

about	beside	in addition to	since
according to	between	in spite of	through
after	but	into	to
along with	by	like	under
among	during	of	until
around	except	off	upon
at	for	on	with
before	from	on account of	within
below	in	over	without

Objective Case Following Prepositions

As you will recall from Chapter 6, pronouns that are objects of prepositions must be in the objective case.

> Marian, *along with* Jan and *her*, arrived later.
> We received pledges *from him* and *her* for the charity bike ride.
> Give the account balances *to* Mr. Love and *him*.

To review further, recall that some prepositions—such as *like, between, but,* and *except*—are particularly likely to lead to confusion in determining pronoun case. Consider the following examples.

> Strictly *between* you and *me* (not *I*), the contract is already signed.
> Applications from individuals *like* Mr. Sheldon and *him* (not *he*) are rare.
> Recommendations from everyone *but them* (not *they*) have arrived.

Fundamental Problems With Prepositions

In even the most casual speech or writing, the following misuses of prepositions should be avoided.

Spot the Blooper

Colorado Springs trafffic sign: "Following to close." (City officials blamed the sign company, which had shortened "Following too closely" because it didn't fit.)

***Of* for *have*.** The verb phrases *should have* or *could have* should never be written as *should of* or *could of*. The word *of* is a preposition and cannot be used in verb phrases.

> Jeremy *should have* (not *should of*) called first.
> He *could have* (not *could of*) given some advance notice.

***Off* for *from*.** The preposition *from* should never be replaced by *off* or *off of*.

> My friend borrowed money *from* (not *off of*) me.
> Doreen said she got the book *from* (not *off* or *off of*) you.

***To* for *too*.** The preposition *to* means "in a direction toward." Do not use the word *to* in place of the adverb *too*, which means "additionally," "also," or "excessively."

Dividends are not distributed *to* shareholders unless declared by the directors.
No dividends were declared because profits were *too* small.
Contributions of services will be accepted *too*.

You will recall that the word *to* may also be part of an infinitive construction.

She is learning *to* program the computer.

Complete the reinforcement exercises for Level I on pp. 234–235.

▶ Troublesome Prepositions

Be particularly careful to use the following prepositions properly.

Among, between. *Among* is usually used to speak of three or more persons or things; *between* is usually used for two.

The disagreement was *between* Stipchek and his partner.
Supplies were distributed *among* the four divisions.

Beside, besides. *Beside* means "next to"; *besides* means "in addition to."

Please sit *beside* me at the assembly.
Besides a preface, you must write an introduction.

Except. The preposition *except,* meaning "excluding" or "but," is sometimes confused with the verb *accept,* which means "to receive."

Everyone *except* Melanie was able to come.
Please *accept* this gift as a token of our appreciation.

In, into. *In* indicates a position or location. *Into* indicates direction or movement to an interior location.

We store copy paper *in* the supply cabinet. (The preposition *in* indicates location.)
Bring the boxes *into* the storeroom. (Preposition *into* indicates movement to an interior location.)

Some constructions may employ *in* as an adverb preceding an infinitive. The two words must then be written separately.

They went *in* to see the manager. (Adverb *in* precedes infinitive *to see.*)

Like. The preposition *like* should be used to introduce a noun or pronoun. Do not use *like* to introduce a clause (a group of words with a subject and a predicate). Use a conjunction like *as* in this case. (Conjunctions will be discussed further in Chapters 14 and 15.)

The copy looks very much *like* the original. (*Like* is used as preposition introducing the noun *original.*)
It looks *as if* (not *like*) it may rain. (*As if* is used to introduce the clause *it may rain.*)
As (not *like*) I said earlier, the order was sent. (Do not use *like* to introduce the clause *I said earlier.*)

Notable Quotable

"Success isn't how far you got, but the distance you travelled from where you started."
—Peter Frame

Study Tip

Look at the word(s) following *like.* If many words follow, chances are they function as a clause; use *as, as if,* or *as though* instead of *like.*

▶ Using Prepositions Efficiently

Necessary Prepositions

Don't omit those prepositions necessary to clarify a relationship. Be particularly careful when two prepositions modify a single object.

> We have every desire *for* and hope *of* an early settlement. (Do not omit *for*.)
> What type *of* coupler do you need? (Do not omit *of*.)
> Mr. Munoz is unsure *of* where to place the machine. (Do not omit *of*.)
> Salaries for temporary positions seem to be higher than *for* permanent positions. (Do not omit *for*.)
> When did you graduate *from* high school? (Do not omit *from*.)*

Unnecessary Prepositions

Omit unnecessary prepositions, particularly the word *of*.

> The book fell *off* the desk. (Not *off of*)
> Leave the package *inside* the door. (Not *inside of*)
> Both Web sites are useful. (Not *of the* Web sites)
> All the letters require stationery. (Not *of the* letters)
> Where is the meeting? (Not meeting *at*)
> She could not help laughing. (Not *help from*)
> Keep the paper *near* the printer. (Not *near to*)

Ending a Sentence With a Preposition

In the past, language authorities warned against ending a sentence (or a clause) with a preposition. In formal writing today most careful authors continue to avoid terminal prepositions. In conversation, however, terminal prepositions are acceptable.

Informal Usage	Formal Usage
What organization is he a member *of*?	*Of* what organization is he a member?
What is the medicine prescribed *for*?	*For* what is the medicine prescribed?
How many forms did you write *on*?	*On* how many forms did you write?
We don't know whom you spoke *to* when you called.	We don't know *to* whom you spoke when you called.

Complete the reinforcement exercises for Level II on pp. 236–238.

LEVEL III

▶ Idiomatic Use of Prepositions

Every language has idioms (word combinations peculiar to that language). These combinations have developed through usage and often cannot be explained rationally. A native speaker usually is unaware of idiom usage until a violation jars his or her ear, such as "He is capable *from* (rather than *of*) violence."

---

* See Hotline Queries on p. 232.

The list below shows words that require specific prepositions to denote precise meanings. This group is just a sampling of the large number of English idioms involving prepositions. Consult a dictionary when you are unsure of the correct preposition to use with a particular word.

acquaint with	You must become *acquainted with* the new equipment.
adept in	Are you *adept in* programming?
adhere to	All employees must *adhere to* certain office rules.
agree to (a proposal)	Did they *agree to* the plan for splitting shifts?
agree with (a person)	In this matter I certainly *agree with* you.
angry at (a thing)	Customers are understandably *angry at* the delay.
angry with (a person)	How can you be *angry with* the child?
bored with	Terry became *bored with* his repetitive duties.
buy from	You may *buy from* any one of several wholesalers.
capable of	She is *capable of* remarkable accomplishments.
comply with	We must *comply with* government regulations.
concur in (an action)	Four countries *concur in* a plan to reduce oil production.
concur with (a person)	Do you *concur with* Andrew in the need for economy?
conform to	These machine parts do not *conform to* the specifications.
contrast with	The white boat *contrasts* sharply *with* the blue ocean.
correspond to (match)	A bird's wing *corresponds to* a man's arm.
correspond with (write)	Madge *corresponds with* several distant friends.
desire for	A *desire for* wealth may create greed.
desirous of	Rogers was *desirous of* acquiring blue-chip investments.
differ from (things)	Computer software *differs from* computer hardware.
differ with (a person)	I *differ with* you in small points only.
different from (not *than*)	This product is *different from* the one I ordered.
disagree with	Do you *disagree with* him?
expert in	Dr. Rand is an *expert in* electronics.
guard against	*Guard against* infection by covering wounds.
identical with (*or* to)	This house key is *identical with* yours.
independent of	Living alone, the young man was *independent of* his parents.
infer from	I *infer from* your remark that you are dissatisfied.
interest in	Jan has a great *interest in* personal computers.
negligent of	*Negligent of* his diet, the old man became ill.
oblivious to *or* of	McClain was *oblivious to* (or *of*) his surroundings.
plan to (*not* on)	We *plan to* expand the marketing of our products.
prefer to	Do you *prefer to* work a four-day week?
reason with	Mr. Miller tried to *reason with* the unhappy customer.
reconcile with (match)	Chequebook figures must be *reconciled with* bank figures.
reconcile to (accept)	He has never become *reconciled to* retirement.
responsible for	William is *responsible for* locking the building.
retroactive to	The salary increase is *retroactive to* last July 1.
sensitive to	Mrs. Choy is unusually *sensitive to* cold.
similar to	Your term paper topic is *similar to* mine.
stand in (*not* on) line	How long have you been *standing in* line?

Hotlink

An excellent place to learn more about prepositions is Capital Community College's site **<http://cctc2. commnet.edu/ grammar/prepositions. htm>**.

Notable Quotable

"When one door of opportunity closes, another opens; however, we often look so long at the closed door that we do not see the one that has been opened for us."
—Helen Keller

talk to (to tell something)	The speaker *talked to* the large group.
talk with (exchange remarks)	After his lecture, the speaker *talked with* club members informally.
tired of	The receptionist gets *tired of* hearing the telephone ring.

Complete the reinforcement exercises for Level III on pp. 239–240.

HOTLINE QUERIES

Question: Another employee and I are collaborating on a report. I wanted to write this: *Money was lost due to poor attendance.* She says the sentence should read *Money was lost because of poor attendance.* My version is more concise. Which of us is right?

Answer: Most language authorities agree with your co-author. *Due to* is acceptable when it functions as an adjective, as in *Success was due to proper timing.* In this sense, *due to* is synonymous with *attributable to.* However, *because of* should introduce adverbial phrases and should modify verbs: *Money was lost because of poor attendance. Because of* modifies the verb phrase *was lost.*

Question: What's wrong with saying *Lisa graduated college last year?*

Answer: The preposition *from* must be inserted for syntactical fluency. Two constructions are permissible: *Lisa graduated from college* or *Lisa was graduated from college.* The first version is more popular; the second is preferred by traditional grammarians.

Question: Should *sometime* be one or two words in the following sentence? *Can you come over (sometime) soon?*

Answer: In this sentence you should use the one-word form. *Sometime* as an adverb means "an indefinite time" *(the convention is sometime in December).* The two-word combination means "a period of time" *(we have some time to spare).*

Question: I saw this printed recently: *Some of the personal functions that are being reviewed are job descriptions, job specifications, and job evaluation.* Is *personal* used correctly here?

Answer: Indeed not! The word *personal* means "private" or "individual" *(your personal letters are being forwarded to you).* The word *personnel* refers to employees *(all company personnel are cordially invited).* The sentence you quote requires *personnel.*

Question: Is there any difference between *proved* and *proven?*

Answer: As a past participle, the verb form *proved* is preferred *(he has proved his point).* However, the word *proven* is preferred as an adjective form *(that company has a proven record). Proven* is also commonly used in the expression *not proven.*

Question: We're writing a letter to our subscribers, and this sentence doesn't sound right to me: *Every one of our subscribers benefit...*

Answer: As you probably suspected, the verb *benefit* does not agree with the subject *one*. The sentence should read as follows: *Every one of our subscribers benefits...* Don't let intervening phrases obscure the true subject of a sentence.

Question: How should I write *industry wide*? It's not in my dictionary.

Answer: A word with the suffix *wide* is usually written solid: *industrywide, nationwide, countrywide, statewide, worldwide* (but *province-wide*).

CHAPTER 13   Reinforcement Exercises

A. (**Self-check**) Select the correct word, and write it in the space provided.

LEVEL I

1. Let's you and I share the cost of the trip between (we, us).   _____

2. Thomas thought that he (should of, should have) been allowed extra time.   _____

3. Bernstein has (to, too) little patience for that job.   _____

4. Everyone seems to have read the book but (I, me).   _____

5. You might be able to get the lecture notes (off of, from) Kathleen.   _____

6. Should a photocopy be made for Mrs. Korkis or (her, she)?   _____

7. Government has (to, too) consider the effects of inflation.   _____

8. Can you borrow a tent (off, from) the Bouchers?   _____

9. With additional study Gregory (could of, could have) earned an A.   _____

10. No one in the group except her and (I, me) will miss the field trip.   _____

Check your answers.

B. Underline any errors you find in the following sentences. Write the correct forms in the spaces provided. Write *C* if the sentence is correct as written.

Example: Performers like Mervin and <u>she</u> are crowd pleasers.   ____*her*____

1. Everyone in the class except he uses the Internet regularly.   _____

2. James could of worked some overtime hours.   _____

3. We got your address off of Tony before he left.   _____

4. Many customers are eager to make appointments with Mr. Jerome or him.   _____

5. Our union said that management's offer was "too little and to late."   _____

6. Diana Bowman told Andrew and me that we should have read the directions more
    carefully.   _____

7. It's to soon to tell if the young tree will bear edible fruit.   _____

8. Along with Tim and I, Mr. De la Torre will check the computer printout.   _____

9. Just between you and me, how many employees will be reassigned?   _____

10. You could of attended the premier showing last evening.   _____

---

1. us 2. should have 3. too 4. me 5. from 6. her 7. to 8. from 9. could have 10. me

11. Our manager, together with Tanya and he, helped to complete the transaction. _____

12. If you could of delivered the disks earlier, we might have finished on time. _____

13. One can always rely upon friends like Renée and she for assistance in time of need. _____

14. Everyone except him and I received the announcement too late to respond. _____

15. To address the letter properly, you must use information off of their stationery. _____

16. Last year we tried to order supplies off of them too. _____

17. All the checkers except she and he have the holiday off. _____

18. Some of the paper is to long for our everyday use. _____

19. If you could have seen the shipment when it arrived, you would of refused it too. _____

20. CEO Christine Gerbig spoke with the marketing manager and I about sales. _____

A. (Self-check) Select the correct word(s).

LEVEL II

1. The inheritance will be divided (between, among) all the heirs.   _____

2. Robert Whitmore moved (in, into) the office next door.   _____

3. Identifying serial numbers are located (inside, inside of) the machines.   _____

4. Located (beside, besides) the computer store is the food court.   _____

5. It looks (like, as if) we'll be working late tonight.   _____

6. You will be billed later if you (except, accept) the shipment.   _____

7. Despite her salary and new title, Helen feels (as, like) a technician.   _____

8. Differences (between, among) the two brothers affected their management styles.   _____

9. The contracts blew (off, off of) the desk when the door was opened.   _____

10. In the work Marcia used many resources (beside, besides) the Web.   _____

Check your answers.

B. In the following sentences cross out unnecessary prepositions and insert any necessary ones.

Examples: What type ^of^ wheel bearings are needed?

Where are you going ~~to~~?

1. The time for submitting entries is over with.

2. A new shopping centre is being built opposite to the college.

3. Who can tell me where the meeting is scheduled at?

4. Dr. Forward had a great interest and an appreciation of all applications of computerization.

5. Do you know if all of the orders have been filled?

6. Special printing jobs must be done outside of the office.

7. Only Mr. Larsen knows where those supplies might be stored at.

8. What style clothes is recommended for the formal dinner?

9. Where shall we move the extra desks and chairs to?

10. besides

1. among 2. into 3. inside 4. beside 5. as if 6. accept 7. like 8. between 9. off

10. Daniel's love and interest in photography led to a gratifying career.

11. As the huge stack of boxes tumbled, Randy couldn't help from laughing.

12. I'm not certain where you want me to take this report to.

13. Please place the new directories inside of the office.

14. We have been informed that the claim is due on April 15.

15. Did Jill say she graduated high school last year?

C. Select the correct word(s).

1. Relief funds were divided (among, between) all earthquake victims. _____

2. (As, Like) the president said, we must increase productivity. _____

3. Sitting (beside, besides) the speaker is the program chair. _____

4. All three candidates have gone (in, into) the conference room. _____

5. Your laptop computer looks just (like, as) mine. _____

6. The advertising campaign looks (like, as if) it will be quite successful. _____

7. Has anyone been (in to, into) see me this morning? _____

8. We cannot (accept, except) the shipment without an invoice. _____

9. After the interview, Lee felt (like, as if) he would be offered the position. _____

10. If he (accepts, excepts) the job, he will have to move to Toronto. _____

11. (Beside, Besides) Randy and Tyler, whom have you invited? _____

12. It looks (like, as if) Dr. Helen Grattan will be the next CEO. _____

D. Write original sentences using these prepositions correctly.

1. (besides) _____

   _____

2. (into) _____

   _____

3. (except) _____

   _____

4. (like) _____

   _____

5. (among) _____

_____

E. The following sentences have prepositions that end clauses. Rewrite the sentences so that the prepositions precede their objects.

Example: Here is the information you asked about.

Here is the information about which you asked. _____

1. Whom did you address the letter to? _____

_____

2. Please find the folder you put the letter in. _____

_____

3. What did I come into this room for? _____

_____

4. We have a number of loyal members we can rely on. _____

_____

5. Which salesperson did these brochures come from?_____

_____

LEVEL III

A. (Self-check) Underline any errors in the use of prepositions in the following sentences, and write a correct form in the space provided. Write *C* if the sentence is correct as written.

1. Al Fisher is exceptionally adept with woodworking. _____

2. We find it impossible to comply to the latest safety regulations. _____

3. In a televised address, the Prime Minister will talk with the nation at 6 p.m. _____

4. Brenda said that she plans on sleeping late during her vacation. _____

5. Mrs. Reich's management style is much different than Mr. Haddad's. _____

6. Ray is very angry at David for divulging the secret. _____

7. How can one reconcile this new business venture with their recent bankruptcy? _____

8. Isolated from neighbours, the hermit was independent with local laws. _____

9. A car very similar with yours is for sale. _____

10. Richard has little interest with data processing. _____

Check your answers.

B. Underline any errors in the use of prepositions in the following sentences, and write a correction in the space provided. Write *C* if the sentence is correct as written.

1. Assertion is not identical to truth. _____

2. Mr. Colotti described how common stock differs with preferred stock. _____

3. Nike officials plan on expanding their market in Latin America. _____

4. Does Mr. Brady concur with other board members in raising tuition? _____

5. Have you become acquainted to your new database sotfware yet? _____

6. That film is much different than what I expected. _____

7. All procedures must adhere with the company manual. _____

8. The white letters on the sign do not sufficiently contrast from the yellow background. _____

9. Do you hire a translator when your company corresponds to Japanese customers? _____

1. adept in 2. comply with 3. talk to 4. plans to sleep 5. different from 6. angry with 7. C 8. independent of 9. similar to 10. interest in

10. Because the franchise is completely standardized, a fast-food restaurant in California may be identical to one in Saskatchewan.

11. We had to increase parking lot security to guard from auto thefts.

12. To conform with departmental procedures, all work must be logged in.

13. Brian learned that Ellen was quite angry at him.

14. We cannot possibly agree with a contract that we have not yet read.

15. The applicant for the position claimed to be an expert on hydraulic systems.

C. Optional Composition. Your instructor may ask you to complete this exercise on a separate sheet. Write ten original sentences using the following expressions: *oblivious of, adhere to, retroactive to, desirous of, independent of, agree with, identical with, differ from, prefer to,* and *was graduated from.* Use a dictionary if necessary.

Editor's Challenge

The following report contains intentional errors in spelling, proofreading, and concepts you have studied thus far. Use standard proofreading marks to show your corrections.

RESULTS OF SMOKING POLICY SURVEY

by Craig Abrams, Human Resources

Background

A number of requests has been received from employees asking that smoking be banned in all buildings. Second hand smoke represent a health risk with significant compensation implications for our company and it's shareholders. To gather information, Human Resources distributed a questionnaire to 58 managerial and supervisory personnel, a total of 52 responses were received.

Findings

A tally of the returned surveys show that a clear majority of our managerial employees favours a non-smoking policy. A total of 42 employees, or nearly 80 per cent of the total survey, indicated there approval of an non-smoking policy. To implement this policy, excellent suggestions were made by respondents. Which are discussed from the attached printouts.

Conclusion

The results of this survey suggests that our managers and supervisors would support a non-smoking policy. They feel that a carefully planned sensitively implemented non-smoking policy could be successful about our organization.

Recommendations

A well managed cessation program should offer support and practical advice to those who want to use the opportunity to quit. Employees should be allowed sometime to take part in group counselling activitys. High visibility displays should promote participation. Whether to provide smoking areas for those employees who do not stop are a matter a committee must work on.

learning.web.ways

Your advertising company has been asked to create promotional material for a hotel in St. John's, Newfoundland. You want to get some basic facts about this province first.

Goal: To use an on-line encyclopedia.

1. With your Web browser on the screen, go to the Canadian Encyclopedia site **<http://www.thecanadianencyclopedia.com>**. Enter the English version of the site.

2. In the search box near the middle of the screen, key your search term, **Newfoundland**.

3. Read the entry about **Newfoundland and Labrador**, and print one page of the article.

4. When did Newfoundland officially join the confederation? What is its largest mountain system? Which two provincial institutes are located in St. John's?

5. To select another on-line encyclopedia, go to the textbook site at **<http://www.buscomm.nelson.com>**. Click **Research Tools** and then **Reference Tools**.

6. From the list of encyclopedias, click on one, and compare the findings for Newfoundland. Print one page.

7. End your session, and turn in all printed pages and your answers to the questions.

1. too 2. as if 3. with 4. among 5. Besides

Conjunctions to Join Equals

OBJECTIVES   When you have completed the materials in this chapter, you will be able to do the following:

LEVEL I
- *Distinguish between simple and compound sentences.*
- *Punctuate compound sentences joined by* and, or, not, *and* but.

LEVEL II
- *Punctuate compound sentences using conjunctive adverbs such as* therefore, however, *and* consequently.
- *Punctuate sentences using parenthetical (interrupting) adverbs such as* therefore, however, *and* consequently.

LEVEL III
- *Recognize correlative conjunctions such as* either ... or, not only ... but also, *and* neither ... nor.
- *Use parallel construction in composing sentences with correlative conjunctions.*

PRETEST

Insert commas and semicolons to punctuate the following sentences correctly.

1. Sales in Ontario have increased therefore we are assigning more sales representatives to that area.
2. It is important however that we also continue to cover all other sales territories adequately.
3. Eleanor Uyeda prefers to remain in Kitchener but Wanda Deen is considering the Windsor area.
4. As many as 20 agents will move nevertheless the transition must be made smoothly.

Circle the letter of the sentence that is more effective.

5. (a) Not only is this copier faster, but it is also cheaper than the other.

   (b) This copier is not only faster but also cheaper than the other.

1. increased; therefore,   2. important, however,   3. Kitchener,   4. move;   nevertheless,   5. b

Conjunctions are connecting words. They may be separated into two major groups: those that join grammatically equal words or word groups and those that join grammatically unequal words or word groups. This chapter will focus on those conjunctions that join equals. Recognizing conjunctions and understanding their patterns of usage will, among other things, enable you to use commas and semicolons more appropriately.

LEVEL I

Hotlink

For a colourful look at "A Brief Explanation of Conjunctions," go to **<http://www.gsu. edu/~wwwesl/egw/ bryson.htm>**. If this site is not available, search for "coordinating conjunctions" with your favourite search engine.

Study Tip

Clauses have subjects and verbs. Phrases do not. Clauses may have phrases within them.

Hotlink

For a thorough overview of phrases and clauses, check out this Trent University handout **<http://www.trentu.ca/ academicskills/unit9. htm>**.

▶ Coordinating Conjunctions

Coordinating conjunctions connect words, phrases, and clauses of equal grammatical value or rank. The most common coordinating conjunctions are *and, or, but,* and *nor.* Notice in these sentences that coordinating conjunctions join grammatically equal elements.

> We think your action is *illogical, unfair,* and *arbitrary.* (Here the word *and* joins equal words.)
>
> Give serious thought *to your letters* and *to reader reaction.* (Here *and* joins equal phrases.)
>
> *Mr. Freeman opens the mail,* but *Miss Dunaway fills the orders.* (Here *but* joins equal clauses.)

Phrases and Clauses

A group of related words without a subject and a verb is called a *phrase.* You are already familiar with verb phrases and prepositional phrases. It is not important that you be able to identify the other kinds of phrases (infinitive, gerund, participial), but it is very important that you be able to distinguish phrases from clauses.

The alarm was coming from another part of the building.

    phrase   phrase   phrase

A group of related words including a subject and a verb is a *clause.*

We interviewed three applicants, and we decided to hire Mr. Lee.

        clause   clause

Karen is interested in a job in marketing, but she wants also to travel.

        clause   clause

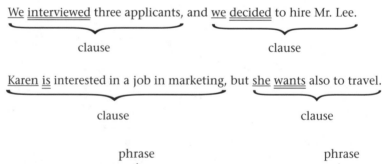

         phrase   phrase

Salaries begin at $35,000 annually, and they can reach over $70,000.

        clause   clause

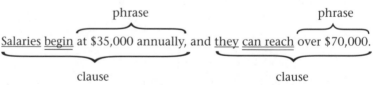

Clauses often contain phrases, as illustrated in the last sentence.

Simple and Compound Sentences

A simple sentence has one independent clause, that is, a clause that can stand alone. A compound sentence has two or more independent clauses.

> We agreed to lease the equipment. (Simple sentence)
> Our Travel Services Department planned the sales trip, but some salespeople also made private excursions. (Compound sentence)

Punctuating Compound Sentences

When coordinating conjunctions join clauses in a compound sentence, a comma precedes the conjunction, unless the clauses are very short (four or fewer words in each clause).

> We can ship the merchandise by air, *or* we can ship it by rail.
> Ship by air *or* ship by rail. (Clauses are too short to require a comma.)

Do not use commas when coordinating conjunctions join compound verbs, objects, or phrases.

> The <u>bank</u> <u>will notify</u> you of each transfer, or <u>it</u> <u>will send</u> you a monthly statement. (Comma used because *or* joins two independent clauses.)
> The <u>bank</u> <u>will notify</u> you of each transfer or <u>will send</u> you a monthly statement. (No comma needed because *or* joins the compound verbs of a single independent clause.)
> <u>Thomas Edison</u> <u>said</u> that colleges should not have to choose between lighting their buildings *and* enlightening their students. (No comma needed because *and* joins the compound objects of the prepositional phrase beginning with *between*.)
> <u>Shareholders</u> <u>are expected</u> to attend the meeting *or* to send in their proxies. (No comma needed because *or* joins the two infinitive phrases.)
> <u>Analyze</u> all your possible property risks, *and* <u>protect</u> yourself with insurance. (Comma needed to join two independent clauses; the subject of each clause is understood to be *you*.)

Complete the reinforcement exercises for Level I on pp. 249–250.

▶ **Conjunctive Adverbs**

LEVEL II

Conjunctive adverbs may also be used to connect equal sentence elements. Because conjunctive adverbs are used to effect a transition from one thought to another, and because they may consist of more than one word, they have also been called *transitional expressions*. The most common conjunctive adverbs and adverb phrases follow.

accordingly	however	on the other hand
consequently	in fact	otherwise
for example	in the meantime	that is
for instance	moreover	then
furthermore	nevertheless	therefore
hence	on the contrary	thus

Hotlink

Also known as transitional words and phrases, conjunctive adverbs get a full airing at the Memorial University Web site **<http://www.mun. ca/writingcentre/ transword.shtml>**. Try the exercise at the bottom of this page, and check your solutions against the Possible Answer Key.

In the following compound sentences, observe that conjunctive adverbs join clauses of equal grammatical value. Note that semicolons (*not* commas) are used before conjunctive adverbs that join independent clauses. Commas should immediately follow conjunctive adverbs of two or more syllables. Note also that the word following a semicolon is not capitalized—unless, of course, it is a proper noun.

> Electricians rewired the equipment room; *nevertheless*, fuses continued to blow.
> Some machines require separate outlets; *consequently*, we installed new outlets.
> Equipment expenditures are high this quarter; *on the other hand*, new equipment will reduce labour costs.
> Complex equipment requires operators who are specialists; *thus* we must train operators to become specialists.
> Competition among computer manufacturers is intensive; *hence* prices have decreased sharply.

Generally, no comma is used after one-syllable conjunctive adverbs such as *hence, thus,* and *then* (unless a strong pause is desired).

▶ Distinguishing Conjunctive Adverbs From Parenthetical Adverbs

Many words that function as conjunctive adverbs may also serve as *parenthetical* (interrupting) *adverbs*. Use semicolons only with conjunctive adverbs that join independent clauses. Use commas to set off parenthetical adverbs that interrupt the flow of a sentence.

> Jackson is, *however*, a fine administrator. (Adverb used parenthetically.)
> Jackson is a fine administrator; *however*, he is a poor fundraiser. (Adverb used to join two independent clauses.)

> The discount will, *furthermore,* be increased after six years.
> Policyholders are eligible for a discount after only three years; *furthermore*, the discount will be increased after six years.

> We believe, *on the other hand*, that cellular phone sales will continue to grow.
> We believe that cellphones are convenient; *on the other hand*, they must be used responsibly.

Complete the reinforcement exercises for Level II on pp. 251–253.

Study Tip

Use a semicolon with a conjunctive adverb only when you are joining two sentences.

LEVEL III

▶ Other Conjunctions

So far we have studied two kinds of conjunctions used to join grammatically equal sentence elements: coordinating conjunctions (used to join equal words, phrases, and clauses) and conjunctive adverbs (used to join grammatically equal clauses in compound sentences). *Correlative conjunctions* form the third and final group of conjunctions that join grammatically equal sentence elements.

Correlative Conjunctions

Correlative conjunctions are always paired: *both ... and, not only ... but (also), either ... or, neither ... nor.* When greater emphasis is desired, these paired conjunctions are used instead of coordinating conjunctions.

> Your glasses are on the counter *or* on the table.
> Your glasses are *either* on the counter *or* on the table. (More emphatic)

In using correlative conjunctions, place them so that the words, phrases, or clauses being joined are parallel in construction.

Parallel:	He was working *either* in Victoria *or* in Nanaimo.
Not parallel:	*Either* he was working in Victoria *or* in Nanaimo.
Parallel:	She was *not only* gracious *but also* kind.
Not parallel:	She was *not only* gracious, *but* she was *also* kind.
Parallel:	I have *neither* the time *nor* the energy for this.
Not parallel:	I *neither* have the time *nor* the energy for this.

Additional Coordinating Conjunctions

At Level I you studied four commonly used coordinating conjunctions: *and, or, nor,* and *but.* Three other coordinating conjunctions should also be mentioned; *yet, for,* and *so.*

The words *yet* and *for* may function as coordinating conjunctions, although they are infrequently used as such.

> We have only two hours left, *yet* we hope to finish.
> The weary traveller was gaunt and ill, *for* his journey had been long and
> arduous.

The word *so* is often informally used as a coordinating conjunction. In more formal contexts the conjunctive adverbs *therefore* and *consequently* should be substituted for the conjunction *so.*

Informal:	The plane leaves at 2:15, *so* they still have time to pack.
Formal:	The plane leaves at 2:15; *therefore,* they still have time to pack.

To avoid using *so* as a conjunction, try starting your sentence with *because* or *although.*

Informal:	Cellphone calls in public can be exasperating, *so* they are banned in some places.
Improved:	*Because* cellphone calls in public can be exasperating, they are banned in some places.

Complete the reinforcement exercises for Level III on pp. 254–255.

Complete the reinforcement exercises for Level III on pp. 254–255.

Notable Quotable

"Great minds have purposes; others have wishes."
—Washington Irving

HOTLINE QUERIES

Question: Please help me decide which *maybe* to use in this sentence: *He said that he (maybe, may be) able to help us.*

Answer: Use the two-word *may be,* which is the verb form. *Maybe* is an adverb that means "perhaps" *(maybe she will call).*

Question: Is it acceptable to key part of an individual's name at the end of one line and carry the rest to the next line?

Answer: Full names may be divided between the first and the last names or after the middle initial. For example, you could key *John R.* on one line and *Williamson* on the next line. Do not, however, separate a short title and a surname (such as *Mr./Williamson*), and do not divide a name (such as *William/son*). By the way, many computer programs make unacceptable line-ending decisions. Be sure to inspect your copy, either on the screen or on the printout, so that you can correct poor hyphenation and unacceptable word separations.

Question: What should the verb in this sentence be? *There (has, have) to be good reasons ...*

Answer: Use the plural verb *have,* which agrees with the subject *reasons.* In sentences that begin with the word *there,* look for the subject after the verb.

Question: Does *Ms.* have a period after it? Should I use this title for all women in business today?

Answer: *Ms.* is probably a blend of *Miss* and *Mrs.,* and it is written with a period following it. Some women in business prefer to use *Ms.,* presumably because it is a title equal to *Mr.* Neither title reveals one's marital status. Many other women, however, prefer to use *Miss* or *Mrs.* as a title. It's always wise, if possible, to determine the preference of the individual.

Question: I just typed this sentence: *He was given a new title in lieu of a salary increase.* I went to my dictionary to check the spelling of *in lieu of,* but I can't find it. How is it spelled and what does it mean?

Answer: The listing in the dictionary is under *lieu,* and the phrase means "in place of" or "instead of." Many authorities today are recommending that such foreign phrases be avoided. It's easier and clearer to say "instead of."

Question: Can you help me with the words *averse* and *adverse?* I've never been able to straighten them out in my mind.

Answer: *Averse* is an adjective meaning "disinclined" or "reluctant" and is generally used with the preposition *to (the little boy was averse to bathing; she is averse to statistical keyboarding). Adverse* is also an adjective, but it means "hostile" or "unfavourable" *(adverse economic conditions halted the company's growth; the picnic was postponed because of adverse weather conditions).* In distinguishing between these two very similar words, it might help you to know that the word *averse* is usually used to describe animate (living) objects.

Question: What should I write: *You are our No. 1 account,* or *You are our number one account?* Should anything be hyphenated?

Answer: Either is correct, but I prefer *No. 1* because it is more easily recognizable. No hyphen is required.

Question: A friend of mine gets upset when I say something like, *I was so surprised by her remark.* She thinks I'm misusing *so.* Am I?

Answer: Your friend is right, if we're talking about formal expression. The intensifier *so* requires a clause to complete its meaning. For example, *I was so surprised by her remark that I immediately protested.* It's like waiting for the other shoe to drop when one hears *so* as a modifier without a qualifying clause. *He was so funny.* So funny that what? *He was so funny that he became a stand-up comedian.*

CHAPTER 14   Reinforcement Exercises

A. **(Self-check)** Select *a, b,* or *c* to identify the sentences below.

LEVEL I

   a. A comma correctly punctuates a compound sentence.

   b. The sentence is not compound; thus the comma should be omitted.

   c. Although the sentence is compound, the clauses are too short to require a comma.

Example: It rained most of the morning, but stopped in the afternoon when the sun began to shine.   *b*

1. The value-added tax is quite popular in Europe, but it has received little support in this country. _____

2. I did not expect a profit, and did not fear a loss. _____

3. Listen well, and look carefully. _____

4. Word processing specialists must possess excellent English skills, and they must be skilled at keyboarding. _____

5. Thank you for applying for admission, and for sending us your résumé. _____

6. The concert did not begin until 8 p.m., but a large crowd began to gather at noon. _____

7. Ms. Phillips keyboards and Mrs. Rogers edits. _____

8. Albert Einstein was four years old before he could speak, and seven years old before he could read. _____

9. Human Resources Director Berman will be interviewing applicants Monday and Tuesday, and will make a decision on the appointment by Friday. _____

10. The city of Bombay originally rested on seven islands, but the islands were joined by landfill long ago. _____

Check your answers.

B. A simple sentence has one independent clause. A compound sentence has two or more independent clauses. Indicate with a check mark whether the following sentences, all of which are punctuated correctly, are simple or compound. *Hint:* A sentence is not compound unless the words preceding and following a conjunction form independent clauses. If these groups of words could not stand alone as sentences, the sentence is not compound.

                                                           Simple   Compound

1. James Thomas wrote a travel report, and he shared its information with other members of the staff. _____ _____

1. a 2. b (not compound because no subject follows *and*) 3. c 4. a 5. b (no comma is needed because this is a simple sentence with two prepositional phrases joined by *and*) 6. a 7. c 8. b (the words following *and* do not form an independent clause) 9. b 10. a

2. James Thomas wrote a travel report and shared its information with other members of the staff. _____ _____

3. We will allow you our discount of 10 per cent and also a cash rebate of over $50 for each purchase. _____ _____

4. The recently constructed corporate headquarters contained attractive executive offices, but the structure had few support facilities for employees. _____ _____

5. The recently constructed corporate headquarters contained attractive executive offices but few support facilities for employees. _____ _____

6. Management trainees are sent to all our branch offices in this country and to some of the branch offices in South America and Europe. _____ _____

7. Children become adults when they stop asking their parents for allowances and begin requesting loans instead. _____ _____

8. Fill in all the answers on the application, and send the form to the human resources director. _____ _____

9. Send copies of the project report to me and to other management personnel in our three subsidiaries. _____ _____

10. Supplies for three offices arrived today, but most of our order will not arrive until later. _____ _____

C. Insert commas where appropriate in the following sentences. Then, in the space provided, indicate the number of commas you have added for each sentence. If no comma is needed, write *0*.

Example: Kevin attended classes on Monday, but he went to the beach on Tuesday. ____1____

1. Some employees think their e-mail should be confidential but courts generally uphold an employer's right to monitor messages. _____

2. Mrs. Sokol authorized the expenditure and directed the purchasing agent to place an order immediately. _____

3. Mr. Peterson was not pleased with the delay but he did not seem to be angry with the vendor. _____

4. Please transcribe this letter and fax it. _____

5. Today's software can detect potentially troublesome words or identify high-pressure sales tactics in e-mail messages. _____

6. Annuities for all contributors may accumulate yearly or may be withdrawn at regular intervals over a five-year period. _____

7. Proverbs are often short in length but they are usually long in experience. _____

8. Raw materials and supplies are available but machinery and equipment must be replaced before production can begin. _____

9. Consider the alternatives and act accordingly. _____

10. You may be interested in a career in this country or you may be interested in working abroad. _____

A. **(Self-check)** In the following sentences selected adverbs and conjunctions have been italicized. Insert commas and semicolons where appropriate. Indicate the number of punctuation marks added to each sentence in the space provided. Be prepared to explain your choices.

LEVEL II

Example: Too many salespeople missed the seminar; *therefore,* attendance will be mandatory in the future.

_____2_____

1. Our Reprographics Department is currently understaffed *thus* we are behind on our production schedule.

_____

2. We are *however* able to make single copies quickly.

_____

3. The bill of lading did not match the order *consequently* the shipment was refused.

_____

4. Property may be insured in excess of its actual value *however* damages will be paid for no more than the actual loss.

_____

5. Kelly did *nevertheless* pick up the printed copies she needed immediately.

_____

6. Ellen Arnold appears to be the best qualified *on the other hand* Diana Percy has excellent recommendations.

_____

7. Jeanette considered the possibility of changing jobs *but* was unwilling to accept the risks involved.

_____

8. Liam *on the other hand* changed jobs whenever the urge impelled him.

_____

9. Our Accounts Receivable Department has written to you three times *however* we have had no response to our letters.

_____

10. Your account is now three months overdue *hence* we have only one alternative left open to us.

_____

Check your answers.

1. (1) understaffed; thus   2. (2) are, however,   3. (2) order; consequently,   4. (2) value; however,   5. (2) did, nevertheless,   6. (2) qualified; on the other hand,   7. (0)   8. (2) Liam, on the other hand,   9. (2) times; however,   10. (1) overdue; hence

B. Insert commas and semicolons where appropriate. Indicate in the space provided the number of punctuation marks added to each sentence. Be prepared to explain your choices.

Example: Some loans must be secured, therefore, the borrower must supply collateral. _____2_____

1. The capital of Canada has changed several times in fact Kingston, Ontario, was capital from 1841 to 1843. _____

2. Microwave relay stations have reduced telephone costs moreover cable and satellite circuits reduce costs even more. _____

3. We are faced nevertheless with unusually expensive communication costs. _____

4. We submitted a low bid but did not get the contract. _____

5. Insurance works according to the law of averages thus increased losses send the average cost of insurance premiums upward. _____

6. The car came with an automatic transmission nevertheless it provided better-than-average gas mileage. _____

7. We are moreover pleased with its manoeuvrability and handling. _____

8. A new directory will be released later in the month in the meantime use the old book and the information service. _____

9. Automobile repair costs are skyrocketing consequently car insurance costs are rising sharply. _____

10. Please place your order immediately or you will not be eligible for the discount. _____

11. Members of our management staff moreover are interested in hiring a consultant to train customer service personnel on the new equipment. _____

12. Data concerning cellular phone use was needed therefore Nokia conducted a survey. _____

13. We are mailing over 3000 questionnaires to business organizations thus we will need a postal permit for metered mail. _____

14. We are currently using envelopes made from kraft paper and find that some of our deliveries are arriving in damaged condition. _____

15. ColorImage for example has produced a program with remarkable graphic features and excellent accessibility. _____

16. The company gave each employee a holiday bonus therefore Christmas cheques were considerably larger this year. _____

17. This apprenticeship program on the contrary combines classroom instruction with on-the-job training. _____

18. The sessions for business managers start on Tuesday but the seminars for sales representatives do not begin until Wednesday. _____

C. Write compound sentences using the conjunctions and conjunctive adverbs shown below.

1. *consequently* _____

_____

2. *but* _____

_____

3. *nevertheless* _____

_____

4. *otherwise* _____

_____

5. *and* _____

_____

6. *moreover* _____

_____

7. *or* _____

_____

8. *then* _____

_____

A. (**Self-check**) Select the more effective version of each of the following sentence pairs. Write its letter in the space provided.

LEVEL III

1. (a) Either she sent the letter on Monday or Tuesday.
   (b) She sent the letter on either Monday or Tuesday.   _____

2. (a) Mr. Kinsman is not able to represent us, and neither is Mrs. Bragg.
   (b) Neither Mr. Kinsman nor Mrs. Bragg is able to represent us.   _____

3. (a) Our objectives are both to improve customer relations and increasing sales.
   (b) Our objectives are both to improve customer relations and to increase sales.   _____

4. (a) She neither called nor explained her absence.
   (b) Neither did she call nor explain her absence.   _____

5. (a) This work order must be completed by Friday, so you may have to work late Thursday.
   (b) This work order must be completed by Friday; therefore, you may have to work late Thursday.   _____

6. (a) Our new copier is not only faster but also cheaper.
   (b) Not only is our new copier faster, but it is also cheaper.   _____

7. (a) Neither did the staff finish the proposals nor the contracts.
   (b) The staff finished neither the proposals nor the contracts.   _____

8. (a) He has no formal education, yet he is very well-read.
   (b) He has no formal education; yet he is very well-read.   _____

9. (a) A three-hour time difference separates us; so you should call immediately.
   (b) A three-hour time difference separates us; therefore, you should call immediately.   _____

10. (a) You must either e-mail or fax the proposal quickly.
    (b) Either you must e-mail or fax the proposal quickly.   _____

Check your answers.

B. Which of these sentence pairs is more effective?

1. (a) Either give the time card to Tina Chang or to me.
   (b) Give the time card either to Tina Chang or to me.   _____

2. (a) Our travel counsellor will both plan your trip and make your reservations.
   (b) Our travel counsellor will both plan your trip and reservations will be made.   _____

3. (a) We have checked every figure carefully; yet the totals do not balance.
    (b) We have checked every figure carefully, yet the totals do not balance.   _____

4. (a) Not only does a product carry an expressed warranty, but it also carries an implied warranty.
    (b) A product carries not only an expressed warranty but also an implied warranty.   _____

5. (a) We must receive either your payment or a reason for nonpayment.
    (b) Either we must receive your payment, or you must give us a reason why you cannot pay.   _____

C. Rewrite the following sentences to make them more effective.

1. Either bankruptcy can be declared by the debtor, or it can be requested by the creditors.

_____

_____

2. Neither the staff was happy with the proposed cutbacks in class offerings, and nor were the students.

_____

_____

3. Not only do banks use computers to sort cheques, but they also use computers for disbursing cash automatically.

_____

_____

D. Optional Composition. Your instructor may ask you to complete this exercise on a separate sheet. Write original sentences that illustrate the following: *a simple sentence, a compound sentence, a parenthetical adverb,* and *a pair of correlative conjunctions.* Write five compound sentences using different conjunctive adverbs. Label each sentence.

Editor's Challenge

The following e-mail message contains intentional errors in spelling, proofreading, punctuation, and language principles covered thus far. Use standard proofreading marks to show necessary corrections.

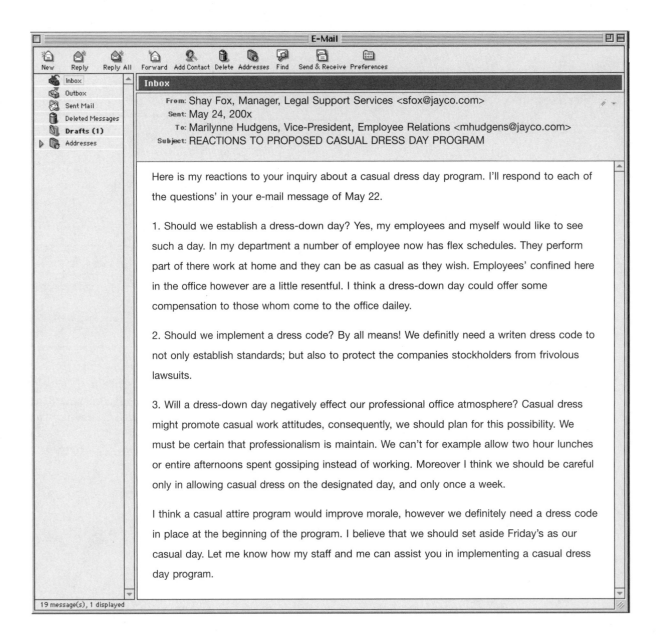

E-Mail

| New | Reply | Reply All | Forward | Add Contact | Delete | Addresses | Find | Send & Receive | Preferences |

Inbox
Outbox
Sent Mail
Deleted Messages
Drafts (1)
Addresses

Inbox

From: Shay Fox, Manager, Legal Support Services <sfox@jayco.com>
Sent: May 24, 200x
To: Marilynne Hudgens, Vice-President, Employee Relations <mhudgens@jayco.com>
Subject: REACTIONS TO PROPOSED CASUAL DRESS DAY PROGRAM

Here is my reactions to your inquiry about a casual dress day program. I'll respond to each of the questions' in your e-mail message of May 22.

1. Should we establish a dress-down day? Yes, my employees and myself would like to see such a day. In my department a number of employee now has flex schedules. They perform part of there work at home and they can be as casual as they wish. Employees' confined here in the office however are a little resentful. I think a dress-down day could offer some compensation to those whom come to the office dailey.

2. Should we implement a dress code? By all means! We definitly need a writen dress code to not only establish standards; but also to protect the companies stockholders from frivolous lawsuits.

3. Will a dress-down day negatively effect our professional office atmosphere? Casual dress might promote casual work attitudes, consequently, we should plan for this possibility. We must be certain that professionalism is maintain. We can't for example allow two hour lunches or entire afternoons spent gossiping instead of working. Moreover I think we should be careful only in allowing casual dress on the designated day, and only once a week.

I think a casual attire program would improve morale, however we definitely need a dress code in place at the beginning of the program. I believe that we should set aside Friday's as our casual day. Let me know how my staff and me can assist you in implementing a casual dress day program.

19 message(s), 1 displayed

Add commas or semicolons to the following sentences.

1. The cost of our raw materials is increasing consequently the price of our product must also increase.

2. We are convinced nevertheless that our products will continue to be competitive in today's market.

3. We are searching for other suppliers and we are trying to reduce transportation costs.

4. One supplier is located in the southern United States however we have been unable to find anyone closer.

Circle the letter of the sentence that is more effective.

5. (a) Neither can we ship the printer or the computer until April 1.

   (b) We can ship neither the printer nor the computer until April 1.

learning.web.ways

You've heard that "cookies" are dangerous and can be used to gather sensitive information from your computer. You decide to find out more.

Goal: To learn about "cookies."

1. With your Web browser on the screen, go to the Cookies and Privacy FAQ site of Netscape Communications Security **<http://www.cookiecentral.com/n_cookie_faq.htm>**.

2. Read over the FAQs (Frequently Asked Questions) and answers. Print three pages.

3. What are cookies? Can they be used to retrieve sensitive data from your computer?

4. End your session by clicking the **X** in the upper right corner of your browser. Turn in all printed pages and your answers.

1. increasing; consequently, 2. convinced, nevertheless, 3. suppliers, 4. United States; however, 5. b

Conjunctions to Join Unequals

15

OBJECTIVES When you have completed the materials in this chapter, you will be able to do the following:

LEVEL I
- *Distinguish among dependent clauses, independent clauses, and phrases.*
- *Recognize subordinating conjunctions and relative pronouns functioning as conjunctions.*

LEVEL II
- *Punctuate introductory and terminal dependent clauses.*
- *Punctuate parenthetical, essential, and non-essential dependent clauses.*

LEVEL III
- *Recognize simple, compound, complex, and compound–complex sentences.*
- *Convert simple sentences into a variety of more complex patterns.*

PRETEST

Insert appropriate commas in the following sentences. Mark *C* if correct.

1. When you finish work tomorrow remember that you must back up all files.
2. If possible we will stop work a little early on Friday.
3. The employee who submits the best suggestion will win the bonus trip.
4. We understand that Kala Jones who works in Legal Services will be leaving next month.
5. Although several applicants passed the test no one has been hired yet.

1. tomorrow, 2. possible, 3. C, 4. Jones, Services, 5. test,

In Chapter 14, we studied conjunctions that joined equal sentence elements such as words, phrases, and clauses. Such equal sentence parts can be joined by coordinating conjunctions (such as *and, or, but*), conjunctive adverbs (such as *therefore, however, consequently*), and correlative conjunctions (such as *either ... or*). Now let's look at a special group of conjunctions that join unequal sentence parts.

▶ Subordinating Conjunctions

To join unequal sentence elements, such as independent clauses and dependent clauses, we use subordinating conjunctions. A list of the most common subordinating conjunctions follows.

after	because	since	until
although	before	so that	when
as	if	that	where
as if	in order that	though	whether
as though	provided (that)	unless	while

You should become familiar with this list of conjunctions, but do not feel that you must at all times be able to recall every subordinating conjunction. Generally, you can recognize a subordinating conjunction by the way it limits or subordinates the clause it introduces. In the clause *because he always paid with cash,* the subordinating conjunction *because* limits the meaning of the clause it introduces. The clause beginning with *because* is incomplete and could not stand alone as a sentence.

▶ Independent and Dependent Clauses

Main clauses that can stand alone are said to be *independent.* They have subjects and verbs and make sense by themselves.

> Business writing should be concise. (One main clause.)
> Business writing should be concise, and it should be clear as well. (Two main clauses.)
> Shauna Cox writes many e-mail messages, but Kathleen Young writes more letters. (Two main clauses.)

Clauses that cannot stand alone are said to be *dependent.* They have subjects and verbs, but they depend upon other clauses for the completion of their meaning. Dependent clauses are often introduced by subordinating conjunctions.

> When Ms. Cox wants a quick reply, she sends an e-mail message.
>   (Dependent clause precedes the main clause.)
> Since Ms. Young writes many letters, she keeps her address file current.
>   (Dependent clause precedes the main clause.)
> Business letters are important because they represent the company.
>   (Dependent clause, *because they represent the company*, comes after the main clause.)

▶ Relative Pronouns

The relative pronouns *who, whom, whose, which,* and *that* actually function as conjunctions when they introduce dependent clauses. *Who* is used to refer to persons. It may introduce essential or non-essential clauses. *That* refers to animals or things and

Notable Quotable

"You can have brilliant ideas, but if you can't get them across, your ideas won't get you anywhere."
—Lee Iacocca, former CEO, Chrysler Corporation

Spot the Blooper

Bank of Montreal advertising slogan: "Get the card that thinks like you."

should be used to introduce essential clauses. *Which* refers to animals or things and should introduce non-essential clauses.

The tricky part is deciding whether a clause is essential or non-essential. Non-essential clauses contain information that the reader does not need to know; the main clause is understandable without this extra information. In some cases, only the writer knows whether a clause is intended to be essential or non-essential. If it is non-essential, it should be set off from the rest of the sentence by commas. You'll learn more about punctuating these sentences shortly.

Study Tip

Dependent clauses should never be written or punctuated as if they were complete sentences.

> Anyone *who* (not *that*) has a computer can create a Web site. (The relative pronoun *who* refers to a person, and it introduces an essential clause.)
>
> A company *that* (not *who* or *which*) values its employees is likely to succeed. (The relative pronoun *that* introduces an essential clause.)
>
> Software giant Microsoft, *which* is headquartered in Redmond, has many other offices in the state of Washington. (The relative pronoun *which* introduces a non-essential clause and is set off by commas.)
>
> Microsoft is the company *that* (not *which*) is headquartered in Redmond. (The relative pronoun *that* introduces an essential clause and requires no commas.)
>
> Lisa Meyers, *who* has excellent recommendations, is applying for a position in our department. (The relative pronoun *who* introduces a non-essential clause and is set off by commas.)

Complete the reinforcement exercises for Level I on pp. 266–268.

▶ Punctuation of Sentences With Dependent Clauses

LEVEL II

Business writers are especially concerned with clarity and accuracy. A misplaced or omitted punctuation mark can confuse a reader by altering the meaning of a sentence. The following guidelines for using commas help ensure clarity and consistency in writing. Some professional writers, however, take liberties with accepted conventions of punctuation, particularly in regard to comma usage. These experienced writers may omit a comma when they feel that such an omission will not affect the reader's understanding of a sentence. Beginning writers, though, are well advised to first develop skill in punctuating sentences by following traditional guidelines.

Introductory Dependent Clauses

Use a comma after a dependent (subordinate) clause that precedes an independent clause.

> *Before* they left the office, they finished the project.
> *Until* he returns, we cannot continue.
> *When* you are ready to start, let me know.

Use a comma after an introductory dependent clause even though the subject and verb may not be stated.

> *As* [it is] expected, the shipment is overdue.
> *If* [it is] possible, send a replacement immediately.
> *When* [they are] printed, your brochures will be distributed.

Spot the Blooper

From classified ads in local newspapers: "LAWNMORE SHOP" and a house for sale with "walking closets."

Terminal Dependent Clauses

Generally, a dependent clause introduced by a subordinating conjunction does not require a comma when the dependent clause falls at the end of a sentence.

> They finished the proposal *before* they left the office.
> We cannot continue *until* he returns.
> Let me know *when* you are ready to start.

If, however, the dependent clause at the end of a sentence interrupts the flow of the sentence and sounds like an afterthought, a comma should be used.

> I know the cancelled cheque was returned, *although* I cannot find it now.
> We will ship the goods within the week, *if* that is satisfactory for you.

Parenthetical Clauses

Within a sentence, dependent clauses that interrupt the flow of the sentence and are unnecessary for the grammatical completeness of the sentence are set off by commas.

> The motion, *unless* you want further discussion, will be tabled at our next meeting.
> At our next meeting, *provided* we have a quorum, the motion will be reconsidered.

Relative Clauses

Dependent clauses introduced by relative pronouns such as *who, that*, and *which* may be essential (restrictive) or non-essential (non-restrictive).

Essential Clauses. An *essential clause* is needed to identify the noun to which it refers; therefore, no commas should separate this clause from its antecedent.

> Any student *who missed the test* must make it up. (Dependent clause needed to identify which students must make up the test.)
> Parking permits *that were issued in the fall* must be validated for the spring. (Dependent clause needed to identify which parking permits must be validated.)

Non-Essential Clauses. A *non-essential clause* supplies additional information that is not needed to identify its antecedent; therefore, commas are used to separate the non-essential information from the rest of the sentence. Notice that two commas are used to set off internal non-essential dependent clauses.

> Amy Kertesz, *who missed the exam,* must make it up. (Dependent clause not needed; the antecedent of the clause, Amy Kertesz, is clearly identified.)
> Lot C parking permits, *which were issued in the fall,* must be validated for the spring. (Dependent clause not needed; the antecedent of the clause, Lot C parking permits, is clearly identified.)

Punctuation Review

The following three common sentence patterns are very important for you to study and understand. Notice particularly how they are punctuated.

Hotlink

The Academic Skills Centre at Trent University offers this comprehensive introduction to relative clauses prepared especially for ESL students **<http://www.trentu.ca/ academicskills/ unit8.htm>**.

Study Tip

Since relative clauses introduced by *that* are always essential, they require no commas.

Independent clause (,) + { and / or / nor / but }	+ *Independent clause.*	(Comma used when a coordinating conjunction joins independent clauses.)

$$\text{Independent clause } (;) + \left\{ \begin{array}{l} \text{therefore,} \\ \text{consequently,} \\ \text{however,} \\ \text{nevertheless,} \end{array} \right\} + \text{Independent clause.}$$

(Semicolon used when a conjunctive adverb joins independent clauses.)

$$\left\{ \begin{array}{l} \text{Since} \\ \text{If} \\ \text{As} \\ \text{When} \end{array} \right\} \text{Dependent clause } (,) + \text{Independent clause.}$$

(Comma used when a dependent clause precedes an independent clause.)

Complete the reinforcement exercises for Level II on pp. 269–270.

▶ Sentence Variety

LEVEL III

To make their messages interesting, good writers strive for variety in sentence structure. Notice the monotony and choppiness of a paragraph made up entirely of simple sentences:

> The United States purchased Alaska from Russia in 1867. The exact boundary of the "panhandle" strip of coastline seemed fairly unimportant. The 1898 Gold Rush made this boundary significant. Both Canadians and Americans wanted to profit from the prospectors and their gold. The boundary dispute became extremely serious. A court of six judges was chosen. It decided 4 to 2 against Canada's version of the boundary. The decision outraged Canadians. One good consequence of this controversy was the International Joint Commission. It was set up in 1909 to settle boundary disputes.

Compare the following version of this paragraph, which uses dependent clauses and other structures to achieve greater sentence variety:

> When the United States purchased Alaska from Russia in 1867, the exact boundary of the "panhandle" strip of coastline seemed fairly unimportant. However, the 1898 Gold Rush made this boundary significant since both Canadians and Americans wanted to profit from the prospectors and their gold. After the boundary dispute had become extremely serious, a court of six judges was chosen and decided 4 to 2 against Canada's version of the boundary. Although the decision outraged Canadians, one good outcome of this controversy was the International Joint Committee, which was set up in 1909 to settle boundary disputes.

Spot the Blooper

From *The Ft. Lauderdale Sun Sentinel:* "Architect Barry Sugerman of North Miami designed this pergola to divert attention from the garage, which is seen walking up to the house from the motorcourt."

Hotlink

The Writing Centre at Wilfrid Laurier University <http://www.wlu.ca/writing/handouts.shtml> has several grammar handouts you can print out. Scroll down the page for the link to Sentence Revision for a Mature Compact Style.

Recognizing the kinds of sentence structures available to writers and speakers is an important step toward achieving effective expression. Let's review the three kinds of sentence structures that you have been studying and include a fourth category as well.

Kind of Sentence	Minimum Requirement	Example
Simple	One independent clause	The United States purchased Alaska from Russia in 1867.
Compound	Two independent clauses	The exact boundary of the "panhandle" strip of coastline seemed fairly unimportant, but the 1898 Gold Rush made this boundary significant.
Complex	One independent clause and one dependent clause	After the boundary dispute had become extremely serious, a court of six judges was chosen.
Compound–complex	Two independent clauses and one dependent clause	When the United States purchased Alaska from Russia in 1867, the exact boundary of the "panhandle" strip of coastline seemed fairly unimportant; however, the 1898 Gold Rush made this boundary significant.

Developing the ability to use a variety of sentence structures to facilitate effective communication takes practice. Start sharpening your skills with the reinforcement exercises for Level III on pp. 271–273.

HOTLINE QUERIES

Question: Can the word *that* be omitted from sentences? For example, *She said [that] she would come.*

Answer: The relative pronoun *that* is frequently omitted in conversation and casual writing. For absolute clarity, however, skilled writers include it.

Question: Is there some rule about putting periods in organization names that are abbreviated? For example, does *IBM* have periods?

Answer: When the names of well-known business, educational, governmental, labour, and other organizations or agencies are abbreviated, periods are normally not used to separate the letters. Thus, no periods would appear in IBM, YWCA, UAW, UN. The names of radio and television stations and networks are also written without periods: CNN, CFRB, CBC, PBS. Geographical abbreviations, however, generally do require periods: U.S.A., U.A.E., S.A. The two-letter state and province abbreviations used in computerized address systems require no periods: NF, ON, SK, CA, NY, OH, and so on.

Question: As a command, which is correct: *lay down* or *lie down*?

Answer: Commands are given in the present tense. You would never tell someone to *closed the door* because commands are not given in the past tense. To say *lay down* (which is the past tense form of *lie*) is the same as saying *closed the door.* Therefore, use the present tense: *lie down.*

Question: In this sentence which word should I use? *Your order will be sent to you in the (later or latter) part of the week.*

Answer: Use *latter.* The word *latter* designates the second of two persons or things. In addition, *latter* can be used to mean "further advanced in time or sequence," or *latter* can be used to contrast with *former.* In your sentence, the *latter* part of the week contrasts with the *former* part of the week.

Question: I have a lot of trouble with verbs in sentences like this: *She was one of approximately 20,000 Canadian women who (was or were) diagnosed with breast cancer last year.*

Answer: You're not alone. Make your verb agree with its antecedent (*women*). One easy way to work with sentences like this is to concentrate on the clause that contains the verb: *Of those Canadian women who were diagnosed with breast cancer last year, she was one.*

CHAPTER 15   Reinforcement Exercises

A. (**Self-check**) Indicate whether the following word groups are phrases *(P)*, independent clauses *(I)*, or dependent clauses *(D)*. (Remember that phrases do not have both subjects and verbs.)

LEVEL I

Example: in the spring of the year   _____P_____

1. when you consider how much time we spent   _____

2. paralegals and administrative assistants worked together   _____

3. at the crack of dawn to finish studying   _____

4. as he stated earlier in the lecture   _____

5. she answered immediately   _____

6. recently they acquired an option to purchase the property   _____

7. before anyone had an opportunity to examine it carefully   _____

8. in the middle of the five-year fiscal period from 1995 to 2000   _____

9. unless the human resources department rejects his application   _____

10. our new pricing schedule takes effect January 1   _____

Check your answers.

B. Indicate whether the following word groups are phrases *(P)*, independent clauses *(I)*, or dependent clauses *(D)*. For the clauses underline the subjects once and the verbs twice.

Example: until <u>we</u> <u>are</u> able to assess the damage   _____D_____

1. as you complete the research   _____

2. in order that students may attend   _____

3. many businesses sell services rather than products   _____

4. on the last line of the contract   _____

5. after he complimented Miss Ross's work   _____

6. she swerved just in time   _____

7. might have been considered   _____

8. since Charles began working as a marketing representative   _____

1. D 2. I 3. P 4. D 5. I 6. I 7. D 8. P 9. D 10. I

9. Division Manager Kelsey analyzed the data   _____

10. during our lunch hour last week   _____

C. After each sentence write the correct word in the space provided. Use the relative pronoun *which* only to introduce non-essential clauses (clauses that require commas).

1. We're shopping for software (that, who, which) we can use without customizing.   _____

2. Is this the horse (who, which, that) broke its leg?   _____

3. Revenue Canada, (who, which, that) processes our income tax returns, is choked with paperwork at the end of April.   _____

4. The Bank of Montreal is known as a company (who, which, that) emphasizes customer service.   _____

5. I have a friend (who, which, that) cannot study alone.   _____

6. Any bank (who, that, which) adds an outside ATM can reduce the number of its inside tellers.   _____

7. Our team, (who, that, which) has authority to set its own work schedules, tries to rotate the hardest jobs.   _____

8. The ruby-throated hummingbird, (who, which, that) measures less than ten centimetres in length, migrates great distances to wintering grounds in the southern U.S. and Mexico.   _____

9. We plan to use our new Web site as a research tool (who, that, which) will enhance our print coverage.   _____

10. Employers are looking for workers (who, that, which) have good vocabularies, grammar, and manners.   _____

D. Sort this group of words into three lists, and write them below: *and, if, but, moreover, although, nor, because, consequently, or, thus, since, however.*

Coordinating Conjunctions	Conjunctive Adverbs	Subordinating Conjunctions
_____	_____	_____
_____	_____	_____
_____	_____	_____
_____	_____	_____

E. Use your imagination to write complete sentences according to the following directions. Remember that clauses must contain subjects and verbs.

1. A sentence using *and* to connect two independent clauses. _____

_____

_____

2. A sentence using *but* to connect two independent clauses. _____

_____

_____

3. A sentence using *because* to introduce a dependent clause. _____

_____

_____

4. A sentence using *although* to introduce a dependent clause. _____

_____

_____

5. A sentence using *after* to introduce a dependent clause. _____

_____

_____

6. A sentence using *and* to join two phrases. _____

_____

_____

A. **(Self-check)** Where appropriate, insert commas in the following sentences. In the space provided after each sentence, indicate the number of commas you have added to that sentence. Do not add any commas that you cannot justify.

LEVEL II

Example: After we hiked to the summit‸ we pitched our tent.   1

1. Tony Molino who recently took out a life insurance policy wanted more security for his family.   _____

2. As predicted interest rates will climb throughout a period of rampant inflation.   _____

3. Supplies for all office equipment which includes computers are now stored in Room 20.   _____

4. A magazine that is featuring the 100 best places to work is now on the newsstands.   _____

5. Annette Ridgeway who was the first salesperson to reach the quota earned a considerable bonus.   _____

6. Any salesperson who sells more than the weekly quota will receive a bonus.   _____

7. If possible send the report that compares your current sales figures with last year's.   _____

8. The latest production model unless it is altered drastically looks as if it will be a winner.   _____

9. Please consider our budget deficit before you make a decision.   _____

10. A profit-sharing plan for employees is now available although I believe the announcement about it will not be made until next week.   _____

Check your answers.

B. Where appropriate, insert commas in the following sentences. In the space provided after each sentence, indicate the number of commas that you added. Be prepared to discuss the reasons for the commas you use.

1. Joseph Farrell who developed an innovative Web site received the top award.   _____

2. A journalist who developed an innovative Web site received the top award.   _____

3. If you have any further questions please contact Mr. Brown.   _____

4. We have received a directive to hold all shipments although I do not know why.   _____

5. I will edit and process the Microsoft order tomorrow morning if that meets with your approval.   _____

6. When completed the newly printed forms will be used for billing.   _____

7. All the information on my personal résumé which I typed myself fills just one page.   _____

8. Although you said my order was shipped ten days ago I have not yet received it.   _____

9. The warranty that you refer to in your recent letter covers only merchandise brought to our shop for repair.   _____

10. Ray Rampersad who works in the Traffic Department received last month's merit award.   _____

11. A secretary who joined our staff only two months ago received this month's merit award.   _____

12. Zone Improvement Program codes which are better known as zip codes were designed in the United States to expedite the sorting and delivery of mail.   _____

13. I would like to give your suggestion more thought when I am not quite so preoccupied.   _____

14. Parliament will surely when it convenes in its regular session take up the defence issue.   _____

15 Before you make a decision consider our strained financial condition.   _____

16 No additional tuition increases can be made if I understand the legislation correctly.   _____

17. In order that we may complete the mailing quickly the address list is being printed from our database.   _____

18. In the coming fiscal year provided that enough funds are available we hope to expand our employee recreation program.   _____

19. The clerk who receives the orders also sets the prices and makes the initial calculations.   _____

20. Marketers that develop advertising targeted at heavy users are attempting to build brand loyalty.   _____

A. **(Self-check)** Indicate the structure of the following sentences by writing the appropriate letter in the spaces provided:

a = Simple sentence   b = Compound sentence
c = Complex sentence   d = Compound–complex sentence

Example: We expect to receive the price list shortly.   _____*a*_____

1. The project manager suggested a new marketing campaign. _____

2. Since it passed the controversial ordinance, the city council has been besieged by calls. _____

3. A decision had to be made soon; therefore, a managers' meeting was scheduled for Monday. _____

4. We have no supplies, and other departments face a similar problem. _____

5. Allen was offered a sales position in Fredericton; therefore, he eagerly made plans to travel to New Brunswick, where he looked forward to beginning his sales career. _____

6. The bank will charge a service fee unless you write fewer cheques. _____

7. The cost of the product increased, but sales continued to climb. _____

8. Although the letter was concise, its message was clear; moreover, it promoted goodwill. _____

9. Alison Stewart, Dee Frome, and Mike Crackower will be transferred. _____

10. Because pictures are worth a thousand words, your report should include photos or graphics. _____

Check your answers.

1.a 2.c 3.b 4.b 5.d 6.c 7.b 8.d 9.a 10.c

B. Rewrite the following groups of simple sentences into *one* sentence for each group. Add coordinating conjunctions, conjunctive adverbs, and subordinating conjunctions as needed to create more effective complex, compound, and compound–complex sentences.

Example: Canadian Tire needed an executive assistant. It advertised in local newspapers. It finally hired a recent graduate. The graduate had excellent skills.

After advertising for an executive assistant in local newspapers, Canadian Tire finally hired a recent

graduate who had excellent skills.

1. Rusty was recently hired as a word processing specialist. She will work for Great-West Life Assurance. Great-West is located in Winnipeg, Manitoba.

_____

_____

_____

2. Each intern is assigned to a senior staff member. The staff member acts as a mentor. The staff member assists the intern with eventual job placement.

_____

_____

_____

3. Makers of the Rolls-Royce plan to open showrooms in Shanghai and Hong Kong. The world's largest market for Rolls-Royce cars is China.

_____

_____

_____

4. Jerry Eichorn recently finished his business degree. He is looking for employment in Alberta. Alberta is Jerry's home.

_____

_____

_____

5. Nancy Burnett is a single parent. She has merchandising experience. Nancy started a mall-based chain of stores. These stores sell fashionable, durable children's clothing.

_____

_____

_____

6. Skilled writers save time for themselves. They also save time for their readers. They organize their ideas into logical patterns. They organize their ideas before sitting down at their computers.

_____

_____

_____

C. **Optional Composition.** Your instructor may ask you to complete this exercise of ten sentences on a separate sheet. Write original sentences that illustrate the following: a simple sentence, a compound sentence, a complex sentence, and a compound–complex sentence. Write original sentences that begin with the following subordinating conjunctions: *if, when, as,* and *since*. In addition, write sentences in which *who* is used to introduce an essential clause and again to introduce a non-essential clause. Label each sentence.

Editor's Challenge

The following memo contains intentional errors in spelling, proofreading, punctuation, and language principles covered thus far. Use standard proofreading marks to show all necessary corrections.

Dee Kirkland Modelling and Dance Studios

MEMORANDUM

DATE: February 21, 200x

TO: Karen Archer Stacy Janisse Eduardo Solano
Robin Haynes Mayer Rubin Tom Winters

FROM: Dee Kirkland

SUBJECT: MARCH 1 FASHION SHOW AT WESTLAND PLAZA HOTEL

Thanks to all of you acceptional students for agreeing to participate in this years fashion show at the Westland Plaza Hotel.

Show time is 8:15 p.m., if possible you should be there at 6:30 to prepare. Rehearsals is scheduled for Tuesday, February 25, and Thursday, February 27, from 5 to 6:15 p.m. Its important for you to be promp!

Participants in the fashion show will not be payed, however, we have a bonus for you. Mr. Lon McHenry who is this years sponsor is one of those people who likes to encourage young models, so he will allow you to by any of the items in the show at 20 per cent below his cost.

The cloths are all from CAL SPORT. Which specializes in informal fashions. Since shoes are not supplied everyone should bring there own casual shoes or running shoes.

Of all the students in the school, I choose you to participate in the show because you have showed excellent potential and professionalism. I want you to treat this show like it was any professional paid job. This fashion show is bigger then any show in the area, please consider it a extension of your training. If you succeed here you can count on farther success as you grow in your career.

POSTTEST

Insert appropriate commas in the following sentences. Mark *C* if the sentence is correct.

1. If the figures are available send them by e-mail to our Halifax branch office. _____

2. When necessary we make rush shipments of products that we have in our immediate inventory. _____

3. The demonstration by Jeremy Jenkins who represents DataTech Products will be Friday. _____

4. Any manager or employee who is unable to attend the Friday demonstration should call me. _____

5. Since many employees are interested in spreadsheet programs they will be discussed first. _____

learning.web.ways

Goal: To learn about privacy policies.

1. With your Web browser on the screen, enter the URL for a search engine, such as **<www.google.com>**. Search for **"privacy policies."** Be sure to use the quotation marks.

2. Select a general article to read, such as "Privacy Policies Spread, but Privacy Doesn't" published by *PC World*.

3. What should a privacy policy include?

4. Inspect the privacy policies at three sites, such as Canada's flagship retailer the Hudson's Bay Company **<http://www.hbc.com/hbc/>**, leading financial institution Toronto Dominion Bank **<http://www.td.com/>**, and software giant Corel Corporation **<http://www.corel.com>**. Look carefully to find a reference to each site's privacy policy. Which company seems to have the most effective policy? Print two pages of the policy you like best.

5. End your session, and submit your printout along with your answers.

1. available, 2. necessary, 3. Jenkins, Products, 4. C 5. programs,

UNIT 4 REVIEW Chapters 12–15 (Self-Check)

Begin your review by rereading Chapters 12 through 15. Then test your comprehension of those chapters by completing the exercises that follow. Compare your responses with those provided at the end of the book.

In the blank provided, write the letter of the word or phrase that correctly completes each of the following sentences.

LEVEL I

1. I've never seen a (a) worse, (b) worst printing job than this. _____

2. In comparing Papa John's and Pizza Palace, we decided that Pizza Palace's delivery service was (a) fastest, (b) faster. _____

3. If you need (a) a, (b) an example of her work, just look at her Web site. _____

4. The technician (a) could have, (b) could of repaired the equipment if she had had the parts. _____

5. The weather was (a) to, (b) too moist for the paint to dry. _____

6. We are fortunate to have exceptional employees like Thomas and (a) him, (b) he. _____

7. We're seeking a bright young person (a) which, (b) whom we can train. _____

8. The group of words *if you will write us* is a(n) (a) phrase, (b) independent clause, (c) dependent clause. _____

Selected words have been underscored in the following sentences. Using the letters below, indicate what punctuation should precede and what should follow the underscored words.

    (a)   , _____   (c) ; _____   (e) no punctuation

    (b)   , _____ ,   (d) ; _____ ,

9. Fran came to Moose Jaw in May <u>but</u> moved to Regina in July. _____

10. Jeffrey might be assigned to work in our legal office <u>or</u> he might be assigned to our administrative headquarters. _____

11. Stop at the crosswalk <u>and</u> look both ways. _____

Write the letter of the word or phrase that correctly completes each sentence.

LEVEL II

12. Before we proceed any (a) further, (b) farther with this matter, I must consult my lawyer. _____

13. The search was conducted (a) house to house, (b) house-to-house. _____

14. If you have (a) less, (b) fewer than ten items, you may use the express checkout. _____

15. Mr. Jefferson said that we had done the work (a) satisfactorily, (b) satisfactory. _____

16. What paper is left must be divided (a) among, (b) between the three offices. _____

17. One of the printers must be moved (a) into, (b) in the outer office. _____

In the following sentences selected words have been underscored. Using the letters below, indicate what punctuation should precede and what should follow the underscored words.

    (a) , _____   (c) _____ ,   (e) no punctuation

    (b) , _____ ,   (d) ; _____ ,

18. Miss Daily's secretarial service was an immediate success <u>consequently</u> she is considering opening a second office. _____

19. <u>In the meantime</u> we learned that many others felt the same way. _____

20. The employee <u>who asked for a transfer</u> will be moving to Sudbury. _____

21. Send all your cheques to Jerry Daniels <u>who is in charge of contributions.</u> _____

22. <u>As reported</u> sales figures for the entire corporation have dropped. _____

Write the letter of the word or phrase that correctly completes each sentence.

LEVEL III

23. Vancouver is larger than (a) any other city, (b) any city on the West Coast. _____

24. Examine carefully the (a) 50 first, (b) first 50 pages of the booklet. _____

25. Despite her meagre income, Sally remained independent (a) of, (b) from her parents. _____

26. You will find that the test questions are not very different (a) than, (b) from some of the review questions. _____

27. The union asked that the salary increase be retroactive (a) to, (b) from the first of the year. _____

In the following sentences selected words have been underscored. Using the letters below, indicate what punctuation should precede and follow the underscored words.

(a)   , _____

(c)   _____ ,

(e) no punctuation

(b)   , _____ ,

(d) ; _____ ,

28. <u>When you called our office last week</u> I was unable to locate the information you requested.   _____

29. I was unable to locate the information you requested <u>when you called our office last week.</u>   _____

30. Sales in your district have risen markedly <u>moreover</u> service requests are decreasing.   _____

Hotline Review

Select the word or phrase that correctly completes the statement, and write its letter in the corresponding blank.

31. Of the two options the (a) later, (b) latter seems preferable.   _____

32. The enclosed text (a) maybe, (b) may be appropriate for your proposed course.   _____

33. We are (a) all ready, (b) already for the department meeting next week.   _____

34. Gerald missed the luncheon (a) due to, (b) because of a prior appointment.   _____

35. (a) I hope that, (b) Hopefully, you now have a better understanding of English grammar.   _____

Memos and E-Mail Messages

Memos and e-mail messages are increasingly important forms of internal communication for most companies today. Organizations are downsizing, flattening chains of command, forming work teams, and empowering rank-and-file employees. Given more power in making decisions, employees find that they need more information. They must collect, exchange, and evaluate information about the products and services they offer. Management also needs input from employees to respond rapidly to local and global market actions. This growing demand for information results in an increasing use of memos and especially e-mail. That's why anyone entering the business world today should know how to write good memos and e-mail messages.

Characteristics of Memos and E-Mail Messages

Memos and e-mail messages have a number of characteristics in common:

- They begin with *To, From, Date,* and *Subject.*
- They generally cover just one topic.
- They are informal.
- They are concise.

Memos and e-mail messages use efficient standard formats, such as you see in Figure 15.1 (page 283). So that they can be acted on separately, memos and e-mail messages should discuss only one topic. Let's say you send your supervisor an e-mail message requesting a copier repair. You also tack on a comment about an article you want to appear in the company newsletter. The supervisor may act on one item and overlook the other. He might also want to forward your request for a copier repair directly to the operations manager, but he has to edit or rekey the message because of the second topic. Thus memos and e-mail messages are most helpful when they cover just one subject.

Because they replace conversation, these messages tend to be informal. They may include first-person pronouns, such as *I* and *me*, as well as occasional contractions, such as *can't* or *haven't.* The tone, however, should not become familiar or unbusinesslike. Moreover, memos and e-mail messages should not be wordy. Concise messages save time and often are more easily understood than longer documents.

Writing Plan

For most informational and procedural messages, follow a direct writing plan that reveals the most important information first. Here are specific tips for writing the subject line, first sentence, body, and closing of memos and e-mail messages.

Subject Line. In the subject line, summarize the message. Although brief, a subject line must make sense and should capture the reader's interest. Instead of *Meeting,* for example, try *Meeting to Discuss Hiring Two New Employees. A* subject line is like a newspaper headline. It should snag attention, create a clear picture, and present an accurate summary. It should not be a complete sentence and should rarely occupy more than one line.

First Sentence. Although an explanation occasionally may precede the main idea, the first sentence usually tells the primary idea of the message. For example, an appropriate first sentence in a memo announcing a new vacation procedure follows:

Here are new guidelines for employees taking two- or three-week vacations between June and September.

The opening of a memo may issue a polite command *(Please answer the following questions about . . .),* make a request *(Please begin research on a summer internship program),* or ask a question *(Can your department complete the printing of a . . .).* Try not to begin with a lengthy explanation. Get to the point as quickly as possible.

Skill Check 4.1 Beginning Memos and E-Mail Messages

Which subject line is better for a memo? Circle its letter.

1. **a.** SUBJECT: Inventory
   b. SUBJECT: Annual Pharmacy Inventory Scheduled for June 2

2. **a.** SUBJECT: This Memo Announces Revised Procedures for Applying for Dental Benefits
   b. SUBJECT: Revised Procedures for Dental Benefits Applications

Which opening sentence is better for a memo?

3. **a.** Employees interested in acquiring and improving computer skills are invited to an in-service training program beginning October 4.
   b. For some time now we have been thinking about the possibility of developing an in-service training program for some of our employees.

4. **a.** We have noticed recently a gradual but steady decline in the number of customer chequing accounts.
   b. Please conduct a study and make recommendations regarding the gradual but steady decline of customer chequing accounts.

5. Write a subject line for a memo that describes the possibility of a new sports scoreboard sponsored by Coca-Cola, a topic to be discussed at the next management council meeting.

   _____

   _____

6. Write a subject line for a memo announcing a demonstration of new software for all employees to be given Thursday, November 16.

   _____

   _____

Body of Message. Provide details of the message in the body. If you are asking for information, arrange your questions in a logical order. If you are providing information, group similar information together. Think about using headings in bold print, such as you see in these paragraphs. They help readers understand, locate, and reference information quickly. You can also improve the readability of any message by listing items with numbers or bullets. Compare the two sets of instructions that follow:

Hard to Read
The instructions for operating our copy machine include inserting your meter in the slot, loading paper in the upper tray, and then copies are fed through the feed chute.

Improved

Here are instructions for using the copy machine:

- Insert your meter in the slot.
- Load paper in the upper tray.
- Feed copies through the feed chute.

Notice that all the items in the preceding bulleted list are parallel in construction. That means that each item uses the same form. All begin with verbs. This kind of balanced writing helps readers anticipate and understand information more readily.

Skill Check 4.2 Listing Information

In the space provided, revise the following paragraph so that it includes an introductory sentence and a list of four items.

We are trying to improve budget planning, and we'd also like to control costs. To accomplish these goals, we must change our procedures for submitting requests in the future for outside printing jobs. The new procedures include first determining your exact printing specifications for a particular job. Then we want you to obtain two estimates for the job. These estimates should be submitted in writing to Kelly. Finally, you may place the outside print order—but only after receiving approval.

_____

_____

_____

_____

_____

_____

_____

_____

Closing a Memo or an E-Mail Message. Memos and e-mail messages frequently end with a (a) request for action, (b) summary of the message, or (c) closing thought. If action on the part of the reader is sought, be sure to spell out that action clearly. A vague request such as *Drop by to see this customer sometime* is ineffective because the reader may not understand exactly what is to be done. A better request might be worded as follows: *Please make an appointment to see Rebecca Johnson before June 2, when she will be leaving.* Notice that an *end date* is given. This technique, particularly when coupled with a valid reason, is effective in prompting people to act.

Another way to close an internal message is by summarizing its major points. A closing summary is helpful if the message is complicated. When no action request is made and a closing summary is unnecessary, the writer may prefer to end the memo with a simple closing thought, such as *I'll appreciate your assistance, What do you think of this proposal?* or *Call me if I may answer questions.* Avoid tired, mechanical phrases such as *Don't hesitate to call on me* or *Thank you for your cooperation.* If you wish to express these thoughts, find a fresh way to say them.

Figure 15.1 (p. 283) shows how the four parts of a writing plan combine to create a readable, efficient inter-office memo. For more information on memo and e-mail formats, see Appendix C.

Special Tips for Sending E-Mail Messages

Instead of using paper to send memos, increasing numbers of business people are turning to e-mail to send internal and external messages. To make the best use of e-mail, you may wish to implement the following suggestions:

Compose off-line. Instead of dashing off hasty messages on-line, take the time to compose off-line. Consider using your word processing program and then uploading your message to the e-mail network. This avoids "self-destructing" on-line (losing all your writing through some glitch or pressing the wrong key).

Get the address right. E-mail addresses are sometimes complex, often illogical, and always unforgiving. Omit one character or misread the letter *l* for the number *1*, and your message bounces. Solution: Use your electronic address book for people you write to frequently. And double-check every address that you key in manually. Also, be sure that you don't reply to a group of receivers when you intend to answer only one.

Keep lines, paragraphs, and messages short. Try to keep your lines under 65 characters in length and your paragraphs no longer than eight lines. Above all, keep your message short. If it requires more than three screens, consider sending it in hard-copy form.

Care about correctness. Senders and receivers of e-mail tend to be casual about spelling, grammar, and usage. However, people are still judged by their writing, and you never know how far your message will travel. Read and edit any message before hitting the "Send" button!

Don't send anything you wouldn't want published. Because e-mail seems like a telephone call or a person-to-person conversation, writers sometimes send sensitive, confidential, inflammatory, or potentially embarrassing messages. Beware! E-mail creates a permanent record that often does not go away even when deleted. And every message is a corporate communication that can be used against you or your employer. Don't write anything that you wouldn't want your boss, your family, or a judge to read.

Special Tips for Replying to E-Mail Messages

Scan all messages in your in-box before replying to each individually. Because subsequent messages often affect the way you respond, read them all first (especially all those from the same individual).

Don't automatically return the sender's message. When replying, cut and paste the relevant parts. Avoid irritating your recipients by returning the entire "thread" (sequence of messages) on a topic.

Revise the subject line if the topic changes. When replying or continuing an e-mail exchange, revise the subject line as the topic changes.

Finally, remember that office computers are meant for work-related communication. Don't use company computers for personal matters. Unless your company specifically allows it, never use your employer's computers for personal messages, personal shopping, or entertainment. Assume that all e-mail is monitored. Employers legally have the right to eavesdrop on employee e-mail messages, and many do.

Figure 15.1
Inter-Office Memo

TO: Michelle Young, Legal Services Department

FROM: Rasheed Polk, Human Resources Department

DATE: May 14, 200x

SUBJECT: Change in Job-Advertising Procedures

Effective today, all advertisements for departmental job openings should be routed through the ———— Human Resources Department.

> Introduces main idea directly.

A major problem resulted from the change in hiring procedures implemented last month. Each ———— department has been placing newspaper advertisements for new hires individually, when all such requests should be centralized in this office. To process applications more efficiently, please follow this procedure:

> Explains why change in procedure is necessary.

1. Write an advertisement for a position in your department.

2. Let Human Resources place the ad in an appropriate newspaper. ————

> Presents new procedure in parallel list.

3. Pick up applicant folders from Human Resources the day following the closing date provided in the ad.

Following these guidelines will save you work and will also enable Human Resources to help ———— you fill your openings more quickly. Call Ann Edmonds at Ext. 351 if you have questions about this procedure.

> Summarizes benefits and names contact person.

Writing Application 4.1. On a separate sheet of paper or, preferably, at a computer, revise the following poorly written memo. It suffers from wordiness, indirectness, and confusing instructions. Include a numbered list in your revised memo, and be sure to improve the subject line.

TO: All Staff Members

FROM: Roy Minami, Manager

DATE: July 11, 200x

SUBJECT: COPIER RULES

Some of you missed the demonstration of the operation of our new Turbo X copier last week. I thought you might appreciate receiving this list of suggestions from the salesperson when she gave the demonstration. This list might also be helpful to other employees who saw the demo but didn't take notes and perhaps can't remember all these pointers. It's sometimes hard to remember how to operate a machine when you do it infrequently. Here's what she told us to do. There are two paper loading trays. Load 8 1/2-×-11-inch or 8 1/2-×-14-inch paper in the two loading trays. The paper should curve upward in the tray. You should take your copy and feed it into the machine face up. However, if you have small sheets or book pages or cut-and-pasted copy, lift the copier door and place your copy face down on the glass.

Before you begin, select the number of copies to be made by pressing the touch selector panel. Don't push too hard. If copies become jammed, open the front door and see where the paper got stuck in the feed path. Remove jammed paper. Oh yes, your meter must be inserted before the machine will operate. We urge you, of course, to make only as many copies as you really need. Keep this list to use again.

Don't hesitate to call on me if you need a private demonstration.

Writing Application 4.2. As Jennifer Tovar, manager, Reprographic Services, write an e-mail message to Kevin Suzuki, manager, Technical Services. You are very worried that one of the computers of your operators may be infected with a virus. The computer belongs to Jackie Jimenez. Jackie says that each time she opens a previously stored document in her Word program, the contents of the document are immediately deleted. Fortunately, because Jackie has backup files, she hasn't lost anything yet. But obviously she can't go on using this computer. You plan to assign Jackie some temporary tasks for the rest of the day; however, she must have her computer up and running by tomorrow. You want a technician to inspect her machine before 5 p.m. today. You know that Kevin likes to learn as much about a computer problem as possible before he sends a technician, so include sufficient details to help him identify the problem.

Writing Application 4.3. As Garth M. Scavone, manager of the Customer Services Division, Molson Breweries, write an e-mail message to Melissa Miller, supervisor, Customer Services. Ask Melissa to draft a form letter that can be sent to groups requesting plant tours. In your memo, explain that the brewery has always encouraged tour groups to see your home plant brewery. However, you cannot sponsor tours at this time because of extensive remodelling. You are also installing a new computer-controlled bottling system. Tours are expected to resume in September. You need a form letter that can be sent to all groups but that can be personalized for individual responses. You want the letter draft by Monday, April 6. The letter should build good customer relations, a primary goal of your tour policy. The letter might enclose a free product coupon and a brochure picturing your operations. Tell Melissa to add any information that she feels would improve the letter.

Punctuating Sentences

Commas

OBJECTIVES   When you have completed the materials in this chapter, you will be able to do the following:

LEVEL I
- *Correctly place commas in series, direct address, and parenthetical expressions.*
- *Use commas correctly in punctuating dates, addresses, geographical items, and appositives.*

LEVEL II
- *Place commas correctly in punctuating independent adjectives, verbal phrases, and prepositional phrases.*
- *Use commas correctly in punctuating independent, introductory, terminal, and non-essential clauses.*

LEVEL III
- *Use commas correctly in punctuating degrees, abbreviations, and numerals.*
- *Use commas to indicate omitted words, contrasting statements, clarity, and short quotations.*

PRETEST

Insert appropriate commas in the following sentences.

1. Our records Mr. Thomas indicate that your order was received May 3 and shipped May 6.

2. We have suppliers in Oshawa Ontario and in Montreal Quebec.

3. The lawyer had reason to believe by the way that the judge was not impartial and might be biased against this case.

4. The information revolution may be responsible for the biggest peacetime economic boom in history but keeping up with the digital flow means being chained to your computer.

5. Although tired employees preferred the evening not the morning in-service training programs.

1. records, Mr. Thomas,   2. Oshawa, Ontario, Montreal,   3. believe, way,   4. history,   5. tired, evening, morning,

When you talk with a friend, you are probably unaware of the "invisible" commas, periods, and other punctuation devices that you are using. In conversation your pauses and voice inflections punctuate your thoughts and clarify your meaning. In writing, however, you must use a conventional set of symbols—punctuation marks—to help your reader understand your meaning.

Over the years we have gradually developed a standardized pattern of usage for all punctuation marks. This usage has been codified (set down) in rules that are observed by writers who wish to make their writing as precise as possible. As noted earlier, some professional writers may deviate from conventional punctuation practices. In addition, some organizations, particularly newspapers and publishing houses, maintain their own style manuals to establish a consistent "in-house" style.

The punctuation guidelines presented in this book represent a consensus of punctuation styles that are acceptable in business writing. Following these guidelines will help you to write with clarity, consistency, and accuracy.

LEVEL I

▶ Basic Comma Guidelines

The most used and misused punctuation mark, the comma, indicates a pause in the flow of a sentence. *Not all sentence pauses, however, require commas.* It is important for you to learn the standard rules for the use of commas so that you will not be tempted to clutter your sentences with needless, distracting commas. Here are the guidelines for basic comma usage.

Study Tip

As you begin to learn about commas, try to name a rule or guideline for every comma you insert. For example, *comma/series, comma/parenthetical,* and so forth.

Series

Commas are used to separate three or more equally ranked (coordinate) elements (words, phrases, or short clauses) in a series. A comma before the conjunction ensures separation of the last two items. No commas are used when conjunctions join all the items in a series.

> Only in June, July, and August is a lifeguard on duty. (Series of words. Notice that a comma precedes *and* but no comma follows the last item, *August.*)
> Marvella conducted the research, organized the data, and wrote the report. (Series of phrases)
> Mrs. Horton is the president, Mr. Travis is the marketing manager, and Miss Zavala is the executive assistant. (Series of clauses)
> We need wireless access to e-mail and Web sites and the home office. (No commas needed when conjunctions are repeated.)

Direct Address

Words and phrases of direct address are set off with commas.

> You must agree, *Mr. Lee,* that Ingrid has done outstanding work.
> I respectfully request, *sir,* that I be transferred.

Parenthetical Expressions

Parenthetical words, phrases, and clauses may be used to create transitions between thoughts. These expressions interrupt the flow of a sentence and are unnecessary for its grammatical completeness; they should be set off with commas, no matter

Hotlink

"The Mystery of the Comma Unveiled," a short handout prepared by the Writing Centre at the University College of the Fraser Valley, is well worth a visit and a bookmark. You'll find it at **<http:// www.ucfv.bc.ca/ writing_centre/comma. htm>**.

where they occur in the sentence. Some common parenthetical expressions are listed below.

accordingly	hence	namely
all things considered	however	needless to say
as a matter of fact	in addition	nevertheless
as a result	incidentally	no doubt
as a rule	in fact	of course
at the same time	in my opinion	on the contrary
by the way	in other words	on the other hand
consequently	in the first place	otherwise
for example	in the meantime	therefore
furthermore	moreover	under the circumstances

> *In addition,* your computer skills are excellent. (At beginning of sentence)
> This report is not, *however,* one that must be classified. (Inside sentence)
> You have checked with other suppliers, *no doubt.* (At end of sentence)

The words in question are set off by commas only when they are used parenthetically and actually interrupt the flow of a sentence. Study the following examples.

> *However* the vote goes, we will abide by the result. (No comma needed after *however.*)
> We have *no doubt* our selling techniques must be revamped. (No commas needed to set off *no doubt.*)

Don't confuse short introductory essential prepositional phrases functioning as adverbs with parenthetical expressions. Notice that the following short phrases are essential and, therefore, require no commas.

> *In the summer* the size of our staff declines. (No comma is needed because the short prepositional phrase answers the question *when*?)
> *At our Madison branch* we will hire additional personnel. (No comma is needed because the short prepositional phrase answers the question *where*?)
> *For this reason* we will be lowering our wholesale prices. (No comma is needed because the short prepositional phrase answers the question *why*?)
> *With your help* our production team can meet its goal. (No comma is needed because the short prepositional phrase answers the question *how*?)

Dates, Addresses, and Geographical Items

When dates, addresses, and geographical items contain more than one element, the second and succeeding elements are normally set off by commas. Study the following illustrations.

Dates

> On January 3 we opened for business. (No comma needed for one element.)
> On January 3, 2001, we opened for business. (Two commas set off second element.)
> On Monday, January 3, 2001, we opened for business. (Commas set off second and third elements.)
> In June, 2001, the reorganization was effected. (Commas set off second element.)
> *OR:* In June 2001 the reorganization was effected. (This alternate style is also acceptable when writing the month and year only.)

Study Tip

Phrases are essential (no commas) when they answer the questions *when? where? why?* or *how?*

Hotlink

The Four Basic Comma Rules are clearly and briefly explained by the Memorial University Writing Centre at **<http://www.mun.ca/ writingcentre/ commarules.shtml>**. The link at the bottom of the page will take you to an on-line exercise that offers a possible solution for each case.

Study Tip

In separating cities and provinces and dates and years, many writers remember the initial comma but forget the final one, as in *My friend from Sherbrooke, Quebec, called.*

Addresses

Send the software to Mr. Chun Wong, 1639 Carling Avenue, Ottawa, Ontario K1A 0G5, before Tuesday. (Commas are used between all elements except the province and postal code, which are in this special instance to be considered a single unit.)

Geographical Items

He moved from St. John's, Newfoundland, to Sydney, Nova Scotia. (Two commas set off the name of a province (or a state) unless it appears at the end of the sentence.)

Appositives

You will recall that appositives rename or explain preceding nouns or pronouns (Chapter 6). An appositive that provides information not essential to the identification of its antecedent should be set off by commas.

Debbie Robinson, *the DataMax sales representative,* is here. (The appositive adds non-essential information; commas set it off.)

The sales representative *Debbie Robinson* is here to see you. (The appositive is needed to identify which sales representative has arrived; therefore, no commas are used.)

One-word appositives are read as a unit with the preceding item and do not require commas.

My husband *Kevin* sometimes uses my computer.

Complete the reinforcement exercises for Level I on pp. 297–298.

Spot the Blooper

From *The Union-Leader* [Manchester, NH] "Prince Louis Ferdinand of Prussia, a grandson of Germany's last emperor who worked in a Detroit auto plant in the 1930s and later opposed Nazi dictator Adolf Hitler, has died at age 86." (Could a comma help clarify who worked in the auto plant? Would the idea be better expressed in two sentences?)

LEVEL II

▶ Special Guidelines for Using Commas

At this level we will review comma usage guidelines that you studied in previous chapters, and we will add one new guideline for the punctuation of prepositional phrases.

Independent Adjectives

Separate two or more adjectives that equally modify a noun (Chapter 12).

An *industrious, ambitious* student came to see me.
On-line customers can conduct *secure, real-time* banking transactions.

Introductory Verbal Phrases

Verbal phrases that precede main clauses should be followed by commas (Chapter 11).

To qualify for the position, you must have two years' experience.
Starting Monday, all sales orders must be in triplicate.

Prepositional Phrases

One or more introductory prepositional phrases totalling five or more words should be followed by a comma.

In the spring of the year, our thoughts may be diverted from academics.
For a period of six months, a new employee is on probation.

Hotlink

For a chatty on-line discussion of commas, go to "Commas: They're Not Just for English Majors Anymore" **<http://parallel.park.uga.edu/~sigalas/Commas/ie.html>**.

Introductory prepositional phrases of fewer than five words require *no* commas.

> *In August* that stock reached its highest price. (Short prepositional phrase requiring no comma)
>
> *In some instances* it will be necessary to increase our price. (Short prepositional phrase requiring no comma)

Do *not* use commas to set off prepositional phrases in other positions when they contain essential information and do not interrupt the sentence.

> Sales for our branches *in the province of British Columbia* have improved. (No commas needed because prepositional phrases tell *where* sales improved and do not interrupt the flow of the sentence.)
>
> We do not *at this time* anticipate any unusual expenses. (No commas needed because prepositional phrase tells *when* no unusual expenses are expected.)

Independent Clauses

When a coordinating conjunction joins independent clauses, use a comma before the coordinating conjunction, unless the clauses are very short (Chapter 14).

> We may have Paul Dean work on that project, *or* we may ask Valerie Lieu.

Introductory Clauses

Dependent clauses that precede independent clauses are followed by commas (Chapter 15).

> *When you have finished,* please return the style manual.
> *If you need help,* please call me in the afternoon.
> *Since we need more clerks,* we will begin advertising.

Terminal Dependent Clauses

Use a comma before a dependent clause at the end of a sentence *only* if the dependent clause is an afterthought.

> Please return the style manual *when you have finished with it.* (No comma needed.)
>
> I plan to leave at 3:30, *if that meets with your approval.* (Dependent clause added as an afterthought.)

Non-Essential Clauses

Use commas to set off clauses that are used parenthetically or that supply information not needed for the grammatical completeness of a sentence.

> An increase in employee salaries, *as you can well understand,* must be postponed until profits improve.
>
> We received a letter from Anne Diga, *who is now living in Red Deer, Alberta.*

Do *not* use commas to set off clauses that contain essential information.

> A student *who is studying English* certainly needs an up-to-date dictionary. (No commas are necessary because the italicized clause is essential; it tells which student needs an up-to-date dictionary.)

Complete the reinforcement exercises for Level II on pp. 299–300.

Notable Quotable

"Both tears and sweat are salty, but they render a different result. Tears will get you sympathy; sweat will get you change."
—Jesse Jackson

Study Tip

The comma after an introductory clause is probably the most frequently missed comma in student writing. Be sure to insert a comma after a clause beginning with *If, When, As, Since,* and so forth.

Hotlink

If your writing suffers from the infamous comma splice, here's another excellent Memorial University page to help you out: **<http://www.mun.ca/writingcentre/commasplices.shtml>**. For more exercises, click on the link at the bottom of the page.

▶ Additional Guidelines for Using Commas

Degrees and Abbreviations

Degrees and professional designations following individuals' names are set off by commas. Abbreviations such as *Jr.* and *Sr.* are not set off by commas unless the individual prefers to use commas.

> Judith Lounsbury, Ph.D., applied for the position of college president.
> Elizabeth Truez, M.D., had a flourishing practice.
> John T. O'Dell Jr. is frequently confused with John T. O'Dell Sr.
> Only Gregory Stoddard, Jr., is unable to participate. (Individual prefers having *Jr.* set off by commas.)

The abbreviations *Inc.* and *Ltd.* are not set off by commas (unless the company's legal name includes the commas).

> DMR Group Inc. is based in Montreal. (Canadian companies' legal names do not as a rule include commas before *Inc.* or *Ltd.*)
> The U.S. firm of Blackstone & Smythe, Inc., exports goods worldwide. (Since this company name includes a comma before *Inc.,* a second comma must follow *Inc.* when it appears in the middle of a sentence.)

Numerals

Unrelated figures appearing side by side should be separated by commas.

> A total of 150, 1990 graduates attended the reception.
> By 2004, 1.3 billion subscribers will be using wireless devices worldwide.

Numbers of more than four digits require commas. Four-digit numbers require commas only when they occur together with larger numbers that must be written with commas.*

> 2760 47,950 6,500,000

However, calendar years, telephone numbers, house numbers, decimals, page numbers, serial numbers, contract numbers, and U.S. zip codes are written without commas within the numerals.

1867	(Calendar year)
(902) 429-0311	(Telephone number)
20586 Victory Avenue	(House number)
.98651	(Decimal)
p. 3561	(Page number)
36-5710-1693285763	(Serial number)
No. 359063420	(Contract number)
02116	(Zip code)

Omitted Words

A comma is used to show the omission of words that are understood.

> Last summer we hired 12 employees; this summer, 3 employees. (Comma shows omission of *we hired* after *summer.*)

---

* *A commonly accepted alternative style is to use spaces rather than commas. Spaces <u>must</u> be used when metric quantities are expressed.*

Spot the Blooper

From *The Boston Globe*: "Then her hair caught fire while sitting in a front seat during a fireworks display."

Spot the Blooper

Sign outside a restaurant in Granada, Mississippi: "LETS EAT SENIOR CITIZENS."

Contrasting Statements

Commas are used to set off contrasting or opposing expressions. These expressions are often introduced by such words as *not, never, but,* and *yet.*

> The nominating committee selected Mr. Cardinal, not Mr. Monroe, as its
> representative. (Two commas set off contrasting statement that appears
> in the middle of sentence.)
> The harder our staff works, the further behind we seem to get. (One comma
> sets off contrasting statement that appears at the end of a sentence.)
> Our budget for equipment this year is reduced, yet quite adequate.

Clarity

Commas are used to separate words repeated for emphasis and words that may be misread if not separated.

> Mr. Long said it was a very, very complex contract.
> Whoever goes, goes at his or her own expense.
> No matter what, you know you have our support.

Short Quotations

A comma is used to separate a short quotation from the rest of a sentence. If the quotation is divided into two parts, two commas are used. (Quotation marks are discussed in Chapter 18, Level III.)

> Mrs. Lara said, "The deadline for the McBride contract is June 6."
> "The deadline for the McBride contract," said Mrs. Lara, "is June 6."

Complete the reinforcement exercises for Level III on pp. 301–302.

Study Tip

Here's a good rule to follow in relation to the comma: *When in doubt, leave it out!*

HOTLINE QUERIES

Question: My boss always leaves out the comma before the word *and* when it precedes the final word in a series of words. Should the comma be used?

Answer: Although some writers omit this comma, present practice favours its use so that the last two items in the series cannot be misread as one item. For example, *The departments participating are Engineering, Accounting, Personnel, and Human Resources.* Without that final comma, the last two items might be read as being one item.

Question: Should I use a comma after the year in this sentence? *In 1999 we began operations.*

Answer: No. Commas are not required after short introductory prepositional phrases unless confusion might result without them. If two numbers, for example, appear consecutively, a comma would be necessary to prevent confusion: *In 1999, 156 companies used our services.*

Question: Are these three words interchangeable: *assure, ensure,* and *insure?*

Answer: Although all three words mean "to make secure or certain," they are not interchangeable. *Assure* refers to persons and may suggest setting someone's

---

mind at rest (*let me assure you that we are making every effort to locate it*). *Ensure* and *insure* both mean "to make secure from loss," but only *insure* is now used in the sense of protecting or indemnifying against loss (*the building and its contents are insured*).

Question: It seems to me that the word *explanation* should be spelled as *explain* is spelled. Isn't this unusual?

Answer: Many words derived from root words change their spellings in their various grammatical forms. Consider these: *maintain, maintenance; repeat, repetition; despair, desperate, desperation; pronounce, pronunciation.*

Question: Is *appraise* used correctly in this sentence? *We will appraise shareholders of the potential loss.*

Answer: No. Your sentence requires *apprise,* which means "to inform or notify." The word *appraise* means "to estimate" (*he will appraise your home before you set its selling price*).

Question: Is an apostrophe needed in this sentence? *The supervisor('s) leaving early on Thursday prevented us from finishing the job by Friday.*

Answer: Yes, the apostrophe is needed: *the supervisor's leaving* … The word *leaving* is a verbal noun (a gerund), and its modifier must be possessive. Other examples of this: *the boy's whistling, the lion's roaring, my friend's driving.*

Question: Which word is correct in this sentence? *The officer (cited, sited, sighted) me for speeding.*

Answer: Your sentence requires *cited,* which means "to summon" or "to quote." *Site* means "a location," as in *a building site* or "to choose a position for" as in *site the proposed school building.* *Sight* means "a view," as in *the building was in sight* or "to see," as in *a ship was sighted.*

CHAPTER 16 Reinforcement Exercises

A. (**Self-check**) In the sentences below insert necessary commas. Indicate in the space provided the number of commas that you inserted. Be prepared to explain the reason for any comma you used.

Example: We believe ˄ on the contrary ˄ that our budget is too low.   2

1. Monday February 5 2001 was the most important date in the history of our company.   _____

2. Hong Kong is on the other hand one of the most densely populated areas in the world.   _____

3. Please see the large selection of trunks briefcases airplane luggage and other travel items in our store.   _____

4. Patti lived in Kingston Ontario before she began working in Hull Quebec.   _____

5. Your student Jim Farwell called this morning.   _____

6. Judith Simpson your business English student also called.   _____

7. In the winter we always hire additional personnel in the warehouse and in the office.   _____

8. Your car Mr. Takeda is not properly registered.   _____

9. We have no doubt that such practices are widespread.   _____

10. Keep your hotel bills and your restaurant and gasoline receipts.   _____

Check your answers.

B. Insert necessary commas in the sentences below. Indicate in the space provided the number of commas that you inserted.

1. As a matter of fact several students asked the same question.   _____

2. Send the Web-enabled cellphone to Mrs. J. D. McKay 4692 Oak Drive Etobicoke Ontario M9B 1L8 as soon as possible.   _____

3. Cynthia Felix the former office manager now has a similar job in Winnipeg Manitoba.   _____

4. We would like of course to have personal letters sent to all the donors.   _____

5. The document was recorded on Tuesday March 21 1993 in Calgary Alberta.   _____

6. We feel however that a job transfer would be appropriate.   _____

7. I understand that your brother Keith is pleased with his new smart phone.   _____

9. (0) 10. (0)

4. (3) Kingston, Ontario, Hull, 5. (0) 6. (2) Simpson, student, 7. (0) 8. (2) car, Mr. Takeda,

1. (3) Monday, February 5, 2001, 2. (2) is, hand, 3. (3) trunks, briefcases, airplane luggage,

8. It is a pleasure to announce that our new wireless phone allows you to download, store, and play songs from the Internet.   _____

9. For you Mrs. Treadwell we have a three months' subscription to the *Financial Times*.   _____

10. Hector Vargas joined the staff in December 1994.   _____

11. It is necessary consequently for you to pay the return postage.   _____

12. Terry Thomas who is a student at Mohawk College is studying office information systems.   _____

13. In the meantime we must make flight reservations immediately.   _____

14. The special fares by the way are available only until July 1.   _____

15. Tanya Collins is president Troy Schumacher is vice-president and Robert Chevrier is secretary.   _____

16. I wonder Ms. Gilford when we may visit the Digby Nova Scotia resort hotels.   _____

17. My cousin Paul will arrive Monday July 17 from Chicoutimi Quebec.   _____

18. Bennie Porter the chief security officer responded to a disturbance that awoke nearly everyone in the buiding at 1:30 a.m.   _____

19. We must as a matter of fact analyze the entire document cycle.   _____

20. I have no doubt in my mind about his competency and integrity.   _____

21. Our latest catalogue contains exceptional selections of jewellery china and linens.   _____

22. Incidentally I feel that we should get an outside opinion.   _____

23. It appears Mr. and Mrs. Ford that you owe additional taxes for 1993 1994 and 1995.   _____

24. I noticed on our company Web site by the way that your friend Charles was promoted.   _____

25. Adam Adler the eminent Toronto architect studied our needs developed a plan and designed our office complex.   _____

LEVEL II

A. (**Self-check**) Insert any necessary commas in the following sentences. In the space provided, indicate briefly the reason for the comma(s). Write *C* if the sentence is correct.

Example: If I were you‸ I would take a part-time job and continue school.   *intro. dependent clause*

1. Jeremy made several constructive imaginative suggestions.   _____

2. To communicate effectively you must be able to express your ideas clearly.   _____

3. In 1983 the company enacted a program of energy conservation.   _____

4. As soon as Anna keyboarded the letter I proofread it and mailed it.   _____

5. By January we are able to predict with considerable accuracy the year's profits.   _____

6. Beginning June 15 the interest on your savings account will be non-taxable.   _____

7. Dr. Johnson attended the conference in London and he then travelled to Spain to vacation.   _____

8. The work in this office is strictly confidential as I am sure you are well aware.   _____

9. The person who answers the telephone sounds alert and responsive.   _____

10. When you have completed this exercise you are to check your answers.   _____

Check your answers.

B. Insert any necessary commas. In the space provided, indicate briefly the reason for the comma(s). Write *C* if the sentence is correct.

1. If we reorganized several branches we could develop a more productive operation.   _____

2. The students had just completed their examinations although many had to leave immediately for their jobs.   _____

3. Whether you do or do not buy please feel free to seek our advice.   _____

4. We are looking for a stable reliable individual who is interested in growing with our organization.   _____

5. In the winter Susan Madarieta who was recently hired away from CyberVision will join the executive staff as chief information officer.   _____

---

6. Renouncing her wealthy social background Florence Nightingale became a nurse and is considered the founder of modern nursing. _____

7. Our current liability insurance in view of the new law that went into effect April 1 needs to be increased. _____

8. Some companies use excellent voice mail systems but other organizations use impersonal systems that frustrate and irritate callers. _____

9. It was a privilege to show you our new offices and we look forward to serving you in the near future. _____

10. In the fall the sports scene is dominated by football. _____

11. Having misplaced her keys Kerry had to retrace her day's activities. _____

12. You have purchased from us often and your payments in the past have always been prompt. _____

13. Before a policy is issued a prospective policyholder is thoroughly investigated. _____

14. In our company a prospective policyholder is thoroughly investigated before a policy is issued. _____

15. The energetic resourceful sales representative was most successful. _____

16. Although it represents a small share of our total sales the loss of the Regina territory would negatively affect our profits. _____

17. Lynda Lee who recently bought a sports car has received three speeding tickets in the past six weeks. _____

18. Before we announce this sale to the general public we are inviting our charge account customers to a one-day presale. _____

19. You were probably concerned about your increased insurance rates but you didn't know where to find adequate coverage at reduced rates. _____

20. The contracts that were finished during the early summer must be revised and resubmitted for consideration at the fall board meeting. _____

21. Planning for the cold months ahead your gas company has developed a plan to equalize your monthly bills. _____

22. We hope that the new year will be prosperous for you and that we may have many more opportunities to serve you. _____

23. At a meeting of our advertising committee we decided to renew our contract for one-page advertisements in your magazine. _____

24. We do not at this time see any reason for continuing this inefficient profitless practice. _____

25. When you need a mortgage loan please check our Web site for competitive rates. _____

LEVEL III

A. (**Self-check**) Insert necessary commas. Indicate briefly in the space provided the reason(s) for the comma(s). Write *C* if the sentence is correct.

1. What it is is a matter of principle. _____

2. The first tract of homes will be available May 15; the second September 1. _____

3. "I am having your policy amended" said Mrs. Bennet "and you will receive the paperwork soon." _____

4. In the fall we will need six operators; in the spring eight. _____

5. Mark Simonton C.A. listed the firm's assets at $873500. _____

6. At least 16 2001 Chevy vans must be serviced. _____

7. We are issuing Policy No. 2176800394 in your name. _____

8. We were expecting Miss Weber not Mr. Allen to conduct the audit. _____

9. "A résumé is a balance sheet without any liabilities" said personnel specialist Robert Half. _____

10. The octogenarians had known each other for a long long time. _____

Check your answers.

B. Insert necessary commas. Indicate briefly in the space provided the reason(s) for the comma(s). Write *C* if the sentence is correct.

1. "Nothing you can't spell" said humorist Will Rogers "will ever work." _____

2. Did you know that on July 23 16 additional workers will be hired? _____

3. On January 1 your Policy No. 8643219 will expire. _____

4. Francisco Torres Sr. was born in 1897 and died in 1980. _____

5. On paper diets often sound deceptively simple. _____

6. The longer we keep the funds invested the greater will be the interest. _____

7. Major responsibility for the loan lies with the signer; secondary responsibility with the co-signer. _____

8. That task must be reserved for experienced never inexperienced employees. _____

1. it is, (clarity)   2. second, (omitted words)   3. amended," Bennet, (short quotation)   4. spring, (omitted words)   [*Note:* Do not use a comma after a short introductory prepositional phrase.]   5. Simonton, C.A., (professional designation) $873,500 (numeral more than four digits)   6. 16, (adjacent numerals)   7. C   8. Weber, Allen, (contrasting statement)   9. liabilities," (short quotation)   10. a long, (clarity)

9. Professor Marcus said "All extra-credit assignments are due May 1." _____

10. In short employees must be more considerate of others. _____

11. Jeff Brady Ph.D. and Dominic Corloni M.D. spoke at the opening session. _____

12. Toyota management was worried because 231 1998 sedans had to be recalled. _____

13. It was Dr. Harris not Dr. Shimada who performed the surgery. _____

14. What it was was an international power struggle. _____

15. Half of the payment for the shipment is due on delivery; the balance in six weeks. _____

16. Although bored students managed to stay awake during the lecture. _____

17. Whatever it is it is not very amusing. _____

18. In Room 201 32 computers and 16 printers are operating. _____

19. Co-operation not criticism is what is needed. _____

20. "Frankly" said Abdul "I don't really understand his motivation." _____

21. The government has announced repairs to more than 21 000 km of highway. _____

22. Lynn Craig D.C. and Annette Bellotti M.D. both have offices in the Queensland Medical Building. _____

23. Level 6 secretaries are eligible for promotion after 12 months of probation; Level 5 secretaries after 18 months. _____

24. Whatever is is right. _____

25. The number of workers this year will not be reduced but only if sales remain good. _____

C. Optional Composition.
Your instructor may ask you to complete this exercise on a separate sheet. This chapter presents many guidelines for using commas. Select ten guidelines that you consider most important, and write original sentences to illustrate their use. Identify each guideline.

Editor's Challenge

The following letter illustrates *simplified* style. Notice that all lines begin at the left margin and that the salutation is replaced by a subject line in all capital letters. The complimentary close is replaced by the writer's name and title or company. This letter contains intentional errors in spelling, proofreading, punctuation, and language principles covered thus far. Use standard proofreading marks to make all necessary corrections.

Adventure Sports, Inc.

8550 Old Dairy Road
Juneau, AK 99801

E-mail: troy@alaska.net
FAX: 907-789-2319

March 7, 200x

Mr. Kevin M. Simpson
433 East Temple
Edmonton, AB T9E 7X5

THANKS FOR YOUR INTEREST IN KAYAK TOURS

Enclosed is a list of current trips and other information, that you requested about our kayak tours in Alaska. To ensure a quality wilderness experience the number of guests on a tour are limited to six people. No special experience is neccesary. Many of our guests have never been in a sea kayak, and are surprised to find that they are very stable. Moreover we teach you safe efficient operation of a kayak.

All equipment, meals and safety gear is included in the trip price. We provide charter transportation from Juneau to the trip location, however you are responsible for getting to Juneau, and for your meals and lodging before and after the trip. To reserve a trip you must make a 50 per cent deposit. We will hold reservations for your party for two weeks. Anyone who must request a refund, will be charged a $50 handling fee. If we must cancel a trip a full refund will be made. In some instances, we must cancel because of to few participants, or dangerous weather.

Our most popular trip is whale watching and kayaking at Pt. Adolphus. This four day trip costs US$1050 which includes boat charter and fairy. We also recommend the glacier tour at Tracy Arm, and our island tour of Pt. Couverdon. By the way custom dates is available for familys or group's of three or more.

Call, write or fax to make your reservations. We look forward to providing you with the wilderness adventure of a lifetime!

Troy M. Donohue

TROY M. DONOHUE, ADVENTURE SPORTS INC.

Enclosure

learning.web.ways

Soon you will be looking for a job. You decide to learn as much as possible about trends in your career area.

Goal: To gather job-search and career information.

1. With your Web browser on the screen, go to the Workopolis site **<http://www.workopolis.com/index.html>** and bookmark it.

2. Familiarize yourself with Workopolis by exploring its **Resources** in the frame on the left. What's the **Tip of the Week**? Jot it down.

3. Enter the **Resource Centre** (top of the screen), and click on **Researching a Company or an Industry**. Scroll down, and click on **Business Information by Sector**. Study the list of industries, and click on the one you expect to join after graduating.

4. Go to its **Industry Profiles** page, and print out the section you find most informative.

5. Using your bookmarks, return to Workopolis. In the keyword search box, enter the job title you are interested in. Scroll down and specify the job category, industry, and city or location to which you want your search to apply. **Search**.

6. Print out a page showing information about your job choice in your province.

7. End your session, and submit your printouts and your answers.

---

1. letter, Mrs. Youngblood, 2. thinks, hand, 3. Clark, Ph.D., King, M.B.A., Banff, Alberta, 4. trained, logical, 5. unsure, Carlson, Ray,

Semicolons and Colons

OBJECTIVES   When you have completed the materials in this chapter, you will be able to do the following:

LEVEL I
- *Use semicolons correctly in punctuating compound sentences.*
- *Use semicolons when necessary to separate items in a series.*

LEVEL II
- *Distinguish between the proper and improper use of colons to introduce listed items.*
- *Correctly use colons to introduce quotations and explanatory sentences.*

LEVEL III
- *Distinguish between the use of commas and semicolons preceding expressions such as* namely, that is, *and* for instance.
- *Understand why semicolons are sometimes necessary to separate independent clauses joined by* and, or, nor, *and* but.
- *Use colons appropriately and be able to capitalize words following colons when necessary.*

PRETEST

Insert appropriate semicolons, colons, and commas in the following sentences.

1. Small businesses often lack credit opportunities therefore the owners of these businesses must raise capital privately.

2. We have engaged as speakers the following individuals Tom Woods Mount Royal College Beverly Linnell Southern Alberta Institute of Technology and Judy O'Shea Lethbridge Community College.

3. Speakers for the morning session are now scheduled speakers for the afternoon session have not yet been arranged.

continued

4. The programming committee however must proceed with plans for the entire conference.

5. Although the committee had many cities from which to choose we decided to limit the selection to the following namely Vancouver, Toronto, or Montreal.

Skilled writers use semicolons and colons to signal readers about the ideas that will follow.

The semicolon is a stronger punctuation mark than a comma, which signifies a pause; but the semicolon is not as strong as a period, which signifies a complete stop. Understanding the use of the semicolon will help you avoid fundamental writing errors, such as the *comma splice* (separating two independent clauses with a comma) and the *run-on sentence* (running two independent clauses together without punctuation).

WARNING! Don't overuse the semicolon. Most independent clauses will end with periods. Join clauses together only when the combined idea improves comprehension.

LEVEL I

▶ Basic Uses of the Semicolon

The semicolon is most frequently used in compound sentences. Many business communicators use a comma when they should be using a semicolon. Study the following examples to make sure you don't make this error.

Independent Clauses Separated by Conjunctive Adverbs

You have already learned that independent clauses separated by a conjunctive adverb or a transitional expression (Chapter 14) are usually joined by a semicolon. Here are some review examples.

> Companies make no profits until they recover costs; *therefore*, most companies use a cost approach in pricing. (Semicolon separates two independent clauses joined by the conjunctive adverb *therefore*.)
>
> Advertising is aimed at increasing sales; *thus* an advertising policy must be formulated with that objective. (Semicolon separates two independent clauses joined by the conjunctive adverb *thus*.)

Independent Clauses Without a Coordinating Conjunction or a Conjunctive Adverb

Two or more closely related independent clauses not separated by a conjunctive adverb or a coordinating conjunction (*and, or, nor, but*) may be joined by a semicolon.

> The licensing company is called the *franchisor*; the dealer is called the *franchisee*.

Study Tip

Remember that a comma is used only after a conjunctive adverb of two syllables or more. And don't capitalize the word following a semicolon unless it's a proper noun.

---

1. opportunities; therefore. 2. individuals; Woods, College; Linnell, Technology; O'Shea, 3. scheduled; 4. committee, however; 5. choose, following; namely,

Our inside teller service closes at 4 p.m.; outside ATM service is available 24 hours a day.

As you learned in Chapter 3, a serious punctuation error results when separate independent clauses are joined by only a comma (a comma splice) or without any punctuation whatsoever (a run-on sentence).

Comma splice: Our inside teller service closes at 4 p.m., outside ATM service is available 24 hours a day.

Run-on sentence: Our inside teller service closes at 4 p.m. outside ATM service is available 24 hours a day.

Series Containing Internal Commas or Complete Thoughts

Semicolons are used to separate items in a series when one or more of the items contain internal commas.

Only the company branches in St. John's, Newfoundland; Sherbrooke, Quebec; and Mississauga, Ontario, are showing substantial profits.

Attending the conference were Teresa Caruana, executive vice-president, Cabrillo Industries; Martin Manheim, president, Servex Corporation; and Joyce Moran, program director, Club Mediterranean.

Semicolons are used to separate three or more serial independent clauses.

The first step consists of surveying all available information related to the company objective so that an understanding of all problems can be reached; the second step consists of interviewing consumers, wholesalers, and retailers; and the third step consists of developing a research design in which the actual methods and procedures to be used are indicated.

A series of short independent clauses, however, may be separated by commas (Chapter 16).

Ease of handling is excellent, passenger comfort is certainly above average, and fuel consumption is the lowest of all cars tested.

Complete the reinforcement exercises for Level I on pp. 313–314.

▶ Basic Uses of the Colon

The colon is most often used to introduce formally listed items, quotations, and explanatory sentences.

Formally Listed Items

Use a colon after an independent clause introducing one item, two items, or a formal list. A list may be shown vertically or horizontally and is usually introduced by such words as *the following, as follows, these,* or *thus.* A colon is also used when such words are implied but not stated.

Creating a company Web site offered the following advantage: improved customer service. (Independent clause introduces single item.)

Some of the most commonly used manufacturers' discounts are *the following*: trade, cash, quantity, and seasonal. (Formal list with introductory expression stated)

Our business uses several private delivery services: United Parcel, Purolator, and Federal Express. (Formal list with introductory expression only implied)

These are a few of the services that a correspondent bank performs for other banks:

1. Collecting cheques and payments
2. Accepting letters of credit and travellers' cheques
3. Making credit investigations (Formal list shown vertically)

Do not use a colon unless the list is introduced by an independent clause. Often, lists function as sentence complements or objects. If the statement introducing the list is not complete, no colon should be used. It might be easiest to remember that lists introduced by verbs or prepositions require no colons (because the introductory statement is incomplete).

Three courses in this program are Accounting 103, Business English 210, and Computer Science 220. (No colon is used because the introductory statement is not complete; the list is introduced by a *to be* verb and functions as a complement.)

Letters were sent to Professor Loncorich, Ms. Harned, and Dr. Konishi. (No colon is used because the introductory statement is not an independent clause; the list functions as an object of the preposition *to*.)

Do not use a colon when an intervening sentence falls between the introductory statement and the list.

Purchase orders are being sent to the following companies. The supplies are needed immediately.

IBM   A.B. Dick
Monroe   Microsoft

(No colon is used after *companies* because an intervening sentence falls between the introductory statement and the list.)

Quotations

Use a colon to introduce long one-sentence quotations and quotations of two or more sentences.

Consumer advocate Sandra Hersh said: "Historically, in our private-enterprise economy, consumers determine what and how much is to be produced through their purchases in the marketplace; hence the needs of consumers are carefully monitored by producers."

Incomplete quotations not interrupting the flow of a sentence require no colon, no comma, and no initial capital letter.

The writer described the new Jackson-Triggs winery as "a vintner's heaven."

Explanatory Sentences

Use a colon to separate two independent clauses if the second clause explains, illustrates, or supplements the first.

The company's newly elected directors were immediately faced with a perplexing dilemma: they had to choose between declaring bankruptcy and investing additional funds in an attempt to recoup previous losses.

The applicants for the position all exhibited one common trait: they were achievers who accepted nothing less than success.

Complete the reinforcement exercises for Level II on pp. 315–316.

▶ Special Considerations in Using Semicolons and Colons

You've just studied basic uses for semicolons and colons. Occasionally, though, these punctuation marks are used in circumstances demanding special attention.

Introductory Expressions Such as *namely*, *for instance*, and *that is*

When introductory expressions (such as *namely, for instance, that is,* and *for example*) immediately follow independent clauses, they may be preceded by either commas or semicolons. Generally, if words following the introductory expression appear at the end of the sentence and form a series or an independent clause, use a semicolon before the introductory expression. If not, use a comma.

Study Tip

Notice that a comma follows *namely, for instance, that is,* and *for example* when these words are used as introductory expressions.

Use semicolons

Numerous fringe benefits are available to employees; *namely*, injury compensation, life insurance, health insurance, dental care, and vision care. (A semicolon is used because *namely* introduces a series at the end of the sentence.)

We offer outstanding prices on flights to Europe; *for example*, flights to Glasgow and Belfast begin at $469. (A semicolon is used because *for example* introduces an independent clause.)

Use commas

Our company is considering better ways to evaluate employees, *for example*, an objective performance appraisal system. (A comma is used because *for example* introduces neither a series nor an independent clause.)

These same introductory expressions (*namely, for instance,* etc.) may introduce parenthetical words within sentences. Usually, commas punctuate parenthetical words within sentences. If the parenthetical words thus introduced are punctuated by internal commas, however, use dashes or parentheses. (Dashes and parentheses are treated in detail in Chapter 18.)

Hotlink

Another helpful handout on colon and semicolon use **<http://www.carleton.ca/wts/handouts/colon_and_semi-colon.htm>** comes from the Carleton University Writing Tutorial Service.

Use commas

The biggest health problems facing workers, *namely,* drug abuse and alcoholism, cost industry over one billion dollars a year. (Parenthetical words contain only two items joined by *and*.)

Use dashes

The pursuit of basic job issues—*for instance,* wages, job security, and working conditions—was the main concern of workers. (Parenthetical words are punctuated with commas.)

Independent Clauses With Coordinating Conjunctions

Normally, a comma precedes a coordinating conjunction (*and, or, nor, but*) when it joins two independent clauses. If either of the independent clauses contains an additional comma, however, the reader might be confused as to where the second independent clause begins. For this reason many writers prefer to use a semicolon, instead of the normally expected comma, to separate independent clauses when either independent clause contains a comma.

> *Use comma*
> We have considered your suggestions carefully, and it appears that they have considerable merit. (Comma precedes coordinating conjunction because no additional punctuation appears within either clause.)

> *Use semicolon*
> On the basis of Comptroller Macon's recommendation, we have considered your suggestions carefully; and it appears that they have considerable merit. (Semicolon precedes coordinating conjunction because a comma appears within one of the independent clauses.)

Other Uses of the Colon

- After the salutation of a business letter
  Dear Mr. Jameson: Ladies and Gentlemen: Dear Mike:

- In expressions of time to separate hours from minutes
  2:45 p.m.   12:01 a.m.

- Between titles and subtitles
  HOW: A Handbook for Office Workers

- Between place of publication and name of publisher
  Choy, Wayson. *The Jade Peony*. Vancouver: Douglas & McIntyre, 1995.

Capitalization Following Colons

Do not capitalize the initial letter of words or of phrases listed following a colon unless the words so listed are proper nouns or appear as a vertical array.

> The four Cs of effective letter writing are the following: clarity, courtesy, conciseness, and correctness.
> These cities will receive heavy promotional advertising: Dauphin, Portage la Prairie, and Selkirk.
> To be legally enforceable, a contract must include at least four elements:
> 1. Mutual assent of all parties
> 2. Parties who are competent
> 3. A consideration
> 4. A lawful purpose

Do not capitalize the first letter of an independent clause following a colon if that clause explains or supplements the first one (unless, of course, the first word is a proper noun).

> You will be interested in our credit card for one special reason: we offer you the opportunity of a full refund of the low annual fee.

Capitalize the first letter of an independent clause following a colon if that clause states a formal rule or principle.

> Experienced negotiators adhere to the following principle: Never cut what you can untie.

For a quotation following a colon, capitalize the initial letter of each complete sentence.

> Commenting on the importance of incorporation, historians Kroos and Seropian said: "A strong case can be made for the proposition that the increased use of the corporation was the most important institutional innovation of the century. The corporate form permeates American business."

▶ A Final Word

Semicolons are wonderful punctuation marks when used carefully and knowingly. After reading this chapter, though, some students are guilty of semicolon overkill. They begin to string together two—and sometimes even three—independent clauses with semicolons. Remember to use semicolons in compound sentences *only* when two ideas are better presented together. Forget about joining three independent clauses with semicolons—too unconventional and too difficult to read. In most instances, independent clauses should end with periods.

Complete the reinforcement exercises for Level III on pp. 317–318.

Hotlink

To check your skill using semicolons, try the quiz at **<http://swt.edu/SLAC/ writing/Semi2.htm>**.

HOTLINE QUERIES

Question: Here's a sentence we need help with: *We plan to present the contract to whoever makes the lowest bid.* My supervisor recommends *whoever* and I suggest *whomever.* Which of us is right?

Answer: Your supervisor. The preposition *to* has as its object the entire clause (*whoever makes the lowest bid*). Within that clause, *whoever* functions as the subject of the verb *makes;* therefore, the nominative case form *whoever* should be used.

Question: When I list items vertically, should I use a comma or semicolon after each item? Should a period be used after the final term? For example,

> *Please inspect the following rooms and equipment:*
> 1. *The control room*
> 2. *The power transformer and its standby*
> 3. *The auxiliary switchover equipment*

Answer: Do not use commas or semicolons after items listed vertically, and do not use a period after the last item in such a list. However, if the listed items are complete sentences or if they are long phrases that complete the meaning of the introductory comment, periods may be used after each item.

Question: Is there a plural form of *plus and minus*?

Answer: The plural form is *pluses and minuses (consider all the pluses and minuses before you make a decison).*

Question: I'm setting up advertising copy, and this sentence doesn't look right to me: *This line of fishing reels are now priced …*

Answer: Your suspicion is correct. The subject of the verb in this sentence is *line;* it requires the singular verb *is.*

Question: I wonder if the possessive is correctly expressed in this sentence that I'm transcribing: *I appreciate the candour of both you and Neil in our conversation.* Shouldn't both *you* and *Neil* be made possessive?

Answer: No. It would be very awkward to say *your and Neil's candour.* It's much better to use the *of* construction, thus avoiding the awkward double possessive.

Question: Is this a double negative: *We can't schedule the meeting because we have no room available?*

Answer: No, this is not regarded as a double negative. In grammar a double negative is created when two negatives appear in a single clause such as *I can't hardly…* or *We don't have nothing.* Avoid such constructions. Your sentence has two negatives, but they are quite acceptable as they are in separate clauses.

CHAPTER 17   Reinforcement Exercises

A. (**Self-check**) For each of the following sentences, underline any errors in punctuation. Then in the space provided, write the correct punctuation mark plus the word preceding it. Write *C* if the sentence is correct.

LEVEL I

Example: Breeding and raising horses can be profitable, consequently, large sums are being invested.

profitable;

1. Horse breeding has become a big business and investors are supplying large sums for thoroughbreds.

_____

2. Most thoroughbreds are sold as yearlings it is usually one year before they can race.

_____

3. Investors' expectations are high therefore, competitive bidding for breeding animals is brisk.

_____

4. Some investors use thoroughbred horses as tax shelters, these investors write off the expenses of maintaining the horses.

_____

5. Mr. Marks invested, Mrs. Hiram was interested, and Mr. Stefansson declined.

_____

6. Important breeding is being conducted at Canada West Ranches, Mt. Lehman, British Columbia; Paddockhurst Stables, Nisku, Alberta; and Sam-Son Farms, Milton, Ontario.

_____

7. Stallions yield the highest prices; but mares can also be extremely expensive.

_____

8. The average auction price has tripled in the last five years profits from breeding have climbed even faster.

_____

9. Several investors may form a syndicate to buy a good horse the syndicate then shares expenses and spreads risks.

_____

10. Horse breeding can be an exciting and profitable venture, thus many investors are choosing horses over stocks and bonds.

_____

Check your answers.

B.   Add any necessary commas or semicolons to the following sentences. (Do not add periods.) In the spaces provided, write the number of punctuation marks you inserted. Write *C* if a sentence is correct as written.

Example: New equipment was ordered eight weeks ago‸ delivery is expected within two weeks.
;

1

1. Consumers expect anytime, anywhere access to businesses therefore wireless cellphone use is growing.

_____

2. Dr. Paulson scheduled appointments every 30 minutes he was assisted by an experienced nurse.

_____

1. business; 2. yearlings; 3. high; 4. shelters; 5. C 6. C 7. prices, 8. years; 9. horse; 10. venture;

3. Buildings swayed lights flickered and dishes rattled. _____

4. Serving on the panel are Pam Rippin marketing director Trinity Sales Evelyn Katusak sales supervisor Broome Products and Timothy Miank market analyst Lansing Enterprises. _____

5. Several members of the staff are near the top of their salary ranges we may have to reclassify their jobs before recommending them for increases. _____

6. Your account is now several months past due consequently it is not possible for us to grant you further extensions. _____

7. The shortest recorded reign of any monarch was that of Louis XIX of France it lasted only 15 minutes. _____

8. Every Christmas we hire a number of temporary office workers hence I am writing to ask you to make this announcement about job openings to your students. _____

9. Jeremy worked Jennifer supervised and Jean entertained. _____

10. Web advertising attempts to reach large international audiences television advertising is aimed at national or local audiences. _____

11. Dawson City was full of fortune hunters at the turn of the century it is now full of tourists, at least during the summer. _____

12. Computer hackers can easily decode short passwords thus passwords should be at least six to eight characters long and be a mix of letters and numerals. _____

13. We are opening a branch office in Drumheller and we hope we will be able to serve you from that office in the future. _____

14. Smart companies assume their computer networks will be broken into consequently they develop computer-use policies to limit the damage. _____

15. Speakers for the afternoon session include Ms. Jana Webb executive vice-president Security Systems Professor David Brewer Schulich School of Business York University and Dr. Jane Mangrum director of research Oshawa Group. _____

16. Our new Instant Cash chequing service allows you to write a cheque for more than the balance in your chequing account we transfer funds automatically to your account. _____

17. Employment opportunities are available in hospitals banks and insurance companies however training is often required. _____

18. Such training nevertheless can usually be completed in six to ten months thus you can begin earning wages in less than a year. _____

19. If you open your account immediately your first 500 cheques will be supplied free moreover you will receive a bonus gift if you are among our first 50 customers. _____

20. Three participating institutions are Nova Scotia Community College Halifax Nova Scotia Keewatin Community College The Pas Manitoba and Red Deer College Red Deer Alberta. _____

A. (Self-check) For each of the following sentences, underline any errors in punctuation. Then in the space provided, write the correct punctuation plus the preceding word. If a colon should be omitted, write *Omit colon*. Write *C* if the sentence is correct.

LEVEL II

Example: Special invitations were sent to: President Owens, Vice-President Spears, and Treasurer Avery.

_____*Omit colon*_____

1. The most outstanding speakers at the national convention were: Judy Dresser, Cathy Cheng, and Carol Engel.

_____

2. The educational trip through Ontario included visits to the following: Black Creek Pioneer Village, Toronto; Old Fort Henry, Kingston; and the Canadian Museum of Civilization, Ottawa.

_____

3. Smart phones are available from the following three companies. Please check on prices:
    Motorola
    Nokia
    Samsung

_____

4. During the presentation the realtor explained; "If you purchase before the start of construction, you can choose from 20 suite layouts; you can also customize your suite. Best of all, you can still take advantage of pre-construction prices."

_____

5. The head of the computer security firm admitted one big problem: finding good people without criminal records.

_____

6. Four of the worst computer passwords are: your first name, your last name, *Password*, and the name of a sports team.

_____

7. We have requests for information from three local companies: Pharma Plus, Waldorf Inc., and Data Control.

_____

8. Because of the urgency of the problem, we have sent fax messages to: Evelyn Dobson, Mary Ringle, and Connie Clark.

_____

9. The most commonly observed holidays are the following: Thanksgiving, Christmas, Boxing Day, New Year's Day, and Labour Day.

_____

10. Arriving late for class, the student offered a convincing excuse: her car had run out of gas three kilometres away.

_____

Check your answers.

1. Omit colon 2. C 3. prices: 4. explained: 5. C 6. Omit colon 7. C 8. Omit colon 9. C 10. C

B. For the following sentences add any necessary but missing punctuation marks. For each sentence indicate in the space provided the number of additions you have made. Write *C* if the sentence is correct as it stands.

Example: Shipments of computer components will be sent to Dallas，Vancouver，Barcelona，and Zurich. _____3_____

1. Three similar types of tropical storms with different names are cyclones typhoons and hurricanes. _____

2. Japan faces a serious economic threat its dependence on oil imports endangers its future economic growth. _____

3. Polygraph examinations generally consist of four parts a pre-examination interview, a demonstration, questioning of the examinee, and a post examination interview. _____

4. Speaking at the convention, humorist Lawrence Peter said "Most hierarchies were established by men who now monopolize the upper levels. This deprives women of their rightful share of opportunities for incompetence." _____

5. The records of the following employees will be reviewed for salary evaluation Please send the records by October 1

    Vicky Peck   Julie Mauer

    Tony Watkins   Ivan Krakowski _____

6. The balance sheet is a statement of assets liabilities and owner's equity. _____

7. Included in our introductory offer are the following coloured file folders self-closing envelopes and erasable ballpoint pens. _____

8. Energy in this country is supplied from a number of sources oil natural gas coal nuclear fission and hydropower. _____

9. For graduation you must complete courses in mathematics, accounting, English, management, and computer applications. _____

10. The law of supply and demand can function only under the following condition producers must know what consumers want. _____

11. Professor Charlotte Cohen asked that research reports contain the following parts introduction body summary and bibliography. _____

12. Additional costs in selling a house are title search, land transfer tax, preparation of documents, and closing fee. _____

13. Warren Bennis said "The factory of the future will have only two employees, a man and a dog. The man will be there to feed the dog. The dog will be there to keep the man from touching the equipment." _____

14. In addition to drilling holes, a good electric drill will also enable you to sand rough surfaces, grind compounds, and polish surfaces. _____

15. Business letters generally include four parts date, inside address, body, and closing. _____

LEVEL III

A. (**Self-check**) Insert necessary punctuation. In the space provided, write the number of punctuation marks that you inserted. Write *C* if the sentence is correct.

1. The local community youth program attracted several employees as volunteers; namely, Pam Wheeler, Benita Washington, Sid Daily, and Samar Hillo. _____

2. Sales personnel may be assigned to a number of countries; for example, India, Brazil, France, and South Africa. _____

3. If she accepts the transfer to Calgary, she will have a better chance of promotion; but if she declines the transfer, her family will not be uprooted. _____

4. The meeting started promptly at 1:15 p.m. and ended at 3:45 p.m. _____

5. Many banks now offer automated transfers from savings to chequing accounts that is money may be kept in an interest-bearing savings account until needed. _____

6. All employees are urged to observe the following rule: When in doubt, consult the company style manual. _____

7. The writer of a research report should include a variety of references; for example, books, periodicals, government publications, and newspapers. _____

8. Debra Reinke considered naming her book *Successful Investing A Complete Guide to Your Financial Future.* _____

9. For the opening session of the convention, the keynote speaker will be systems analyst Norma Patterson; and for the afternoon general membership meeting, the speaker will be union representative Judith R. Rice. _____

10. You may repay your loan according to one of the following plans: the annual plan, the semi-annual plan, the quarterly plan, or the weekly plan. _____

Check your answers.

B. For the following sentences add any necessary but missing punctuation marks. For each sentence indicate in the space provided the number of additions you have made. Mark *C* if correct.

Example: If she completes the proposal, Ms. Upchurch will fly to Ottawa on Tuesday; if not, she will leave on Thursday. _____3_____

1. When completing your résumé be sure to include relevant activities for example intern experience work-study experience and volunteer work. _____

1. C 2. C 3. C 4. C 5. (2) accounts; that is, 6. C 7. C 8. (1) *Investing:* 9. C 10. C

2. Because of his extended service abroad Edward Mautz was selected to head the export division and because of her outstanding sales experience Barbara Malom was selected to head the marketing division. _____

3. Karen Epstein remarked that she always found whatever she was looking for in her favourite dictionary namely the *Gage Canadian Dictionary*. _____

4. One of the titles I'm considering for my book is *Your First Résumé A Complete Guide to Strategies and Techniques*. _____

5. Some punctuation marks require a great deal of instruction and practice for example commas colons and semicolons. _____

6. Three times have been designated for the interviews Thursday at 630 p.m. Friday at 330 p.m. and Monday at 10 a.m. _____

7. An author, composer, or photographer may protect his or her product with a government-approved monopoly namely a copyright. _____

8. Our school operates on the quarter system that is the school year is divided into four equal quarters. _____

9. Franca Santin enjoyed her current position as sales representative very much but when a competing company offered her a substantial increase in salary she found it very tempting. _____

10. Stories circulated about Henry Ford founder of the Ford Motor Company Lee Iacocca former CEO Chrysler Motor Company and Shoichiro Toyoda former chief Toyota Motor Company. _____

C. Optional Composition.

Your instructor may ask you to complete this exercise on a separate sheet. Write about your experience using the Internet and e-mail. For example: *I generally use the Internet for e-mail; however, I plan to get better at using it for research.* Write three original sentences illustrating basic uses of semicolons. Write one sentence using *namely* with a semicolon preceding it. Write three original sentences illustrating basic uses of colons. Compose a list arranged vertically, and write an introduction to it using an independent clause that requires a colon. Label each of the sentences.

Editor's Challenge

The following progress report contains intentional errors. Use proofreader's marks to indicate corrections.

★LONESTAR PRODUCTIONS ★

TO: Patrick M. Young
FROM: Kellie Whitford
DATE: May 2, 200x
SUBJECT: SITES FOR *BODEGA BAY* TELEFILM

This memo describes the progress of my search for a appropriate rustic home, villa, or farmhouse. To be used for the wine country sequences in the upcoming telefilm *Bodega Bay*. As you requested three sites has been selected for you to inspect on May 21.

Background. To prepare for this assignment I consulted Director Mario Polero who gave me his preferences for the sight. He wants a picturesque home, that is located near grape vineyards, moreover he would like woods in the background. I also consulted Producer Tucker Setterberg who told me that the site must accommodate 55 to 70 production crew members for approximately three weeks of filming. Jocelyn Garcia who is our telefilm accountant requested that the cost of the site not exceed $24,000, for a three week lease.

Work Completed. For the past eight days I have searched the Niagara Peninsula in the southern Ontario wine country. Since this area is rich with history I was able to locate many possibilities including: turn-of-the-century estates, Victorian mansions and rustic farmhouses. One of the best sites is the Country Meadows Inn a 97 year old farmhouse, with a breathtaking view of vallies and woods. The most promising towns are the following Niagara-on-the-Lake, St. Catharines and Pelham.

Work to Be Completed. In the next few days I'll search the Ontario countryside, and inspect winerys such as: Jackson-Triggs, Hillebrand, and Inniskillin. Many of the older winerys has charming structures, however they also attract tourists, and crowds of people.

By May 14, you'll have my final report, that describes the three better locations.

Add appropriate semicolons, colons, and commas.

1. Most students prefer morning classes consequently we schedule many courses before noon.

2. The following instructors have been chosen to represent their schools at the professional meeting Ian Mason Cégep de Jonquière Patricia Parnall Sir Sandford Fleming College and Kay Oxford George Brown College.

3. All morning sessions begin at 9 a.m. all afternoon sessions commence at 1 p.m.

4. Because we have little time before the deadline we are forced to choose from among the top vendors for example IBM, AST, or Hewlett-Packard.

5. We feel however that more time should be allowed for major equipment purchase decisions.

learning.web.ways

You're now ready to hunt for a job, and you decide to start with on-line listings.

Goal: To learn to locate job listings.

1. With your Web browser on the screen, key <**http://www.monster.ca**>.

2. First bookmark the Monster.ca site, and then click **How to Use Monster**. What features does this service offer? What can you learn and practise at this site?

3. Return to the site's main page by clicking the **Back** button of your Web browser.

4. Click **Search Jobs**, and scroll down the **Location Search** box to select a location of your choice.

5. Now scroll down the **Category Search** box, and select the field you're interested in. Finally, in the **Keyword Search**, enter the title of the job you're looking for.

6. Study the jobs listed, and print this page. Click on one or more of the listed vacancies, and print a page describing a job vacancy you like.

7. End your session, and submit the two printed pages.

Other Punctuation

OBJECTIVES   When you have completed the materials in this chapter, you will be able to do the following:

LEVEL I
- *Use periods to correctly punctuate statements, commands, indirect questions, and polite requests.*
- *Use periods to correctly punctuate abbreviations, initials, and numerals.*
- *Use question marks and exclamation points correctly.*

LEVEL II
- *Recognize acceptable applications of the dash.*
- *Use parentheses to de-emphasize material.*
- *Explain when to use commas, dashes, or parentheses to set off non-essential material.*
- *Correctly punctuate and capitalize material set off by parentheses and dashes.*

LEVEL III
- *Correctly use double and single quotation marks.*
- *Correctly place other punctuation marks in relation to quotation marks.*
- *Use brackets, underscores, and italics appropriately.*

PRETEST

Use proofreading marks to insert appropriate punctuation in the following sentences.

1. Will you please send certificates to Wanda Allenton and Paula Brin

2. Miss Lee Mrs Adams and Mr Simon have been appointed to the YMCA committee

3. Ottawa Quebec City and Montreal these are the only cities receiving deliveries f o b

continued

4. The chapter entitled Telecommunication Today was the best one in the book Current Office Technology

5. Did Professor Scholl say There will be no class Tuesday

This chapter teaches you how to use periods, question marks, and exclamation points correctly. It also includes suggestions for punctuating with dashes, parentheses, single and double quotation marks, brackets, underscores, and italics.

LEVEL I

Notable Quotable

"There's not so much to be said about the period except that most people don't reach it soon enough."
—William Zinsser, writing expert

Hotlink

If your learning style is visual, you may find the following Punctuation Pattern Sheet from University College of the Fraser Valley very helpful. Print it out from
<http://www.ucfv.bc.ca/writing_centre/punctsht.htm>.

▶ Uses for the Period

The period is used to punctuate sentences, abbreviations, and numerals. The following guidelines will help you use the period correctly.

To Punctuate Sentences

Use a period at the end of a statement, a command, an indirect question, or a polite request. Although it may have the same structure as a question, a polite request ends with a period.

> Ali Mazahri was promoted to a position with increased salary and responsibilities. (Statement)
> Send our latest catalogue and price list to them. (Command)
> Marilyn asked whether we had sent the price list. (Indirect question)
> Would you please send me an introductory sample. (Polite request)

To Punctuate Abbreviations

Because of their inconsistencies, abbreviations present problems to writers. The following suggestions will help you organize certain groups of abbreviations and will provide many models. In studying these models, note the spacing, capitalization, and use of periods. Always consult a good dictionary or style manual when in doubt.

Use periods after most abbreviations beginning with lower-case letters.

a.m. (ante meridiem)	i.e. (that is)
e.g. (for example)	ft. (foot or feet)
c.o.d. (cash on delivery)	f.o.b. (free on board)

Exceptions: mph (miles per hour), wpm (words per minute).

Use periods for most abbreviations containing capital and lower-case letters.

Dr. (Doctor)	Mr. (Mister)
Esq. (Esquire)	No. (Number)
Ms. (blend of Miss and Mrs.)	Sat. (Saturday)

---

1. Brin. 2. Lee, Mrs. Adams, Mr. committee. 3. Ottawa, Quebec City, Montreal—these f.o.b. 4. "Telecommunication Today" Current Office Technology. 5. say, "There Tuesday"?

Use periods with abbreviations that represent academic degrees, geographical expressions, and initials of a person's first and middle names.

B.A. (bachelor of arts)
M.B.A. (master of business administration)
M.D. (doctor of medicine)
Ph.D. (doctor of philosophy)

S.A. (South America)
U.K. (United Kingdom)
U.S.A. (United States of America)
Mr. J. A. Jones (initials)

Do *not* use periods for most capitalized abbreviations.

CEO (chief executive officer)
CFO (chief financial officer)
CPU (central processing unit)
EST (Eastern Standard Time)
FYI (for your information)
IBM (International Business Machines)
ID (identification)
OCR (optical character reader)

RAM (random-access memory)
RRSP (registered retirement savings plan)
SASE (self-addressed, stamped envelope)
SIDS (sudden infant death syndrome)
SOP (standard operating procedure)
UNEF (United Nations Emergency Force)
VCR (video cassette recorder)

Study Tip

Most abbreviations fall into this group. Note capitalized letters, lack of periods, and tight spacing.

Note: Do not confuse metric symbols with abbreviations. As symbols, they require no periods: kg (kilogram), mm (millimetre), km (kilometre), etc.

To Punctuate Numerals

For a monetary sum use a period (decimal point) to separate dollars from cents.

The two items in question, $13.92 and $98.07, were both charged in the month of October.

Use a period (decimal point) to mark a decimal fraction.

Although a moderate voter turnout was predicted, only 18.6 per cent of registered voters actually voted.

▶ Uses for the Question Mark

To Punctuate Direct Questions

Use a question mark at the end of a direct question.

What qualities are necessary for a person to become a successful administrator?
Have you compiled the figures requested by Techdata, Inc.?

Study Tip

Use a period after a polite request if you expect an action rather than a yes-or-no answer.

Do not punctuate polite requests with question marks. These sentences are considered commands or "please do" statements. A polite request asks the reader to perform a specific action and is usually answered by an action rather than a verbal response.

Will you please mail your cheque in the enclosed envelope.

To Punctuate Questions Appended to Statements

Place a question mark after a question that is appended to a statement (a tag question). Use a comma to separate the statement from the question.

They have already established a Web site, haven't they?
This personnel announcement should be sent by e-mail, don't you think?

Hotlink

To improve your punctuation, use the printer-friendly version of this handout from the University of Guelph. It's hosted by the English Commons at **<http:// www.learningcommons. uoguelph.ca/writing/ fastfax/punctuation. htm>**. Scroll down for the link to the print version of the page.

To Indicate Doubt

A question mark within parentheses may be used to indicate a degree of doubt about some aspect of a statement.

> The accounting department needs two(?) temporary clerks.
> A beginning salary of $3,500(?) per month is possible.

▶ Uses for the Exclamation Point

The exclamation point is an emphatic mark of punctuation reserved for strong feelings. It is seldom seen in business writing.

To Express Strong Emotion

After a word, phrase, or clause expressing strong emotion, use an exclamation point. In business and other formal writing, however, exclamation points should be used sparingly.

> Impossible! We understood the deadline to be tomorrow.
> What a day! Will 5 p.m. never come?
> It is incredible that my watch is still working after such punishment!

Do not use an exclamation point after mild interjections such as *oh* and *well*.

> Well, it seems we have little choice in the matter.

Complete the reinforcement exercises for Level I on pp. 330–331.

LEVEL II

▶ Uses for the Dash

The dash is a legitimate and effective mark of punctuation when used according to accepted conventions. As an emphatic punctuation mark, however, the dash loses effectiveness when it is overused. In typewritten or simple word processing–generated material, a dash is formed by typing two hyphens with no space before, between, or after the hyphens or by typing one hyphen with a space both before and after. In printed or desktop publishing–generated material, a dash appears as a solid line (an *em* dash). Study the following suggestions for and illustrations of appropriate uses of the dash.

To Set Off Parenthetical Elements

Within a sentence parenthetical elements are usually set off by commas. If, however, the parenthetical element itself contains internal commas, use dashes (or parentheses) to set it off.

> Sources of raw materials—farming, mining, fishing, and forestry—are all dependent on energy.
> Four efficient secretaries—Priscilla Alvarez, Vicky Evans, Yoshiki Ono, and Edward Botsko—received cash bonuses for outstanding performance in their departments.

To Indicate an Interruption

An interruption or abrupt change of thought may be separated from the rest of a sentence by a dash.

> The shipment will be on its way—you have my word—by Wednesday.
> Send the disks by Friday—no, we must have them sooner.

Sentences with abrupt changes of thought or with appended afterthoughts can usually be improved through rewriting.

To Set Off a Summarizing Statement

Use a dash (not a colon) to separate an introductory list from a summarizing statement.

> Variety of tasks, contact with people, opportunity for advancement—these are what I seek in a job.
> Running, hiking, and reading—those are Rudy's favourite pastimes.

To Attribute a Quotation

Place a dash between a quotation and its source.

> "English is the language of men ever famous and foremost in the achievements of liberty." — John Milton.
> "A man has no worse enemy than himself." —Cicero.

▶ Uses for Parentheses

Parentheses are useful to set off non-essential sentence elements. Careful writers avoid overusing parentheses because they distract readers.

To Set Off Non-Essential Sentence Elements

Generally, non-essential sentence elements may be punctuated in three ways: (1) with commas, to make the lightest possible break in the normal flow of a sentence; (2) with dashes, to emphasize the enclosed material; and (3) with parentheses, to de-emphasize the enclosed material.

> One of the blueprints, which appears on page 7, shows the internal structure of the engine clearly. (Normal punctuation.)
> One of the blueprints—which appears on page 7—shows the internal structure of the engine clearly. (Dashes emphasize enclosed material.)
> One of the blueprints (which appears on page 7) shows the internal structure of the engine clearly. (Parentheses de-emphasize enclosed material.)

Explanations, references, and directions are often enclosed in parentheses.

> The bank's current business hours (10 a.m. to 3 p.m.) will be extended in the near future (to 6 p.m.).
> We recommend that you use hearing protectors (see our comment on p. 618) when using this electric drill.

Hotlink

The University of Victoria Writer's Guide at **<http://web.uvic.ca/wguide/Pages/GrammarToc.html>** has separate sections on parentheses and dashes at the bottom of the page. Follow the links.

Spot the Blooper

From a box of Post cereal: "Everyday's a new adventure with Katy."

Additional Considerations

If the material enclosed by parentheses is embedded within another sentence, a question mark or exclamation point may be used where normally expected. Do not, however, use a period after a statement embedded within another sentence.

> We have tickets to *The Chorus Girl* (have you seen it?) on the evening of March 9. (A question mark concludes a question enclosed by parentheses and embedded in another sentence.)
>
> The fire alarm sounded (but no one responded!) during the middle of our final exam. (An exclamation mark concludes an exclamation enclosed by parentheses and embedded in another sentence.)
>
> An air conditioner cools space (this will be discussed in detail in the next chapter) by removing heat from it. (A period is not used at the end of a statement enclosed by parentheses and embedded in another sentence.)

If the material enclosed by parentheses is not embedded in another sentence, use whatever punctuation is required. Note that the item in parentheses begins with a capital letter.

> Report writers must document all references. (See the appendix for a guide to current documentation formats.)
>
> In less than ten years, the price of that article has tripled. (Who would have thought it possible?)

In sentences involving expressions within parentheses, a comma, semicolon, or colon that would normally occupy the position occupied by the second parenthesis is then placed after that parenthesis.

> When I return from my trip (in late June), I will begin work on the feasibility study. (Comma follows parenthesis.)
>
> Your application for a credit card was received before the deadline (November 1); however, you did not supply two financial references. (Semicolon follows parenthesis.)

Complete the reinforcement exercises for Level II on pp. 332–333.

LEVEL III

▶ Uses for Quotation Marks

Quotation marks help readers understand what words were written or spoken by somebody else. They may also be used to enclose short expressions, definitions, and titles.

To Enclose Direct Quotations

Double quotation marks are used to enclose direct quotations. Unless the exact words of a writer or speaker are being repeated, however, quotation marks are not employed.

> "There is a world market for about five computers," said IBM founder Thomas J. Watson. (Direct quotation enclosed.)
>
> Dwight Moody said that character is what you are in the dark. (Indirect quotation requires no quotation marks.)

Capitalize only the first word of a direct quotation.

> "The office staff," said Mrs. Rogers, "has now reached its full complement."
> (Do not capitalize the word *has*.)

To Enclose Quotations Within Quotations

Single quotation marks (apostrophes on most keyboards) are used to enclose quoted passages cited within quoted passages.

> Sharon Miles remarked, "In business writing I totally agree with Aristotle, who said, 'A good style must, first of all, be clear.'" (Single quotation marks within double quotation marks)

To Enclose Short Expressions

Slang, words used in a special sense, and words following *stamped* or *marked* are often enclosed within quotation marks.

> Cheryl feared that her presentation would "bomb." (Slang)
> In Web terminology robots are referred to as "bots." (Word used in a special sense)
> The package was stamped "Handle with Care." (Words following *stamped*)

To Enclose Definitions

Quotation marks are used to enclose formal definitions of words or expressions. The word or expression being defined should be underscored or set in italics.

> The Latin word *ergo* means "therefore" or "hence."
> Business people use the term *working capital* to indicate an "excess of current assets over current debts."

To Enclose Titles

Quotation marks are used to enclose titles of subdivisions of literary and artistic works such as magazine and newspaper articles, chapters of books, poems, lectures, and songs. Names of entire books, magazines, pamphlets, newspapers, plays, movies, and television series, however, are set in italics, underscored, or sometimes keyed in all capital letters. Names of Web sites are also sometimes set in italics.

> Office administration students should familiarize themselves with the section of *The Gregg Reference Manual* entitled "Glossary of Computer Terms."
> One source of information for your term paper might be the magazine article "Cross-Training of Key Personnel," which appeared in *Newsweek*.
> The episode "Turnabout Intruder," in which a vengeful woman took mental control of Kirk's body, ended the *Star Trek* TV series.

Additional Punctuation Considerations

Periods and commas are always placed inside closing quotation marks, whether single or double. Semicolons and colons are, on the other hand, always placed outside quotation marks.

> Betty Pearman said, "I'm sure the package was marked 'Fragile.'"
> The article is entitled "Bad Business of Banks," but we can't locate the magazine in which it appeared.

Hotlink

For an on-line explanation of the use of quotation marks, visit the Purdue Online Writing Lab **<http://owl.english. purdue.edu/handouts/ grammar/g_quote. html>**.

Spot the Blooper

Toilet tissue advertisement heard on the radio: "For less changes, double your Royale."

The contract stipulated that "both parties must accept arbitration as binding"; therefore, the decision reached by the arbitrators is final.

Three dates have been scheduled for the seminar called "E-Commerce and You": April 1, May 3, and June 5.

Question marks and exclamation points may go inside or outside closing quotation marks, as determined by the form of the quotation.

Jeanette said, "How may I apply for that position?" (Quotation itself is a question; question mark goes inside quotation marks.)

"The next time your cellphone rings," fumed Mr. Bradley, "we will ask you to leave!" (Quotation is an exclamation.)

Do you know who it was who said, "Money is more trouble than it's worth"? (Incorporating sentence asks question; quotation does not.)

I can't believe that the cheque was stamped "Insufficient Funds"! (Incorporating sentence is an exclamation; quotation is not.)

When did the manager say, "Who wants to reserve a summer vacation?" (Both incorporating sentence and quotation are questions. Use only one question mark inside the quotation marks.)

▶ Uses for Brackets

Within quotations, brackets are used by writers to enclose their own inserted remarks. Such remarks may be corrective, illustrative, or explanatory. Brackets are also used within quotations to enclose the word *sic*, which means *thus* or *so*. This Latin word is used to emphasize the fact that an error obvious to all actually appears *thus* in the quoted material.

"A British imperial gallon," reported Miss Sedgewick, "is equal to 1.2 U.S. gallons [4.54 litres]."

"The company's reorganization program," wrote President Theodore Bailey, "will have its greatest affect [*sic*] on our immediate sales."

▶ Uses for the Underscore or Italics

The underscore (underline) or italics are normally used for titles of books, magazines, newspapers, and other complete works published separately, as already mentioned. In addition, words under discussion in a sentence and used as nouns are italicized or underscored.

Creative Financing, the latest book by Thomas Manley, was favourably reviewed in *The Wall Street Journal*.

Two of the most frequently misspelled words are *calendar* and *separate*. (Words under discussion used as nouns.)

Complete the reinforcement exercises for Level III on pp. 334–335.

Hotlink

For a really extensive overview of punctuation, go to the Grammar Tutorials at the University of Calgary, **<http://www.ucalgary.ca/UofC/eduweb/grammar/>**.

Study Tip

With today's sophisticated software programs, you can, like professional printers, use italics instead of underscoring for titles and special words.

HOTLINE QUERIES

Question: We can't decide whether the period should go inside quotation marks or outside. At the end of a sentence, I have typed the title "Positive Vs. Negative Values." The author of the document I'm typing wants the period outside because she says the title does not have a period in it.

Answer: When a period or comma falls at the same place quotation marks would normally fall, the period or comma is always placed inside the quotation marks, regardless of the content of the quotation. (In Britain a different style is observed; a few Canadian writers may use that style.)

Question: I'm not sure where to place the question mark in this sentence: *His topic will be "What Is a Good Health Plan (?)"* Does the question mark go inside the quotation marks? Also, should a comma precede the title of the talk?

Answer: First, the question mark goes inside the quotation mark because the quoted material is in the form of a question. Be sure that you do not use another end punctuation mark after the quotation mark. Second, do not use a comma preceding the title because the sentence follows normal subject–verb–complement order. No comma is needed to separate the verb and the complement.

Question: Is it correct to say *Brad and myself were chosen … ?*

Answer: No. Use the nominative case pronoun *I* instead of *myself*.

Question: What salutation should I use when addressing a letter to Sister Mary Elizabeth?

Answer: The salutation of your letter should be *Dear Sister Mary Elizabeth*. For more information on forms of address, consult a good dictionary or reference manual.

Question: Is anything wrong with saying *someone else's car*?

Answer: Although it may sound somewhat awkward, the possessive form is acceptable. The apostrophe is correctly placed in *else's*.

Question: I've looked in the dictionary, but I'm still unsure about whether to hyphenate *stepsister*.

Answer: Do not hyphenate family terms containing the prefixes *step* or *grand* (*stepsister, stepdaughter, granddaughter*). Always hyphenate such terms involving the prefix *great* or the suffix *in-law* (*great-uncle, son-in-law, brother-in-law*). In reading your dictionary, notice that centred periods may be used to indicate syllables (grand•moth•er); hyphens are used to show hyphenated syllables (*great-aunt*).

Question: Can you tell me what sounds strange in this sentence and why? *The building looks like it was redesigned.*

Answer: The word *like* should not be used as a conjunction, as has been done in your sentence. Substitute *as if* (*the building looks as if it was redesigned*).

CHAPTER 18   Reinforcement Exercises

A. **(Self-check)** In the spaces provided after each sentence, indicate whether a period, question mark, or exclamation point is needed. Use the symbol. If no additional punctuation is required, write *C*.

LEVEL I

Example: May I please have your answer by return mail⊙   _____⊙_____

1. Would you give me your latest price figure for a ream of 16-pound bond paper   _____

2. What an amazingly complex situation this has become   _____

3. You are not using this printer, are you   _____

4. Has anyone checked to see if the mail has been distributed   _____

5. Send for your complimentary brochure today   _____

6. Help! Smoke is coming from my keyboard   _____

7. Juanita asked if she should come in at 7 a.m. to complete the work for LaserPro Ltd.   _____

8. Oh, I don't believe we should worry about it at this time   _____

9. I wonder whether he received my e-mail message   _____

10. Will you please keep one copy and return the other to me   _____

Check your answers.

B. In the following sentences all punctuation has been omitted. Insert commas, periods, question marks, colons, and exclamation points. The words have extra space between them so that punctuation may be inserted easily. Use a caret (∧) to indicate most insertions. In the space at the right, indicate the number of punctuation marks inserted. Consult a reference manual or a dictionary for abbreviation style if necessary.

Example: Will you please add Mr⊙ T⊙ G⊙ Skaggs Jr⊙ to the address list⊙   _____5_____

1. I wonder if William R Templeton was hired as C I O at Intel, Inc   _____

2. Common abbreviations like a m and p m often appear in business correspondence   _____

3. Dr Iva Jeffreys was recently named C E O at Laurentian Enterprises   _____

4. You did place an ad in the classified section didn't you   _____

5. It was Miss Jenkins not Mrs Reed who was to receive the c o d shipment   _____

6. What a dilemma the latest C R T C regulations have created   _____

A. 1. ? 2. ! 3. ? 4. ? 5. . 6. ! 7. C 8. . 9. . 10. .

7. Stop Don't touch that switch

8. Deliver the signed contracts to Mr C P Ryan before 5 p m

9. If I B M offers a full-service contract we would be interested

10. What a great day for lunch in the park

11. Darren asked if most automobiles were delivered f o b Windsor

12. I sent my congratulations on the completion of Peter's M B A degree

13. The Toronto office pipes in radio station C F R B because the manager Ms Buckley prefers that station

14. He often uses the abbreviations *e g* and *i e* in his e-mail messages

15. Will you please R S V P before Friday September 30

16. Some authorities wonder if the I Q of school-age children is affected by T V

17. Has the erroneous charge of $45 95 been removed from my account

18. The following individuals have agreed to serve Dr Lyn Clark Ms Deborah Kitchin and Professor Marilyne Hudgens

19. Capt G Maxwell asked if he could serve in Germany

20. Why we have not heard from the C F O is a mystery to me

21. You did check the U R L for that Web site didn't you

22. Among the speakers are Michael Hartman M D and Gail Nemire R N (*Don't forget the commas.*)

23. Since the funds were earned in the U K I must consult my C A about taxes

24. Virginia T Laws Ph D who is a well-known communications consultant will address the group at 10 a m

25. Wow I have finally finished this exercise

A. (**Self-check**) In the space provided, write the letter of the best version of each sentence.

LEVEL II

1. (a) Reading, travelling, and jogging: these are my favourite activities.
   (b) Reading, travelling, and jogging—these are my favourite activities.
   (c) Reading, travelling, and jogging; these are my favourite activities. _____

2. (a) "Civilization and profits go hand in hand." —Calvin Coolidge
   (b) "Civilization and profits go hand in hand," Calvin Coolidge
   (c) "Civilization and profits go hand in hand: Calvin Coolidge _____

3. (a) I was forty minutes late (would you believe it) to the exam.
   (b) I was forty minutes late (would you believe it?) to the exam.
   (c) I was forty minutes late (would you believe it) to the exam? _____

4. (Emphasize parenthetical element.)
   (a) Currently our basic operating costs: rent, utilities, and wages, are 10 per cent higher than last year.
   (b) Currently our basic operating costs (rent, utilities, and wages) are 10 per cent higher than last year.
   (c) Currently our basic operating costs—rent, utilities, and wages—are 10 per cent higher than last year. _____

5. (a) Loading and unloading film (see page 23 in the manual) must be done carefully.
   (b) Loading and unloading film, see page 23 in the manual, must be done carefully.
   (c) Loading and unloading film: see page 23 in the manual, must be done carefully. _____

6. (a) Recently you applied for a position (legal secretary); however, you did not indicate for which branch your application is intended.
   (b) Recently you applied for a position; (legal secretary) however, you did not indicate for which branch your application is intended.
   (c) Recently you applied for a position (legal secretary;) however, you did not indicate for which branch your application is intended. _____

7. (Emphasize.)
   (a) Sales, sales, and more sales: that's what we need to succeed.
   (b) Sales, sales, and more sales—that's what we need to succeed.
   (c) Sales, sales, and more sales; that's what we need to succeed. _____

8. (De-emphasize.)
   (a) Ramps will be closed on three Toronto-area highways—Highway 427, Highway 27, and Highway 401—during the summer.
   (b) Ramps will be closed on three Toronto-area highways, Highway 427, Highway 27, and Highway 401, during the summer.
   (c) Ramps will be closed on three Toronto-area highways (Highway 427, Highway 27, and Highway 401) during the summer. _____

Check your answers.

1.b 2.a 3.b 4.c 5.a 6.a 7.b 8.c

B. Insert dashes or parentheses in the following sentences. In the space provided after each sentence, write the number of punctuation marks you inserted. Count each parenthesis and each dash as a single mark.

Example: (Emphasize.) Three of the biggest problems with e-mail --privacy, overuse, and etiquette --will be discussed.   2

1. (De-emphasize.) The modernized production of Shakespeare's *As You Like It* have you read the reviews? will be opening here very shortly. _____

2. Fingerprints, mug shots, and arrest records these are now stored on microforms by law enforcement officers. _____

3. "Do not squander time, for that is the stuff life is made of." Benjamin Franklin _____

4. (Emphasize.) Three branch assistant managers Augusta Jones, James Redman, and Candi Herman will be promoted this month. _____

5. (De-emphasize.) Three branch assistant managers Augusta Jones, James Redman, and Candi Herman will be promoted this month. _____

6. (De-emphasize.) As soon as you are able to make an appointment try to do so before December 30, we will process your insurance forms. _____

7. Quality copies, low cost, ease of operation, speedy output what more could a customer want in an economical office copy machine? _____

8. Funds for the project will be released on the following dates see Section 12.3 of the original grant: January 1, March 14, and June 30. _____

9. (De-emphasize.) Although one of the traditionally favoured teams England, Germany, Italy, or Brazil will probably win the World Cup, the host country is always a sentimental favourite. _____

10. The warranty period for this cordless drill is limited to sixty 60 days. _____

C. Using three different forms of punctuation, correctly punctuate the following sentence. In the space provided, explain how the three methods you have employed differ.

1. Numerous considerations all of which are fully described in our report prompted the closure of the outlet.

2. Numerous considerations all of which are fully described in our report prompted the closure of the outlet.

3. Numerous considerations all of which are fully described in our report prompted the closure of the outlet.

Explanation: _____

_____

_____

_____

_____

A. (**Self-check**) Indicate whether the following statements are true (*T*) or false (*F*).

LEVEL III

1. Quotation marks are used to enclose the exact words of a writer or speaker. _____

2. The names of books, magazines, pamphlets, and newspapers may be underscored or enclosed in quotation marks. _____

3. Periods and commas are always placed inside closing quotation marks. _____

4. Parentheses are used by writers to enclose their own remarks inserted into a quotation. _____

5. A quotation within a quotation is shown with single quotation marks. _____

6. Semicolons and colons are always placed inside closing quotation marks. _____

7. The underscore is used in handwriting to emphasize words that would be italicized in printed copy. _____

8. If both a quotation and its introductory sentence are questions, use a question mark before the closing quotation marks. _____

9. The word *sic* is used to show that a quotation is free of errors. _____

10. A single quotation mark is keyed by using the apostrophe key. _____

Check your answers.

B. Many, but not all, of the following sentences contain direct quotations. None have any punctuation. Insert all necessary punctuation.

Example: ⟨ital⟩ The word <u>asset</u> means ˇ"an item of monetary value⊙."

1. In our five-year projections said the general manager we plan to expand marketing and distributing to the East Coast

2. Careful speakers use the word mad to mean insane

3. Dr Graham's chapter entitled Drawing the World Together appeared in the book Global Links

4. Did Mr Le Sage say Where are the printers that need to be repaired

5. In his speech the software billionaire said Our goal is to link the world irregardless *sic* of national boundaries and restrictions.

6. Melissa said that she hoped we would call her if we needed assistance

7. Although he was somewhat worried about the interview Jerry told his friends that he was cool

1. T   2. F   3. T   4. F   5. T   6. F   7. T   8. T   9. F   10. T

8. The postal worker said Shall I stamp your package Fragile

9. Did you see the article What People Earn in last week's Parade magazine

10. The expression persona non grata means one who is not acceptable

11. After banging on the elevator doors repeatedly Mrs Lowe shouted Please help us

12. Has anyone seen the extra copy of the sheet music for All You Need Is Love

13. The title of the article is Automation in the Office however the author may change the title later

14. This copy machine said the sales representative will reproduce charts books and large-size originals

15. The three most important links at the Globex Online Web site are the following About Us Success Stories and Resources

C. Insert all necessary punctuation. These sentences review Levels I, II, III.

1. Would you please send a copy of the current catalogue to Globex Ltd

2. Eating studying and working these are Mike's principal activities

3. Regular cleaning of the tape head see Chart 2 in the operating manual is necessary for best performance

4. (Emphasize.) Two of our best researchers Darlene McClure and Judith Ehresman were hired by our competitor

5. (De-emphasize.) Stereo systems for cars these include amplifiers tape decks speakers FM receivers and CD players have blossomed into a lucrative specialty market

6. (Direct quote.) Was it President Martin who said What can't be cured must be endured

7. The word copyright literally means right to copy

8. Mary Gooderham's fascinating article on virtual reality in The Globe and Mail was entitled The Next Best Thing to Being

9. The envelope marked Confidential was delivered to the wrong office

10. (Direct quote.) Did Alicia say Where is our supply of printer cartridges

D. Optional Composition. On a separate sheet type or write a paragraph describing your favourite job. Try to include as many of the punctuation marks you have studied as possible. Include commas, semicolons, periods, question marks, exclamation points, dashes, parentheses, quotation marks, italics, and possibly even brackets. Include a quotation from your boss. Make up the name of a book or article that you could publish about this job.

Editor's Challenge

The following letter contains intentional errors in concepts you have studied thus far. It also contains a few spelling errors. Use standard proofreading marks to show all necessary corrections. Notice that this letter is addressed to a company; hence the writer doesn't know whom to address in the salutation. The simplified style avoids this problem.

GLOBAL IMPORTERS INC.
814 John Street, Suite 205
Kelowna, BC V1Y 5S7

West Coast Foods Ltd.
729 Leland Street
Maple Ridge, BC V2X 7L3

YOUR MAY 3 PURCHASE ORDER NO 14902

All the in stock items requested in your recent purchase order were ship to you Friday May 8 from our Vancouver warehouse.

Because of unseasonably wet weather in February; this springs supply of black teas from Sri Lanka are extremely limited. We have none of these fine tea on hand at present, however, we expect a small shipment to arrive by August 1.

We do have in our warehouse a stock of select black teas from the following sources, south China Japan and south India. Indian teas as you are well aware do not always meet some of our customers high standards. Which is why we hesitate to advice you to except the Indian tea as a substitute. Chinese and Japanese teas though are generally well regarded.

In fact one of our customers recently said "Our best sales are now from Chinese black tea. Another importer wrote "We are delighted with the recent shipment of Japanese black tea". Moreover an article in the January 8 issue of The new york times described the healthful affects of Japanese tea.

Please call us toll free at 1-800-321-8993 to tell us whether you wish to wait for the Sri Lankan black tea or whether you prefer the immediate supply of black tea from: China, Japan, or India.

BRIAN W. LEE, MANAGER

Use proofreading marks to insert necessary punctuation.

1. Will you please send me a copy of the book entitled Office Careers Today

2. When did we receive this envelope marked Confidential

3. The only guests who have not sent RSVPs are Miss Lee Mrs Gold and Mr Sims

4. The word principal was misused in the chapter entitled Writing Persuasive Letters

5. Did Professor Miles say How many students expect to miss the test Friday

learning.web.ways

You've just discovered that the company where you wish to apply uses a computer to scan all incoming résumés. You decide to learn more about electronic résumés.

Goal: To learn more about electronic résumés.

1. With your browser on the screen, go to Kamloops Career and Technology Centre **<http://www.kmlp.kctc.bc.ca/resumes/scan.html>**.

2. Read the information on scannable résumés. What are the techniques you should use in preparing a scannable résumé? Print two pages from the Web site.

3. Click on **Scannable Resume**. What is distinctive about the model résumé shown?

4. Use the browser's **Back** button once, and click on **Internet Resources**, and select the **Scannable Resumes** link from **Basics**.

5. Read about keyword résumés. How can you determine the keywords for your profession?

6. End your session, and submit your printouts and answers to the questions from this exercise.

1. Office Careers Today. 2. "Confidential"? 3. Lee, Mrs. Gold, Mr. Sims. 4. principal "Writing Persuasive Letters." 5. say, "How Friday?"

UNIT 5 REVIEW Chapters 16–18 (Self-Check)

First, review Chapters 16 through 18. Then, test your comprehension of those chapters by completing the exercises that follow and comparing your responses with those shown at the end of the book.

Insert necessary punctuation in the following sentences. Write *C* if the sentence is correct.

LEVEL I

1. Under no circumstances Mr. Greenwood will your complaints be disregarded. _____

2. However the matter is resolved, the goodwill of the customer is paramount. _____

3. Our Sales Department is concerned with the financing delivery and installation of our products. _____

4. A student who studies diligently and masters the principles will score well on the examination. _____

5. Our management team feels on the other hand that it must hold the line on benefits and salaries. _____

6. The sales representative Walter S. Anderson presented a thorough report. _____

Select (a), (b), or (c) to indicate the correctly punctuated sentence.

7. (a) Some of the equipment is stored in the warehouse other equipment is now in transit.
   (b) Some of the equipment is stored in the warehouse, other equipment is now in transit.
   (c) Some of the equipment is stored in the warehouse; other equipment is now in transit. _____

8. (a) Seminar participants are arriving from Calgary, Alberta, Regina, Saskatchewan, and Winnipeg, Manitoba.
   (b) Seminar participants are arriving from Calgary, Alberta; Regina, Saskatchewan; and Winnipeg, Manitoba.
   (c) Seminar participants are arriving from Calgary; Alberta; Regina; Saskatchewan; and Winnipeg; Manitoba. _____

9. (a) Investments should turn a profit; however, security is also important.
   (b) Investments should turn a profit, however, security is also important.
   (c) Investments should turn a profit; however security is also important. _____

10. (a) Would you please send the shipment c.o.d.
    (b) Would you please send the shipment c.o.d.?
    (c) Would you please send the shipment cod? _____

Select (a), (b), or (c) to indicate the best version of each sentence.

11. (a) It was investigated by the R.C.M.P., wasn't it?
    (b) It was investigated by the RCMP, wasn't it?
    (c) It was investigated by the RCMP wasn't it?   _____

12. (a) Wow! A total of 89.9 per cent of the voters approved!
    (b) Wow, a total of 89 point 9 percent of the voters approved!
    (c) Wow. A total of 89.9 per cent of the voters approved!   _____

13. (a) We are looking for three qualities in an employee; honesty, intelligence, and
        experience.
    (b) We are looking for three qualities in an employee, honesty, intelligence, and
        experience.
    (c) We are looking for three qualities in an employee: honesty, intelligence, and
        experience.   _____

14. (a) Thus far, we have received brochures from Compaq, IBM, and Dell.
    (b) Thus far, we have received brochures from, Compaq, IBM, and Dell.
    (c) Thus far, we have received brochures from: Compaq, IBM, and Dell.   _____

15. (a) Mr. Jenkins said, "We used to depend on fixed-rate mortgages."
    (b) Mr. Jenkins said: "We used to depend on fixed-rate mortgages."
    (c) Mr. Jenkins said; "We used to depend on fixed-rate mortgages."   _____

16. (a) The spokesperson compared three other railways: Canadian National, Canadian
        Pacific, and Amtrak, with VIA Rail.
    (b) The spokesperson compared three other railways—Canadian National, Canadian
        Pacific, and Amtrak—with VIA Rail.
    (c) The spokesperson compared three other railways, Canadian National, Canadian
        Pacific, and Amtrak, with VIA Rail.   _____

17. (a) Cameras, VCRs, and cellphones—these are only some of the products we carry.
    (b) Cameras, VCRs, and cellphones: these are only some of the products we carry.
    (c) Cameras, VCRs, and cellphones, these are only some of the products we carry. _____

18. Emphasize:
    (a) Only three products: cameras, VCRs, and camcorders account for 70 per cent of
        our total sales.
    (b) Only three products—cameras, VCRs, and camcorders—account for 70 per cent of
        our total sales.
    (c) Only three products (cameras, VCRs, and camcorders) account for 70 per cent of
        our total sales.   _____

19. (a) Notable members of the fund's honorary committee were June Callwood, St. Clair
        Balfour, and Paul Beeston.
    (b) Notable members of the fund's honorary committee were: June Callwood, St. Clair
        Balfour, and Paul Beeston.
    (c) Notable members of the fund's honorary committee were—June Callwood, St.
        Clair Balfour, and Paul Beeston.   _____

20. De-emphasize:
  (a) A pilot project—refer to page 6 of the report—may help us justify the new system.
  (b) A pilot project, refer to page 6 of the report, may help us justify the new system.
  (c) A pilot project (refer to page 6 of the report) may help us justify the new system. _____

Select (a), (b), or (c) to indicate the correctly punctuated sentence.

21. (a) In short employees must be extremely courteous.
  (b) In short—employees must be extremely courteous.
  (c) In short, employees must be extremely courteous. _____

22. (a) The aim of our company is to build, not destroy, customer goodwill.
  (b) The aim of our company is to build: not destroy, customer goodwill.
  (c) The aim of our company is to build, not destroy customer goodwill. _____

23. (a) Only one department submitted its report on time, namely the Legal Department.
  (b) Only one department submitted its report on time, namely, the Legal Department.
  (c) Only one department submitted its report on time: namely, the Legal Department. _____

24. (a) The location of the convention has been narrowed to three sites, namely Victoria, Vancouver, and Seattle.
  (b) The location of the convention has been narrowed to three sites; namely, Victoria, Vancouver, and Seattle.
  (c) The location of the convention has been narrowed to three sites; namely Victoria, Vancouver, and Seattle. _____

25. (a) The computer was producing "garbage," that is, the screen showed gibberish.
  (b) The computer was producing "garbage"; that is, the screen showed gibberish.
  (c) The computer was producing "garbage;" that is, the screen showed gibberish. _____

26. (a) A cartel is defined as a "group of companies acting to control prices."
  (b) A "cartel" is defined as a 'group of companies acting to control prices.'
  (c) A *cartel* is defined as a "group of companies acting to control prices." _____

27. (a) *HomeOffice,* a magazine for small business owners, recently featured an article entitled *Coping with Copiers.*
  (b) *HomeOffice,* a magazine for small business owners, recently featured an article entitled "Coping with Copiers."
  (c) "HomeOffice," a magazine for small business owners, recently featured an article entitled *Coping with Copiers.* _____

28. (a) "An ombudsman, said Sally Sirakides, is an individual hired by management to investigate and resolve employee complaints."
  (b) "An ombudsman," said Sally Sirakides, "Is an individual hired by management to investigate and resolve employee complaints."
  (c) "An ombudsman," said Sally Sirakides, "is an individual hired by management to investigate and resolve employee complaints." _____

29. (a) Who was it who said, "A penny saved is a penny earned."?
  (b) Who was it who said, "A penny saved is a penny earned?"
  (c) Who was it who said, "A penny saved is a penny earned"? _____

30. (a) Did the office manager really say, "Stamp this package 'Confidential'?"

(b) Did the office manager really say, "Stamp this package 'Confidential'"?

(c) Did the office manager really say, "Stamp this package "Confidential"?

_____

Hotline Review

Write the letter of the word or phrase that correctly completes each sentence.

31. Every measure has been taken to (a) ensure, (b) insure your satisfaction.

_____

32. Because few shareholders were (a) appraised, (b) apprised of the CEO's total salary package, no complaints were heard.

_____

33. My partner and (a) I, (b) me, (c) myself have signed an agreement.

_____

34. Have you ever been (a) cited, (b) sited, (c) sighted for a speeding violation?

_____

35. We give our Web address to (a) whoever, (b) whomever requests it.

_____

Informational Business Letters

Business letters are forms of external communication. That is, they deliver information to individuals outside an organization. Business letters may request information, respond to requests, make claims, seek adjustments, order goods and services, sell goods and services, recommend individuals, develop goodwill, or achieve many other goals. All business people have to write business letters of various kinds, but a majority of those letters will be informational.

Characteristics of Business Letters

Writers of good business letters—whether the messages are informational, persuasive, or bad news—are guided by the four Cs: conciseness, clarity, correctness, and courtesy. In earlier Writer's Workshops, you learned techniques for making your writing concise and clear. You've also studied many guidelines for correct grammar and usage throughout this textbook. At this point we'll review some of these techniques briefly as they relate to business letters.

Conciseness. Concise letters save the reader's time by presenting information directly. You can make your letters concise by avoiding these writing faults: (a) wordy phrases (such as *in addition to the above* and *in view of the fact that*), (b) excessive use of expletives (such as *There are four reasons that explain . . .* or *It is a good plan*), (c) long lead-ins (such as *This message is to inform you that* or *I am writing this letter to*), (d) needless adverbs (such as *very, definitely, quite, extremely,* and *really*), and (e) old-fashioned expressions (such as *attached please find* and *pursuant to your request*).

Clarity. Business letters are clear when they are logically organized and when they present enough information for the reader to understand what the writer intended. Informational letters are usually organized directly with the main idea first. Clarity can be enhanced by including all the necessary information. Some authorities estimate that one-third of all business letters are written to clarify previous correspondence. To ensure that your letters are clear, put yourself in the reader's position and analyze what you have written. What questions may the reader ask? Does your information proceed logically from one point to another? Are your sentences and paragraphs coherent?

Correctness. Two aspects of correctness are accuracy of facts and accuracy of form. In regard to facts, good business writers prepare to write by gathering relevant information. They collect supporting documents (previous letters, memos, and reports), they make inquiries, they jot down facts, and they outline the message. Correct letters require thorough preparation. In the same manner, correct letters require careful proofreading and attention to form. Typographical errors, spelling irregularities, and grammatical faults distract the reader and damage the credibility of the writer. Correct business letters also follow one of the conventional formats, such as block, modified block, or simplified style, shown in Appendix C.

Courtesy. You develop courtesy in business letters by putting yourself in the place of the reader. Imagine how you would like to be treated, and show the same consideration and respect for the individual receiving your message. The ideas you express and the words used to convey those ideas create an impression on the reader. Be alert to words that may create a negative feeling, such as *you claim, unfortunately, you neglected, you forgot, your complaint,* and so forth. Create a positive feeling by presenting your message from the point of view of the reader. Try to use the word *you* more than the words *I* and *we*. Create a positive tone in business letters by using conversational language. How can you make your writing sound like conversation? Think of your reader as if he or she were sitting across from you having a friendly chat. Avoid formal, pretentious, and stuffy language, such as *the undersigned is pleased to grant your request*. In your business messages you can develop goodwill toward your company and toward yourself by putting yourself in the place of the reader, by developing a friendly tone, and by using conversational language.

Skill Check 5.1 Reviewing the Four Cs

1. Which of the following is most concise?
   (a) Due to the fact that we had a warehouse fire, your shipment is delayed.
   (b) This is to inform you that your shipment will be delayed.
   (c) Because of a warehouse fire, your shipment is delayed.
   (d) There was a warehouse fire, which explains why your shipment is delayed.   _____

2. Which of the following is clear and logical?
   (a) If the strike is not settled quickly, it may last a while.
   (b) Flying over the rain forests of Indonesia, the trees form a solid and menacing green carpet.
   (c) This is not to suggest that Kingston, Oshawa, and London are not the most affordable areas for housing.
   (d) Prince Charles complained that the citizens of Britain speak and write their language poorly.   _____

3. Which of the following is grammatically correct?
   (a) We hope that you and he will be in town for our next seminar.
   (b) A host of ethical issues involve business, including e-mail privacy, whistleblowing, and mission statements.
   (c) We must develop a policy on returning merchandise. So that they know about it before they are made.
   (d) Jeffrey has twenty years experience in the software industry.   _____

4. Which of the following is most courteous?
   (a) During your interview, I informed you that if we were not successful in finding a suitable candidate, I would contact you.
   (b) We appreciate receiving your letter describing your treatment by our store security personnel.
   (c) In your letter of June 1, you claim that you were harassed by our store security personnel.
   (d) Unfortunately, we are unable to complete your entire order because you neglected to provide a shirt size.   _____

5. Which of the following sounds most conversational?
   (a) Attached herewith is the form you requested.
   (b) Pursuant to your request, we are forwarding the form you requested.
   (c) Under separate cover we are sending the form you requested.
   (d) You'll receive the form you requested in a separate mailing.   _____

Writing Plan

Most business letters have three parts: opening, body, and closing. This three-part writing plan will help you organize the majority of your business messages quickly and effectively.

Opening. The opening of a business letter may include a subject line that refers to previous correspondence or summarizes the content of the message. A subject line should make sense but should not be a complete sentence; it is not followed by a period.

The first sentence of a business letter that requests or delivers information should begin directly with the main idea. If you are asking for information, use one of two approaches. Ask the most important question first, such as *Do you have a two-bedroom cottage on Devil's Lake available for the week of July 8–15?* A second approach involves beginning with a summary statement, such as *Please answer the following questions regarding. . . .* If the letter delivers information, begin with the most important information first, such as *Yes, we have a two-bedroom cottage on Devil's Lake available for . . .* or *Here is the information you requested regarding . . . .* Most informational business letters should *not* begin with an explanation of why the letter is being written.

Body. The body of the letter provides explanations and additional information to clarify the first sentence. Use a separate paragraph for each new idea, being careful to strive for concise writing.

If the message lends itself to enumeration, express the items in a bulleted or numbered list. Be certain, of course, to construct the list so that each item is parallel.

Think about the individual reading your message. Will that person understand what you are saying? Have you included enough information? What may seem clear to you may not be so evident to your reader. In responding to requests, don't hesitate to include more information than was requested—if you feel it would be helpful.

Maintain a friendly, conversational, and positive tone.

Closing. Business letters that demand action should conclude with a specific request, including end dating if appropriate. That is, tell the reader when you would like the request complied with, and, if possible, provide a reason (for example, *Please send me this information by June 1 so that I can arrange my vacation*).

Letters that provide information may end with a summary statement or a pleasant, forward-looking thought (for example, *I hope this information helps you plan your summer vacation*). Business organizations may also use the closing to promote products or services.

Avoid ending your letters with mechanical phrases such as *If I can be of further service, don't hesitate to call on me,* or *Thanks for any information you can provide.* Find a fresh way to express your desire to be of service or to show appreciation.

Figure 18.1 illustrates the application of the writing plan to an information request. Notice that the subject line summarizes the main topic of the letter, while the first paragraph provides more information about the reason for writing. The body of the letter explains the main idea and includes a list of questions so that the reader can see quickly what information is being requested. The closing includes an end date with a reason.

Skill Check 5.2 Reviewing the Writing Plan

In the space provided, write a, b, or c to identify the letter part where each of the following might logically be found.

(a) Opening   (b) Body   (c) Closing

1. Explanation and details   _____

2. Subject line that summarizes main idea   _____

3. End dating with reason   _____

4. Enumerated or bulleted list   _____

5. Main idea   _____

6. Summary statement or forward-looking thought _____

Figure 18.1
Information Request Letter

GraphicPros

264 South Halsted Street
Mississauga, ON L5T 3K8
FAX (905) 568-2210   VOICE (905) 568-8319   INTERNET: http://www.graphicpros.com

March 5, 200x

Ms. Kesha Scott
Micro Supplies and Software
4671 Main Street
Saskatoon, SK S7K 3G3

Dear Ms. Scott:

Summarizes main idea — SUBJECT: AVAILABILITY AND PRICE OF EQUIPMENT SECURITY DEVICES

Introduces purpose immediately — Please provide information and recommendations regarding security equipment to prevent the theft of office computers, keyboards, monitors, faxes, and printers.

Explains need for information — Our office now has 18 computer workstations and 6 printers that we must secure to desks or counters. Answers to the following questions will help us select the best devices for our purpose.

Groups open-ended questions into list for quick comprehension and best feedback

1. What device would you recommend that can secure a workstation consisting of a computer, monitor, and keyboard?

2. What expertise and equipment are required to install and remove the security device?

3. How much is each device? Do you offer quantity discounts, and, if so, how much?

Courteously provides end date and reason — Because our insurance rates will be increased if the security devices are not installed before May 12, we would appreciate your response by March 20.

Sincerely,

Brent R. Barnwell

Brent R. Barnwell
Office Manager

Writing Application 5.1 On a separate sheet of paper or, preferably, at a computer, revise the following poorly written letter. Use block style (every line starts at the left margin) and mixed punctuation. This is a personal business letter; follow the format shown in Figure C.3 in Appendix C (see page 443), inserting your own address in the return address block. Remember that the following letter is poorly written. Improve it!

Writer's street address
City, Province Postal Code
Current date

Ms. Barbara L. George
Manager, Rainbow Resort
1102 West Island Road
Omemee, ON K0L 2W1

Dear Ms. George:

I saw an advertisement recently in *Sunset* magazine where Rainbow Resort rents houseboats. My family and I (there are three kids and my wife and me) would like to take a vacation on a houseboat from July 17 through July 24 on the Trent-Severn Waterway. We've never done this before but it sounds interesting.

Please send me any information you may have. I'll have to make my vacation plans soon.

I have no idea how much this might cost. If we rent a houseboat, my wife wants to know do you provide bedding, dishes, pots and pans, and the like? I'm wondering about navigating a houseboat. Will I have to take a course or training on how to operate it? It may be too difficult for me to run. Where can we travel on the Waterway in one of your houseboats? What if we decide to stay on more than one week? I actually have two weeks of vacation, but we may want to travel in our RV part of the time. Does insurance come with the rental fee? My kids want to know if it has TV.

Yours,

Leslie E. Childers

Leslie E. Childers

Writing Application 5.2 Assume you are Barbara George. Write a response to Mr. Childers' letter. Use modified block style and mixed punctuation. Tell Mr. Childers that the rental fee, which is $175 per day or $1000 per week, does include insurance. You have a houseboat available for July 17–24, but definite reservations must be made for that time and for the week following, if Mr. Childers decides to stay two weeks. Your houseboats can travel through 20 lakes, canals, and rivers. Rainbow Resort provides bedding, dishes, and kitchenware. Yes, each houseboat has a TV set. You also provide an AM/FM radio and a CD player. Your houseboats accommodate four to ten people, and you require a deposit of $500 for a one-week reservation. Reservations must be received by June 1 to ensure a July vacation. Your houseboats are easy to operate. No special training is required, but you do give each operator about 30 minutes of instruction. Send Mr. Childers a brochure describing Rainbow Resort and the memorable holiday he and his family can enjoy. The scenery and attractions are good.

Writing Application 5.3 Write a personal business letter in response to the following problem. For your home office you ordered a combination telephone/answering machine called the Execudyne Remote 2010. Instead of trouble-some cassette tapes, the Execudyne used solid-state microchips to record both incoming and outgoing messages. It had many attractive features, and you were eager to try it. When it arrived, however, you plugged it in and discovered that an irritating static sound interfered with every telephone call you made or received. Eventually you discovered that the static occurred only when the fluorescent light fixtures over your desk were turned on. When the lights were on, the telephone picked up static, making telephone calls impossible. You returned the telephone January 15 by UPS surface mail to ElectroWare Ltd., the mail order supplier from whom you purchased the unit. You still have a copy of the invoice, which states that merchandise may be returned for any reason within 30 days after purchase. You also have the UPS receipt proving that you returned it. However, your MasterCard statement (Acct. No. 5390-3390-2219-0002) has not shown a credit for the return. Both your February and March statements show no credit for $188.90. You're wondering what happened. Did ElectroWare receive the returned telephone? Why hasn't your account been credited? If they did not receive the machine, you want UPS to trace it. Write to ElectroWare Ltd., 22121 Crystal Creek Boulevard, Lethbridge, Alberta T9L 3T2. You have complied with ElectroWare's instructions regarding returning merchandise, and you want the company to credit your account. You do not want another telephone/answering machine. Be sure to open your letter with a direct request for the action you want taken.

Writing With Style

6

Capitalization

OBJECTIVES When you have completed the materials in this chapter, you will be able to do the following:

LEVEL I
- *Distinguish between common and proper nouns for purposes of capitalization.*
- *Decide when to capitalize proper adjectives and when not to.*

LEVEL II
- *Properly capitalize personal titles, numbered items, and points of the compass.*
- *Correctly capitalize departments, divisions, committees, government terms, product names, and literary titles.*

LEVEL III
- *Capitalize beginning words, celestial bodies, and ethnic references.*
- *Apply special rules in capitalizing personal titles and terms.*

PRETEST

Use proofreading marks to show any letters that should be capitalized in the sentences below.

1. Last spring mother took classes in history, computer technology, english, and psychology.

2. The canadian medical association's executive will meet in the manitoba room of the hilton hotel on march 25.

3. After receiving a bachelor's degree from york university, sharon became assistant to the human resources manager at general motors of canada.

continued

4. Our company president and vice-president met with several supervisors on the west coast last week.

5. The booklet provided by revenue canada explains the use of form T2202.

Rules governing capitalization reflect conventional practices; that is, they have been established by custom and usage. By following these conventions, a writer tells a reader, among other things, what words are important. In earlier times writers capitalized most nouns and many adjectives at will; few conventions of capitalization or punctuation were then consistently observed. Today most capitalization follows definite rules that are fully accepted and practised at all times.

Within many large organizations, capitalization style may be prescribed in a stylebook. Dictionaries are also helpful in determining capitalization practices, but they do not show all capitalized words. To develop skill in using capitals, study the rules and examples shown in this chapter.

LEVEL I

Career Tip

Many large companies publish style manuals showing their preferred capitalization and the spelling of frequently used terms. One of the first tasks of new employees is to become familiar with the company style manual.

▶ Basic Rules of Capitalization

Proper Nouns

Capitalize proper nouns, including the *specific* names of persons, places, schools, streets, parks, buildings, religions, holidays, months, nicknames, agreements, and so forth. Do *not* capitalize common nouns that make *general* reference.

Proper Nouns	Common Nouns
Jackson Turner	a young man on the basketball team
Mexico, United States	neighbouring countries of Canada
Canadore College, University of British Columbia	a community college and a university
Grand Avenue Park	a park in town
Catholic, Moslem	representatives of two religions
Empire Room, Royal Inn	a room in a hotel
Canada Day, Easter	holidays
Humber River Bridge	a bridge over a river
Fairview Mall	a large shopping centre
Parliament, the Senate	components of government
January, February, March	first three months of the year
the Great One, the Big Apple	nicknames of people and places
Stipulation of Interest Agreement	an agreement between companies
The Online English Grammar Clinic	a Web site
Microsoft Word	a word processing program

1. Mother English 2. Canadian Medical Association's Manitoba Room Hilton Hotel March 3. York University Sharon General Motors of Canada 4. West Coast 5. Revenue Canada Form

Proper Adjectives

Capitalize most adjectives that are derived from proper nouns.

Arabic alphabet	Keynesian economics
British thermal unit	Roman numeral
Danish pastry	Socratic method
Greek symbols	Victorian furniture

Do not capitalize those few adjectives originally derived from proper nouns that have become common adjectives (without capitals) through usage. Consult your dictionary when in doubt.

china dishes	italic type
diesel engine	mandarin collar
french fries	manila folder
homburg hat	raglan sleeves

Study Tip

Most proper nouns retain their capital letters when they become adjectives—for example, French toast, Russian roulette, Persian cat, Spanish moss, Italian marble, and Swedish massage.

Beginning of Sentence

Capitalize the first letter of a word beginning a sentence.

Inventory and sales data are transmitted electronically.

Geographic Locations

Capitalize the names of *specific* places such as provinces, cities, mountains, valleys, lakes, rivers, oceans, and geographic regions. Capitalize words like *county, state,* and *region* when they follow the proper nouns.

Ontario, British Columbia	Red River, Mississippi River
Port Hood, Quebec City	Atlantic Ocean, Indian Ocean
Rocky Mountains	the Prairies, the Maritimes
Lake Michigan, Labrador Sea	New England
James Bay	European Community (EC)
Huron County, York Region	New York State
Manitoba Escarpment	Okanagan Valley

66 99

Notable Quotable

"A genius is a talented person who does his homework."
—Thomas Edison

Organization Names

Capitalize the principal words in the names of all business, civic, educational, governmental, labour, military, philanthropic, political, professional, religious, social, and sports organizations.

Professional Secretaries International	Federation of Saskatchewan Indian Nations
Royal Canadian Legion	Liberal Party, Canadian Alliance
Canadian Union of Public Employees	Communications Satellite Corporation
Business Development Bank of Canada	Electric Vehicle Association
Canadian Red Cross	The Hospital for Sick Children*
National Hockey League	The Boeing Company*

---

* *Capitalize the *only* when it is part of an organization's official name (as it would appear on the organization's stationery).*

Generally, do not capitalize *company, association, board,* and other shortened name forms when they are used to replace full organization names. If these shortened names, however, are preceded by the word *the* and are used in formal or legal documents (contracts, bylaws, minutes, etc.), they may be capitalized.

> Did you know that the *company* will pay certain medical benefits? (Informal document)
>
> The Treasurer of the *Association* is herein authorized to disburse funds. (Formal document)

Academic Courses and Degrees

Capitalize the names of numbered courses and specific course titles. Do not capitalize the names of academic subject areas unless they contain a proper noun.

> Professor Rose Waxman is scheduled to offer Psychology 104 in the spring.
>
> All accounting majors must take business English and business law.
>
> Becky expects to enrol in Keyboarding 12, Office Administration 32, and Accounting 28.
>
> My most interesting classes are history, business management, and business French.

Capitalize abbreviations of academic degrees whether they stand alone or follow individuals' names. Do not capitalize general references to degrees.

> Aleksandar hopes to earn B.Sc. and M.Sc. degrees.
>
> The university offers bachelor's and master's degrees.
>
> Sylvia Sasot, Ph.D., teaches there.
>
> New employees include Joanne Duncan, M.S.W., and Thomas Wong, M.A.

Seasons

Do not capitalize seasons unless they are personified (i.e., referred to as if alive).

> Last winter we drew lots for summer vacations. (Usual reference)
>
> "Come, Winter, with thine angry howl ..."—Burns (Personification)

Complete the reinforcement exercises for Level I on pp. 360–361.

Study Tip

Course titles with numbers are usually capitalized (*Marketing 101*). Those without numbers usually are not capitalized (*marketing*).

LEVEL II

▶ Special Rules of Capitalization

Titles of People

a. Capitalize personal titles when they precede names.

Aunt Gertrude	Budget Director Magee
Councillor Mendler	Mayor Rasmussen
Commander Howard Rogers	Chief Dan George
Rabbi David Cohen	Prince Charles

b. Capitalize titles in addresses and closing lines.

Mr. Kenneth Miller   Very sincerely yours,
Executive Vice-President, Planning
Energy Systems Technology
112 Ellery Street   Patricia Barr
Victoria, BC V8W 3K5   Sales Supervisor

c. Capitalize titles of high-ranking national or international officials.

the Prime Minister   the Chief Justice
the President of the United States   an audience with the Queen
the visit of the Pope   the Secretary of State

d. Do not capitalize titles following names.

Leon Jones, president of Atlas Chemical Company
Rose Valenzuela, supervisor, Word Processing Centre
Davonne Adams, office manager

e. Generally, do not capitalize titles appearing alone.

The president of that company was made chair of the board.
Refer the problem to the vice-president or to the human resources manager.

f. Do not capitalize titles when they precede or follow appositives (unless they represent special high rank, as in c).*

Our cost accountant, Mona Chase, submitted her revised figures.
Gary Bauer, vice-president, controls all hiring.

The capitalization of business titles can be summarized in one rule: Capitalize business titles *only* when they precede personal names and are not followed by appositives, as in this case: *Personnel Director Roslyn Katz.*

g. Do not capitalize family titles used with possessive pronouns or articles.

my mother   the aunt
his father   a cousin

But do capitalize titles of close relatives when they are used without pronouns— as names are used.

Please call Father immediately.
This is Grandmother's brooch.

Numbered and Lettered Items

Capitalize nouns followed by numbers or letters (except in page, paragraph, line, and verse references).

Gate 69, Flight 238   Form 2900-4   Building I-63-B
Invoice No. 15891   Volume II, Appendix A   Supplement No. 3
page 6, line 12   County Road 56   Order 1034

Study Tip

Capitalize only the first word in salutations (*My dear Ms. Jones*) and complimentary closes (*Very truly yours*).

Study Tip

Notice that titles of high rank are capitalized whether they precede, follow, or replace a name.

Hotlink

Using this Capital Community College Web page <**http://webster. commnet.edu/ grammar/capitals. htm**>, you can access a Microsoft® PowerPoint® presentation on the use of capital letters, a list of capitalization rules with examples, and an on-line quiz to help you test your mastery of this subject.

* *You will recall that appositives rename or explain previously mentioned nouns or pronouns.*

Points of the Compass

Capitalize *north, south, east, west,* and their derivatives when they represent *specific* regions. Do not capitalize the points of the compass when they are used in directions or in general references.

the Middle East, the Far East	heading east on the turnpike
the West, the Midwest (of the United States)	to the west of town
	eastern Ontario, western regions
the East, the West Coast	southern Manitoba
Easterners, Southerners	northern towns

Departments, Divisions, and Committees

Capitalize the names of departments, divisions, or committees within *your own* organization. Outside your organization capitalize only specific department, division, or committee names.

> Send your employment application to their human resources department.
> A steering committee has not yet been named.
> Dr. Nguyen is director of the Northeast Division of Barco.
> Sue works in *our* Communication Services Department.
> Grievances are referred to *our* Personnel Practices Committee.

Governmental Terms

Do not capitalize the words *federal, government, national, provincial,* or *state* unless they are part of a specific title.

> Neither the provincial government nor the federal government would fund the proposal.
> The legislative body in Quebec is called the National Assembly.

Product Names

Capitalize product names only when they represent trademarked items. Frequently used product names, like many in the following list, are shown in dictionaries and labelled as trademarked or proprietary terms. Except in advertising, common names following manufacturers' names are not capitalized.

Coke, Coca-Cola	Jeep	Plasticine
Duo-Tang folder	Kleenex	Q-tip
DuPont Teflon	Kodak camera	Ray-Ban sunglasses
Formica counter	Magic Marker	Styrofoam cup
IBM computer	Pepsi	Whirlpool washer

Literary and Artistic Titles

Capitalize the principal words in the titles of books, magazines, newspapers, articles, movies, plays, songs, poems, and reports. Do *not* capitalize articles (*a, an, the*), short conjunctions (*and, but, or, nor*), and prepositions of fewer than four letters (*in, to, by, for,* etc.) unless they begin or end the title.

> Quinn's *Making the Most of Your Money* (Book)
> Smith's *Easy World Wide Web—Worth Waiting For* (Book with preposition at end of title)

HOW: A Handbook for Office Workers (Book with title and subtitle)
The Globe and Mail (Newspaper)
Frank Capra's *It Happened One Night* (Movie)
"How to Get the Most From a Placement Service" (Magazine article)
"Stand by Me" (Song)

Complete the reinforcement exercises for Level II on pp. 362–363.

▶ Additional Rules of Capitalization

LEVEL III

Beginning Words

In addition to capitalizing the first word of a complete sentence, capitalize the first words in quoted sentences, independent phrases, enumerated items, and formal rules or principles following colons.

> John F. Kennedy said, "Man is the most extraordinary computer of all."
>   (Quoted sentence)
> No, not at the present time. (Independent phrase)
>
> Big utilities formed an alliance to sell the following:
>   1. Electricity
>   2. Natural gas
>   3. Energy management services (Enumerated items)
>
> Our office manager responded with his favourite rule: Follow the company
>   stylebook for correct capitalization. (Rule following colon)

Celestial Bodies

Capitalize the names of celestial bodies such as Jupiter, Saturn, and Neptune. Do not capitalize the terms *earth, sun,* or *moon* unless they appear in a context with other celestial bodies.

> Where on earth did you find that ancient typewriter?
> Venus and Mars are the closest planets to Earth.

Ethnic References

Terms that relate to a particular culture, language, or race are capitalized.

> The Dene are the Athapaskan-speaking First Nations peoples, including the
>   Chipewyan, Dogrib, Gwich'in, and Slave groups.
> In Hawaii, Oriental and Western cultures merge.
> Both English and Hebrew are spoken by Jews in Israel.
> The politician wasn't popular with French-Canadian voters.*

"99

Notable Quotable

"A determined person is one who, when he or she gets to the end of the rope, ties a knot and hangs on."
—Joe L. Griffith

---

* *Hyphenate terms such as* French-Canadian *and* African-American *when used as adjectives. Do not hyphenate these terms when they are nouns.*

Spot the Blooper

Words Following *marked* and *stamped*

Capitalize words that follow the words *marked* and *stamped*.

> For greater care in transport, the package was stamped "Fragile."
> That bill was marked "Paid in Full" on September 15.

Special Uses of Personal Titles and Terms

a. Generally, titles are capitalized according to the specifications set forth earlier. However, when a title of an official appears in that organization's minutes, bylaws, or other official documents, it may be capitalized.

> The Controller will have authority over college budgets. (Title appearing in bylaws)
> By vote of the shareholders, the President is empowered to implement a stock split. (Title appearing in annual report)

b. When the terms *ex, elect, late,* and *former* are used with capitalized titles, they are not capitalized.

> The projections of ex-Vice-President Baldwin have proven exceedingly accurate.
> Mayor-elect Ross addressed the city council.
> The Prime Minister appointed former Governor General Ramon Hnatyshyn to the commission.

c. Titles are capitalized when used in direct address, except for terms like *sir, madam, ladies,* and *gentlemen.*

> May I ask, Doctor, what the prognosis is?
> You, ladies and gentlemen, are well aware of the gravity of the situation.

Complete the reinforcement exercises for Level III on pp. 364–365.

HOTLINE QUERIES

Question: I don't know how to describe the copies made from our copy machine. Should I call them *Xerox* copies or something else?

Answer: They are *Xerox* copies only if made on a Xerox copier. Copies made on other machines may be called *xerographic* copies, *machine* copies, or *photocopies.*

Question: In the doctor's office where I work, I see the word *medicine* capitalized, as in *the field of Medicine.* Is this correct?

Answer: No. General references should not be capitalized. If it were part of a title, as in the Northwestern College of *Medicine,* it would be capitalized.

Question: I work for the National Therapy Association. When I talk about *the association* in a letter, should I capitalize it?

Answer: No. When a shortened form of an organization name is used alone, it is generally not capitalized. In formal or legal documents (contracts, bylaws, printed announcements), however, it may be capitalized.

Question: I work for a provincial agency, and I'm not sure what to capitalize or hyphenate in this sentence: *Provincial agencies must make forms available to <u>non-English speaking</u> applicants.*

Answer: When a prefix is joined to a word that must be capitalized, the prefix is usually followed by a hyphen and the capital letter is retained, as in *anti-American, mid-July,* or *pre-Confederation.* In your example because the word *speaking* combines with *English* to form a single-unit adjective, it should be hyphenated. Thus the expression should be typed *non-English-speaking applicants.*

Question: When we use a person's title, such as *business manager,* in place of a person's name, shouldn't the title always be capitalized?

Answer: No. Business titles are capitalized only when they precede an individual's name, as in *Business Manager Smith.* Do not capitalize titles when they replace an individual's name: *Our business manager will direct the transaction.*

Question: How do you spell *marshal,* as in the Grand Marshal of the Rose Bowl Parade?

Answer: The preferred spelling is with a single *l: marshal.* In addition to describing an individual who directs a ceremony, the noun *marshal* refers to a high military officer or a city law officer who carries out court orders (*the marshal served papers on the defendant*). As a verb, *marshal* means "to bring together" or "to order in an effective way" (*the lawyer marshalled convincing arguments*), and the preferred spelling is with a double *l* before the ending *-ing* or *-ed.* The similar-sounding word *martial* is an adjective and means "warlike" or "military" (*martial law was declared after the riot*).

CHAPTER 19   Reinforcement Exercises

A. **(Self-check)** In the following sentences, use standard proofreading marks to correct errors you find in capitalization. Use three short lines (≡) under a lower-case letter to indicate that it is to be changed to a capital letter. Draw a diagonal (/) through a capital letter you wish to change to a lower-case letter. Indicate at the right the total number of changes you have made in each sentence. If no changes are needed, write *0*.

LEVEL I

Example: The /bandit Henry McCarthy was also known as Billy the kid.   2

1. One of the World's largest trading businesses is the japanese sumimoto corporation.   _____

2. Born in Timiskaming county, Wilson grew up in the province of Manitoba.   _____

3. All Ford Motor Company Cars and Light Trucks carry a Warranty.   _____

4. Isaac Bantu is studying spanish, accounting, Management, and Keyboarding.   _____

5. Use India ink to make dark headings on the manila folders.   _____

6. Pelee island is located on the canadian side of lake erie.   _____

7. Regulations of transport canada resulted in costly expenses for the Company.   _____

8. Salt lake city, in the State of Utah, was founded by Brigham Young and a small Party of Mormons in 1847.   _____

9. All sales representatives of the Company met in the Sheraton room of the Red lion inn.   _____

10. both the house of commons and the Senate passed consumer protection laws.   _____

Check your answers.

B. Use proofreading marks to correct any capitalization errors in these sentences. Indicate the total number of changes at the right. If no changes are needed, write *0*.

1. Because he was interested in Computer Technology, Craig took computer mathematics I, general physics I, and computer circuitry II.   _____

2. Representatives from the methodist, presbyterian, baptist, and catholic faiths will hold a Conference in St. petersburg beach, florida.   _____

3. Rex Mackey was sent to our port Dover branch office for the Month of August, but he hopes to return in September.   _____

4. The newspaper reports that Joe Fujimoto, ph.d., has joined your Company. _____

5. Expansion of the internet has seriously affected business at The Boeing Company. (The word *the* is part of the company name.) _____

6. Last Fall Ms. Adams took out a policy with the Prudential life insurance company. (The word *the* is part of the company name.) _____

7. Work schedules will have to be adjusted in november for remembrance day. _____

8. All company representatives gathered in quebec city in the champlain room of the holiday inn for the spring sales meeting. _____

9. The windy city is attractive to many American Tourists as well as to increasing numbers of european and canadian visitors. _____

10. Professor Daruty employed the socratic method of questioning students to elicit answers about Business Management. _____

11. After driving through New York state, we stayed in New York city and visited the Empire State building. _____

12. Because she had a cold, Marg asked me to pick up cough syrup and kleenex at the corner store. _____

13. Kay Randolph completed the requirements for a bachelor's degree at Simon Fraser university. _____

14. The report contained some roman numerals and many greek symbols in the engineering equations. _____

15. Last spring my political science class visited the tishman building in westwood village. _____

A. (Self-check) Use proofreading marks to correct errors you find in capitalization. Indicate at the right the total number of changes you make.

LEVEL II

Example: Project manager Harold Gross was promoted to Vice-President.   _____3_____

1. Henry Davis, supervisor of our legal department, travelled to the east coast over the holidays. (Note use of *our*.)   _____

2. Please consult figure 52D in appendix B for instructions in computing the depreciation of equipment.   _____

3. We will ask sales manager Sperazza to be chair of an investigative committee.   _____

4. Both mother and aunt grace received Radio Shack Cordless Phones as Christmas gifts.   _____

5. The fishing industry in the Pacific northwest is affected by recent federal regulations.   _____

6. The business manager and the vice-president attended an e-business seminar in southern Alberta.   _____

7. My Uncle recommended that I read the article entitled "how management is guided by research."   _____

8. Address the envelope to Ms. Maris Sheaffer, director, employee services, Omega Corporation, 304 Hilyard Street, Edmonton, Alberta T6J 5G4.   _____

9. The pope was reported in good condition after his fall in the Vatican.   _____

10. Centron oil company, with headquarters in western Texas, distributes its products throughout the entire northern hemisphere.   _____

Check your answers.

B. Use proofreading marks to correct errors in the sentences below. Indicate the number of changes you make for each sentence.

1. Harley Lee, vice-president of Manufacturers trust company, asked his Executive Assistant to direct the united way office contributions.   _____

2. My sister, my cousin, and I will fly to visit mother, father, and uncle Eduardo over the Spring holidays.   _____

3. Marcia Morrow, formerly with our office products department, recently published *Word processing from infancy through the 90s*.   _____

1. Legal Department East Coast (4) 2. Figure Appendix (2) 3. Sales Manager (2) 4. Mother Aunt Grace cordless phones (5) 5. Northwest (1) 6. (0) 7. uncle How Management Is Guided by Research (3) 8. Director Employee Services (3) 9. Pope (1) 10. Oil Company (2)

4. When the prime minister entertained the queen, stringent security measures were effected. _____

5. You will find a discussion of keynesian economics in volume II on page 71, starting with line 11. _____

6. The Sales Manager of Datacom hurried to gate 16 to catch flight 263 to Fredericton. _____

7. The director of purchasing, Harvey Gross, ordered Victor Calculators and Sony Recorders. _____

8. The letter is addressed to Paul Jorgensen, director of research and development, blum corporation, p.o. box 58, gulfport, florida 33707. _____

9. May Co.'s ad featured Royal Manor Dishes and teflon-coated pans. _____

10. Overtime compensation for Carmen Corregas was referred to our industrial relations department. _____

11. Kristen shopped for kleenex tissues and kodak film at her local zellers. _____

12. Daphne Mainprize, curator, gave a talk in the stephen leacock museum on old brewery bay outside Orillia, Ontario. _____

13. Business Manager Edward Davis devised a procedure for expediting Purchase Orders from Area D Offices. _____

14. Douglas ordered a big mac, french fries, and a coca-cola for lunch. _____

15. David Kane is now supervising our entire west coast division. _____

16. As stated in Part II of the Contract, sun life assurance company pays claims related to injuries only. _____

17. The new Cantel model 100 cellular phone will be demonstrated at the national office products show at the bonaventure hotel next fall. _____

A. (Self-check) Use proofreading marks to indicate necessary changes. Write the total number of changes at the right.

LEVEL III

Example: Mercury, venus, earth, and Mars are ɸense and solid.

_____3_____

1. Because the package was marked "fragile," we handled it carefully.

_____

2. The guiding principle of capitalization is this: capitalize *specific* names and references, but do not capitalize *general* references.

_____

3. Members of both asian and hispanic cultures participated in the city's celebration.

_____

4. The Late Prime Minister Lester Pearson is remembered for his efforts to obtain world peace at the united nations.

_____

5. The most frequently typed documents in a Lawyer's office are the following:
   1. affidavits
   2. wills and trusts
   3. briefs

_____

6. Spacecraft from earth have recently been sent to the planets Mars, Jupiter, and Venus.

_____

7. Oversupply of canadian dollars causes the dollar's value to decline compared with the american dollar, the german mark, the swiss franc, the japanese yen, and the french franc.

_____

8. We have Ex-Councillor Lupus and Mayor-Elect Lanham scheduled for the Remembrance day festivities.

_____

9. You, Sir, are in danger of being held in contempt of court.

_____

10. The Organization's bylaws state, "The Secretary of the Association will submit an agenda two weeks before each meeting."

_____

Check your answers.

B. Use proofreading marks to indicate necessary changes. Write the total number of changes at the right.

1. As the Sun beat down on the crowd, the Vice-Chancellor continued his graduation address.

_____

2. Would you like a ride home? yes, thank you very much.

_____

3. Our Advertising Agency operates according to this rule: you must spend money to make money.

_____

1. Fragile (1) 2. Capitalize (1) 3. Asian Hispanic (2) 4. late United Nations (3)
5. lawyer's Affidavits Wills Briefs (4) 6. Earth (1) 7. Canadian American German Swiss
Japanese French (6) 8. ex-Councillor Mayor-elect Day (3) 9. sir (1) 10. organization (1)

4. William noticed that the english spoken by asians in hong kong sounded quite british. _____

5. Please take the file marked "budget" to the Business Manager's office. _____

6. The Minutes of the last meeting show that the Vice-President, acting on behalf of the President, conducted the meeting despite the lack of a quorum. _____

7. Mayor-Elect Hudson sat beside Ex-Mayor Benedict and councillor Waller at the morning Ceremony. _____

8. How much, professor, does the Final Exam count? _____

9. Some factors I am considering in seeking a job are the following:
   1. income
   2. geographical location
   3. job security _____

10. Benjamin Disraeli provided England with its National motto when he said, "something will turn up." _____

C. Review of Levels I, II, and III. Select (a) or (b) to indicate correct capitalization.

1. (a) our marketing manager   (b) our Marketing Manager   _____

2. (a) Rogers pass   (b) Rogers Pass   _____

3. (a) awarded a Bachelor's degree (b) awarded a bachelor's degree _____

4. (a) courses in English and sociology   (b) courses in english and sociology   _____

5. (a) the Pacific Room at the Marriott   (b) the pacific room at the Marriott   _____

6. (a) French fries and a pepsi-cola   (b) french fries and a Pepsi-Cola   _____

7. (a) a file marked "urgent"   (b) a file marked "Urgent"   _____

8. (a) avoid the sun's rays   (b) avoid the Sun's rays   _____

9. (a) the prime minister's TV speech   (b) the Prime Minister's TV speech   _____

10. (a) exit from highway 5   (b) exit from Highway 5   _____

D. Optional Compositions. Your instructor may ask you to complete these exercises on a separate sheet. (1) Write ten original sentences that contain at least 20 properly capitalized words, not counting the first word. (2) On a separate sheet write one or two paragraphs summarizing an article from a local newspaper. Choose an article with as many capital letters as possible. Apply the rules of capitalization you learned in this chapter.

Editor's Challenge

The following letter/progress report contains intentional errors reflecting the concepts you have studied thus far. It also contains a few spelling errors. Use standard proofreading marks to show all necessary corrections.

HOLST BROTHERS CONSTRUCTION

2230 DUNSMUIR AVE.
OTTAWA ON K1A 2J7   (613) 828-4493

Ms. Danielle M. Forrester
President, Interior Design Institute
504 Richmond Street
Ottawa, ON K1N 7B7

Dear Ms. Forrester:

Here is a brief report about our work with the cheviot hills residence being prepared as the showcase house for the interior design institute. The renovation and remodelling is progressing on schedule, and should be ready for the photographers from metropolitan home magazine june 1.

Past Progress

During the Fall the work crew completed the following tasks, removal of all wood shingles, repair of the plywood roof base and installation of a permawear tile roof. In december we replaced damaged window facings we also repaired the plumbing in two baths and the kitchen. As you requested we investigated italian marble for the entry and spanish tiles for the patio. A price sheet for those items are enclosed.

Current Progress

At present we are concentrating on the Living Room which required ceiling repair and electrical rewiring, see page 6 of your blueprints. The pyramid skylight has been installed in the library, however, we had to alter two bookcases in doing so. After consulting the President and General Manager of our company, a decision was made that we should absorb some of the extra costs involved, however, other off budget items will be your responsibility.

Future Schedule

In February we expect to complete all the interior finish work, the painters will apply two coats of anderson no. 343 wall primer. I believe that Ms. Chin and Mr. Darwin whom you suggested would be decorating the downstairs, could begin there work february 15. Just have them call my Supervisor or I to arrange the exact date.

Sincerely yours,

Irena Overmeyer

Irena Overmeyer

Underline any letter that should be capitalized.

1. Both the president and the human resources manager were fluent in french and english.

2. Judy studied english literature, accounting, and sociology at the university of alberta.

3. The engineers will meet in the algonquin room of the four points Sheraton next thursday.

4. Although we ordered a model 500 sony calculator, we received a model 400 calculator.

5. My mother, my father, and uncle michael will spend the easter holidays with us.

learning.web.ways

You have written a super résumé, and now you want to write a terrific application letter to introduce your résumé. You know that many Web sites offer tips on writing cover letters.

Goal: To improve your employment application letters.

1. With your Web browser on the screen, first visit the Canadian Careers site **<http://www.canadiancareers.com/resandcl.html>**.

2. Read the **Cover Letter Guide**, and print a copy.

3. In your browser's location box, enter The University of Waterloo's Career Services URL **<http://www.adm.uwaterloo.ca/infocecs/CRC/manual-home.html>**. Bookmark this site, and find the **Letters** section of its **Career Development** manual.

4. Read this section, and jot down the tips you did not learn from the **Cover Letter Guide**.

5. End your session. Submit your printout and tips.

1. French English 2. English University of Alberta 3. Algonquin Room Four Points Thursday 4. Model 500 Sony Model 400 5. Uncle Michael Easter

Numbers

OBJECTIVES When you have completed the materials in this chapter, you will be able to do the following:

LEVEL I
- *Choose correctly between figure and word forms to express general numbers, money, and numbers beginning sentences.*

- *Express dates, clock time, addresses, and telephone numbers appropriately.*

LEVEL II
- *Use the correct form in writing related numbers, consecutive numbers, periods of time, and ages.*

- *Use the correct form in expressing numbers in conventional phrases, with abbreviations and symbols, and as round numbers.*

LEVEL III
- *Express correctly weights, measures, and fractions.*

- *Use the correct form in expressing percentages, decimals, and ordinals.*

PRETEST

Examine the expression of numbers in the following sentences. Should word or figure form be used? Underline any incorrect form, and write an improved form in the blank provided. For example, which is preferred: *$10* or *ten dollars?*

1. On the fifth of September at five p.m., our 1st computer left the assembly line. _____

2. When Roxanne reached 18 years of age, she assumed ownership of over fifty ha of property in two provinces. _____

3. Please take eleven dollars to pick up 20 forty-eight-cent stamps at the post office. _____

continued

Just as capitalization is governed by convention, so is the expression of numbers. Usage and custom determine whether numbers are to be expressed in the form of a figure (for example, 5) or in the form of a word (for example, *five*). Numbers expressed as figures are shorter and more easily comprehended, yet numbers used as words are necessary in certain instances. The following guidelines are observed in expressing numbers that appear in written *sentences*. Numbers that appear in business communications such as invoices, statements, and purchase orders are always expressed in figures.

LEVEL I

Study Tip

To remember it better, some people call this the "Rule of Ten": Words for one through ten; figures for 11 and above.

▶ Basic Guidelines for Expressing Numbers

General Rules

The numbers *one* through *ten* are generally written as words. Numbers above *ten* are written as figures.

> The jury consisted of *nine* regular members and *one* alternate.
> The *37* spoiled questionnaires were discarded.

Numbers that begin sentences are written as words. If a number involves more than two words, however, the sentence should be rewritten so that the number no longer falls at the beginning.

> *Twenty-three* investors provided capital for the down payment.
> A total of *320* distributors agreed to market the product. (Not: *Three hundred twenty* distributors agreed to market the product.)

Money

Sums of money $1 or greater are expressed as figures. If a sum is a whole dollar amount, most business writers omit the decimal and zeros (whether or not the amount appears with fractional dollar amounts).

> Although he budgeted only *$20*, Mike spent *$34.50* for the gift.
> Our monthly statement showed purchases of *$7.13, $10, $43.50, $90,* and *$262.78*.

Sums less than $1 are written as figures that are followed by the word *cents*. If they are part of sums greater than $1, use a dollar sign and a decimal instead of the word *cents*.

---

1. 5th 5 p.m. first 2. eighteen 50 ha 3. $11 twenty 48-cent 4. 20 cars May 2 4 cars 5. 23 cm by 30 cm $2 million

Lisa said she had only *65 cents* with her.

Supplies for the project were listed at *$1.35, $.99, $2.80, $1,* and *$.40.*

Dates

In dates, numbers that appear after the name of the month are written in cardinal figures (*1, 2, 3,* etc.). Those that stand alone or appear before the name of a month are written in ordinal figures (*1st, 2nd, 3rd,* etc.).

> The meeting is scheduled for *October 5* in our office.
>
> On the *2nd* day of January and again on the *18th,* we called for service.

In business documents dates generally take the following form: month, day, year. An alternative form, used primarily in military and international correspondence, begins with the day of the month.

> The contract was originally signed *25 June 1994.*

Some business organizations also prefer this international date style for its clarity since it separates the numerical date of the month from the year.

Clock Time

Figures are used when clock time is expressed with *a.m.* or *p.m.* Omit the colon and zeros with whole hours. When exact time is expressed with *o'clock,* either figures or words may be used.

> The first shift starts at *8 a.m.,* and the second begins at *3:30 p.m.*
>
> At *four* (or *4*) *o'clock* in the afternoon, we'll announce the winner.

Addresses and Telephone Numbers

Except for the number *One,* house and building numbers are expressed as figures.

> 805 Fiske Avenue   27321 Riverside Drive
>
> One Victoria Boulevard   1762 Cone Street

Street names that involve the number *ten* or a lower number are written entirely as words, unless the original form is known to contradict this guideline. In street names involving numbers greater than *ten,* the numeral portion is written as figures. If no compass direction (*North, South, East, West*) separates a house number from a street number, the street number is expressed in ordinal form (*–st, –d, –th*).

> 503 Second Street
>
> 11901 Ninth Avenue
>
> 2320 West 11 Street
>
> 613 North 102 Avenue
>
> 327 39th Avenue (Use *th* when no compass direction separates house
>   number and numerical portion of street name.)

Telephone and fax numbers are expressed with figures. When used, the area code is placed in parentheses preceding the telephone number. As an alternate form, the area code may be separated from the telephone number by a hyphen.

> Please call us at *828-1100* for further information.
>
> You may reach me at *(306) 685-4321, Ext. 281,* after 9:30 a.m.
>
> Call our toll-free number at 800-340-3281 for the latest sports updates.

Complete the reinforcement exercises for Level I on pp. 377–379.

Study Tip

If your company has a style manual, check it for number preferences. Larger companies may prescribe the figure or word form they prefer for often-used numbers.

Spot the Blooper

From *The Suburban & Wayne Times:* "Cases of Lyme disease, which is transmitted by deer-carrying ticks, are on the rise." (What unintended meaning resulted from the unneeded hyphen?)

▶ **Special Guidelines for Expressing Numbers**

Related Numbers

Numbers used similarly in the same document are considered related and should be expressed as the largest number is expressed. Thus if the largest number is greater than *ten,* all the numbers should be expressed as figures.

> Only *3* companies out of *147* neglected to return the survey form.
> Of the *35* documents processed, *9* letters and *3* memoranda were urgent.

Unrelated numbers within the same document are written as words or figures according to the general guidelines presented earlier in this chapter.

> The *two* studies included *22* employees working in *three* separate offices.
> The *two* bridges carry at least *10,000* cars during the *four* peak traffic hours.

Consecutive Numbers

When two numbers appear consecutively and both modify a following noun, readers may misread the numbers because of their closeness. You should (a) rewrite the expression or (b) express one number in word form and the other in figure form. Use word form for the number that may be expressed in fewer words. If both numbers have an equal count, spell out the first number and place the second one in figures.

> We offered to publish *400 thirty*-page brochures. (Use word form for the number that may be expressed in the fewest words.)
> The economist divided the era into *four 25*-year periods.
> Please purchase *thirty 10*-cm galvanized nails for the job. (Use word form for the first number since both have an equal word count.)

Periods of Time

Periods of time that can be expressed in one or two words are usually written in word form. However, figures may be used to achieve special emphasis in expressing business concepts such as discount rates, interest rates, warranty periods, credit terms, loan periods, and payment terms.

> *Word form*
> Mrs. Martino has been with our firm for over *thirty-five* years.
> We agreed to keep the book for only *fifteen* days.
>
> *Figure form (would require more than two words)*
> After a *183-day* strike, workers returned to their jobs.
>
> *Figure form (business concept)*
> The warranty period is limited to *2* years.
> For payment within *30* days, a cash discount is provided.

Ages and Anniversaries

Ages and anniversaries that can be written out in one or two words are generally expressed in word form. Figures are used when an age (a) appears immediately after a name, (b) is expressed in exact years and months, or (c) is used in a technical sense.

> When he was *forty-one,* Mr. Selnig became the company's president.
> This year marks the *twenty-fifth* anniversary of the company's founding.

Grace Siebold, *63,* plans to retire in two years.
The child was adopted when he was *3* years and *8* months old.

Numbers Used in Conventional Phrases, With Abbreviations, and With Symbols

Numbers used in conventional phrases are expressed as figures.

page 4	Policy 04-168315	Area Code 819
Room 14	Volume 5	Section 16
Option 3	Form 1040	Bylaw 96-221

Numbers used with abbreviations are expressed as figures.

Apt. 16	Serial No. 265188440	Nos. 199 and 202
Ext. 245	Account No. 286-32-5891	Social Insurance No. 412 434 456

Notice that the word *number* is capitalized and abbreviated when it precedes a number. Notice, too, that no commas are used in serial, account, and policy numbers.

Symbols (such as #, %, ¢) are usually avoided in contextual business writing (sentences). In other business documents where space is limited, however, symbols are frequently used. Numbers appearing with symbols are expressed as figures.

15% 44¢ #10 nails 2/10, n/60

Round Numbers

Round numbers are approximations. They may be expressed in word or figure form, although figure form is shorter and easier to comprehend.

Almost *400* (or *four hundred*) employees signed the petition.
At last count we had received about *20* (or *twenty*) reservations.

For ease of reading, round numbers in the millions or billions should be expressed with a combination of figures and words.

The Prime Minister asked for a budget cut of *$2 billion.*
In its lawsuit IBM made available to the government *69 million* documents.
Nearly *1.2 million* imported cars were sold last year.

Complete the reinforcement exercises for Level II on pp. 380–382.

▶ Additional Guidelines for Expressing Numbers

The following guidelines will help you use appropriate forms for weights and measurements, fractions, percentages and decimals, and ordinals.

Weights and Measurements

Weights and measurements are expressed as figures.

The truck needed *80* L of gasoline and *2* L of oil.
A microfiche card measures *4* by *6* inches (about *10* by *15* cm).
The announcement gave the baby's weight as *7* pounds *14* ounces.

Study Tip

Figures are easier to understand and remember than words. That's why business terms, even for numbers under ten, are generally written as figures.

- You earn a *2 per cent* discount if your bill is paid within *10 days* of purchase.
- High interest rates are offered even on *6-* and *9-month* certificates of deposit.
- Your loan must be repaid within *60 days* in accordance with its terms.

Spot the Blooper

From *The Denver Post*: "The Allied Jewish Federation, which overseas the fund drive, hopes to raise $5.5 million."

In sentences in non-technical writing, the nouns following weights and measurements are spelled out if they refer to traditional units of measurement (for example, *7 pounds 14 ounces*) but should not be spelled out if they refer to metric units of measure (10 by 15 *cm*). For business forms, charts, and technical writing, symbols or abbreviations are used.

57 kg   17°C   100 km   2 lb.   5 tbsp.   9′ × 12′   #10

Canada adopted SI (Système international d'unités, commonly referred to as the metric system) in 1971, but examples here include traditional forms such as *pound* and *foot* because they are still in common use.

Note that the metric/SI system uses symbols rather than abbreviations. No periods are used unless the symbol falls at the end of a sentence. Abbreviations for traditional units of measure are now commonly written without periods as well.

Fractions

Simple fractions are expressed as words and are hyphenated.

> Over *three-fourths* of the students attended the lecture.
> A *two-thirds* majority is needed to carry the measure.

Complex fractions appearing in sentences may be written either as figures or as a combination of figures and words.

> The microcomputer will execute a command in *1 millionth* of a second. (Combination of words and figures is easier to comprehend.)
> Flight records revealed that the emergency system was activated at *13/200* of a second after the pilot was notified. (Figure form is easier to comprehend.)

Mixed fractions (whole numbers with fractions) are always expressed by figures.

> The office desks were expected to be *35¼* inches long, not *35½* inches. (Notice that no space follows a whole number when a keyboard fraction is used.)
> The envelope measured *3 5/8* inches by *6 1/2* inches. (Notice that fractions that must be keyed with slashes are separated from their related whole numbers.)

When fractions that are constructed with slashes appear with key fractions, be consistent by using the slash construction for all the fractions involved.

Percentages and Decimals

Percentages are expressed with figures that are followed by the expression *per cent*. The per cent sign (%) is used only on business forms or in statistical presentations.

> Interest rates have been as low as *6 per cent* and as high as *19 per cent*.
> The report states that *52 per cent* of the workers joined the union.

Decimals are expressed with figures. If a decimal does not contain a whole number (an integer) and does not begin with a zero, a zero should be placed before the decimal.

> Daryl Thomas set a record when he ran the race in *9.86* seconds. (Contains a whole number.)
> Close examination revealed the settings to be *.005* of an inch off. (Begins with a zero.)

Spot the Blooper

Sign posted in bank: "Canada Trust Branch 538 is proud to present a RSP seminar on Tuesday, January 20."

Hotlink

This superb handout on Number Usage in the Business World <http://www.uvsc.edu/owl/handouts/number-usage.html> comes from Utah Valley State College. For a printer-friendly version, click on the link at the top of the page.

Less than *0.1* per cent of the operating costs will be borne by taxpayers. (Zero placed before decimal that neither contains a whole number nor begins with a zero.)

Ordinals

Although ordinal numbers are generally expressed in word form (*first, second, third,* etc.), three exceptions should be noted: (1) figure form is used for dates appearing before a month or appearing alone, (2) figure form is used for street names involving numbers greater than *ten,* and (3) figure form is used when the ordinal would require more than two words.

> *Most ordinals*
> The company is celebrating its *fortieth* anniversary.
> Before the *eighteenth* century, spelling was not standardized.
> Of *237* sales representatives, Joanna ranked *second* in total sales.
> A woman, Jeanne Sauvé, became the *twenty-third* Governor General in 1984.
>
> *Dates*
> Your payment must be received by the *30th* to qualify for the cash discount.
> We experienced a power outage on the *2nd* of June.
>
> *Streets*
> A traffic light was installed on *Second* Street.
> The customer service division has been moved to *35th* Street.
>
> *Larger ordinals*
> Our bank ranks *103rd* in terms of capital investments.

Complete the reinforcement exercises for Level III on pp. 383–385.

Complete the reinforcement exercises for Level III on pp. 383–385.

"

Notable Quotable

"Patience is the greatest of all shock absorbers. The only thing you can get in a hurry is trouble."
—Lord Thomas R. Dewar

HOTLINE QUERIES

Question: I recently saw the following format used by a business to publish its telephone number on its stationery and business cards: 647.582.0903. Is it now an option to use periods in telephone numbers?

Answer: I've recently seen this format used, particularly in graphics design. It seems to be a stylistic affectation, perhaps reflecting European influences. To some, the style is upscale and chic; to others, it's just confusing. Telephone numbers written in the traditional formats are most readily recognized. That's why it's best to stick with parentheses or hyphens: (647) 582-0903 or 647-582-0903.

Question: I'm never sure when to hyphenate numbers, such as *thirty-one.* Is there some rule to follow?

Answer: When written in words, the numbers *twenty-one* through *ninety-nine* are hyphenated. Numbers are also hyphenated when they form compound adjectives and precede nouns (*ten-year-old* child, *16-storey* building, *four-year* term, *30-day* lease).

Question: I've always been confused by *imply* and *infer.* Which is correct in this sentence: We (*imply* or *infer*) from your letter that the goods are lost.

Answer: In your sentence use *infer. Imply* means "to state indirectly." *Infer* means "to draw a conclusion" or "to make a deduction based on facts." A listener or reader *infers.* A speaker or writer *implies.*

Question: Should I put quotation marks around figures to emphasize them? For example, *Your account has a balance of "$2,136.18."*

Answer: Certainly not! Quotation marks are properly used to indicate an exact quotation, or they may be used to enclose the definition of a word. They should not be used as a mechanical device for added emphasis.

Question: I'm an engineer, and we have just had a discussion in our office concerning spelling. I have checked the dictionary, and it shows *usage.* Isn't this word ever spelled *useage?*

Answer: No. The only spelling of *usage* is without the internal *e.* You are probably thinking of the word *usable,* which does have a variant spelling—*useable.* Both forms are correct, but *usable* is recommended for its simplicity. Incidentally, if the word *usage* can be replaced by the word *use,* the latter is preferred (*the use* (not *usage*) *of ink pens is declining*).

Question: How should I spell the word *lose* in this sentence? *The employee tripped over a (lose* or *loose) cord.*

Answer: In your sentence use the adjective *loose,* which means "not fastened," "not tight," or "having freedom of movement." Perhaps you can remember it by thinking of the common expression *loose change*, which suggests unattached, free coins jingling in your pocket. If you *lose (mislay)* some of those coins, you have less money and fewer *o's.*

Question: My manager is preparing an advertisement for a charity event. She has written this: *Donors who give $100 dollars or more receive plaques.* I know this is not right, but I can't exactly put my finger on the problem.

Answer: The problem is in *$100 dollars.* That is like saying *dollars dollars.* Drop the word *dollars* and use only the dollar sign: *Donors who give $100 or more....*

CHAPTER 20   **Reinforcement Exercises**

A. **(Self-check)** Choose (a) or (b) to complete the following sentences.

LEVEL I

1. We are able to finish only (a) 11, (b) eleven letters by noon.   _____

2. (a) 15, (b) Fifteen applicants responded to the advertisement.   _____

3. The office will reopen on the (a) 14th, (b) fourteenth of June.   _____

4. Duplicating this brochure will cost (a) 4 cents, (b) $.04 per page.   _____

5. Ellen has collected (a) $20.00, (b) $20 for the gift.   _____

6. His address is listed as (a) Three, (b) 3 Meadowlark Drive.   _____

7. Financial institutions are clustered on (a) Seventh, (b) 7th Avenue.   _____

8. Send the letter to (a) 320 27th Street, (b) 320 27 Street.   _____

9. She said that a ream of paper would cost (a) $6, (b) six dollars.   _____

10. We plan to meet at (a) 9:00 a.m., (b) 9 a.m. Tuesday   _____

Check your answers.

B. Assume that the following phrases appear in business correspondence. Write the preferred forms in the spaces provided. If a phrase is correct as shown, write *C*.

Example: 8930 23 Avenue   _8930 23rd Avenue_

1. fourteen clerks	_____	**11.** thirty-three desks	_____
2. Tenth Street	_____	**12.** January 22nd	_____
3. $.09 per issue	_____	**13.** 12655 32nd Street	_____
4. 7 e-mail messages	_____	**14.** 12655 West 32nd Street	_____
5. June ninth	_____	**15.** two executives	_____
6. 5th Avenue	_____	**16.** twenty-four dollars	_____
7. $6.59, 98 cents, and $30.00	_____	**17.** 7 Hampton Square	_____
8. the eighteenth of September	_____	**18.** 1 Hampton Square	_____
9. 9:00 p.m.	_____	**19.** sixty-six rooms	_____
10. eight o'clock	_____	**20.** 7 o'clock	_____

1.a 2.b 3.a 4.a 5.b 6.b 7.a 8.a 9.a 10.b

---

21. (military style) May 15, 2002 _____   **26.** ninety cents _____

22. 2742 8th Street _____   **27.** 18307 Eleventh Street _____

23. six thirty p.m. _____   **28.** three p.m. _____

24. the fourth of May _____   **29.** 21 chapters _____

25. one hundred dollars _____   **30.** 3 laptops _____

C. Rewrite these sentences, correcting any errors you note.

1. On January thirteenth Alex submitted the following petty cash disbursements: $2.80, 99 cents, $3.00, and 25 cents.

_____

_____

_____

2. Elizabeth James moved from seventeen sixteen Sunset Drive to one Bellingham Court.

_____

_____

_____

3. 21 pages of *The Gregg Reference Manual* are devoted to rules for expressing numbers.

_____

_____

_____

4. On the 28 of January, I sent you 3 e-mail messages about restricting Internet use.

_____

_____

_____

5. If you have only thirty dollars, why are you considering the model that costs $49.99?

_____

_____

_____

6. Regular work breaks are scheduled at 10:00 a.m. in the morning and again at 3:30 p.m. in the afternoon.

_____

_____

_____

7. We want to continue operations through the thirtieth, but we may be forced to close by the twenty-second.

_____

_____

_____

8. 362 contracts had been signed before the June 1st deadline.

_____

_____

_____

A. **(Self-check)** Select (a) or (b) to complete each of the following sentences.

1. We are working on (a) three 16-page, (b) 3 sixteen-page booklets. _____

2. Elliot Walker has worked there for (a) twenty-seven, (b) 27 years. _____

3. A seminar on investing is being held in (a) Room Two, (b) Room 2. _____

4. Of the 650 envelopes sent, (a) nine, (b) 9 were returned. _____

5. Although she is only (a) 21, (b) twenty-one, Miss Love was appointed manager. _____

6. Current sales have reached (a) $2 million, (b) $2,000,000. _____

7. You can obtain Form (a) ten twenty, (b) 1020 by calling us. _____

8. Next week our company celebrates its (a) 25th, (b) twenty-fifth anniversary. _____

9. Your short-term loan covers a period of (a) 60, (b) sixty days. _____

10. The serial number on my monitor is (a) 85056170, (b) 85,056,170. _____

Check your answers.

B. For the following sentences underscore any numbers or words that are expressed inappropriately. Write the correct forms in the spaces provided. If a sentence is correct as written, write *C*.

Example: We need 16 60-cent stamps to complete the mailing. _____*sixteen*_____

1. The advisory committee is composed of 17 members, of whom five are supervisors, three are consultants, and nine are technicians. _____

2. To qualify for the federal grant, we submitted 3 100-page proposals. _____

3. Protected by steel armour, today's undersea telephone cables are expected to last 25 years. _____

4. Seven transatlantic cables can carry nearly 2,000,000 simultaneous phone calls. _____

5. The following policy Nos. are listed for John Daley: No. 1355801 and No. 1355802. _____

6. Model 8,400 costs $10,000 and can be leased for $275 a month. _____

7. A revolutionary new light bulb will reduce the demand for electricity by 8,000,000,000 kilowatt hours per year. _____

8. Of the 65 typed pages, nine pages need minor revisions and six pages require heavy revision. _____

1.a 2.a 3.b 4.b 5.b 6.a 7.b 8.b 9.a 10.a

9. John Edwards, forty-one, and Maria Gomez, thirty-three, were interviewed for the two executive positions. _____

10. On page twenty-two of Volume two, the total sales are listed at nearly $22 million. _____

11. All three electrical appliances have warranties limited to ninety days. _____

12. The total book club membership of eight hundred thousand received the four bonus books. _____

13. Only 43 of the 57 staff members could attend the two training sessions. _____

14. Bill Gates' Lake Washington mansion features a wall of twenty-four video screens, parking for twenty cars, and a reception hall for one hundred people. _____

15. When she is 21 years old, Ms. Enrico will inherit $1.3 million. _____

16. It took 12 inspection teams to review and rewrite thirty thousand pages of deeds, options, leases, and bills of sale. _____

17. The old man was 93 years old, but he said he felt as if he were fifty-three. _____

18. With 4 pickups daily, the delivery service serves two thousand employees in 45 departments. _____

C. Assume that the following phrases appear in business correspondence. Write the preferred forms in the spaces provided. If a phrase is correct as shown, write *C*.

1. four rooms with eleven computers and fifteen desks

_____

2. two twenty-five kg weights

_____

3. loan periods of sixty days

_____

4. Martha Diamond, fifty-eight, and John Diamond, sixty-one

_____

5. Account No. 362,486,012

_____

6. three point two billion dollars

_____

7. Room Five

_____

8. a period of seventeen years

_____

9. ninety-one books

_____

10. about two hundred guests

_____

11. four point four million people

_____

12. Section three point two

_____

13. insurance for 15 computers, 12 printers, and 3 DVD players

_____

14. a child two years five months old

_____

15. warranty period of two years

_____

A. **(Self-check)** Choose (a) or (b) to complete the following sentences.

LEVEL III

1. The rides are restricted to people taller than (a) 4'10", (b) 4 feet 10 inches. _____

2. Over (a) four-fifths, (b) 4/5 of the workers approved the pact. _____

3. The profit margin is expected to be (a) 16 per cent, (b) 16%. _____

4. Next year marks this company's (a) 40th, (b) fortieth anniversary. _____

5. Newspaper advertising accounts for about (a) one third, (b) one-third of all advertising dollars. _____

6. The company warehouses are now located on (a) Sixty-second, (b) 62nd Street. _____

7. We need a rug measuring (a) 3 by 4 m, (b) three by four m. _____

8. This year's maintenance costs are only (a) 0.5, (b) .5 per cent above last year's. _____

9. Did you order (a) five, (b) 5 L of oil? _____

10. The elevator stops at the (a) 14th, (b) fourteenth floor. _____

Check your answers.

B. Rewrite the following sentences with special attention to appropriate number usage.

1. Located in California, "Superman the Escape," the world's fastest roller coaster, travels one hundred miles per hour and is forty-one storeys high.

_____

_____

2. Swiss engineers used precise instruments to ensure that Superman's three thousand feet of steel track were within 0.05 inches of specifications.

_____

_____

3. The director announced a budget cut of almost $3,000,000.00.

_____

_____

1. b   2. a   3. a   4. b   5. b   6. b   7. a   8. a   9. b   10. b

4. In California's 19th Congressional District, Magic Mountain is thirty miles north of Los Angeles and attracts over eight hundred thousand visitors each summer.

_____

_____

5. Approximately 3/4 of every dollar contributed goes to charity.

_____

_____

6. Our company ranks one hundred seventh in terms of total exports.

_____

_____

7. Invoices that are paid before the tenth will receive a two per cent cash discount.

_____

_____

8. At least seven-tenths of the members attended the May tenth meeting when we approved the budget of thirty-five thousand dollars.

_____

_____

9. In the year 2,002 our nation celebrated its one hundred thirty-fifth anniversary.

_____

_____

10. A stock that costs fifty dollars a share and pays four dollars in dividends will yield an eight per cent return.

_____

_____

C. Optional Compositions. (1) Your instructor may ask you to complete this exercise on a separate sheet. Select ten number rules from this chapter. Write one sentence illustrating each rule. Label each rule. (2) In your local newspaper find ten sentences with numbers. Write those sentences on a separate sheet. After each one, explain what usage rule the number style represents. Strive to find examples illustrating different rules.

Editor's Challenge

The following e-mail message contains intentional errors representing language principles covered thus far. Use standard proofreading marks to make corrections.

E-Mail

New | Reply | Reply All | Forward | Add Contact | Delete | Addresses | Find | Send & Receive | Preferences

- Inbox
- Outbox
- Sent Mail
- Deleted Messages
- **Drafts (1)**
- Addresses

Inbox

From: Courtney Coleman
Sent: November 29, 200x
To: Ryan T. O'Neill, Vice-President
Subject: Summary of Internship Survey of Chain Restaurant Desserts

As an intern here at Midland Food Services I appreciate the opportunity you give me to informally investigate desserts offered by major chain restaurants. At our October 20th meeting of interns you mentioned that desserts are suppose to be fun. And that many of the chains were missing a big opportunity to develop a desert business.

To complete my internship project No. three I visited 10 of the biggest and best chains in Toronto and bought and taste all there desserts. I rated them on a scale of one to ten. Over a period of 5 weeks I tried over fifty desserts in 12 restaurants. Although my full report will be submitted shortly here is a brief summary of the dramatic, but disappointing, results.

- Surprisingly the average dessert score was only four point two on a 10-point scale. I rated them for taste, texture, portability, healthfulness and freshness of concept.
- 1/2 of the chains still have "hot apple pies." A leftover from the 1960's. These "pies" are largely dough with an overpowering taste of cinnamon and sugar. They have 280 calories with fifteen grams of fat. Thats more then a Cheeseburger or a order of French Fries!
- 1/3 of the chains offered chocolate chip cookies, they cost between ninety-nine cents and two dollars and contain another 15 grams of fat and three hundred or more calories.

The best chain dessert I encountered was "Fudge Grande, Choco Taco" from Taco bell. It was innovative, fun, good tasting, portable, relevant and refreshing. However the best restaurant dessert I've ever ate is a Chewy-Choco-Caramel-Marshmallow-Popcorn Bar offered by my college cafeteria.

The full findings of my informal survey is in three eleven-page reports. That I will distribute at the next Midland internship meeting Tuesday December 12th.

19 message(s), 1 displayed

Underline numbers that are expressed inappropriately. Write corrected forms in the space provided.

1. It took Revenue Canada seven years to collect the 750,000 dollars owed by the 2 companies.

_____

_____

2. Before the third of the month, we had received seventeen calls regarding the bicycle we advertised for twenty dollars.

_____

_____

3. The department had eighteen employees, and they shared four telephones, ten file cabinets, and seven computers.

_____

_____

4. Professor Yeoman reported that five hundred students enrolled, an increase of ten per cent over last year.

_____

_____

5. We will need ten fifty-page booklets before December 1st.

_____

_____

1. $750,000 two 2. 3rd 17 3. 18 4. 500 10 per cent 5. 50-page December 1

learning.web.ways

You've sent out your résumés and landed a couple of promising interviews. But you'd like to learn more about what to expect and how to answer interview questions.

Goal: To learn how to be more successful in employment interviewing.

1. With your Web browser on the screen, go to the Job-Interview Web site **<http://www.job-interview.net>**, and bookmark it.

2. Click **Interview Tips** (top of screen), and scroll down to identify the site recommended for further exploration.

3. Follow the recommended link, and familiarize yourself with the material on the interview process provided by **Human Resources Development Canada**. (You may want to bookmark this site, too, in fact.)

4. Print out the section you find most useful or informative.

5. Use the browser **Back** button to return to Job-Interview.net. Explore other articles on interviewing.

6. Using your bookmarks, go to the University of Waterloo's Career Services URL **<http://www.adm.uwaterloo.ca/infocecs/CRC/manual-home.html>**. Select the link for **Job/Work Interviews**. What two additional tips can you find about interviewing on this site? Write them down.

7. End your session, and submit your printout and answers.

Effective Sentences

21

OBJECTIVES When you have completed the materials in this chapter, you will be able to do the following:

LEVEL I
- *Eliminate wordy phrases and redundant words.*
- *Use the active voice in writing efficient sentences.*
- *Compose unified sentences by avoiding excessive detail and extraneous ideas.*

LEVEL II
- *Write clear sentences using parallel construction for similar ideas.*
- *Place words, phrases, and clauses close to the words they modify.*
- *Avoid ambiguous pronoun references such as* this, that, *and* which.

LEVEL III
- *Achieve emphasis by subordinating secondary ideas to primary ideas.*
- *Recognize and use concrete words instead of abstract words.*
- *Use transitional expressions (such as* therefore, however, *and* for example) *to develop coherence between thoughts.*

PRETEST

Rewrite the following sentences to eliminate problems in parallelism, redundancy, modification, reference, conciseness, and coherence.

1. In view of the fact that we are moving, we are not renewing the contract.

_____

_____

2. By totalling every column separately, the error was quickly located.

_____

_____

3. Lisa had to empty the cash register, count the cash, and the doors had to be locked.

_____

_____

4. I would like your final decision by June 1.

_____

_____

5. The new computer is for the desk in the outer office, which was delivered yesterday.

_____

_____

Business people value efficient, economical writing that is meaningful and coherent. Wordy communication wastes the reader's time; unclear messages confuse the reader and are counterproductive. In the business world, where time is valuable, efficient writing is demanded. You can improve your writing skills by emulating the practices of good writers. Most good writers begin with a rough draft that they revise to produce a final version. This chapter shows you how to revise your rough draft sentences to make them efficient, clear, emphatic, and coherent.

1. Since we are moving, we are not renewing the contract.   2. By totalling every column separately, we located the error quickly.   3. Lisa had to empty the cash register, count the cash, and lock the doors.   4. I would like your final decision by June 1.   5. The new computer, which was delivered yesterday, is for the outer office.

▶ Writing Efficient Sentences

Revising Wordy Phrases

Sentences are efficient when they convey a thought directly and economically—that is, in the fewest possible words. Good writers excise all useless verbiage from their writing. Most of these examples are also in the Unit 2 Writer's Workshop.

Wordy Phrases	**Efficient Substitutes**
along the lines of	like
at the present time	now
at this point in time	now
due to the fact that	because
for the purpose of	for
in connection with	about
in spite of the fact that	even though
in the amount of	for
in the event that	if
in the final analysis	finally
in the near future	soon
in the neighbourhood of	approximately
in terms of	regarding
in view of the fact that	since
until such time as	until
with a view to	to
with reference to	about
with regard to	about

Notice that the revised versions of the following wordy sentences are more efficient.

Wordy:	*Due to the fact that* fire damaged our warehouse, we must delay some shipments.
More efficient:	*Because* fire damaged our warehouse, we must delay some shipments.
Wordy:	Please send your cheque *in the amount of* $45.
More efficient:	Please send your cheque *for* $45.
Wordy:	We expected *in the neighbourhood of* 25 applicants.
More efficient:	We expected *approximately* 25 applicants.

Eliminating Redundant Words

Words that are needlessly repetitive are said to be "redundant." Writers can achieve greater efficiency (and thus more effective sentences) by eliminating redundant words or phrases.

Redundant:	The examples shown in Figure 2 illustrate letter styles.
More efficient:	Figure 2 shows letter styles.
Redundant:	The seminar covers only the fundamental basics.
More efficient:	The seminar covers only the basics (or, only the fundamentals).
Redundant:	As a rule, we generally approve all such requests.
More efficient:	We generally approve all such requests.

Hotlink

You'll find a few basic but indispensable tips on writing clear and concise sentences at this Carleton University site <http://www.carleton.ca/wts/handouts/Clear_Concise_Sentences.htm>.

Redundant:	The committee co-operated together to settle the issue.
More efficient:	The committee co-operated to settle the issue.

Using the Active Voice

Sentences that use active verbs are more economical—and, of course, more direct—than those using passive verbs. (See Chapter 8 for a review of passive and active voices.)

Passive:	Your account *has been credited* with your recent payment.
Active:	We *credited* your account with your recent payment.
Passive:	At our next meeting your request *will be considered.*
Active:	At our next meeting we *will consider* your request.
Passive:	Our Products Division *was informed* by you that you want an office copier.
Active:	You *informed* our Products Division that you want an office copier.

Writing Unified Sentences

A sentence is unified if it contains only closely related ideas. When extraneous or unrelated ideas appear in a sentence, they confuse the reader. Sentences lacking unity can be improved by clarifying the relationship between the ideas, by excising the extraneous ideas, or by shifting the unrelated ideas to separate sentences.

Lacks unity:	It is easy for you to do your Christmas shopping, and we offer three unique catalogues.
Improved:	Because we offer three unique catalogues, it is easy for you to do your Christmas shopping.
Lacks unity:	I certainly appreciate the time you spent with me in our interview last week, and I am enrolling in a computer science course this summer.
Improved:	I certainly appreciate the time you spent with me last week. Because of our interview, I am enrolling in a computer science course this summer.
Lacks unity:	Retailers must have a system of inventory control, and they must keep current on reorders.
Improved:	To be able to keep current on reorders, retailers must have a system of inventory control.

The inclusion of excessive detail can also damage sentence unity. If many details are necessary for overall clarity, put them in an additional sentence.

Excessive detail:	One of the nation's leading suppliers of pure bottled water mails thousands of computerized statements every month, along with a variety of inserts including overdue payment notices and pieces that are meant to be advertising and promotions, which became very costly in terms of both cash flow and personnel time.

Spot the Blooper

Announcer's voice on a TV ad for Ford: "What is it about Ford cars that makes it the best-selling car in America?"

Notable Quotable

"I have never thought of myself as a good writer. Anyone who wants reassurance of this should read one of my first drafts. But I'm one of the world's greatest rewriters."
—James Michener

Improved:	One of the nation's leading suppliers of pure bottled water mails thousands of monthly computerized statements, overdue notices, and promotional information. This mailing operation has become costly and time-consuming.
Excessive detail:	A report can be important, but it may not be effective or be read because it is too long and bulky, which will also make it more difficult to distribute, to store, and to handle, as well as increasing its overall cost.
Improved:	An important report may be ineffective because it is too long. Its bulk may increase its cost and make it difficult to read, handle, distribute, and store.

Complete the reinforcement exercises for Level I on pp. 398–400.

▶ Writing Clear Sentences

LEVEL II

Clear sentences immediately convey their central thought. Good writers achieve sentence clarity by the use of parallel construction, the avoidance of misplaced modifiers, and the use of unambiguous pronoun references.

Developing Parallel Construction

Sentence clarity can be improved by expressing similar ideas with similar grammatical structures. For example, do not use *ing* words for two of the ideas in a list and a *to* verb for the third idea: *reading, eating, and studying* (not *to study*). Use nouns with nouns, verbs with verbs, phrases with phrases, and clauses with clauses. In the following list, use all verbs: *the machine sorted, stamped, and counted* (not *and had a counter*). For phrases, the wording for all parts of the list should be matched: *safety must be improved in the home, in the classroom, and on the job* (not *and for office workers*).

Faulty:	Steel filing cabinets are best for durability, ease of cleaning, and they resist fire better.
Improved:	Steel filing cabinets are best for durability, ease of cleaning, and fire resistance. (Matches nouns.)
Faulty:	Composing, revising, and then to retype—these are necessary steps in report writing.
Improved:	Composing, revising, and retyping—these are necessary steps in report writing. (Matches *ing* nouns.)

Avoiding Misplaced Modifiers

As you will recall, modifiers are words, phrases, or clauses that limit or restrict other words, phrases, or clauses. To be clear, modifiers must be placed carefully, so that the words modified by them are obvious. When a modifier is placed so that it does not appear to be modifying the word or words intended to be modified, that modifier is said to be *misplaced*. In Chapter 11 introductory verbal modifiers were discussed. An introductory verbal modifier is sometimes misplaced simply by being at the beginning of the sentence. Consider how the introductory verbal modifier makes the following sentence nonsensical: *Walking down the street, the building was the tallest I had ever seen.*

Spot the Blooper

"The patient's pelvis was fractured by being thrown from a car."

Hotlink

You'll find a whole page on Ambiguous Modifiers (including misplaced modifiers) in the Sentence Elements section fo the University of Calgary's on-line English Grammar Guide at **<http://www.ucalgary. ca/UofC/eduweb/ grammar/>.** Click on "Sentence Elements" and follow the link to "Ambiguous Modifier."

Spot the Blooper

"Being moribund on arrival at the hospital, the doctor could do nothing for the patient."

After all, the building was not doing the walking. In positions other than the beginning of a sentence, misplaced modifiers may also interfere with sentence clarity.

Faulty:	We provide a map for all visitors *reduced to a one-inch scale.*
Improved:	For all visitors we provide a map *reduced to a one-inch scale.*
Faulty:	Employees did not hear the alarm *working busily on the rush printing job.*
Improved:	Employees *working busily on the rush printing job* did not hear the alarm.
Faulty:	You can install these wall pockets on flat surfaces *with screws or double-foam tape.*
Improved:	*With screws or double-foam tape,* you can install these wall pockets on flat surfaces.

Improving Pronoun References

Sentence confusion results from the use of pronouns without clear antecedents (refer to Chapter 7 for a discussion of *antecedent*). Be particularly careful with the pronouns *this, that, which,* and *it.* Confusion often results when these pronouns have as their antecedents an entire clause; such confusion can usually be avoided by substituting a noun for the pronoun or by following the pronoun with a clarifying noun (or nouns).

Faulty:	Installation of a computerized billing system has improved our cash flow and reduced our accounts receivable. *This* helps our entire operation run more efficiently and profitably.
Improved:	Installation of a computerized billing system has improved our cash flow and reduced our accounts receivable. *The new system* helps our entire operation run more efficiently and profitably.
Faulty:	We have a policy of responding to customer inquiries and orders on the same day they are received. *That* keeps us busy and keeps our customers satisfied.
Improved:	We have a policy of responding to customer inquiries and orders on the same day they are received. *That policy* keeps us busy and keeps our customers satisfied.
Faulty:	Our engineering projects require work on thousands of details that need constant updating and access to technical data, supplies, and references, *which* is why an open office design allowing team interaction is essential.
Improved:	Our engineering projects require work on thousands of details that need constant updating and access to technical data, supplies, and references. *These needs* explain why an open office design allowing team interaction is essential.

Complete the reinforcement exercises for Level II on pp. 401–403.

▶ Writing Emphatic and Coherent Sentences

In your writing you can achieve emphasis and coherence by using clause subordination, concrete words, and effective transitions.

Emphasis Through Subordination

Subordination is a technique used by skilful writers to show the relationship between unequal ideas. Appropriate emphasis can be achieved by using subordinate conjunctions, such as *if, because, since,* and *when,* and relative pronouns, such as *who, which,* and *that,* to introduce secondary ideas or incidental information. Principal ideas should appear in independent clauses, and less important ideas should be expressed in subordinate or dependent clauses.

Principal idea:	Compucorp recently entered the microcomputer market.
Secondary idea:	Compucorp is a division of Intel.
Sentence:	Compucorp, which is a division of Intel, recently entered the microcomputer market.
Principal idea:	Your account is now three months overdue.
Secondary idea:	You have been a good customer in the past.
Sentence:	Although you have been a good customer in the past, your account is now three months overdue.
Principal idea:	A credit card holder is not liable for more than $50 in unauthorized purchases.
Secondary idea:	The credit card holder must give notice to the issuer of the card.
Sentence:	If a credit card holder gives notice to the issuer of the card, the holder is not liable for more than $50 in unauthorized purchases.

Did You Know?

The language of the Information Age is English. More than 80 per cent of all the information stored in the more than 100 million computers around the world is stored in English. And 85 per cent of all international telephone conversations are conducted in English.

Emphasis Through the Use of Concrete Words

As you know, concrete words (see Chapter 4) refer to specific persons, places, concepts, and actions. They bring to mind sharp images and arouse strong feelings. Abstract words, such as *honesty, freedom,* and *utilization,* because they refer to general ideas, do not call forth immediate sensory reactions or feelings. Use concrete words and constructions to make your writing emphatic, persuasive, and unambiguous.

Abstract:	Your shipment will be sent *soon.*
Concrete:	Your shipment will be sent *October 1.*
Abstract:	Our candidate won by a *substantial margin.*
Concrete:	Our candidate won by a *2-to-1 margin.*
Abstract:	The utilization of *computer capabilities* helped us reduce costs.
Concrete:	*Computerized filing* and *billing* helped us reduce costs.
Abstract:	The Model DC-161 copier produces your first copy *quickly.*
Concrete:	The Model DC-161 copier produces your first copy *in five seconds.*

Career Tip

Use concrete words when you wish to emphasize or promote an idea. Use abstract words to soften bad news.

Hotlink

For some basic advice on coherent, unified paragraphs, visit this Carleton University Web page <http://www.carleton.ca/wts/handouts/Paragraphs.htm>.

When an abstract word is necessary, its meaning can often be enhanced by the addition of clarifying words.

Abstract:	During the hearing, no one questioned Mr. Turner's *loyalty.*
Concrete:	During the hearing, no one questioned Mr. Turner's *loyalty to the company.*

Coherence Through the Use of Transitional Words or Phrases

Orderly and consistent development of ideas leads to coherence. Coherence between sentences can be attained by the use of transitional expressions such as *therefore, in this way, in addition, for example, however, moreover, for this reason,* and *on the other hand.* Such words and phrases serve as flags to signal the reader that ideas are being contrasted or amplified. Notice that transitional words and phrases in the following sentences help the reader connect successive ideas.

> We improved customer services as a result of spending less time on clerical chores. *Moreover,* we reduced storage charges for shipments held up because of incorrect documentation.

> Our company stands ready to help you in the event of loss or damage to your microfilm records. *For example,* we have salvaged thousands of feet of muddied, tangled rolls of microfilm after floods.

> A blank endorsement enables anyone in possession of a cheque to cash it. A special endorsement, *on the other hand,* enables only a specific person to negotiate the cheque.

> When the federal government purchases goods on a cost-plus contract, it requires detailed accounting reports. *In this way,* it can monitor the production operations and costs.

Complete the reinforcement exercises for Level III on pp. 404–405.

HOTLINE QUERIES

Question: I just typed this sentence: *You will see in our manual where multiple bids must be obtained.* Somewhere from my distant past I seem to recall that *where* should not be used this way. Can you help me?

Answer: You're right. *Where* should not be substituted for the relative pronoun *that.* In your sentence, use *that.* A similar faulty construction to avoid is the use of *while* for *although* (*although* (not *while*) *I agree with his position, I disagree with his procedures*).

Question: When the company name *Halperin, Inc.,* appears in the middle of a sentence, is there a comma following *Inc.?*

Answer: Current authorities recommend the following practice in punctuating *Inc.* and *Ltd.:* Do not use commas to set off such expressions unless the company does so itself. Canadian companies, unlike U.S. companies, seldom use commas in this position. If the company does use a comma before an expression like *Inc.,* however, then a comma also follows *Inc.* whenever it is followed by other words in a sentence (*we received from Kent, Inc., its latest catalogue*).

Question: Where should the word *sic* be placed when it is used?

Answer: *Sic* means "thus" or "so stated," and it is properly placed immediately following the word or phrase to which it refers. For example, *The kidnappers placed a newspaper advertisement that read, "Call Monna [sic] Lisa." Sic* is used within a quotation to indicate that a quoted word or phrase, though inaccurately spelled or used, appeared thus in the original. *Sic* is italicized and placed within brackets.

Question: Which is correct: *I feel* (*bad* or *badly*)?

Answer: *Bad* is an adjective meaning "not good," "ill," "regretful," etc. *Badly* is an adverb meaning "in a bad manner," "poorly," or "greatly." Your sentence appears to require *bad* (*I feel ill*), unless you mean that your sense of touch is impaired (*I feel poorly*).

Question: Should I capitalize *French* dressing?

Answer: Yes. Adjectives derived from proper nouns are capitalized (*French* dressing, *German* shepherd, *Danish* furniture). A few very well-known adjectives, however, are not capitalized (*pasteurized* milk, *china* plates).

Question: In a business report is it acceptable to write the following: *Most everyone agrees* ,,,?

Answer: In this construction *most* is a shortened form of *almost.* Although such contractions are heard in informal speech, they should not appear in business writing. Instead, use the longer form: *Almost everyone agrees* ....

CHAPTER 21   Reinforcement Exercises

A. **(Self-check)** In the following sentences, inefficient phrases have been underlined. In the space provided after each sentence, suggest a more efficient substitute for each underlined phrase.

LEVEL I

Example: In the event that the alarm sounds, please leave in an orderly manner.

_____if_____

1. In view of the fact that you have not responded to our letters, we have no alternative.

_____

2. We must at the present time send your account to our collection agency.

_____

3. Due to the fact that a strike has temporarily closed our factory, deliveries are delayed.

_____

4. We find it necessary to inform all customers with regard to delivery delays.

_____

5. In the event that you are unable to attend, please notify us at once.

_____

6. We have received your cheque in the amount of $450.

_____

7. In spite of the fact that production costs are rising, we have tried to maintain our current pricing schedule.

_____

8. We find that we must at this point in time reconsider our prices.

_____

9. For the purpose of more efficient record keeping, we will begin writing invoices in triplicate.

_____

10. If the estimate is in the neighbourhood of $100 or less, the repair can be made immediately.

_____

Check your answers.

B. Rewrite the following sentences to eliminate redundancies.

Example: Her solution made absolutely perfect sense.

Her solution made perfect sense.

1. Tim's report appears to contain all the basic essentials.

_____

_____

2. Our modern office equipment is up to date in every feature.

_____

_____

1. Since 2. now 3. Because 4. about 5. If 6. for 7. Even though/Although 8. now 9. For 10. approximately/about

3. Any pages with corrections that are visible to the eye must be retyped.

_____

_____

4. In an explanation at the beginning of the article, the author explained his position.

_____

_____

C. Make the following sentences more efficient and more direct by using the active voice.

Example: The invoice was sent by our organization ten days ago.

_We sent the invoice ten days ago._____

1. Better service is received by our customers who read the instruction booklet.

_____

_____

2. Your order is now being processed by our Shipping Department.

_____

_____

3. Apparently my account was not credited by you with my cheque for $35.

_____

_____

4. A charge account has been opened for you by us at our store.

_____

_____

D. The following sentences lack unity. Improve them by reorganizing the ideas or by shifting extra details to separate sentences.

Example: We are installing a centralized dictation system, and our current transcription production is days behind schedule.

Because we are installing a centralized dictation system, we are days behind in our current

_transcription production._____

1. The keynote speaker will be Dr. Jay S. Cook, and vendors will display their products following the keynote address.

_____

_____

2. We have placed a lien on your property, and your payment is 60 days past due, which explains the lien.

_____

_____

3. We are one of the nation's largest office products distributors, and you can save 15 to 50 per cent on your word processing supplies for your office which we supply to our 260,000 customers who are satisfied from coast to coast because we have been in business for the past twenty years satisfying our customers.

_____

_____

_____

_____

A. (Self-check) In the sentences below, the underlined words illustrate the following: (a) faulty parallel construction, (b) faulty phrase placement, or (c) faulty pronoun reference. After each sentence write the letter that best indicates the sentence fault.

LEVEL II

Example: Our objectives are to increase production, reduce costs, and <u>improving the quality of our work.</u>

_a_

1. We use a four-part delivery ticket, with three copies made in various weights; <u>this</u> is the basis of our billing system.

_____

2. Aluminum construction is lightest, wood is cheapest, and <u>the strongest is steel.</u>

_____

3. Please complete the enclosed questionnaire sent to typical families <u>concerning detergent preferences.</u>

_____

4. Our new billing system totals all balances, gives weekly reports, and <u>statements are printed.</u>

_____

5. Centralized inspection in one area and floor inspection along the assembly line improve product quality; <u>it</u> is useful when precise standards must be met.

_____

6. Automatic cash transfers can be made only on the written authority of the customer <u>from a chequing account.</u>

_____

7. Computing, coding, recording, and <u>storage</u>—these are functions of data processing.

_____

8. The three basic elements of a computer are input, processor, and output units, <u>which</u> can be obtained in a variety of configurations.

_____

9. The next time you travel for business or for pleasure, charge everything to your credit card <u>anywhere in the world.</u>

_____

10. Our objectives are to make our shares profitable, to operate efficiently, and <u>developing good employee relations.</u>

_____

Check your answers.

B. Rewrite the following sentences so that they demonstrate parallel construction.

1. The job description lists these duties: answering the telephone, making appointments, and data must be collected for reports.

_____

_____

_____

2. This department requires more personnel, better facilities, and our equipment should be up to date.

_____

_____

3. Business letters should be written concisely, clearly, and with accuracy.

_____

_____

4. In filing, the use of colour can increase productivity significantly by providing faster retrieval, reducing the number of lost files, and improvement of employee morale.

_____

_____

_____

C. Rewrite these sentences to remedy misplaced modifiers.

1. The customer wrote a cheque for his purchase with insufficient funds.

_____

_____

2. Any person may recover damages from the manufacturer of a product who is injured by a product.

_____

_____

3. Our coat resembles the original trenchcoat for the soldiers of the First World War designed by Englishman Thomas Burberry.

_____

_____

4. Since we installed insulation, we have saved up to 25 per cent on our heating costs in our attic and walls.

_____

_____

D. Rewrite the following sentences to avoid faulty pronoun references.

1. Mrs. Valdez suggested that we try a four-day work week on an experimental basis for one month. _That_ received considerable employee support.

_____

_____

_____

2. Our Reprographics Division produces thousands of company letterheads, booklets, and brochures; *this* demands expert equipment and personnel.

_____

_____

_____

3. Our equipment is outmoded, production is costly, and orders are slow, *which* is why we are forced to cut back.

_____

_____

_____

4. Kathleen speaks both French and Japanese fluently, *which* is why we are offering her a job.

_____

_____

_____

A. (**Self-check**) After each of the following sentences, write *T* (true) or *F* (false).

LEVEL III

1. Appropriate subordination of secondary ideas is a technique of skilful writers.   _____

2. The word *therefore* might be used as a transition between related ideas.   _____

3. *Implementation* is an example of a concrete word.   _____

4. The word *although* may be used to introduce a principal idea in an independent clause.   _____

5. Transitional expressions serve as flags to signal changes in the presentation of ideas.   _____

6. The use of concrete words makes writing more persuasive and emphatic.   _____

7. Coherence is achieved when sentences and their parts are related logically.   _____

8. Principal ideas should appear in independent clauses.   _____

9. *Utilization* is an example of an abstract word.   _____

10. Abstract words are as effective as concrete words.   _____

Check your answers.

B. Shown below are sets of principal ideas and secondary ideas. For each set, write a sentence combining, with appropriate emphasis, both ideas.

<u>Principal Idea</u>	<u>Secondary Idea</u>
1. Margot Franssen believes that retailers should get involved in community projects, social issues, and environmental concerns.	Margot Franssen has been president of The Body Shop Canada since the mid-1980s.

_____

_____

2. La Cité collégiale offers more than 80 post-secondary programs.	La Cité collégiale is the first French-language college of applied arts and technology in Ontario.

_____

_____

_____

1. T 2. T 3. F 4. F 5. T 6. T 7. T 8. T 9. T 10. F

3. Critics say Barbie promotes unhealthy stereotypes.

Mattel has sold more than a billion dolls from its long-lived Barbie line.

_____

_____

4. Pierre Elliott Trudeau's *Memoirs* was on the bestseller list for several months.

Memoirs cost $35 in hardcover.

_____

_____

5. Alexander Shanks invented the first effective lawnmower in 1842.

Alexander Shanks was a Scot.

_____

_____

C. Rewrite the following sentences, making the italicized words concrete. Supply any information needed.

Example: Our organization is improving *conservation.*

Our organization is improving conservation of natural gas, electricity, and paper supplies.

1. We will send your order *as soon as possible.*

_____

_____

2. When we have further information, we will *contact* you.

_____

_____

3. This course includes English *fundamentals.*

_____

_____

4. Nancy Venables gave birth to a healthy *baby* in a *local hospital.*

_____

_____

D. Optional Composition. Your instructor may ask you to complete this exercise on a separate sheet. Write four original sentences that use the following transitional expressions to develop coherence: *therefore, however, consequently,* and *in addition.* Write a sentence with a misplaced modifier; then show how it can be remedied. Label all sentences.

Editor's Challenge

The following abstract is a summary of a long report. It contains errors reflecting the concepts you have studied thus far. Use proofreading marks to show all necessary corrections. Be especially alert to wordy expressions that could be condensed.

ABSTRACT

On the date of November 10th Dennis W. Wilbur, Director, human resources development authorized a study for the purpose of learning whether or not employment equity guidelines for women is being met at Globex enterprises.

A research program was developed to make investigation into each divisions hiring practices. In the neighbourhood of twenty-three thousand employee records was searched to determine date of employment, division and gender. Statistics Canada data were examined by way of comparison.

The following findings in regard to the aforementioned study resulted;

- Halifax is five % above the numerical goals for the three year period
- Regina is seven % below the numerical goals for the three year period
- St.John's is two % above the numerical goals (but figures were available for only five hundred of 2,256 employees

On the basis of these findings the compliance committee recommend the development of (1) A intensive recruiting program to search for and bring qualified females into the Regina division and (2) The development of a training program to train females for drafting and design positions in Regina. The Regina Division should hire two females for every 1 male until such time as 16 extra females are hire. In view of the fact that a training program may cost as much as five hundred thousand dollars, we further recommend that a committee be established at this point in time to investigate funding.

Rewrite the following sentences to correct problems in parallelism, redundancy, modification, reference, conciseness, and coherence.

1. We are at this point in time ready to sign a contract.

   _____

   _____

2. Speeding down the highway, the brakes were suddenly applied.

   _____

   _____

3. First and foremost, you must reserve a meeting room.

   _____

   _____

4. All sales reports must be complete, concise, and written with accuracy.

   _____

   _____

5. Our benefit package is appealing to older employees with both dental and vision care services.

   _____

   _____

   _____

learning.web.ways

Goal: To familiarize yourself with salary-negotiating techniques before your first job interview.

1. With your Web browser on the screen, go to **<http://www.canadiancareers.com/salary.html>**.

2. Read the first section, and jot down three ways you can learn about the current salary scale in the job sector you're interested in.

3. Using the link provided, visit WetFeet.com. What other tips on how to negotiate a salary can you find there? Write down one of them, and return to CanadianCareers.com.

4. Visit one of the Web sites listed on CanadianCareers.com for your salary research, and jot down the entry-level salaries in your field quoted there.

5. Using the **Back** button of your browser, return to CanadianCareers.com, and click on the link to the International Salary Calculator. Find out the salaries in your field in a couple of other cities in case you are offered an out-of-town job. Jot this information down.

6. End your session, and submit your research results.

UNIT 6 REVIEW Chapters 19–21 (Self-Check)

First, review Chapters 19 through 21. Then test your comprehension of those chapters by completing the exercises that follow. Compare your responses with those shown at the end of the book.

Select (a) or (b) to describe the group of words that is more acceptably expressed.

LEVEL I

1. (a) courses in Business Law, Spanish, and Sociology   (b) courses in business law, Spanish, and sociology _____

2. (a) living in York county   (b) living in York County _____

3. (a) the Province of Alberta   (b) the province of Alberta _____

4. (a) during summer vacation   (b) during Summer vacation _____

5. (a) a victorian home   (b) a Victorian home _____

6. (a) the 22nd of June   (b) the twenty-second of June _____

7. (a) twenty dollars   (b) $20 _____

8. (a) on 11th Street   (b) on Eleventh Street _____

9. (a) on December 15th   (b) on December 15 _____

10. (a) at this point in time   (b) now _____

11. (a) about   (b) with reference to _____

12. (a) in the near future   (b) soon _____

Select (a) or (b) to describe the group of words that is more acceptably expressed.

LEVEL II

13. (a) your Aunt and Uncle   (b) your aunt and uncle _____

14. (a) travel north on Highway 10   (b) travel North on Highway 10 _____

15. (a) our manager, Joe Bertuccio   (b) our Manager, Joe Bertuccio _____

16. (a) their receiving department   (b) their Receiving Department _____

17. (a) a message from Mia Cook, Sales Director   (b) a message from Mia Cook, sales director _____

18. (a) a message from Sales Director Cook   (b) a message from sales director Cook _____

19. (a) for the next two years   (b) for the next 2 years   _____

20. (a) 2 twenty-five page booklets   (b) two 25-page booklets   _____

21. (a) nine computers
serving 14 offices   (b) 9 computers serving 14 offices   _____

Each of the following sentences illustrates one of these sentence faults:

a = faulty parallel construction (such as *running, walking,* and *to ride*)

b = faulty phrase placement (phrase not close to word(s) it modifies)

c = faulty pronoun reference (pronoun such as *this, that, it* lacking clear antecedent)

Write the letter that describes the sentence fault in each of the next three sentences.

22. We installed fabric divider panels in the office to provide privacy, reduce sound, and they made the office more attractive.   _____

23. Michelle stood at the lectern on the stage looking at the audience with a blank mind and a dry mouth.   _____

24. Poor ventilation, inadequate light, and hazardous working conditions were cited in the complaint. It must be improved before negotiations continue.   _____

(On a separate sheet of paper, rewrite the above sentences to rectify their faults.)

Select the correct group of words below, and write its letter in the space provided.

LEVEL III

25. (a) our chief executive
officer, Mr. Spiros   (b) our Chief Executive
Officer, Mr. Spiros   _____

26. (a) Mayor-Elect Joan White   (b) Mayor-elect Joan White   _____

27. (a) a package stamped
"photographs"   (b) a package stamped
"Photographs"   _____

28. (a) our 28th anniversary   (b) our twenty-eighth anniversary   _____

29. (a) less than 0.1 per cent   (b) less than .1 per cent   _____

30. (a) 4 L of ice cream   (b) four L of ice cream   _____

31. (a) a 10% return   (b) a 10 per cent return   _____

32. (a) on his 20th birthday   (b) on his twentieth birthday   _____

33. (a) a 2/3 interest   (b) a two-thirds interest   _____

34. (a) the bright moon   (b) the bright Moon   _____

Hotline Review

Write the letter of the word or phrase that correctly completes each sentence.

35. May I (a) imply, (b) infer from your remark that you will not be able to attend the meeting? _____

36. He made five (a) photocopies, (b) Xerox copies on the new Minolta machine. _____

37. The workers wore (a) lose, (b) loose clothing. _____

38. She paused to (a) marshal, (b) marshall, (c) martial her thoughts. _____

Short Reports

Reports are a fact of life in the business world today. They are important because they convey needed information, and they help decision makers solve problems. Organizing information into a meaningful report is an important skill you will want to acquire if your field is business.

Characteristics of Reports

As an introduction to report writing, this workshop focuses on the most important characteristics of reports. You'll learn valuable tips about the format, data, headings, and writing plan for short business reports.

Format. How should a business report look? Three formats are commonly used. *Letter format* is appropriate for short reports prepared by one organization for another. A letter report, as illustrated in Figure 21.1, is like a letter except that it is more carefully organized. It includes side headings and lists where appropriate. *Memo format* is common for reports written within an organization. These internal reports look like memos—with the addition of side headings. *Report format* is used for longer, more formal reports. Printed on plain paper (instead of letterhead or memo forms), these reports begin with a title followed by carefully displayed headings and subheadings.

Data. Where do you find the data for a business report? Many business reports begin with personal observation and experience. If you were writing a report on implementing flex-time for employees, you might begin by observing current work schedules and by asking what schedules employees preferred. Other sources of data for business reports include company records, surveys, questionnaires, and interviews. If you want to see how others have solved a problem or collect background data on a topic, you can consult magazines, journals, and books. Much information is available electronically through on-line library indexes or from searching databases and the Internet.

Headings. Good headings in a report highlight major ideas and categories. They guide the reader through a report. In longer reports they divide the text into inviting chunks, and they provide resting places for the eyes. Short reports often use *functional heads* (such as *Problem, Summary, and Recommendations*). Longer reports may employ *talking heads* (such as *Short-Term Parking Solutions*) because they provide more information to the reader. Whether your heads are functional or talking, be sure they are clear and parallel. For example, use *Visible Costs* and *Invisible Costs* rather than *Visible Costs* and *Costs That Don't Show*. Don't enclose headings in quotation marks, and avoid using headings as antecedents for pronouns. For example, if your heading is *Laser Printers,* don't begin the next sentence with *These produce high-quality output ....*

Figure 21.1
Short Report—Letter Format

Liberty Environmental Inc.
2593 North Glebe Road
Calgary, AB T2T 4T1 (403) 356-1094

October 9, 200x

Ms. Sharon J. Goode
Richmond Realty Inc.
3390 Chester Avenue
Calgary, Alberta T3S 1K7

Dear Ms. Goode:

At the request of Richmond Realty, I have completed a preliminary investigation of its Mountain Park property listing. The following findings and recommendations are based on my physical inspection of the site, official records, and interviews with officials and persons knowledgeable about the site.

Findings and Analyses

My preliminary assessment of the Mountain Park listing and its immediate vicinity revealed rooms with damaged floor tiles on the first and second floors of 2539 Mountain View Drive. Apparently, in recent remodelling efforts, these tiles had been cracked and broken. Examination of the ceiling and attic revealed possible contamination from asbestos. The insulation material surrounding the hot-water storage tank was in poor condition.

Located on the property is Mountain Technology, a possible hazardous waste generator. Although I could not examine its interior, this company has the potential for producing hazardous material contamination. Moreover, several large dumpsters in the parking area collect trash and debris from surrounding businesses. Because these dumpsters were uncovered, they pose a risk to the general public.

Recommendations

To reduce its potential environmental liability, Richmond Realty should take the following steps in regard to its Mountain Park listing:

- Conduct an immediate asbestos survey at the site, including inspection of ceiling insulation material, floor tiles, and insulation around a gas-fired heater vent pipe at 2539 Mountain View Drive.

- Prepare an environmental audit of the generators of hazardous waste currently operating at the site, including Mountain Technology.

- Obtain lids for the dumpsters situated in the parking areas and ensure that the lids are kept closed.

If you would like to discuss the findings or recommendations in this report, please call me and I will be glad to answer your questions.

Sincerely,

Scott R. Evans

Scott R. Evans

Skill Check 6.1 Reviewing the Characteristics of Short Reports

Select a letter to indicate the best format for the report described.

(a) Memo format   (b) Letter format   (c) Report format

1. A short report to a company from an outside consultant   _____

2. A short report from a product manager to her boss   _____

3. A long report describing a company's diversity program   _____

4. If you were writing a report to persuade management to purchase more computers, the best way to begin collecting data would be to
   a. observe current use
   b. consult books and journals
   c. search the Internet   _____

5. Which combination of report headings is best?
   a. Delivery costs, Suppliers
   b. Reduction of delivery costs, Recommendations
   c. "Delivery costs," "Supply Costs"
   d. Reducing delivery costs, Finding new suppliers   _____

Writing Plan for a Short Report

Short reports often have three parts: introduction, findings, and recommendations. If the report is purely informational, a summary may be made instead of recommendations.

Introduction. This part of a report may also be called *Background*. In this section, you'll want to explain why you are writing. You may also (a) describe what methods and sources were used to gather information and why they are credible, (b) provide any special background information that may be necessary, and (c) offer a preview of your findings.

Findings. This section may also be called *Observations, Facts, Results,* or *Discussion.* Important points to consider in this section are organization and display. You may wish to organize the findings (a) chronologically (for example, to describe the history of a problem), (b) alphabetically (if you were, for example, evaluating candidates for a position), (c) topically (for example, discussing sales by regions), or (d) from most to least important (such as listing criteria for evaluating equipment). To display the findings effectively, you could (a) use side headings, (b) number each finding, (c) underline or boldface the key words, or (d) merely indent the paragraphs.

Summary or Recommendations. Some reports just offer information. Such reports may conclude with an impartial summary. Other reports are more analytical, and they generally conclude with recommendations. These recommendations tell readers how to solve the problem and may even suggest ways to implement the necessary actions. To display recommendations, number each one and place it on a separate line.

Notice that the letter report in Figure 21.1 includes an introduction, findings and analyses, and recommendations.

Writing Application 6.1 Organize the following information into a short letter report. As Cynthia M. Chavez, president, Chavez and Associates, you have been hired as a consultant to advise the St. Catharines City Council. The City Council has asked you and your associates to investigate a problem with Willow Park Beachway.

In 1979 St. Catharines constructed a 12-foot pathway, now called the Willow Park Beachway. It was meant originally for bicycle riders, but today it has become very popular for joggers, walkers, bikers, in-line skaters, skateboarders, sightseers, and animal owners walking their dogs. In fact, it's become so popular that it is dangerous. Last year the St. Catharines Police Department reported an amazing 65 collisions in the area. And this does not count the close calls and minor accidents that no one reported. The City Council wants your organization to identify the problem and come up with some workable recommendations for improving safety.

As you look into the matter, you immediately decide that the council is right. A problem definitely exists! In addition to the many pedestrians and riders, you see that families with rented pedal-powered surreys clog the beachway. Sometimes they even operate these vehicles on the wrong side. Your investigation further reveals that bicyclists with rental bikes do not always have bells to alert walkers. And poor lighting makes nighttime use extremely dangerous. You've noticed that conditions seem to be worst on Sundays. This congestion results from nearby art and crafts fairs and sales, attracting even more people to the crowded area.

Your investigation confirms that the beachway is dangerous. But what to do about it? In a brainstorming session, your associates make a number of suggestions for reducing the dangers to users. By the way, the council is particularly interested in lessening the threat of liability to the city. One of your associates thinks that the beachway should be made at least 15 or more feet wide. Another suggests that the beachway be lighted at night. Someone thinks that a new path should be built, on the beach side of the existing beachway; this path would be for pedestrians only. Educating users about safety rules and etiquette would certainly be wise for everyone. One suggestion involves better striping or applying colours to designate different uses for the beachway. And why not require that all rental bicycles be equipped with bells? One of the best recommendations involved hiring uniformed "beach hosts" who would monitor the beachway, give advice, offer directions, and generally patrol the area.

In a short report, outline the problem and list your recommendations. Naturally, you would be happy to discuss your findings and recommendations with the St. Catharines City Council.

Developing Spelling Skills

A

▶ Why Is English Spelling So Difficult?

No one would dispute the complaint that many English words are difficult to spell. Why is spelling in our language so perplexing? For one thing, our language has borrowed many of its words from other languages. English has a Germanic base upon which a superstructure of words borrowed from French, Latin, Greek, and other languages of the world has been erected. For this reason, its words are not always formed by regular patterns of letter combinations. In addition, spelling is made difficult because the pronunciation of English words is constantly changing. Today's spelling was standardized nearly 300 years ago, but many words are pronounced differently today than they were then. Therefore, pronunciation often provides little help in spelling. Consider, for example, the words *sew, dough, hoe,* and *row.*

Canadian writers, unlike U.S. and British writers, have a choice of spelling styles. Currently, most Canadians use a primarily British spelling style (the *our* and *re* ending for words like *honour* and *centre*, for example); others use a primarily U.S. style (*or* and *er* for *honor* and *center*). This text uses British forms, but *The Canadian Oxford Dictionary* and *Gage Canadian Dictionary* indicate that both styles are acceptable in most cases. The spelling style chosen depends on custom and on the preference of the individual or on the requirements of the workplace. Above all, consistency within any single piece of writing is important. If you choose *our* and *re* spellings, you must use these throughout a document; it is incorrect to have, for example, both *honour* and *honor* in the same piece.

▶ What Can Be Done to Improve One's Spelling?

Spelling is a skill that can be developed, just as arithmetic, keyboarding, swimming, and other skills can be developed. Because the ability to spell is a prerequisite for success in business and in many other activities, effort expended to acquire this skill is effort well spent.

Three traditional approaches to improving spelling have met with varying degrees of success.

1. Rules or Guidelines
The spelling of English words is consistent enough to justify the formulation of a few spelling rules, perhaps more appropriately called guidelines since the generalizations in question have exceptions. Such guidelines are, in other words, helpful but not infallible.

2. Mnemonics

Another approach to improving your ability to spell involves the use of mnemonics or memory devices. For example, you might associate the word *principle* with the word *rule*, to form in your mind a link between the meaning and the spelling of *principle*. Mnemonics can be an effective device for the improvement of spelling only if you make a real effort to develop the necessary memory hooks.

3. Rote Learning

A third approach to the improvement of spelling centres on memorization. You study the word until you can readily reproduce it in your mind's eye.

▶ The 1-2-3 Spelling Plan

Proficiency in spelling is not attained without concentrated effort. Here's a plan for mastering the correct spelling of the 400 commonly misspelled words and word pairs included in this appendix. For each word, try this 1-2-3 approach.

1. Is a spelling guideline applicable? If so, select the appropriate guideline and study the word in relation to that guideline.
2. If no guideline applies, can a memory device be created to aid in the recall of the word?
3. If neither a guideline nor a memory device will work, the word must be memorized. Look at the word carefully. Pronounce it. Write it or repeat it until you can visualize all its letters in your mind's eye.

Before you try the 1-2-3 plan, become familiar with the six spelling guidelines that follow. These spelling guidelines are not intended to represent all the possible spelling rules appearing in the various available spelling books. These six guidelines are, however, among the most effective and helpful of the recognized spelling rules.

Guideline 1: Words Containing *ie* or *ei*

Although there are exceptions to it, the following familiar rhyme can be helpful.

  (a) Write *i* before *e*
  (b) Except after *c*,
  (c) Or when sounded like *a*
     As in *neighbour* and *weigh*.

Study these three lists of words, which illustrate the three parts of the rhyme.

(a) *i* Before *e*		(b) Except After *c*	(c) or When Sounded Like *a*
achieve	ingredient	ceiling	beige
belief	mischief	conceit	eight
believe	niece	conceive	freight
brief	piece	deceit	heir
cashier	relief	deceive	neighbour
chief	shield	perceive	reign
convenient	sufficient	receipt	sleigh
field	thief	receive	their
friend	view		vein
grief	yield		weight

Exceptions: These exceptional *ei* and *ie* words must be learned by rote or with the use of a mnemonic device. Note that many of them contain the long *e* sound.

caffeine	forfeit	protein
either	height	seize
financier	leisure	sleight
foreign	neither	weird

Guideline 2: Words Ending in *e*

For most words ending in an *e*, the final *e* is dropped when the word is joined to a suffix (ending) that begins with a vowel (such as *ing, able,* or *al*). The final *e* is retained when a suffix that begins with a consonant (such as *ment, less, ly,* or *ful*) is joined to such a word.

Final *e* Dropped	**Final *e* Retained**
advise, advisable	approximate, approximately
arrive, arrival	arrange, arrangement
believe, believing	care, careless
care, caring	definite, definitely
cure, curable	hope, hopeless
desire, desirable	like, likely
disperse, dispersal	require, requirement
hope, hoping	sincere, sincerely
receive, receiving	time, timeless
value, valuable	use, useful

Exceptions: The few exceptions to this spelling guideline are among the most frequently misspelled words. As such, they deserve special attention. Notice that they all involve a dropped final *e*.

argument	truly
ninth	wholly

Guideline 3: Words Ending in *ce* or *ge*

When *able* or *ous* is added to words ending in *ce* or *ge*, the final *e* is retained if the *c* or *g* is pronounced softly (as in *peace* or *change*).

advantage, advantageous	change, changeable
courage, courageous	service, serviceable
outrage, outrageous	manage, manageable

Guideline 4: Words Ending in *y*

Words ending in a *y* that is preceded by a consonant normally change the *y* to *i* before all suffixes except those beginning with an *i*.

Change *y* to *i* Because *y* Is Preceded by a Consonant	Do Not Change *y* to *i* Because *y* is Preceded by a Vowel
accompany, accompaniment	annoy, annoying, annoyance
apply, appliance	attorney, attorneys
carry, carried, carriage	employ, employer, employment
company, companies	stay, staying, stayed
dry, drier, driest	valley, valleys
duty, dutiful	
empty, emptiness	**Do Not Change *y* to *i* When Adding *ing***
forty, fortieth	
hurry, hurries	accompany, accompanying
industry, industrious	apply, applying
secretary, secretaries	satisfy, satisfying
study, studied, studious	study, studying
	try, trying

Exceptions: day, daily; gay, gaily; mislay, mislaid; pay, paid; shy, shyly.

Guideline 5: Doubling a Final Consonant

If one-syllable words or two-syllable words accented on the second syllable end in a single consonant preceded by a single vowel, the final consonant is doubled before the addition of a suffix beginning with a vowel.

Although complex, this spelling guideline is extremely useful and therefore well worth mastering. Many spelling errors can be avoided by applying this guideline.

One-Syllable Words	Two-Syllable Words
bag, baggage	acquit, acquitting, acquittal
can, canned	admit, admitted, admitting
drop, dropped	begin, beginner, beginning
fit, fitted	commit, committed, committing
get, getting	control, controller, controlling
man, manned	defer, deferred (BUT deference*)
plan, planned	excel, excelled, excelling
run, running	occur, occurrence, occurring
shut, shutting	prefer, preferring (BUT preferable*)
slip, slipped	recur, recurred, recurrence
swim, swimming	refer, referring (BUT reference*)
ton, tonnage	regret, regrettable

Here is a summary of conditions necessary for application of this guideline:

1.   The word must end in a single consonant.
2.   The final consonant must be preceded by a single vowel.
3.   The word must be accented on the second syllable (if it has two syllables).

Words derived from *offer, differ, suffer, widen, deepen,* and *benefit* are not governed by this guideline because they are accented on the first syllable. The same is true of *cancel, equal,* and *travel;* however, since British spelling doubles the final *l* in these words (e.g., *travelled, travelling, traveller*), most Canadians make exceptions to the guideline in these cases.

_____

* *Because the accent shifts to the first syllable, the final consonant is not doubled.*

Guideline 6: Prefixes and Suffixes

For words in which the letter that ends the prefix is the same as the letter that begins the main word (such as in *dis-similar*), both letters must be included. For words in which a suffix begins with the same letter that ends the main word (such as in *cool-ly*), both letters must also be included.

Prefix	Main Word	Main Word	Suffix
dis	satisfied	accidental	ly
il	literate	clean	ness
ir	responsible	cool	ly
mis	spell	even	ness
mis	state	incidental	ly
un	necessary	mean	ness

On the other hand, do not supply additional letters when adding prefixes to main words.

Prefix	Main Word
dis	appearance (not dissapperance)
dis	appoint
mis	take

Probably the most important guideline you can follow in spelling correctly is to use the dictionary whenever in doubt.

400 Most Frequently Misspelled Words and Word Pairs*
(Divided into 20 lists of 20 words each)

List 1	List 2	List 3
absence	afraid	applying
acceptance	against	approaches
accessible	aggressive	appropriate
accidentally	all right	approximately
accommodate	almost	arguing
accompaniment	alphabetical	argument
accurately	already	arrangement
accustom	although	article
achievement	amateur	athlete
acknowledgement/	among	attack
acknowledgment**	amount	attendance, attendants
acquaintance	analysis	attitude
acquire	analyze/analyse	attorneys
across	angel, angle	auxiliary
actually	annoyance	basically
adequately	annual	beautiful
admitted	answer	before
adolescence	apologized	beginning
advantageous	apparent	believing
advertising	appliance	benefited
advice, advise†		

---

* *Compiled from lists of words most frequently misspelled by students and business people.*

** *This type of listing (with a slash) indicates that British and American versions are both accepted in Canada. The first of each pair is the version more frequently used, according to* The Canadian Oxford Dictionary.

† *Pairs listed in this manner (separated by commas) are homonyms or commonly confused word pairs. Consult your dictionary for meanings.*

List 4

biggest
breath, breathe
brief
business
calendar
capital, capitol
career
careless
carrying
cashier
ceiling
certain
challenge
changeable
chief
choose, chose
cloths, clothes
column
coming
committee

List 5

companies
competition
completely
conceive
conscience
conscientious
conscious
considerably
consistent
continuous
controlling
controversial
convenience
council, counsel
cylinder
daily
deceive
decision
define
dependent

List 6

description
desirable
destroy
development
difference
dining
disappearance
disappoint
disastrous
discipline
discussion
disease
dissatisfied
distinction
divide
doesn't
dominant
dropped
due
during

List 7

efficient
eligible
embarrass
encourage
enough
environment
equipped
especially
exaggerate
exceed
excellence
except
exercise
existence
experience
explanation
extremely
familiar
fascinate
favourite/favorite

List 8

February
fictitious
field
finally
financially
foreigner
fortieth
forty, fourth
forward, foreword
freight
friend
fulfill/fulfil
fundamentally
further
generally
government
governor
grammar
grateful
guard

List 9

happiness
hear, here
height
heroes
hopeless
hoping
huge
humorous
hungry
ignorance
imaginary
imagine
immediately
immense
importance
incidentally
independent
indispensable
industrious
inevitable

List 10

influential
ingredient
initiative
intelligence
interest
interference
interpretation
interrupt
involve
irrelevant
irresponsible
island
jealous
judgment/judgement
kindergarten
knowledge
laboratory
labourer/laborer
laid
led, lead

List 11

leisurely
library
licence/license (noun)
license (verb)
likely
literature
lives
loneliness
loose, lose
losing
luxury
magazine
magnificence
maintenance
manageable
manoeuvre/maneuver
manner
manufacturer
marriage
mathematics

List 12

meant
mechanics
medicine
medieval
mere
miniature
minutes
mischief
misspell
mistake
muscle
mysterious
naturally
necessary
neighbour/neighbor
neither
nickel
niece
ninety
ninth

List 13

noticeable
numerous
obstacle
occasionally
occurrence
offered
official
omitted
operate
opinion
opportunity
opposite
ordinance
organization
origin
original
paid
pamphlet
parallel
particular

List 14

passed, past
pastime
peaceable
peculiar
perceive
performance
permanent
permitted
persistent
personal, personnel
persuading
phase, faze
philosophy
physical
piece
planned
pleasant
poison
political
possession

List 15

possible
practical
precede
preferred
prejudice
preparation
prevalent
principal, principle
privilege
probably
proceed
professor
prominent
proving
psychology
pursuing
quantity
quiet, quite
really
receipt

List 16

receiving
recognize
recommend
reference
referring
regard
relative
relieving
religious
reminiscent
repetition
representative
requirement
resistance
responsible
restaurant
rhythm
ridiculous
sacrifice
safety

List 17

satisfying
scenery
schedule
science
secretaries
seize
sense, since
sentence
separation
sergeant
serviceable
several
shining
shoulder
sight, site, cite
significance
similar
simply
sincerely
source

List 18

speak, speech
specimen
stationary, stationery
stopped
stories, storeys
straight, strait
strenuous
stretch
strict
studying
substantial
subtle
succeed
success
sufficient
summary
supposed
surprise
suspense
swimming

List 19

syllable
symbol
symmetrical
synonymous
technique
temperament
temperature
tendency
than, then
their, there, they're
themselves
theories
therefore
thorough
though
through
together
tomorrow
tragedies
transferred

List 20

tremendous
tried
truly
undoubtedly
unnecessary
until
unusual
useful
using
vacuum
valuable
varies
vegetable
view
weather, whether
weird
were, where
wholly, holy
writing
yield

Developing Vocabulary Skills

If you understand the meanings of many words, you can be said to have a "good vocabulary." Words are the basis of thought. We think with words, we understand with words, and we communicate with words.

A large working vocabulary is a significant asset. It allows us to use precise words that say exactly what we intend. In addition, we understand more effectively what we hear and read. A large vocabulary also enables us to score well on employment and intelligence tests. Lewis M. Terman, who developed the Stanford-Binet IQ tests, believes that vocabulary is the single best indicator of intelligence.

In the business world, where precise communication is extremely important, surveys show a definite correlation between vocabulary size and job performance. Skilled workers, in the majority of cases, have larger vocabularies than unskilled workers. Supervisors know more words than the workers they direct, and executives have larger vocabularies than employees working for them.

Having a good vocabulary at our command doesn't necessarily ensure our success in life, but it certainly gives us an advantage. Improving your vocabulary will help you expand your options in an increasingly complex world.

Vocabulary can be acquired in three ways: accidentally, incidentally, and intentionally. Setting out intentionally to expand your word power is, of course, the most efficient vocabulary-building method. One of the best means of increasing your vocabulary involves the use of index cards: when you encounter an unfamiliar word, write it on a card and put the definition of the word on the reverse side of the card. Just five to ten minutes of practice each day with such cards can significantly increase your vocabulary.

Your campaign to increase your vocabulary can begin with the 20 lists of selected business terms and words of general interest included in this appendix. You may already know partial definitions for some of these words. Take this opportunity to develop more precise definitions for them. Follow these steps in using the word lists:

1. Record the word on an index card.

2. Look up the word in your dictionary. Compare the dictionary definitions of the word with the definition alternatives shown after the word in your copy of *Canadian Business English*. Select the correct definition, and write its letter in the space provided in your textbook. (The definitions provided in your textbook are quite concise but should help you remember the word's most common meaning.)

3. On the reverse side of your card, write the phonetic spelling of the word and the word's part of speech. Then write its definition, using as much of the dictionary definition as you find helpful. Try also to add a phrase or sentence illustrating the word.

4. Study your index cards often.

5. Try to find ways to use your vocabulary words in your speech and writing.

List 1

1. adjacent = (a) previous, (b) similar, (c) overdue, (d) nearby _____

2. ambivalence = having (a) uncertainty, (b) ambition, (c) compassion, (d) intelligence _____

3. belligerent = (a) overweight, (b) quarrelsome, (c) likable, (d) believable _____

4. contingent = (a) conditional, (b) allowable, (c) hopeless, (d) impractical _____

5. decadent = in a state of (a) repair, (b) happiness, (c) decline, (d) extreme patriotism _____

6. entitlement = (a) label, (b) tax refund, (c) screen credit, (d) legal right _____

7. equivalent = (a) subsequent, (b) identical, (c) self-controlled, (d) plentiful _____

8. paramount = (a) foremost, (b) high mountain, (c) film company, (d) insignificant _____

9. plausible = (a) quiet, (b) acceptable, (c) notorious, (d) negative _____

10. unilateral = (a) powerful, (b) harmonious, (c) one-sided, (d) indelible _____

List 2

1. affluent = (a) rich, (b) slippery, (c) persistent, (d) rebellious _____

2. autocrat = one who (a) owns many cars, (b) is self-centred, (c) has great power, (d) collects signatures _____

3. benevolent = for the purpose of (a) religion, (b) doing good, (c) healing, (d) violence _____

4. entrepreneur = (a) business owner, (b) traveller, (c) salesperson, (d) gambler _____

5. impertinent = (a) stationary, (b) bound to happen, (c) obsolete, (d) rude and impudent _____

6. imprudent = (a) unwise, (b) crude, (c) vulnerable, (d) lifeless _____

7. mediator = one who seeks (a) overseas trade, (b) profits, (c) safe investment, (d) peaceful settlement _____

8. preponderance = (a) thoughtful, (b) exclusive right, (c) superiority, (d) forethought _____

9. recipient = (a) receiver, (b) respondent, (c) voter, (d) giver _____

10. reprehensible = (a) disobedient, (b) independent, (c) blameworthy, (d) following _____

List 3

1. affable = (a) cheap, (b) pleasant, (c) strange, (d) competent _____

2. consensus = (a) population count, (b) attendance, (c) tabulation, (d) agreement _____

3. criterion = (a) standard, (b) command, (c) pardon, (d) law _____

4. diligent = (a) gentle, (b) industrious, (c) prominent, (d) intelligent _____

5. hydraulic = operated by means of (a) air, (b) gasoline, (c) liquid, (d) mechanical parts _____

6. hypothesis = (a) triangle, (b) promulgation, (c) highest point, (d) theory _____

7. phenomenon = (a) imagination, (b) rare event, (c) appointment, (d) clever saying _____

8. reticent = (a) reserved, (b) strong-willed, (c) inflexible, (d) disagreeable _____

9. sanctuary = a place of (a) healing, (b) refuge, (c) rest, (d) learning _____

10. stimulus = something that causes (a) response, (b) light, (c) pain, (d) movement _____

List 4

1. beneficiary = one who (a) receives a licence, (b) creates goodwill, (c) receives proceeds, (d) makes friends _____

2. constrain = (a) restrict, (b) filter, (c) use, (d) inform _____

3. corroborate = (a) contradict, (b) recall, (c) erode, (d) confirm _____

4. dun = a demand for (a) legal action, (b) payment, (c) credit information, (d) dividends _____

5. equitable = (a) fair, (b) profitable, (c) similar, (d) clear _____

6. fluctuate = (a) rinse out, (b) magnetize, (c) violate, (d) rise and fall _____

7. indolent = (a) self-indulgent, (b) lazy, (c) pampered, (d) uncertain _____

8. nullify = (a) disappear, (b) imitate, (c) invalidate, (d) enhance _____

9. obsolete = (a) ugly, (b) outmoded, (c) audible, (d) scant _____

10. stabilize = to make (a) pleasant, (b) congenial, (c) traditional, (d) firm _____

List 5

1. arbitrate = (a) decide, (b) construct, (c) conquer, (d) ratify _____

2. coalition = (a) deliberation, (b) allegiance, (c) adherence, (d) alliance _____

3. collate = (a) assemble, (b) denounce, (c) supersede, (d) answer back _____

4. conglomerate = combination of (a) executives, (b) companies, (c) investments, (d) countries _____

5. franchise = (a) fictitious reason, (b) right, (c) obligation, (d) official announcement _____

6. logistics = (a) speculations, (b) analytic philosophy, (c) reasonable outcome, (d) details of operation _____

7. proxy = authority to (a) act for another, (b) write cheques, (c) submit nominations, (d) explain _____

8. subsidiary = (a) below expectations, (b) country dominated by another, (c) company controlled by another, (d) depressed financial condition _____

9. termination = (a) end, (b) inception, (c) identification, (d) evasive action _____

10. virtually = (a) absolutely, (b) precisely, (c) almost entirely, (d) strictly _____

List 6

1. affiliate = (a) trust, (b) attract, (c) effect, (d) join _____

2. alter = (a) perform religious ceremony, (b) isolate, (c) attribute, (d) modify _____

3. boisterous = (a) noisily exuberant, (b) masculine, (c) cheerful, (d) brusque _____

4. configuration = (a) stratagem, (b) foreign currency, (c) form, (d) comprehension _____

5. conveyance = (a) vehicle, (b) transformation, (c) baggage, (d) consortium _____

6. infringe = (a) ravel, (b) decorate with border, (c) encroach, (d) margin _____

7. jurisdiction = (a) science of law, (b) enunciation, (c) justice, (d) authority _____

8. non-partisan = (a) unbiased, (b) antisocial, (c) ineffective, (d) untenable _____

9. parity = (a) price index, (b) justice under law, (c) plenitude, (d) equality of purchasing power _____

10. usury = (a) method of operation, (b) implementation, (c) illegal interest, (d) customary _____

List 7

1. anonymous = (a) multiplex, (b) powerless, (c) vexing, (d) nameless _____

2. cartel = (a) combination to fix prices, (b) ammunition belt, (c) partnership to promote competition, (d) placard _____

3. conjecture = (a) coagulation, (b) gesticulation, (c) guesswork, (d) connection _____

4. disparity = (a) unlikeness, (b) separation, (c) lack of emotion, (d) repudiation _____

5. environment = (a) urban area, (b) zenith, (c) surroundings, (d) latitude _____

6. impetus = (a) oversight, (b) stimulus, (c) hindrance, (d) imminence _____

7. portfolio = a list of (a) books, (b) security analysts, (c) corporations, (d) investments _____

8. quiescent = (a) presumptuous, (b) latent, (c) immoderate, (d) volatile _____

9. surrogate = (a) substitute, (b) accused, (c) authenticate, (d) suspension _____

10. tariff = (a) marsupial, (b) announcement, (c) ship, (d) duty _____

List 8

1. accrue = (a) conform, (b) accumulate, (c) diminish, (d) multiply _____

2. amortize = (a) pay off, (b) reduce, (c) romance, (d) kill _____

3. commensurate = (a) infinitesimal, (b) erroneous, (c) reliable, (d) proportional _____

4. consortium = (a) configuration, (b) partnership or association, (c) royal offspring, (d) rental property _____

5. discernible = (a) perceptive, (b) pretentious, (c) recognizable, (d) dissident _____

6. frugal = (a) thrifty, (b) wasteful, (c) judicious, (d) profligate _____

7. pecuniary = (a) rudimentary, (b) eccentric, (c) financial, (d) distinctive _____

8. retract = (a) disavow, (b) reorganize, (c) reciprocate, (d) hide _____

9. scrutinize = (a) cheerfully admit, (b) baffle, (c) persist, (d) examine carefully _____

10. tenacious = (a) falling apart, (b) holding fast, (c) immobile, (d) chagrined _____

List 9

1. amiable = (a) contumacious, (b) impetuous, (c) feasible, (d) likeable _____

2. credible = (a) plausible, (b) deceitful, (c) religious, (d) financially sound _____

3. defendant = one who (a) sues, (b) answers suit, (c) judges, (d) protects _____

4. dissipate = (a) accumulate, (b) partition, (c) liquefy, (d) scatter or waste _____

5. incentive = (a) impediment, (b) support, (c) motive, (d) remuneration _____

6. innocuous = (a) harmless, (b) injected, (c) facetious, (d) frightening _____

7. oust = (a) install, (b) instigate, (c) shout, (d) expel _____

8. pittance = (a) tiny amount, (b) tithe, (c) abyss, (d) pestilence _____

9. plaintiff = one who (a) defends, (b) is sad, (c) sues, (d) responds _____

10. superfluous = (a) extraordinary, (b) very slippery, (c) shallow, (d) more than enough _____

List 10

1. adroit = (a) ideal, (b) resilient, (c) witty, (d) skilful _____

2. derogatory = (a) minimal, (b) degrading, (c) originating from, (d) devious _____

3. escrow = (a) international treaty, (b) public registration, (c) licensed by state, (d) type of deposit _____

4. facsimile = (a) principle, (b) prototype, (c) exact copy, (d) counterfeit _____

5. inordinate = (a) unwholesome, (b) excessive, (c) unimportant, (d) treacherous _____

6. logical = (a) reasoned, (b) irrelevant, (c) lofty, (d) intricate _____

7. malfeasance = (a) prevarication, (b) injury, (c) superstition, (d) misconduct _____

8. noxious = (a) pernicious, (b) unusual, (c) pleasant, (d) inconsequential _____

9. résumé = (a) budget report, (b) minutes of meeting, (c) photo album, (d) summary of qualifications _____

10. spasmodic = (a) paralyzing, (b) intermittent, (c) internal, (d) painful _____

List 11

1. animosity = (a) happiness, (b) deep sadness, (c) hatred, (d) study of animals _____

2. caveat = (a) headwear, (b) warning, (c) neckwear, (d) prerogative _____

3. conscientious = (a) meticulous, (b) productive, (c) cognizant, (d) sophisticated _____

4. cosmopolitan = (a) provincial, (b) multicoloured, (c) heavenly, (d) worldly _____

5. decipher = (a) preclude, (b) decode, (c) demise, (d) reproach _____

6. euphemism = (a) religious discourse, (b) facial expression, (c) figure of speech, (d) indirect expression _____

7. fraudulent = (a) loquacious, (b) candid, (c) deceitful, (d) despotic _____

8. peripheral = (a) supplementary, (b) imaginary, (c) visionary, (d) supernatural _____

9. pungent = (a) knowledgeable, (b) wise religious man, (c) acrid, (d) vulnerable _____

10. requisite = (a) essential, (b) demanding, (c) skilful, (d) discreet _____

List 12

1. ad valorem = (a) esteemed, (b) genuine, (c) recompense, (d) proportional _____

2. carte blanche = (a) white carriage, (b) credit terms, (c) full permission, (d) geographical expression _____

3. de facto = (a) prejudicial, (b) actual, (c) valid, (d) unlawful _____

4. esprit de corps = (a) group enthusiasm, (b) strong coffee, (c) central authority, (d) government overturn _____

5. modus operandi = (a) method of procedure, (b) practical compromise, (c) business transaction, (d) flexible arbitration _____

6. per capita = per unit of (a) income, (b) population, (c) birth, (d) household _____

7. per diem = (a) daily, (b) weekly, (c) yearly, (d) individually _____

8. prima facie = (a) self-taught, (b) apparent, (c) principal, (d) artificial _____

9. status quo = (a) haughty demeanour, (b) steadfast opinion, (c) position of importance, (d) existing condition _____

10. tort = (a) rich cake, (b) extended dream, (c) wrongful act, (d) lawful remedy _____

List 13

1. acquit = (a) discharge, (b) pursue, (c) interfere, (d) impede _____

2. annuity = (a) yearly report, (b) insurance premium, (c) tuition refund, (d) annual payment _____

3. complacent = (a) appealing, (b) self-satisfied, (c) sympathetic, (d) scrupulous _____

4. contraband = (a) discrepancy, (b) opposing opinion, (c) smuggled goods, (d) ammunition _____

5. insolvent = (a) uncleanable, (b) unexplainable, (c) bankrupt, (d) unjustifiable _____

6. malicious = marked by (a) good humour, (b) ill will, (c) great pleasure, (d) injurious tumour _____

7. negligent = (a) careless, (b) fraudulent, (c) unlawful, (d) weak _____

8. nominal = (a) enumerated, (b) beneficial, (c) extravagant, (d) insignificant _____

9. rescind = (a) consign, (b) oppose, (c) repeal, (d) censure _____

10. stringent = (a) rigid, (b) expedient, (c) compliant, (d) resilient _____

List 14

1. affirm   = (a) business organization, (b) validate, (c) elevate, (d) encircle   _____

2. exonerate   = (a) commend, (b) declare blameless, (c) banish, (d) emigrate   _____

3. expedite   = (a) elucidate, (b) get rid of, (c) amplify, (d) rush   _____

4. hamper   = (a) impede, (b) delineate, (c) release, (d) assuage   _____

5. implement   = (a) suppress, (b) ameliorate, (c) carry out, (d) attribute   _____

6. induce   = (a) teach, (b) construe, (c) persuade, (d) copy   _____

7. obliterate   = (a) obstruct, (b) prevent, (c) minimize, (d) erase   _____

8. quandary   = a state of (a) doubt, (b) certainty, (c) depression, (d) apprehension   _____

9. surmount   = (a) hike, (b) overcome, (c) interpret, (d) specify   _____

10. veracity   = (a) truthfulness, (b) swiftness, (c) efficiency, (d) persistence   _____

List 15

1. aggregate   = constituting a (a) hostile crowd, (b) word combination, (c) total body or amount, (d) sticky mass   _____

2. ambiguous   = (a) peripatetic, (b) uncertain, (c) enterprising, (d) deceptive   _____

3. amend   = (a) alter, (b) pray, (c) praise, (d) utter   _____

4. apportion   = (a) sanction, (b) ratify, (c) estimate, (d) divide   _____

5. collaborate = (a) scrutinize, (b) co-operate, (c) surrender, (d) accumulate   _____

6. ingenuity   = (a) innocence, (b) torpor, (c) cleverness, (d) self-composure   _____

7. irretrievable = not capable of being (a) sold, (b) identified, (c) explained, (d) recovered   _____

8. lenient   = (a) liberal, (b) crooked, (c) benevolent, (d) explicit   _____

9. retrench   = (a) dig repeatedly, (b) reduce, (c) reiterate, (d) enlighten   _____

10. trivial   = (a) composed of three parts, (b) momentous, (c) paltry, (d) economical   _____

List 16

1. audit = (a) examine, (b) speak, (c) exchange, (d) expunge _____

2. arrears = (a) retreat, (b) gratuity, (c) overdue debt, (d) option _____

3. curtail = (a) obstruct, (b) restore, (c) rejuvenate, (d) cut short _____

4. encumber = (a) grow, (b) substantiate, (c) burden, (d) illustrate _____

5. exemplify = (a) segregate, (b) divulge, (c) illustrate, (d) condone _____

6. extension = (a) unusual request, (b) prolonged journey, (c) haphazard results, (d) extra time _____

7. fortuitous = (a) accidental, (b) courageous, (c) radical, (d) assiduous _____

8. innovation = (a) reorganization, (b) occupancy, (c) change, (d) solution _____

9. syndicate = (a) union of writers, (b) council of lawmakers, (c) group of symptoms, (d) association of people _____

10. venture = (a) speculative business transaction, (b) unsecured loan, (c) stock split, (d) gambling debt _____

List 17

1. acquiesce = (a) gain possession of, (b) confront, (c) implore, (d) comply _____

2. enumerate = (a) articulate, (b) list, (c) enunciate, (d) see clearly _____

3. erratic = (a) pleasurable, (b) wandering, (c) exotic, (d) serene _____

4. expedient = serving to promote (a) fellowship, (b) one's own interests, (c) good of others, (d) speedy delivery _____

5. feasible = (a) authentic, (b) profuse, (c) practicable, (d) extraneous _____

6. literal = (a) exact, (b) devout, (c) apropos, (d) noticeable _____

7. lucrative = (a) providential, (b) swift, (c) pleasant, (d) profitable _____

8. negotiable = (a) essential, (b) adequate, (c) transferable, (d) economical _____

9. nonchalant = (a) dull, (b) cool, (c) unintelligent, (d) sagacious _____

10. reconcile = (a) settle or resolve, (b) calculate, (c) modify, (d) remunerate _____

1. byte = (a) dental occlusion, (b) computer storage, (c) digits processed as a unit, (d) type font _____

2. disk = (a) magnetic storage medium, (b) print wheel, (c) computer belt, (d) program _____

3. execute = (a) eradicate, (b) inquire, (c) oppose, (d) carry out _____

4. memory = (a) printer logic, (b) computer information-storage capacity, (c) automatic printout, (d) software _____

5. menu = list of (a) parts, (b) options, (c) serial numbers, (d) vendors _____

6. microfiche = sheet of (a) computer printouts, (b) microimages, (c) reduced digits, (d) tiny cards _____

7. program = (a) alphabetical list, (b) computer log, (c) coded instructions, (d) microprocessor _____

8. prompt = (a) reminder, (b) code, (c) function, (d) format _____

9. retrieve = (a) acquiesce, (b) instruct, (c) remove code, (d) recover information _____

10. software = (a) equipment, (b) programs, (c) plastic component, (d) solid-state semiconductor _____

List 19

1. apprehensive = (a) knowledgeable, (b) fearful, (c) reticent, (d) autonomous _____

2. circumspect = (a) cautious, (b) uncertain, (c) co-operative, (d) frugal _____

3. collateral = (a) revenue, (b) secret agreement, (c) book value, (d) security for a loan _____

4. insinuation = (a) disagreeable proposal, (b) indirect suggestion, (c) elucidating glimpse, (d) flagrant insult _____

5. liaison = (a) legal obligation, (b) treaty, (c) connection between groups, (d) quarantine _____

6. procrastinate = (a) predict, (b) reproduce, (c) postpone, (d) advance _____

7. ratification = the act of (a) confirming, (b) reviewing, (c) evaluating, (d) inscribing _____

8. renovate = (a) renegotiate, (b) restore, (c) supply, (d) deliver _____

9. saturate = to fill (a) slowly, (b) dangerously, (c) as expected, (d) to excess _____

10. vendor = (a) seller, (b) manufacturer, (c) trader, (d) coin collector   _____

List 20

1. abhorrent = (a) extremely disagreeable, (b) attractive, (c) valueless, (d) adducible   _____

2. appraisal = (a) general information, (b) certification, (c) estimation, (d) approval   _____

3. collusion = (a) secret agreement, (b) direct conflict, (c) partial exclusion, (d) original artwork   _____

4. commingle = (a) swindle, (b) mix, (c) separate, (d) communicate   _____

5. dissolution = (a) intemperance, (b) solubility, (c) unsolvable, (d) separation   _____

6. ensue = (a) change subtly, (b) relinquish, (c) track down, (d) follow   _____

7. rejuvenate = to make (a) youthful, (b) slender, (c) sturdy, (d) impregnable   _____

8. stipulation = (a) permission, (b) requirement, (c) rejection, (d) concurrence   _____

9. subsidy = (a) scholarship, (b) financial assistance, (c) payment due, (d) unacknowledged payment   _____

10. tenuous = (a) flimsy, (b) indecisive, (c) cautious, (d) firm   _____

Reference Guide to Document Formats

C

Business documents carry two kinds of messages. Verbal messages are conveyed by the words chosen to express the writer's ideas. Non-verbal messages are conveyed largely by the appearance of a document. If you compare an assortment of letters and memos from various organizations, you will notice immediately that some look more attractive and more professional than others. The non-verbal message of professional-looking documents suggests that they were sent by people who are careful, informed, intelligent, and successful. Understandably, you're more likely to take seriously documents that use attractive stationery and professional formatting techniques.

Over the years certain practices and conventions have arisen regarding the appearance and formatting of business documents. Although these conventions offer some choices (such as letter and punctuation styles), most business letters follow standardized formats. To ensure that your documents carry favourable non-verbal messages about you and your organization, you'll want to give special attention to the appearance and formatting of your letters, envelopes, memos, and fax cover sheets.

▶ Letter Parts

Professional-looking business letters are arranged in a conventional sequence with standard parts. Following is a discussion of how to use these letter parts properly. Figure C.1 illustrates the parts in a block-style letter.

Letterhead

Most business organizations use 8 1/2- by 11-inch paper printed with a letterhead displaying their official name, address, and telephone and fax numbers.

Dateline

On letterhead paper you should place the date two lines below the last line of the letterhead or 2 inches from the top edge of the paper (line 13). On plain paper place the date immediately below your return address. Since the date appears 2 inches from the top, start the return address an appropriate number of lines above it. The most common dateline format is as follows: *June 9, 2002*. Don't use *th*, etc., when the date is written this way. For European or military correspondence, use the following dateline format: *9 June 2002*. Notice that no commas are used.

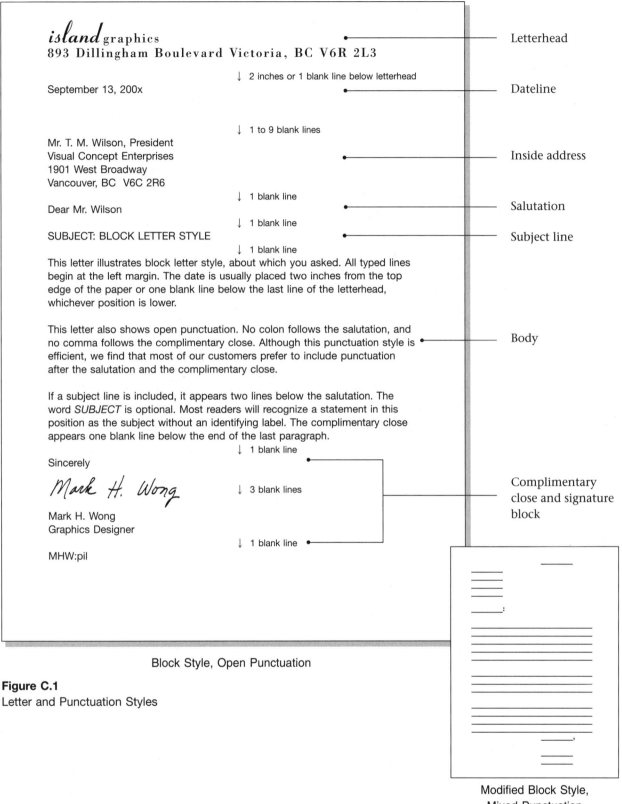

island graphics
893 Dillingham Boulevard Victoria, BC V6R 2L3 — Letterhead

↓ 2 inches or 1 blank line below letterhead

September 13, 200x — Dateline

↓ 1 to 9 blank lines

Mr. T. M. Wilson, President
Visual Concept Enterprises — Inside address
1901 West Broadway
Vancouver, BC V6C 2R6

↓ 1 blank line

Dear Mr. Wilson — Salutation

↓ 1 blank line

SUBJECT: BLOCK LETTER STYLE — Subject line

↓ 1 blank line

This letter illustrates block letter style, about which you asked. All typed lines
begin at the left margin. The date is usually placed two inches from the top
edge of the paper or one blank line below the last line of the letterhead,
whichever position is lower.

This letter also shows open punctuation. No colon follows the salutation, and
no comma follows the complimentary close. Although this punctuation style is — Body
efficient, we find that most of our customers prefer to include punctuation
after the salutation and the complimentary close.

If a subject line is included, it appears two lines below the salutation. The
word *SUBJECT* is optional. Most readers will recognize a statement in this
position as the subject without an identifying label. The complimentary close
appears one blank line below the end of the last paragraph.

↓ 1 blank line

Sincerely

Mark H. Wong   ↓ 3 blank lines   Complimentary
                                                                           close and signature
Mark H. Wong   block
Graphics Designer

↓ 1 blank line

MHW:pil

Block Style, Open Punctuation

Figure C.1
Letter and Punctuation Styles

Modified Block Style,
Mixed Punctuation

Addressee and Delivery Notations

Delivery notations such as *FAX TRANSMISSION, OVERNIGHT DELIVERY, CONFIDEN-TIAL,* or *CERTIFIED MAIL* are typed in all capital letters two line spaces above the inside address.

In block-style letters, as shown in Figure C.1, all lines begin at the left margin. In modified block-style letters, as shown at the right of Figure C.1, the date is centred or aligned with the complimentary close and signature block, which start at the centre. The date may also be backspaced from the right margin. Paragraphs may be blocked or indented. Mixed punctuation includes a colon after the salutation and a comma after the complimentary close.

Inside Address

Type the inside address—that is, the address of the organization or person receiving the letter—single-spaced, starting at the left margin. The number of lines between the dateline and the inside address depends on the size of the letter body, the type size (point or pitch size), and the length of the typing lines. Generally, one to nine blank lines are appropriate.

Be careful to duplicate the exact wording and spelling of the recipient's name and address on your documents. Usually, you can copy this information from the letterhead of the correspondence you are answering. If, for example, you are responding to *Jackson & Perkins Company,* don't address your letter to *Jackson and Perkins Corp.*

Always be sure to include a courtesy title such as *Mr., Ms., Mrs., Dr.,* or *Professor* before a person's name in the inside address—for both the letter and the envelope.

Attention Line

An attention line allows you to send your message officially to an organization but to direct it to a specific individual, office, or department. However, if you know an individual's complete name, it's always better to use it as the first line of the inside address and avoid an attention line. Here are two common formats for attention lines:

MultiMedia Enterprises	MultiMedia Enterprises
2931 St. Laurent	Attention: Marketing Director
Montreal, QC H2F 3C2	2931 St. Laurent
	Montreal, QC H2F 3C2
ATTENTION MARKETING DIRECTOR	

Attention lines may be typed in all caps or with upper- and lower-case letters. The colon following *Attention* is optional. Notice that an attention line may be placed one blank line below the address block or printed as the second line of the inside address. You'll want to use the latter format if you're composing on a word processor because the address block may be copied to the envelope and the attention line will not interfere with the last-line placement of the postal code. (Mail can be sorted more easily if the postal code appears in the last line of a typed address.)

Whenever possible, use a person's name as the first line of an address instead of putting that name in an attention line. Some writers use an attention line because they fear that letters addressed to individuals at companies may be considered private. They worry that if the addressee is no longer with the company, the letter may be forwarded or not opened. Actually, unless a letter is marked "Personal" or "Confidential," it will very likely be opened as business mail.

Salutation

For most letter styles place the letter greeting, or salutation, one blank line below the last line of the inside address or the attention line (if used). If the letter is addressed to an individual, use that person's courtesy title and last name (*Dear Mr. Lanham*). Even if you are on a first-name basis (*Dear Leslie*), be sure to add a colon (not a comma or a semicolon) after the salutation. Do not use an individual's full name in the salutation (not *Dear Mr. Leslie Lanham*) unless you are unsure of gender (*Dear Leslie Lanham*).

For letters with attention lines or those addressed to organizations, the selection of an appropriate salutation has become more difficult. Formerly, *Gentlemen* was used generically for all organizations. With increasing numbers of women in business management, however, *Gentlemen* became problematic. Because no universally acceptable salutation has emerged as yet, you'll probably be safest with *Ladies and Gentlemen* or *Gentlemen and Ladies*. Better yet, address your message to a specific person.

Subject and Reference Lines

Although experts suggest placing the subject line one blank line below the salutation, many businesses actually place it above the salutation. Use whatever style your organization prefers. Reference lines often show policy or file numbers; they generally appear one blank line above the salutation.

Body

Most business letters and memoranda are single-spaced, with double line spacing between paragraphs. Very short messages may be double-spaced with indented paragraphs.

Complimentary Close

Typed one blank line below the last line of the letter, the complimentary close may be formal (*Very truly yours*) or informal (*Sincerely yours* or *Cordially*). The simplified letter style omits a complimentary close.

Signature Block

In most letter styles the writer's typed name and optional identification appear two to three blank lines below the complimentary close. The combination of name, title, and organization information should be arranged to achieve a balanced look. The name and title may appear on the same line or on separate lines, depending on the length of each. Use commas to separate categories within the same line, but not to conclude a line. Women may choose to include *Ms., Mrs.,* or *Miss* before their names. Parentheses are optional. Men do not use *Mr.* before their names.

Sincerely yours,   Cordially yours,

Jeremy M. Wood, Manager   Casandra Baker-Murillo
Technical Sales and Services   Executive Vice-President

Some organizations include their names in the signature block. In such cases the organization name appears in all caps one blank line below the complimentary close, as shown here:

Cordially,

LITTON COMPUTER SERVICES

Ms. Shelina A. Simpson
Executive Assistant

Reference Initials

If used, the initials of the typist and writer are typed one blank line below the writer's name and title. Generally, the writer's initials are capitalized and the typist's are lower-cased, but this format varies.

Enclosure Notation

When an enclosure or attachment accompanies a document, a notation to that effect appears one blank line below the reference initials. This notation reminds the typist to insert the enclosure in the envelope, and it reminds the recipient to look for the enclo-sure or attachment. The notation may be spelled out (*Enclosure, Attachment*), or it may be abbreviated (*Enc., Att.*). It may indicate the number of enclosures or attachments, and it may also identify a specific enclosure (*Enclosure: Form 1099*).

Copy Notation

If you make copies of correspondence for other individuals, you may use *cc* to indicate courtesy copy or carbon copy, *pc* to indicate photocopy, or merely *c* for any kind of copy. A colon following the initial(s) is optional.

Second-Page Heading

When a letter extends beyond one page, use plain paper of the same quality and colour as the first page. Identify the second and succeeding pages with a heading con-sisting of the name of the addressee, the page number, and the date. Use either of the following two formats:

Ms. Rachel Lawson   2   May 3, 200x

Ms. Rachel Lawson
Page 2
May 3, 200x

Both headings appear on line 7 (one inch from top edge) followed by two blank lines to separate them from the continuing text. Avoid using a second page if you have only one line or the complimentary close and signature block to fill that page.

Plain-Paper Return Address

If you prepare a personal or business letter on plain paper, place your address immedi-ately above the date, as shown in Figure C.2. Do not include your name; you will type (and sign) your name at the end of your letter. If your return address contains two lines, begin typing it about 2 inches from the top edge of the paper. Avoid abbrevia-tions except for a two-letter province abbreviation.

For letters prepared in the block style, type the return address at the left margin. For modified block-style letters, start the return address at the centre to align with the complimentary close.

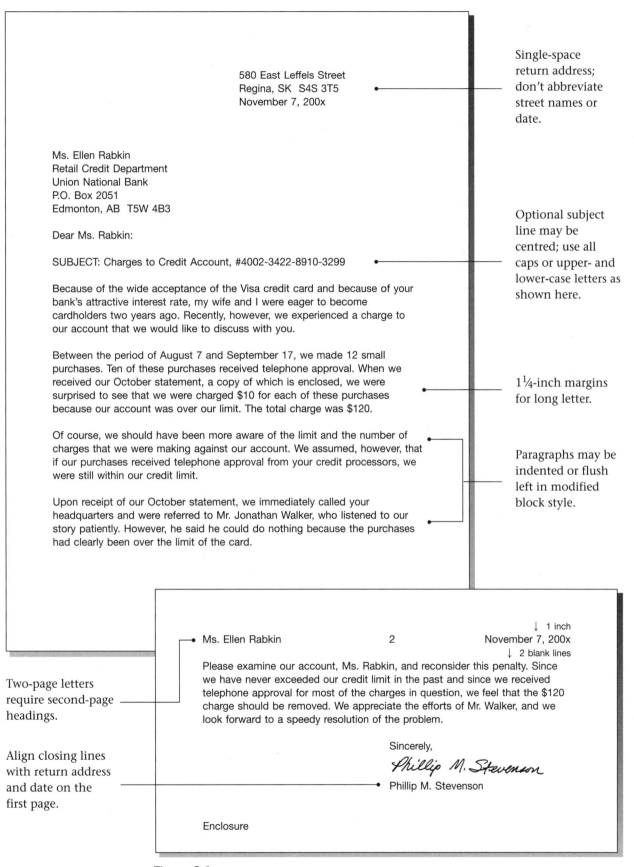

Single-space return address; don't abbreviate street names or date.

Optional subject line may be centred; use all caps or upper- and lower-case letters as shown here.

1¼-inch margins for long letter.

Paragraphs may be indented or flush left in modified block style.

Two-page letters require second-page headings.

Align closing lines with return address and date on the first page.

580 East Leffels Street
Regina, SK S4S 3T5
November 7, 200x

Ms. Ellen Rabkin
Retail Credit Department
Union National Bank
P.O. Box 2051
Edmonton, AB T5W 4B3

Dear Ms. Rabkin:

SUBJECT: Charges to Credit Account, #4002-3422-8910-3299

Because of the wide acceptance of the Visa credit card and because of your bank's attractive interest rate, my wife and I were eager to become cardholders two years ago. Recently, however, we experienced a charge to our account that we would like to discuss with you.

Between the period of August 7 and September 17, we made 12 small purchases. Ten of these purchases received telephone approval. When we received our October statement, a copy of which is enclosed, we were surprised to see that we were charged $10 for each of these purchases because our account was over our limit. The total charge was $120.

Of course, we should have been more aware of the limit and the number of charges that we were making against our account. We assumed, however, that if our purchases received telephone approval from your credit processors, we were still within our credit limit.

Upon receipt of our October statement, we immediately called your headquarters and were referred to Mr. Jonathan Walker, who listened to our story patiently. However, he said he could do nothing because the purchases had clearly been over the limit of the card.

↓ 1 inch
Ms. Ellen Rabkin   2   November 7, 200x
↓ 2 blank lines
Please examine our account, Ms. Rabkin, and reconsider this penalty. Since we have never exceeded our credit limit in the past and since we received telephone approval for most of the charges in question, we feel that the $120 charge should be removed. We appreciate the efforts of Mr. Walker, and we look forward to a speedy resolution of the problem.

Sincerely,

Phillip M. Stevenson

Phillip M. Stevenson

Enclosure

Figure C.2
Letter on Plain Paper, Modified Block Style

▶ Letter Styles

Business letters are generally prepared in one of three formats. The most popular is the block style, but the simplified style has much to recommend it.

Block Style

In the block style, shown in Figure C.1, all lines begin at the left margin. This style is a favourite because it is easy to format.

Modified Block Style

The modified block style differs from block style in that the date and closing lines appear in the centre, as shown at the bottom of Figure C.1. The date may be (1) centred, (2) begun at the centre of the page (to align with the closing lines), or (3) backspaced from the right margin. The signature block—including the complimentary close, writer's name and title, or organization identification—begins at the centre. The first line of each paragraph may begin at the left margin or may be indented five or ten spaces. All other lines begin at the left margin.

Simplified Style

Introduced by the Administrative Management Society a number of years ago, the simplified letter style, shown in Figure C.3, requires little formatting. Like the block style, all lines begin at the left margin. A subject line appears in all caps two blank lines below the inside address and two blank lines above the first paragraph. The salutation and complimentary close are omitted. The signer's name and identification appear in all caps four blank lines below the last paragraph. This letter style is efficient and avoids the problem of appropriate salutations and courtesy titles.

▶ Letter Placement

Business letters should be typed so that they are framed by white space. The most attractive placement results with side margins of 1 1/4 to 1 1/2 inches. However, some organizations prefer business writers to use standard margins of 1 inch (the defaults of many word processing programs). To balance a letter on the page, you can adjust the number of lines between the dateline and the address block (one to nine blank lines depending on the letter length).

▶ Punctuation Styles

Two punctuation styles are commonly used for letters. *Open* punctuation, shown with the block-style letter in Figure C.1, contains no punctuation after the salutation or complimentary close. *Mixed* punctuation, shown with the modified block style letter in Figure C.1, requires a colon after the salutation and a comma after the complimentary close. Many business organizations prefer mixed punctuation, even in a block-style letter. If you choose mixed punctuation, be sure to use a colon—not a comma or semicolon—after the salutation. Even when the salutation is a first name, the colon is appropriate.

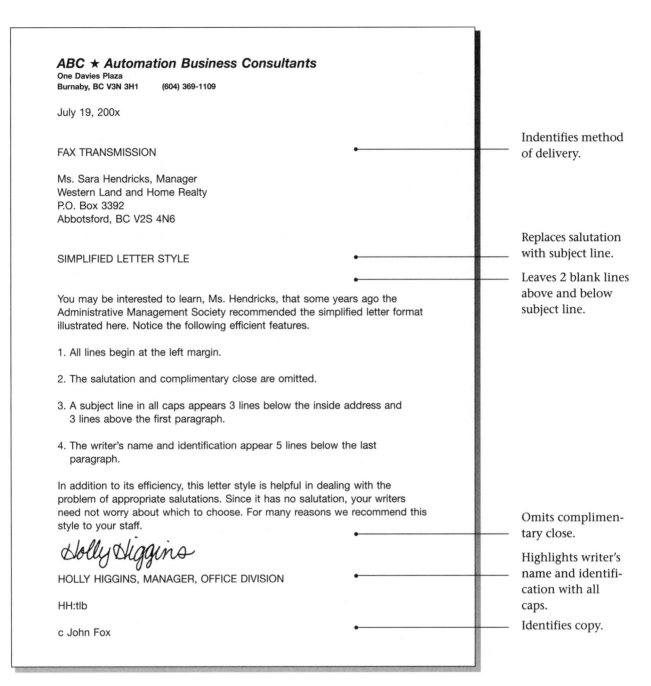

ABC ★ Automation Business Consultants
One Davies Plaza
Burnaby, BC V3N 3H1   (604) 369-1109

July 19, 200x

FAX TRANSMISSION   Indentifies method
                                                             of delivery.

Ms. Sara Hendricks, Manager
Western Land and Home Realty
P.O. Box 3392
Abbotsford, BC V2S 4N6

SIMPLIFIED LETTER STYLE   Replaces salutation
                                                             with subject line.

                                                             Leaves 2 blank lines
                                                             above and below
                                                             subject line.

You may be interested to learn, Ms. Hendricks, that some years ago the
Administrative Management Society recommended the simplified letter format
illustrated here. Notice the following efficient features.

1. All lines begin at the left margin.

2. The salutation and complimentary close are omitted.

3. A subject line in all caps appears 3 lines below the inside address and
   3 lines above the first paragraph.

4. The writer's name and identification appear 5 lines below the last
   paragraph.

In addition to its efficiency, this letter style is helpful in dealing with the
problem of appropriate salutations. Since it has no salutation, your writers
need not worry about which to choose. For many reasons we recommend this
style to your staff.   Omits complimen-
                                                             tary close.

Holly Higgins

HOLLY HIGGINS, MANAGER, OFFICE DIVISION   Highlights writer's
                                                             name and identifi-
                                                             cation with all
HH:tlb   caps.

                                                             Identifies copy.
c John Fox

Figure C.3
Simplified Letter Style

▶ Envelopes

An envelope should be printed on the same quality and colour of stationery as the letter it carries. Because the envelope introduces your message and makes the first
impression, you need to be especially careful in addressing it. Moreover, how you fold
the letter is important.

Return Address

The return address is usually printed in the upper left corner of an envelope, as shown in Figure C.4. In large companies some form of identification (the writer's initials, name, or location) may be typed above the company name and return address. This identification helps return the letter to the sender in case of non-delivery. On an envelope without a printed return address, single-space the return address in the upper left corner. Beginning 1/4 inch from the top and 1/2 inch from the left edge, type the writer's name, title, company, and mailing address.

Mailing Address

On legal-sized No. 10 envelopes (4 1/8 by 9 1/2 inches), begin the address 2 inches from the top and about 4 1/4 inches from the left edge, as shown in Figure C.4. For small envelopes (3 5/8 by 6 1/2 inches), begin typing about 2 1/2 inches from the left edge.

Canada Post Corporation recommends that addresses be typed in all caps without any punctuation. This CPC style, shown in the small envelope in Figure C.4, was originally developed to facilitate scanning by optical character readers. Today's OCRs, however, are so sophisticated that they scan upper- and lower-case letters easily. Many companies today do not follow the CPC format because they prefer to use the same format for the envelope as for the inside address. If the same format is used, writers can take advantage of word processing programs to "copy" the inside address to the envelope, thus saving keystrokes and reducing errors. Having the same format on both the inside address and the envelope also looks more professional and consistent. For

No. 10 envelope,
Upper- and lower-case format

No. 6¾ envelope, CPC upper-case format

Figure C.4
Envelope Formats

---

these reasons you may choose to use the familiar upper- and lower-case combination format. But you will want to check with your organization to learn its preference.

Folding

The way a letter is folded and inserted into an envelope sends additional non-verbal messages about a writer's professionalism and carefulness. Most business people follow the procedures shown here, which produce the least number of creases to distract readers.

For large No. 10 envelopes, begin with the letter face up. Fold slightly less than one-third of the sheet toward the top, as shown below. Then fold down the top third to within 1/3 inch of the bottom fold. Insert the letter into the envelope with the last fold toward the bottom of the envelope.

For small No. 6 3/4 envelopes, begin by folding the bottom up to within 1/3 inch of the top edge. Then fold the right third over to the left. Fold the left third to within 1/3 inch of the last fold. Insert the last fold into the envelope first.

▶ Memoranda

Some offices use memo forms imprinted with the organization name and, optionally, the department or division names, as shown in Figure C.5. Although the design and arrangement of memo forms vary, they usually include the basic elements of *TO, FROM, DATE,* and *SUBJECT*. Large organizations may include other identifying headings, such as *FILE NUMBER, FLOOR, EXTENSION, LOCATION,* and *DISTRIBUTION*.

Because of the difficulty of aligning computer printers with preprinted forms, many business writers use a standardized memo template (sometimes called a "wizard"). This template automatically provides attractive headings with appropriate spacing and formatting. Other writers store their own preferred memo formats. Either method eliminates alignment problems.

If no printed or stored computer forms are available, memos may be typed on company letterhead or on plain paper, as shown in Figure C.6. On a full sheet of paper, start on line 13; on a half sheet, start on line 7. Double-space and type in all caps the guide words: *TO:, FROM:, DATE:, SUBJECT:*. Align all the fill-in information two spaces after the longest guide word (*SUBJECT:*). Leave three lines after the last line of the heading, and begin typing the body of the memo. Like business letters, memos are single-spaced.

Memos are generally formatted with side margins of 1 1/4 inches, or they may conform to the printed memo form.

FIRST FEDERAL BANK
Mortgage Department

Interoffice
Memorandum

TO:

FROM:

DATE:

SUBJECT:

PYRAMID, INC.
Internal Memo

TO: DATE:

FROM: FILE:

SUBJECT:

Figure C.5
Printed Memo Forms

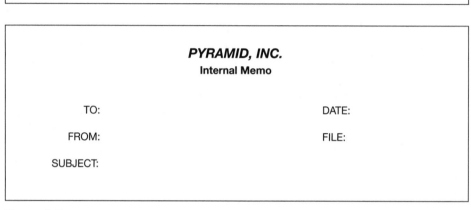

↓ 2 inches
MEMO

TO: Dawn Stewart, Manager   DATE: February 3, 200x
                 Sales and Marketing

FROM: Jay Murray, Vice-President
                 Operations

SUBJECT: TELEPHONE SERVICE REQUEST FORMS
                        ↓ 2 blank lines

To speed telephone installation and improve service within the Bremerton facility, we are starting a new application procedure.

Service request forms will be available at various locations within the three buildings. When you require telephone service, obtain a request form at one of the locations that is convenient for you. Fill in the pertinent facts, obtain approval from your division head, and send the form to Brent White. Request forms are available at the following locations:

Figure C.6
Memo on Plain Paper

▶ E-Mail Messages

Because e-mail is a developing communication medium, formatting and usage are still fluid. The following suggestions, illustrated in Figure C.7, may guide you in setting up the parts of an e-mail message, but always check with your organization to observe its practices.

To Line

Include the receiver's e-mail address after *To*. Some writers personalize the line somewhat by naming the receiver first, followed by that person's e-mail address in angle brackets, such as *Marilyn Lammers <mlammers@accountpro.com>*.

From Line

Most systems automatically include your name and e-mail address after *From*.

Cc

Insert the e-mail address of anyone who is to receive a copy of the message. *Cc* stands for *carbon copy* or *courtesy copy*. Don't be tempted, though, to send needless copies just because it's so easy.

Bcc

Include here the e-mail address of anyone who is to receive a copy of the message without the receiver's knowledge. *Bcc* stands for *blind carbon copy*. Writers are also

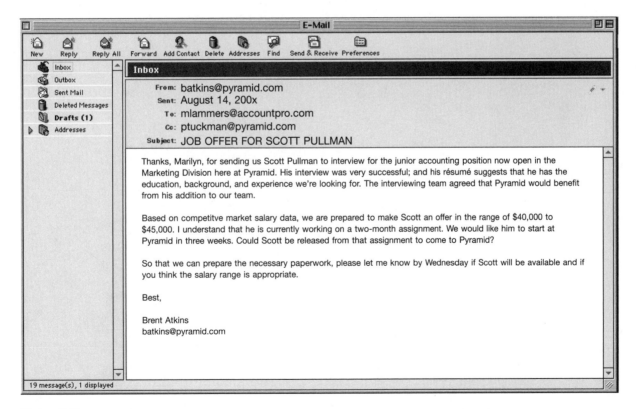

Figure C.7
Typical E-Mail Message

using the *bcc* line for mailing lists. When a message is being sent to a number of people and their e-mail addresses should not be revealed, the *bcc* line works well to conceal the names and addresses of all receivers.

Subject

Identify the subject of the memo briefly. Be sure to include enough information to be clear and compelling.

▶ Fax Cover Sheet

Documents transmitted by fax are usually introduced by a cover sheet, such as that shown in Figure C.8. As with memos, the format varies considerably. Important items to include are (1) the name and fax number of the receiver, (2) the name and fax number of the sender, (3) the number of pages being sent, and (4) the name and telephone number of the person to notify in case of unsatisfactory transmission.

When the document being transmitted requires little explanation, you may prefer to attach an adhesive note (such as a Post-it™ fax transmittal form) instead of a full cover sheet. These notes carry essentially the same information as shown in our printed fax cover sheet. They are perfectly acceptable in most business organizations and can save considerable paper and transmission costs.

```
                          FAX TRANSMISSION

      DATE: _____      FAX
      TO:   _____      NUMBER:_____
            _____
            _____
                                       FAX
      FROM: _____      NUMBER:_____

      NUMBER OF PAGES TRANSMITTED INCLUDING THIS COVER SHEET:____

      MESSAGE:



      If any part of this fax transmission is missing or not clearly received, please call:

      NAME: _____

      PHONE:_____
```

Figure C.8
Fax Cover Sheet

Self-Help Exercises

CONTENTS

NAME _____

Nearly every student who takes business English says, "I wish I had more exercises to try my skills on." Because of the many requests, we provide this set of self-help exercises for extra reinforcement. Immediate feedback is an important ingredient in successful learning. Therefore, a key to these exercises begins on p. 525. Don't check the key, of course, until you complete each exercise.

Use a current dictionary to complete the following exercise.

1. *Amanuensis* originally meant
   (a) deterioration of sight
   (c) a servant with secretarial duties
   (b) coarse herbs including pigweeds
   (d) a female warrior _____

2. An *autocrat* is one who enjoys
   (a) owning many cars
   (c) democratic relationships
   (b) ruling by himself or herself
   (d) racing automobiles _____

3. The words *in so much as* should be written
   (a) in so much as
   (c) insomuch as
   (b) in somuchas
   (d) in somuch as _____

4. The word *logistics* is
   (a) plural but may be used with a singular verb
   (c) singular
   (b) plural and always requires a plural verb
   (d) neither singular nor plural _____

5. The abbreviation *Mme* stands for
   (a) madame
   (c) master in mechanical engineering
   (b) mademoiselle
   (d) monsieur _____

6. In grammar the word *neuter* means
   (a) asexual
   (c) neither feminine nor masculine
   (b) neutral
   (d) both feminine and masculine _____

7. The word *(non)productive* should be written
   (a) non-productive
   (c) non productive
   (b) nonproductive
   (d) non-Productive _____

8. When the word *notwithstanding* is used to mean "nevertheless," it functions as what part of speech?
   (a) conjunction
   (c) preposition
   (b) adverb
   (d) adjective _____

9. The plural of the word *proxy* is
   (a) proxies'
   (c) proxy's
   (b) proxys
   (d) proxies _____

10. In Sri Lanka a *rupee* is a monetary unit equal to
    (a) 10 cents
    (c) 50 cents
    (b) 100 cents
    (d) $2 _____

NAME _____

Worksheet 1

A. This exercise is designed to help you develop a better understanding of the parts of speech. Using Chapter 2, write a brief definition or description of the eight parts of speech listed here. Then list three words as examples of each part of speech.

	Brief Definition	**Three Examples**		
1. noun	names person, place, thing, concept	Anthony	paper	truth
2. pronoun				
3. verb				
4. adjective				
5. adverb				
6. preposition				
7. conjunction				
8. interjection				

B. Fill in the parts of speech for all the words in these sentences. Use a dictionary if necessary.

I immediately called Greg, and he waited for the manager with me.

1. I _____

2. immediately _____

3. called _____

4. Greg _____

5. and _____

6. he _____

7. waited _____

8. for _____

9. the _____

10. manager _____

11. with _____

12. me _____

Gosh, the computer and printer processed this lengthy report in twenty seconds!

13. Gosh _____

14. the _____

15. computer _____

16. and _____

17. printer _____

18. processed _____

19. this _____

20. lengthy _____

21. report _____

22. in _____

23. twenty _____

24. seconds _____

We arrived promptly, but the committee meeting started late.

25. We _____

26. arrived _____

27. promptly _____

28. but _____

29. the _____

30. committee _____

31. meeting _____

32. started _____

33. late _____

Worksheet 2

Fill in the parts of speech for all the words in these sentences. Use a dictionary if necessary.

I sold property in Fredericton, but one transaction is still not complete.

1. I _____
2. sold _____
3. property _____
4. in _____

5. Fredericton _____
6. but _____
7. one _____
8. transaction _____

9. is _____
10. still _____
11. not _____
12. complete _____

Oh, did Lee really think he could change that method of operation?

13. Oh _____
14. did _____
15. Lee _____
16. really _____

17. think _____
18. he _____
19. could _____
20. change _____

21. that _____
22. method _____
23. of _____
24. operation _____

The old accounting system was neither accurate nor efficient, but one company had used it faithfully for the past forty years.

25. The _____
26. old _____
27. accounting _____
28. system _____
29. was _____
30. neither _____
31. accurate _____

32. nor _____
33. efficient _____
34. but _____
35. one _____
36. company _____
37. had _____
38. used _____

39. it _____
40. faithfully _____
41. for _____
42. the _____
43. past _____
44. forty _____
45. years _____

Kerry quietly slipped into an empty seat during the long class film.

46. Kerry _____
47. quietly _____
48. slipped _____
49. into _____

50. an _____
51. empty _____
52. seat _____
53. during _____

54. the _____
55. long _____
56. class _____
57. film _____

3 SENTENCES: ELEMENTS, PATTERNS, TYPES Self-Help Exercises

Worksheet 1
Locating Subjects and Verbs

Action verbs tell what the subject is doing or what is being done to the subject. For each of the following sentences, locate the action verb and underline it twice. Then locate the subject of the verb and underline it once.

To locate the subject, use the verb preceded by *who?* or *what?* In the example the verb is *answered.* To help you find the subject, ask *who answered?*

Example: A <u>group</u> of applicants <u>answered</u> the advertisement.

1. One of our top salespeople sold $2 million worth of life insurance.

2. The speaker in the afternoon session made a dynamic presentation.

3. Our telephones rang constantly during the sales campaign.

4. In the winter we will hire four new workers for this department.

5. Our management team built a sound program of sales and service.

6. The most successful salespeople received trips to Hawaii.

7. In the meantime, our personnel manager will send you an application form.

8. Last week we released our new line of office supplies.

9. One of the vice-presidents was given a promotion recently.

10. Today's computers require managers to think with new clarity and precision.

Linking verbs (such as *am, is, are, was, were, be, being,* and *been*) often join to the sentence words that describe or rename the subject. In the following sentences, underline the linking verbs twice and the subjects once.

Examples: <u>E.J. Todd</u> <u>was</u> president of the organization last year.
In the morning the <u>air</u> <u>is</u> cool.

11. Mr. Thomas is the office manager for Ryerson Metals Corporation.

12. The new copiers are very dependable.

13. Mrs. Seymour is the best person for the job.

14. Dul Youn Hu has been office manager for nine years.

15. Our new offices are much brighter than our previous ones.

Worksheet 2
Sentence Patterns

Finish the sentences below in the patterns indicated.

Subject–Verb

Example: Birds _____*sing*_____ .

1. The audience_____ .

2. Rain _____ .

3. Car horns_____ .

4. The burglar alarm _____ .

5. In 1945 World War II _____ .

6. Last year's sales _____ .

Subject–Action Verb–Object

Example: The sales director made ____*a call*____ .

7. Our salesperson sold a _____ .

8. The secretary typed a _____ .

9. Ricky mailed the _____ .

10. I telephoned _____ .

11. Someone locked _____ .

12. The clerk filed all the _____ .

Subject–Linking Verb–Complement

Example: She is very _____*friendly*_____ .

Jim could have been the ___*manager*___ .

13. Sales have been _____ .

14. Susan is the new _____ .

15. Last year the owner was_____ .

16. I am _____ .

17. The writer could have been_____ .

18. The caller was _____ .

Compose original sentences in the following patterns.

19. (Subject–verb) _____

20. (Subject–verb) _____

21. **(**Subject–action verb–object)_____

_____

22. (Subject–action verb–object)_____

_____

23. (Subject–linking verb–complement)_____

_____

Worksheet 3
Sentence Types

From the list below select the letter that accurately describes each of the following groups of words. If the groups of words need end punctuation marks, add them.

a = fragment   d = question
b = statement   e = exclamation
c = command

1. The management of a multinational corporation with branch offices in several cities   _____

2. Send me a brochure describing your latest camping equipment   _____

3. Will you be working next weekend or during the week   _____

4. The work schedule is usually posted late in the week   _____

5. Wow, he ran 98 yards for a touchdown   _____

6. If you have an opportunity to be promoted to a managerial position   _____

7. For a generous return on your funds, invest in second trust deeds   _____

8. In all levels of business, written and spoken English is extremely important in achieving success   _____

9. Because it is difficult to improve your language skills on your own   _____

Sentence Faults

From the list below select the letter that accurately describes each of the following groups of words.

a = correctly punctuated sentence   c = comma splice
b = fragment   d = run-on sentence

10. I'll have the answer soon, first I must make a telephone call.   _____

11. If you consider all the pros and cons before you make a decision.   _____

12. We have no idea what to order only Dunia Sanchez can do that.   _____

13. Your entire department is entitled to overtime compensation.   _____

14. You check the current address list, and I'll check the old one.   _____

15. You check the current address list, I'll check the old one.   _____

16. You check the current address list I'll check the old one.   _____

17. Although we have complete confidence in our products and prices.   _____

18. When you return from the conference, please submit a brief report describing what you learned.   _____

19. We must focus our charitable contributions on areas that directly relate to our business, therefore we are unable to send a cheque this year.   _____

20. If you agree that this memo accurately reflects our conversation.   _____

NAME _____

Write the preferred plural forms of the nouns shown below. Use a dictionary if necessary.

LEVEL I

1. giraffe	_____	**16.** woman	_____
2. foot	_____	**17.** mismatch	_____
3. switch	_____	**18.** taxi	_____
4. Bush	_____	**19.** loaf (of bread)	_____
5. box	_____	**20.** annex	_____
6. language	_____	**21.** belief	_____
7. fax	_____	**22.** Ross	_____
8. sandwich	_____	**23.** storm	_____
9. income tax	_____	**24.** ranch	_____
10. child	_____	**25.** Jones	_____
11. success	_____	**26.** Chavez	_____
12. conveyer	_____	**27.** letter	_____
13. dress	_____	**28.** business	_____
14. branch	_____	**29.** computer	_____
15. recommendation	_____	**30.** wish	_____

Write the preferred plural forms of the nouns shown below. Use a dictionary if necessary.

LEVEL II

1. wharf	_____	**8.** amt.	_____
2. chief of police	_____	**9.** faculty	_____
3. 1980	_____	**10.** by-product	_____
4. Wolf	_____	**11.** entry	_____
5. embargo	_____	**12.** looker-on	_____
6. cm	_____	**13.** company	_____
7. size 10	_____	**14.** knife	_____

15. court-martial   _____

16. A   _____

17. Sherman   _____

18. memo   _____

19. valley   _____

20. zero   _____

21. life   _____

22. yr.   _____

23. Murphy   _____

24. runner-up   _____

25. oz.   _____

26. journey   _____

27. M.B.A.   _____

28. wolf   _____

29. Kelly   _____

30. minority   _____

LEVEL III

Write the preferred plural forms of the nouns shown below. Use a dictionary if necessary.

1. datum   _____

2. thesis   _____

3. bacterium   _____

4. Chinese   _____

5. parenthesis   _____

6. Miss Soltan (informal)   _____

7. alumna   _____

8. Mr. West and Mr. Turner (formal)   _____

9. genus   _____

10. news   _____

11. p. (page)   _____

12. f. (and following pages)   _____

13. larva   _____

14. Mrs. Smythe and Mrs. Webb (formal)   _____

15. criterion   _____

Select the correct word in parentheses, and complete the sentences in your own words.

16. The goods produced in that factory (is, are) _____

17. Politics in Ottawa (is, are) _____

18. Several (formula, formulas) _____

19. Four separate (analysis, analyses) _____

20. In the business curriculum Economics I (is, are) _____

NAME _____

Worksheet 1

Before you begin this exercise, review the five-step plan for placing apostrophes:

1. Look for possessive construction. (Usually two nouns appear together.)

2. Reverse the nouns. (Use a prepositional phrase, such as *interest of three years*.)

3. Examine ownership word. (Does it end in an *s* sound?)

4. If the ownership word is singular, add an apostrophe and *s*.

5. (a) If the ownership word is plural and ends in *s*, add only an apostrophe.
   (b) If the ownership word is plural but does not end in *s*, add both an apostrophe and an *s*.

Using apostrophes, change the following prepositional phrases into possessive constructions.

Example: interest of three years   *three years' interest*

1. books of all students   _____

2. office of this company   _____

3. toys of the children   _____

4. rent of two months   _____

5. mansion of the movie star   _____

6. feelings of all the neighbours   _____

7. the landing of the pilot   _____

8. agreement of both partners   _____

9. notebook of Jeffrey   _____

10. strengths of the department   _____

11. time of two years   _____

12. customs of those people   _____

13. merger of last week   _____

14. credit from the bank   _____

15. savings of citizens   _____

16. mountains of Canada   _____

17. requirements of the employer   _____

18. résumés of all candidates   _____

19. policies of the government   _____

20. fees of both lawyers   _____

Worksheet 2

Write the correct possessive form of the word in parentheses in the space provided.

1. Applicants will have at least a (year) wait for an apartment.   _____

2. Several (drivers) inquiries prompted the posting of a better sign.   _____

3. We found the (carpenter) tools after he left the building.   _____

4. The electronics store installed a hidden video camera to observe a suspected (thief) activities.   _____

5. The (day) news headlines are given every 15 minutes on CTV News 1.   _____

6. Our new (employees) cafeteria is busy from 11 a.m. to 1 p.m.   _____

7. Only the (CEO) car may be parked in the special zone.   _____

8. Most (readers) letters supported the magazine's editorial position.   _____

9. Where is the (caller) message?   _____

10. All (authors) rights are protected by copyright law.   _____

Correct any errors in the following sentences by underlining the errors and writing the correct forms in the spaces provided. If a sentence is correct as written, write *C*.

11. Many of the secretaries desks had dictionaries and reference manuals on them.   _____

12. The names of these customers are not alphabetized.   _____

13. Some of the countrys biggest manufacturers are being investigated.   _____

14. This account has been credited with four months interest.   _____

15. Certainly your organizations voice mail system is excellent.   _____

16. The vice-presidents resignation left a vital position unfilled.   _____

17. Are you researching your familys genealogy?   _____

18. I am prepared to protest the bill of my lawyer, William Glass.   _____

19. In three years time the software paid for itself.   _____

20. Not a single farmers crop was undamaged by the storm.   _____

21. A citizens committee was formed to address parking problems.   _____

22. One years interest on the account amounted to $120.   _____

23. Each customers complimentary game tickets were mailed today.   _____

24. Childrens clothing is on the first floor.   _____

25. The announcement of new benefits for employees was made in the supervisors memo.   _____

Correct any errors in the following sentences by underlining the errors and writing the correct forms in the spaces provided. If the sentence is correct as written, write *C*.

1. The document required the notary publics signature as well as his seal. _____

2. At least one companies' records are up to date. _____

3. After school Juan stopped at the stationers for supplies. _____

4. My uncle's lawyer's suggestions in this matter were excellent. _____

5. The desk's top had to be refinished by a skilled woodworker. _____

6. We borrowed my aunt's and uncle's motor home. _____

7. All R.N.s' uniforms must now be identical. _____

8. This month's expenses are somewhat less than last months. _____

9. Debbie's and Julie's DVD players came from the same store. _____

10. The president's secretary's telephone number has been changed. _____

11. Have you called the new sales' representative? _____

12. My two brothers-in-law's beards are neat and well trimmed. _____

13. Three birds nests fell to the ground during the windstorm. _____

14. I'm going over to Ricks to pick him up. _____

15. We spent our vacation enjoying Quebecs' historical sights. _____

16. CBC's report on the vote was better than any other network's. _____

17. Anderson's and Clark's transcription book is outstanding. _____

18. The Los Angeles' symphony planned an evening of Beethoven. _____

19. The two architects licences were issued together. _____

20. Our sales this year are greater than last years. _____

21. All RCMP agents must pass rigorous security investigations. _____

22. Diana's and Graham's marriage licence was lost. _____

23. The Prime Minister answered all the reporters questions carefully. _____

24. Workers said they expected a days pay for an honest days work. _____

25. Robin and John's new car came with a five-year warranty. _____

Write the correct forms of the words shown in parentheses.

Example: The (Stivers) cat is missing.
      _____Stiverses'_____

1. I see that (someone else) books also got wet.
      _____

2. Lee (Ross) office is on the south side of the campus.
      _____

3. Both (class) test results were misplaced.
      _____

4. Beth (Saunders) home is farther away than anyone else's.
      _____

5. The bank is reconsidering the (Rodriguez) loan application.
      _____

6. I have no idea where (Les) car is parked.
      _____

7. Only my (boss) desk is cluttered.
      _____

8. The other (boss) desks are rather neat.
      _____

9. Did you hear that the (Abramovich) are moving?
      _____

10. Several (actress) costumes were so valuable that insurance policies were taken out to insure them.
      _____

11. I think that was Mr. (Harris) parking spot you just took.
      _____

12. Mrs. (Burns) history class met outside on that balmy day.
      _____

13. Who is (James) partner for the laboratory experiment?
      _____

14. That (waitress) station consists of four tables.
      _____

15. None of the (Garvey) belongings were missing.
      _____

16. Have you visited the (Morris) vacation home?
      _____

17. Only Mrs. (Betz) car remained in the parking lot.
      _____

18. It looks as if the (Walker) home is getting a new roof.
      _____

19. Miss (Simons) new Internet connection provides instant access.
      _____

20. Mr. (Jones) property is on Kelton Avenue.
      _____

21. Professor (White) lecture was well organized and informative.
      _____

22. Have you seen the (Williams) four-room tent that they took camping last weekend?
      _____

23. We heard that the (Kimball) may be moving.
      _____

NAME _____

Worksheet 1

LEVEL I

List seven pronouns that could be used as subjects of verbs.

1. _____   4. _____   7. _____

2. _____   5. _____

3. _____   6. _____

List seven pronouns that could be used as objects of verbs or objects of prepositions.

8. _____   11. _____   14. _____

9. _____   12. _____

10. _____   13. _____

Pronouns as Subjects

Select the correct pronoun to complete each sentence below. All the omitted pronouns function as subjects of verbs.

15. Mrs. Georges and (I, me) submitted purchase requisitions.   _____

16. We thought that the manager and (she, her) would attend.   _____

17. Will you and (he, him) be going to the sales meeting?   _____

18. Mr. North and (they, them) expect to see you Saturday.   _____

19. It is difficult to explain why Bob and (her, she) decided to move.   _____

20. Of all the applicants only (we, us) agreed to be tested now.   _____

21. We believe that Rudolf and (she, her) deserve raises.   _____

22. After Ms. Barko and (he, him) had returned, customers were handled more rapidly. _____

23. Only you and (her, she) will participate in the demonstration.   _____

24. Did you hear that the sales manager and (he, him) will be promoted?   _____

25. Professor Smith suggested that you and (I, me) work together on a report.   _____

Worksheet 2

Personal Pronouns as Objects

Select the correct pronoun to complete each sentence below. All omitted pronouns function as objects of verbs or prepositions. Prepositions have been underlined to help you identify them.

1. Just <u>between</u> you and (I, me), our branch won the sales trophy. _____

2. Michelle said that she had seen you and (he, him) at the airport. _____

3. We hope to show (they, them) the billing procedure this afternoon. _____

4. Everybody <u>but</u> (I, me) is ready to leave. _____

5. Have you talked <u>with</u> Brad and (her, she) about this change? _____

6. We need more workers <u>like</u> Maria and (him, he) to finish the job. _____

7. All supervisors <u>except</u> Mrs. Young and (her, she) approved the plan. _____

8. This insurance program provides you and (they, them) with equal benefits. _____

9. Terms of the settlement were satisfactory <u>to</u> (we, us). _____

10. Every operator <u>but</u> Molly and (I, me) had an opportunity for overtime. _____

Possessive Case Pronouns

Remember that possessive case pronouns (*yours, his, hers, its, whose, theirs,* etc.) do not contain apostrophes. Do not confuse these pronouns with the following contractions: *it's* (it is), *there's* (there is), *who's* (who is), and *you're* (you are). In the following sentences, select the correct word.

11. Do you think (its, it's) necessary for us to sign in? _____

12. Is (theirs, their's) the white house at the end of the street? _____

13. The contract and all (its, it's) provisions must be examined. _____

14. (There's, Theirs) a set of guidelines for us to follow. _____

15. Jack's car and (hers, her's) are the only ones left in the lot. _____

16. The cheque is good only if (its, it's) signed. _____

17. I was told that Sue's and (yours, your's) were the best departments. _____

18. (Who's, Whose) umbrella is that lying in the corner? _____

19. Most car registrations were sent April 1, but (our's, ours) was delayed. _____

20. (You're, Your) taking Don's place, aren't you? _____

Select the correct pronoun to complete these sentences.

LEVEL II

1. Do you expect Mr. Jefferson and (they, them) to meet you? _____

2. No one could regret the error more than (I, me, myself). _____

3. These photocopies were prepared by Charles and (she, her). _____

4. (We, Us) policyholders are entitled to group discounts. _____

5. Procrastination disturbs Steven as much as (I, me, myself). _____

6. Universal Parcel is hiring James and (I, me, myself) for the summer. _____

7. Have you corresponded with the authors, Dr. Lee and (she, her)? _____

8. On that project no one works as hard as (he, him, himself). _____

9. Everyone but Mr. Foster and (he, him) can help customers if necessary. _____

10. Do you know if Gary and (I, me, myself) signed it? _____

11. Only Erik (he, himself, hisself) knows what is best for him. _____

12. We asked two women, Denise and (she, her), to come along. _____

13. The proceeds are to be divided among Mr. Shelby, Mrs. Huerra, and (she, her). _____

14. Miss Greerson thinks that Mr. Campbell is a better salesperson than (she, her). _____

15. All property claims must be submitted to my lawyer or (I, me, myself) before April 15. _____

16. The result was acceptable to both management and (us, we, ourselves). _____

17. At a keyboard no one is more accurate than (she, her). _____

18. The best time for you and (he, him) to enrol is in January. _____

19. The president and (I, me, myself) will inspect the facility. _____

20. Everyone except Keven and (I, me, myself) was able to join the program. _____

21. Send an application to Human Resources or (I, me, myself) immediately. _____

22. (She and I, Her and me, Her and I) are among the best-qualified candidates. _____

23. Have you invited Jon and (she, her, herself) to our picnic? _____

Worksheet 1

LEVEL III

Remember that pronouns that rename the subject and that follow linking verbs must be in the nominative case (It was he who placed the order). When the infinitive *to be* has no subject (and that subject must immediately precede the infinitive *to be*), the pronoun that follows must be in the nominative case (My sister is often taken to be I). *No subject = nominative.*

In the following sentences, select the correct word.

1. It must have been (her, she) who called this morning. _____

2. I certainly would not like to be (he, him). _____

3. Do you think that it was (they, them) who complained? _____

4. Tram answered the telephone by saying, "This is (her, she)." _____

5. Mrs. Richards thought the salesperson to be (he, him). _____

6. If you were (she, her), would you take the job? _____

7. Cecile is sometimes taken to be (her, she). _____

8. Jim said that yesterday's driver could have been (he, him). _____

9. Miss Soriano asked Frank and (I, me, myself) to help her. _____

10. Was it (they, them) who made the contribution? _____

11. The most accurate proofreader seems to be (he, him). _____

12. Producer Edwards would not allow me to be (he, him) in the production. _____

13. Mr. Fox wants to assign you and (her, she) the project. _____

14. Are you sure it was (I, me) who was called to the phone? _____

15. The visitor was thought to be (she, her). _____

16. If it had not been (she, her) who made the announcement, I would not have believed it. _____

17. How could anyone have thought that Margaret was (I, me)? _____

18. I do not wish to discourage either you or (he, him). _____

19. If anyone is disappointed, it will be (I, me, myself). _____

20. What makes Joan wish to be (she, her)? _____

21. Do you think it was (he, him) who made the large contribution? _____

22. Mr. Egal selected you and (he, him) because of his confidence in your abilities. _____

23. If it had been (she, her), we would have recognized her immediately. _____

24. Everyone thought the new manager would be (she, her). _____

25. Because the president is to be (he, him), Mr. Kaczynski will act as CEO. _____

Worksheet 2

Select the correct word to complete the following sentences.

1. Only the president and (he, him) can grant leaves of absence. _____

2. The manager mistook Danielle to be (I, me). _____

3. The body of the manuscript is followed by (its, it's) endnotes. _____

4. Our staff agreed that you and (she, her) should represent us. _____

5. How can you believe (us, we) to be guilty? _____

6. I'm not sure (their's, there's) enough time left. _____

7. Everyone thought the new manager would be (he, him). _____

8. My friend and (I, me) looked for jobs together. _____

9. This matter will be kept strictly between you and (I, me). _____

10. Good students like you and (she, her) are always prepared. _____

11. Judge Waxman is fully supported by (we, us) consumers. _____

12. We agreed that (your, you're) the best person for the job. _____

13. Send the announcement to Ms. Nguyen and (she, her) today. _____

14. All employees except Kim and (he, him) will be evaluated. _____

15. Many locker combinations are listed, but (your's, yours) is missing. _____

16. Apparently the message was intended for you and (I, me, myself). _____

17. Was it (he, him, himself) who sent the mystery e-mail message? _____

18. The bank is closed, but (it's, its) ATM is open. _____

19. Please submit the report to (him or me, he or I) before May 1. _____

20. (There's, Theirs) only one path for us to follow. _____

21. For you and (he, him), I would suggest careers in marketing. _____

22. These personnel changes certainly affect you and (I, me, myself). _____

23. My friend and (I, me, myself) are thinking of a trip to Cuba. _____

24. Only two branches plan to expand (they're, their) display rooms. _____

25. The operator thought it was (she, her) calling for assistance. _____

26. Because you are a member of the audit review team, you have a better overall picture of the operations than (I, me, myself).   _____

27. Though you may not agree with our decision, I hope you'll support Todd and (I, me, myself) in our effort to get the job done.   _____

28. Some of the recent decisions made by (us, we) supervisors will be reviewed by the management council when it meets in January.   _____

29. I wonder if it was (she, her) who sent the anonymous e-mail message about additional company downsizing.   _____

30. Do you think (theirs, their's, there's) any reason to change our computer passwords every month?   _____

NAME _____

Pronouns must agree with the words for which they substitute. Don't let words and phrases that come between a pronoun and its antecedent confuse you.

Examples: Every one of the women had *her* forms ready. (Not *their*.)
The supervisor, along with four assistants, offered *his* support. (Not *their*.)

Select the correct word(s) to complete these sentences.

1. Mrs. Kennedy, in addition to many other members of the staff, sent (her, their) best wishes. _____

2. Every employee must have (his, her, his or her, their) physical examination completed by December 31. _____

3. After a job well done, everyone appreciates (his, her, his or her, their) share of credit. _____

4. Several office workers, along with the manager, announced (his or her, their) intention to vote for the settlement. _____

5. Individuals like Mr. Herndon can always be depended on to do (his, his or her, their) best in all assignments. _____

6. If a policyholder has a legitimate claim, (he, she, he or she, they) should contact us immediately. _____

7. Every one of the employees brought (his or her lunch, their lunches) to the outdoor event. _____

8. When a customer walks into our store, treat (him, her, him or her, them) as you would an honoured guest in your home. _____

9. Carolyn Davis, along with several other sales representatives, volunteered to demonstrate (her, his or her, their) latest equipment. _____

10. A few of the members of the touring group, in addition to the guide, wanted (his or her picture, their pictures) taken. _____

11. Any female member of the project could arrange (her, their) own accommodations if desired. _____

12. Every player on the men's ball team complained about (his, his or her, their) uniform. _____

Rewrite this sentence to avoid the use of a common-gender pronoun. Show three versions.

Every employee must obtain his parking permit in the personnel office.

13. _____

14. _____

15. _____

Underline any pronoun–antecedent errors in the following sentences. Then write a corrected form in the space provided. If a sentence is correct, write *C*.

1. Either Miss Monahan or Miss Chavez left their machine on Friday. _____

2. The Canadian Medical Association has not yet published it's opinion of the therapy. _____

3. Every clerk, every manager, and every executive will be expected to do their part in making the carpooling program a success. _____

4. Someone left his book on the chair. _____

5. Neither one of the men wanted to have their remarks quoted. _____

6. Every one of the delegates to the women's conference was wearing their name tag. _____

7. The vice-president and the marketing director had already made their reservations. _____

8. Each of the pieces of equipment came with their own software. _____

9. The firm of Higgins, Thomas & Keene is moving their offices to Warner Plaza. _____

10. Every manager expects the employees who report to them to be willing to earn their salaries. _____

11. Neither of the women had her driver's licence in the car. _____

12. We hoped that someone in the office could find their copy of the program. _____

13. Either the first customer or the second one did not pay their bill. _____

14. If everybody will please take their seats, we can get started. _____

15. The faculty agreed to publicize their position on budget cuts. _____

16. We saw that HomeCo reduced their prices on lawn mowers. _____

17. Few of the printers had the sale price marked on it. _____

18. Every one of the male employees immediately agreed to a small cut in their contract. _____

19. Each bridesmaid will pay for their own gown. _____

20. All managers and employees know that she or he must boost productivity. _____

Worksheet 1

In selecting *who* or *whom* to complete the sentences below, follow these five steps:

Example: We do not know (who, whom) the contract names.

1.   Isolate the *who* clause: (*who, whom*) the contract names

2.   Invert to normal subject–verb order: the contract names (*who, whom*)

3.   Substitute pronouns: the contract names *him*/the contract names *her*

4.   Equate: the contract names *whom*

5.   Complete: We do not know *whom* the contract names.

1.   (Who, Whom) will you invite to your party?   _____

2.   Rick Nash is the student (who, whom) the teacher asked to make an oral report.   _____

3.   Do you know (who, whom) will be taking your place?   _____

4.   To (who, whom) did she refer in her letter?   _____

5.   Did Mr. Glade say (who, whom) he wanted to see?   _____

6.   Dr. Truong is a man (who, whom) everyone respects.   _____

7.   (Who, Whom) was president of your organization last year?   _____

8.   (Who, Whom) do you want to work with?   _____

9.   (Who, Whom) has the best chance to be elected?   _____

10.   I know of no one else (who, whom) plays so well.   _____

In choosing *who* or *whom* to complete these sentences, ignore parenthetical phrases such as *I think, we know, you feel,* and *I believe.*

11.   Julie is a person (who, whom) I know will be successful on the job.   _____

12.   The personnel director hired an individual (who, whom) he thought would be the best performer.   _____

13.   Is Freda Hastings the dealer (who, whom) you think I should call?   _____

14.   Major Kirby, (who, whom) I think will be elected, is running in the next election.   _____

15.   (Who, Whom) do you believe will be given the job?   _____

Worksheet 2

In the following sentences, selecting *who, whom, whoever,* or *whomever* first requires isolating the clause within which the pronoun appears. Then, within the clause, determine whether a nominative or objective case pronoun is required.

Example: Give the package to (whoever, whomever) opens the door. (*He* or *she* opens the door = *whoever* opens the door.)

1. A bonus will be given to (whoever, whomever) sells over $100,000. _____

2. Discuss the problem with (whoever, whomever) is in charge of the program. _____

3. We will interview (whoever, whomever) you recommend. _____

4. You may give the tickets to (whoever, whomever) you wish. _____

5. Johnson said to give the parking pass to (whoever, whomever) asked for it. _____

6. The committee members have promised to co-operate with (whoever, whomever) is selected to chair the committee. _____

7. Please call (whoever, whomever) you believe can repair the machine. _____

8. (Whoever, Whomever) is nominated for the position must be approved by the full membership. _____

9. Reservations have been made for (whoever, whomever) requested them in advance. _____

10. (Whoever, Whomever) is chosen to lead the delegation will command attention in the convention. _____

In choosing *who* or *whom* to complete these sentences, be especially alert to pronouns following the linking verbs. Remember that the nominative *who* is required as a subject complement.

Example: Was it (who, whom) I thought it was? (It was *he* = *who*.)

11. (Who, Whom) is the customer who wanted a replacement? _____

12. The visitor who asked for me was (who, whom)? _____

13. Was the new CEO (who, whom) we thought it would be? _____

14. The winner will be (whoever, whomever) is tops in sales. _____

15. For (who, whom) was this new printer ordered? _____

Worksheet 3

In the following sentences, select the correct word.

1. (Who, Whom) did you call for assistance? _____

2. Mr. Lincoln, (who, whom) we thought would never be hired, did well in his first assignment. _____

3. By (who, whom) are you currently employed? _____

4. You should hire (whoever, whomever) you feel has the best qualifications. _____

5. Did the caller say (who, whom) he wanted to see? _____

6. The man (who, whom) I saw yesterday walked by today. _____

7. (Whoever, Whomever) is first on the list will be called next. _____

8. The secretary sent notices to customers (who, whom) she felt should be notified. _____

9. Is the manager (who, whom) we thought it would be? _____

10. The manager praised the clerk (who, whom) worked late. _____

11. She is the one (who, whom) Kevin helped yesterday. _____

12. Many of us thought Jamie Alison was a nice person with (who, whom) to work. _____

13. (Who, Whom) is Stacy often mistaken to be? _____

14. (Who, Whom) did you say to call for reservations? _____

15. Please make an appointment with (whoever, whomever) you consider to be the best internist. _____

16. Here is a list of satisfied customers (who, whom) you may wish to contact. _____

17. (Whoever, Whomever) is suggested by Mr. Arthur must be interviewed. _____

18. The candidate (who, whom) the party supports will win. _____

19. Jas is one on (who, whom) I have come to depend. _____

20. For (who, whom) are these contracts? _____

21. To (who, whom) did you say I should address this letter? _____

22. Do you know (who, whom) their sales representative is? _____

23. Bonus cheques go to (whoever, whomever) increases sales by 25 per cent. _____

24. Rodney Wilson, (who, whom) was our first choice, was appointed. _____

NAME _____

Fill in the answers below with information found in your text.

1. What kind of action verb directs action toward a person or thing?   _____

2. What kind of action verb does not require an object to complete its action?   _____

3. What kind of verb links to the subject words that rename or describe the subject?   _____

4. What do we call the nouns, pronouns, and adjectives that complete the meaning of a sentence by renaming or describing the subject?   _____

In each of the following sentences, indicate whether the underlined verb is transitive (*T*), intransitive (*I*), or linking (*L*). In addition, if the verb is transitive, write its object. If the verb is linking, write its complement. The first two sentences are followed by explanations to assist you.

5. James <u>ran</u> along the dirt path back to his home. (The verb *ran* has no object to complete its meaning. The phrase *along the dirt path* tells where James ran; it does not receive the action of the verb.)   _____

6. It <u>might have been</u> Fran who called yesterday. (The verb phrase ends with the linking verb *been*. The complement is *Fran,* which renames the subject *it*.)   _____

7. Jane <u>filed</u> the address cards of our most recent customers.   _____

8. Customers <u>crowded</u> into the store at the beginning of the sale.   _____

9. Sherry <u>was</u> a lifeguard at the pool last summer.   _____

10. Levi Strauss first <u>sold</u> pants to miners in San Francisco in the 1800s.   _____

11. The bank <u>sent</u> your cancelled cheques last week.   _____

12. Chocolate fudge ice cream <u>tastes</u> better than chocolate mint.   _____

13. Do you think it <u>was</u> he who suggested the improvement?   _____

14. We <u>walked</u> around the shopping mall on our lunch hour.   _____

15. Our company recruiter <u>asks</u> the same questions of every candidate.   _____

16. Many corporations <u>present</u> gifts to important foreign clients.   _____

17. This dictionary <u>is</u> the best on the market for office workers.   _____

18. All employees <u>listened</u> intently as the CEO discussed annual profits.   _____

19. Ellen <u>feels</u> justified in asking for a raise.   _____

20. Customers <u>have</u> high expectations from most advertised products.   _____

Worksheet 1

Transitive verbs that direct action toward an object are in the active voice. Transitive verbs that direct action toward a subject are in the passive voice. Writing that incorporates active voice verbs is more vigorous and more efficient than writing that contains many passive voice verbs. To convert a passive voice verb to the active voice, look for the doer of the action. (Generally the agent of the action is contained in a *by* phrase.) In the active voice the agent becomes the subject.

For each of the following sentences, underline the agent (doer of the action). Write that word in the space provided. Then rewrite the sentence changing the passive voice verb to active voice. Your rewritten version should begin with the word (and its modifiers) that you identified as the agent.

Agent

1. The mail was not picked up by our mail carrier yesterday. _____

_____

_____

2. Our order was shipped last week by Mattel. _____

_____

_____

3. Beginning next week, withdrawals must be authorized by Mrs. Bradford. _____

_____

_____

4. Bill was asked by Mr. Stern to be responsible for turning out the lights at the end of the day. _____

_____

_____

5. Employees who travel a great deal were forced by management to surrender their frequent-flyer awards. _____

_____

_____

Worksheet 2

Some sentences with passive voice verbs do not identify the doer of the action. Before these sentences can be converted, a subject must be provided. Use your imagination to supply subjects, and rewrite the sentences in the spaces provided.

Passive: Interest will be paid on all deposits. (*By whom?* By First Federal.)
Active: First Federal will pay interest on all deposits.

By Whom?

1. The letters must be completed before 5 p.m.   _____

_____

_____

2. Cheques were written on an account with insufficient funds.   _____

_____

_____

3. Our computer was programmed to total account balances.   _____

_____

_____

4. Decisions were made in the courts that affected the daily lives of all Canadians.   _____

_____

_____

5. When home video games were first introduced, it was thought that they were too expensive to sell in mass quantities.   _____

_____

_____

6. Cash discounts are given only when orders are paid immediately with cash.   _____

_____

_____

7. Employees working with computers were warned to change their passwords frequently.   _____

_____

_____

8. For shipments sent in our packaging materials, the value is limited to $500.   _____

_____

LEVEL III

Write the correct answers in the spaces provided.

1. If I (was, were) you, I would complete my degree first. _____

2. The personnel director recommended that Jeff (be, is) hired with the condition that he continue college courses at night. _____

3. If Mr. Greer (was, were) in the office yesterday, he did not sign the cheques. _____

4. One of the shareholders moved that a committee (be, is) constituted to study the problem immediately. _____

5. If the manager were here, he (will, would) sign the work order and we could proceed. _____

6. The civil defence chief suggested that all homes (are, be) stocked with an emergency supply of food and water. _____

7. Joyce said that if she (was, were) the travel agent, she would have planned the trip differently. _____

8. It has been moved and seconded that funds (are, be) allocated for repairs. _____

9. Dr. Washington suggested that the patient (rest, rests) for the next two days. _____

10. Angela wished that she (was, were) able to fly to Vancouver to visit her sister. _____

11. If Mrs. Balfour (was, were) in my position, she would probably do the same thing. _____

12. Hendricks suggested that the cafeteria (is, be) opened earlier so that swing-shift employees could use it. _____

13. Under the circumstances, even if the voter registration drive (was, were) successful, we might lose the election. _____

14. The professor recommended that everyone (meet, meets) in the parking lot before the field trip. _____

15. He acts as though he (was, were) the only employee who wants the weekend off. _____

16. After consulting management, our manager suggested that all employees (are, be) given three-week vacations. _____

17. If the fax machine (was, were) working, you could have the figures immediately. _____

18. If Ron (was, were) at the sales meeting, I missed him. _____

19. Laurie uses credit cards as if she (was, were) an heiress. _____

20. It has been moved and seconded that the meeting (is, be) adjourned. _____

NAME _____

Select the correct verb.

1. Did you tell me that your brother's name (is, was) Martin?   _____

2. The accident (occured, occurred) late last evening.   _____

3. Mr. Anderson said that the car you are driving (is, was) red.   _____

4. Are your sure that her maiden name (is, was) Spitnale?   _____

5. We were taught that an ounce of prevention (is, was) worth a pound of cure.   _____

In the space provided, write the correct form of the verb indicated in parentheses.

Example: Joan (carry) the heavy books every day. (present tense)   _____carries_____

6. Canadian firms (plan) to expand their markets abroad. (present)   _____

7. A Kentucky Fried Chicken franchise (sell) American-style fast food in Japan. (future)   _____

8. The giant Mitsubishi conglomerate (supply) the Colonel with chicken in Japan. (past)   _____

9. The marketing director (study) possible sales sites in foreign countries. (past)   _____

10. We (analyze) such factors as real estate, construction costs, and local attitudes toward fast food. (future)   _____

11. Management (apply) a complex formula to forecast the profitability of the new business. (past)   _____

12. We (consider) the vast differences between the two cultures. (past)   _____

13. A local franchise (vary) the side dishes to accommodate cultural preferences. (present)   _____

14. Kentucky Fried Chicken (insist) on retaining its original recipe in foreign stores. (present)   _____

15. It (appeal) to the average customer in Japan. (future)   _____

16. Doing business in Japan (require) appreciation of rituals and formalities. (present)   _____

17. In East Asia the presentation of business cards (demand) special attention to ceremony. (future)   _____

Worksheet 1

Select the correct verb.

1. The condition of the streets has (became, become) intolerable. _____

2. Ice (froze, freezed) in the pipes last night. _____

3. Before leaving on her vacation, Mrs. Stanton (hid, hide) her silver and other valuables. _____

4. Have you (chose, chosen) a location for the new equipment? _____

5. Three new homes were recently (builded, built) on Fairfax Avenue. _____

6. After he had (drank, drunk) two glasses of milk, he asked for more. _____

7. We must have (forgot, forgotten) the keys. _____

8. Are you sure you have (gave, given) him the correct combination? _____

9. André and the others had (went, gone) on the hike earlier. _____

10. The smaller dog was (bit, bitten) by a larger neighbourhood dog. _____

Underline any errors in the following sentences. Write the correct form in the space provided. Write *C* if the sentence is correct as written. Do not add helping verbs.

Example: After we <u>run</u> out of food, we had to return to camp headquarters. _____*ran*_____

11. We had ate a small snack before we ordered dinner. _____

12. Yesterday the birds sung sweetly. _____

13. Mr. Gazdik was stricken just as he left the witness stand. _____

14. Hundreds of mushrooms sprung up after the rain. _____

15. Many people were shook by the minor earthquake yesterday. _____

16. Tracy had wore her new boots only twice. _____

17. He had wrote a large portion of his report before leaving. _____

18. Their car was stole from its parking place overnight. _____

19. Because of a threatening storm, she should have took a cab. _____

20. If we had went to the movie premier, we would have seen the stars. _____

Worksheet 2

Lie–Lay

Use the chart below to help you select the correct form of *lie* or *lay* in these sentences.

Present	Present Participle	Past	Past Participle
lie (rest)	lying (resting)	lay (rested)	lain (have, has, or had rested)
lay (place)	laying (placing)	laid (placed)	laid (have, has, or had placed)

Example: This afternoon I must (rest) down before dinner.   _____ *lie* _____

1. I am sure that I (placed) the book on the desk yesterday.   _____

2. Andrea angrily told her dog to (rest) down.   _____

3. This month's bills have been (resting) in the drawer for weeks.   _____

4. Bill has (placed) his books on the desk near the entrance.   _____

5. The worker was (placing) concrete blocks on the foundation.   _____

6. This evening I must (rest) down before we leave.   _____

7. Yesterday I (rested) on my bed for an hour before dinner.   _____

8. (Place) the papers in a stack over there.   _____

9. The candy has (rested) on the shelf for several weeks.   _____

10. Let the fabric (rest) there for several hours until it dries.   _____

Now try these sentences to test your skill in using the forms of *lie* and *lay.*

11. Will you be able to (lie, lay) down before dinner?   _____

12. How long have these papers been (laying, lying) here?   _____

13. Please tell your very friendly dog to (lay, lie) down.   _____

14. Will the mason (lay, lie) bricks over the concrete patio?   _____

15. The contract has (laid, lain) in our file for over two months.   _____

16. Yesterday I (laid, lay) down in the afternoon.   _____

17. Mothers complain about clothes that are left (laying, lying) around.   _____

18. Returned books (lie, lay) in a pile at the library until the staff can return them to the stacks.   _____

19. I'm sure I (laid, layed, lied) my keys on this counter.   _____

20. When you were (lying, laying) the groceries down, did you see my keys?   _____

Keep your textbook handy so that you can look up the verb tenses required in the following sentences.

LEVEL III

Example: By June 1 you (employ) here one full year. (future perfect, passive) ___will have been employed___

1. McDonald's (open) many restaurants in foreign countries. (present perfect) _____

2. McDonald's (plan) to start a franchise. (present progressive) _____

3. We (call) for service at least three times before a repairperson arrived. (past perfect) _____

4. She (work) on that project for the past six months. (present perfect) _____

5. We (see) the very first screening of the documentary. (past progressive) _____

6. The mayor (sign) the proclamation at this afternoon's public ceremony. (future progressive) _____

7. The water main (broke) by the bulldozer working on street repairs. (past perfect, passive) _____

8. I (see) two good movies recently. (present perfect) _____

9. We (consider) the installation of a new e-mail system. (present progressive) _____

10. The Queen's message (hear) all across the country. (past progressive, passive) _____

The next sentences review Level II.

11. The alarm had (rang, rung) three times before we responded. _____

12. Yesterday we (drank, drunk) two litres of milk. _____

13. You must (chose, choose) new stationery for the office. _____

14. The car has been (drove, driven) many kilometres. _____

15. Steve claims he (saw, seen) the report yesterday. _____

16. If Chris had (went, gone) earlier, he would have told us. _____

17. Sue said she (seen, saw) an accident on her way to work. _____

18. The tour guide asked if everyone had (ate, eaten). _____

19. Dr. White had (wrote, written) four letters about his new car. _____

20. The price of our shares (raised, rose) again yesterday. _____

NAME _____

Worksheet 1

LEVEL I

For each of the following sentences, cross out any phrase that comes between a verb and its subject. Then select the correct verb and write it in the space provided.

Example: One ~~of the most interesting books on all the lists~~ (is, are) *Becoming a Millionaire at 21.*

                                        is

1. Many Internet sites on the prohibited list (provide, provides) games or amusement that employees may not access. _____

2. The supervisor, together with two technicians, (is, are) working on the faulty circuit. _____

3. This company's supply of raw materials (come, comes) from South America. _____

4. A good many workers in addition to Martha (think, thinks) the work shifts should be rearranged. _____

5. Everyone except you and John (is, are) to repeat the test. _____

6. The table as well as two chairs (was, were) damaged. _____

7. A list with all the customers' names and addresses (is, are) being sent. _____

8. Other equipment, such as our terminals and printers, (need, needs) to be re-evaluated. _____

9. One of the local newspapers (has, have) a bargain box. _____

10. Several copies of the report (is, are) being prepared for distribution. _____

11. The furniture, as well as all the equipment including computers, (is, are) for sale. _____

12. Effects of the disease (is, are) not known immediately. _____

13. Three salespeople, in addition to their district sales manager, (has, have) voiced the same suggestion. _____

14. Profits from his home business (is, are) surprising. _____

15. Every one of the potential businesses that you mention (sounds, sound) good. _____

16. A shipment of 8000 drill sets (was, were) sent to four warehouses. _____

17. Everyone except the evening employees (is, are) coming. _____

18. We learned that two subsidiaries of the corporation (is, are) successful. _____

19. Officials in several levels of government (has, have) to be consulted. _____

20. A letter together with several enclosures (was, were) mailed yesterday. _____

Worksheet 2

For each of the following sentences, underline the subject. Then select the correct verb and write it in the space provided.

Example: Here (is, are) a <u>copy</u> of the findings for your files.   _____is_____

Suggestion: If you know that a subject is singular, temporarily substitute *he, she,* or *it* to help you select the proper verb. If you know that a subject is plural, temporarily substitute *they* for the subject.

1. The flow of industrial goods (travel, travels) through different distribution channels than does the flow of consumer goods.   _____

2. Here (is, are) the newspaper and magazines you ordered.   _____

3. Coleman, Harris & Juarez, Inc., one of the leading management consultant firms, (is, are) able to accept our business.   _____

4. The books on the open shelves of our company's library (is, are) available to all employees.   _____

5. There (appear, appears) to be many significant points omitted from the report.   _____

6. The various stages in the life cycle of a product (is, are) instrumental in determining profits for that product.   _____

7. No one except the Cunninghams (was, were) able to volunteer.   _____

8. A member of the organization of painters and plasterers (is, are) unhappy about the recent settlement.   _____

9. The size and design of its container (is, are) influential in the appeal of a product.   _____

10. Just one governmental unit from the local, provincial, or national levels (is, are) all we need to initiate the project.   _____

11. United Airlines (has, have) been able to increase service while cutting costs.   _____

12. Only two seasons of the year (provide, provides) weather that is suitable for gliding.   _____

13. (Has, Have) the moving van of the Wongs arrived yet?   _____

14. At present the condition of the company's finances (is, are) extremely strong as a result of the recent bond sale.   _____

15. Incoming mail from three flights (is, are) now being sorted.   _____

16. The salary of Marie Ouellette, along with the earnings of several other employees, (has, have) been increased.   _____

17. One of the best designs (appear, appears) to have been submitted by your student.   _____

For each of the following sentences, underline the subject. Then select the correct word and write it in the space provided.

1. Most of the salary compensation to which he referred (is, are) beyond basic pay schedules. _____

2. The Committee on Youth Activities (has, have) enlisted the aid of several well-known athletes. _____

3. Each young man and young woman (deserve, deserves) an opportunity to participate in local athletics. _____

4. Either your company or one of your two competitors (is, are) going to win the government contract. _____

5. All the work for our Special Products Division (is, are) yet to be assigned. _____

6. Either of the two small businesses (is, are) able to secure a loan. _____

7. City council members (was, were) sharply divided along partisan lines. _____

8. Neither the packing list nor the two invoices (mention, mentions) the missing ottoman. _____

9. Every one of your suggestions (merit, merits) consideration. _____

10. Our survey shows that (everyone, every one) of the owner-managed businesses was turning a profit. _____

11. Either Steven or you (is, are) expected to return the call. _____

12. Each of the machines (has, have) capabilities that are suitable for our needs. _____

13. Mrs. Roberts said that most of the credit for our increased sales (belong, belongs) to you. _____

14. First on the program (is, are) the group of Indo-European folk dancers. _____

15. Some of the enthusiasm (is, are) due to the coming holiday. _____

16. After 10 p.m. the staff (has, have) to use the front entrance only. _____

17. (Was, Were) any of the supervisors absent after the holiday? _____

18. Many a young clerk and secretary (has, have) been helped by our in-service training programs. _____

19. We were informed that neither management nor the employees (has, have) special privileges. _____

20. Most of the work that was delivered to us four days ago (is, are) completed. _____

Select the correct word for each sentence.

LEVEL III

1. Reed says that 25 metres of plastic pipe (has, have) been ordered. _____

2. The number of women in the labour force (is, are) steadily increasing. _____

3. Phillip said that he is one of those individuals who (enjoy, enjoys) a real challenge. _____

4. Over two-thirds of the stock issue (was, were) sold immediately after it was released. _____

5. Gerald is the only one of the four applicants who (was, were) prepared to complete the application form during the interview. _____

6. That most offices are closed on weekends (is, are) a factor that totally escaped Mr. Brotherton. _____

7. The majority of the employees (favour, favours) the reorganization plan. _____

8. Telephones (is, are) one item that we must install immediately. _____

9. At least four-fifths of the women in the audience (is, are) willing to participate in the show. _____

10. How could it be I who (am, is) responsible, when I had no knowledge of the agreement until yesterday? _____

11. Let it be recorded that on the second vote the number of members in favour of the proposal (is, are) less than on the first vote. _____

12. Only half of the box of disks (is, are) left in the supply cabinet. _____

13. Are you one of those people who (like, likes) to sleep late? _____

14. I'm sure that it is you who (is, are) next on the list. _____

15. It looks as if 20 inches of extra cord (is, are) what we need. _____

16. Our office manager reports that a number of printers (need, needs) repair. _____

17. At least one-third of the desserts purchased for the party (was, were) uneaten. _____

18. Hiking in Europe and sailing to Scandinavia (is, are) what I plan for my future vacations. _____

19. Dr. Paramanathan is one of our e-mail users who (complain, complains) about the system. _____

20. Whoever submitted an application earliest (has, have) the right to be interviewed first. _____

NAME _____

LEVEL I

A verb form ending in *ing* and used as a noun is a gerund.

>   *Passing* the examination is important. (Gerund used as a subject.)

A noun or pronoun modifying a gerund should be possessive.

>   *Your* passing the examination is important.

Don't confuse verbals acting as nouns with those acting as adjectives.

>   The man *passing* the test received his licence. (*Passing* functions as an adjective describing *man*.)

>   The man's *passing* the test is important. (Verbal noun *passing* functions as the subject of the verb *is*.)

In the following sentences, underline the gerunds and write their modifiers in the space provided. If a sentence contains no gerund, write *None*.

>   **Example:** It is your <u>smoking</u> that disturbs the others. _____*your*_____

1. This job offer is contingent on your passing our physical examination. _____

2. Our office certainly did not approve of his investing in high-risk securities. _____

3. It was Mr. Cortina's gambling that caused him to lose his job. _____

4. The increase in sales is directly related to our placing the staff on a commission basis. _____

Some of the remaining sentences contain gerunds. If any error appears in the modifier, underline the error and write the correct form in the space provided. If the sentence is correct, write *C*.

>   **Example:** Mrs. Feng was instrumental in <u>us</u> acquiring the Collins account. _____*our*_____

5. His recent award is directly related to Mr. Frank receiving a promotion. _____

6. The individual receiving the award could not be present to accept it. _____

7. Do you think you criticizing the manager had anything to do with your transfer? _____

8. We deeply appreciate you calling us to give us this news. _____

9. Is it Mr. Davidson writing that makes the message illegible? _____

10. It appears that us faxing the company is the only logical action to take at this time. _____

11. An employee taking a message must write clearly. _____

12. Mrs. Fackler said that me working overtime was unnecessary this weekend. _____

13. The employees working overtime this week will receive their overtime salary in next month's cheques. _____

A verbal form used as an adjective (to describe or modify nouns and pronouns) is called a participle. When a participle, either as a separate word or as part of a phrase, introduces an independent clause, the participle or its phrase should be followed by a comma. When a phrase containing a participle interrupts the flow of a sentence with non-essential information, it should be set off with commas. The following sentences are punctuated correctly. Underline the participles and participial phrases.

LEVEL II

1. While preparing the report, Isabelle verified all calculations.

2. Surrounded, the enemy troops raised a white flag.

3. Mr. Wilson, seeing his opportunity, brought up the subject of employee fringe benefits.

4. Our new records management system, installed just two months ago, is saving us money.

5. Miss Strawn, rereading the article several times, could not believe her eyes.

6. Opening a new account, Mr. and Mrs. Sams both filled out signature cards.

7. Irritated, the manager raised his voice.

8. A person opening a new account is required to have a valid signature card on file.

For each of the following sentences, add any commas necessary to punctuate verbal forms or phrases. In the space provided, write the comma(s) and preceding words. If a sentence is correct, write C.

Example: Comptroller Duffy, restricted by federal guidelines, revised many budget procedures.   _Duffy, guidelines,_

9. After choosing a model we placed our equipment order.   _____

10. Mr. Dallas consulting his local stockbroker opened an account.   _____

11. Reading a stock market ticker tape requires some training.   _____

12. Displaying security transactions large ticker-tape screens may be found in most brokerage houses.   _____

13. An executive representing a local brokerage firm called me.   _____

14. Terry Sanderson representing a local brokerage firm called me.   _____

15. Acting on her own behalf Miss Delgado placed an order for 100 shares of stock.   _____

From the pairs of sentences that follow, select the sentence that is more logically stated. Write its letter in the space provided.

LEVEL III

1. (a) Hurriedly proofreading the report, three errors were found by Minako.
   (b) Hurriedly proofreading the report, Minako found three errors.   _____

2. (a) To get to the meeting quickly, a shortcut was taken by Mike.
   (b) To get to the meeting quickly, Mike took a shortcut.   _____

3. (a) In investing money in the stock market, one must expect risks.
   (b) In investing money in the stock market, risks must be expected.   _____

4. (a) While looking for Ann's number, the telephone rang and I heard Ann's voice.
   (b) While looking for Ann's number, I answered the phone and heard Ann's voice.   _____

5. (a) After filling out an application, the personnel manager gave me an interview.
   (b) After filling out an application, I was given an interview by the personnel manager.   _____

6. (a) Driving erratically down the street, the driver was stopped by the officer.
   (b) Driving erratically down the street, the officer stopped the driver.   _____

7. (a) To receive a certificate, 30 hours of training must be completed.
   (b) To receive a certificate, a student must complete 30 hours of training.   _____

Check your answers. Using the better versions of the above sentence pairs as models, rewrite the following sentences to make them logical. Add words as necessary, but retain the verbal expressions as sentence openers.

8. Completing the examination in only 20 minutes, a perfect score was earned by Maria.   _____

_____

_____

9. To locate the members' names and addresses, a current directory was used._____

_____

_____

10. Driving through the desert, the highway seemed endless.   _____

_____

11. To stay in touch with customers, telephone contacts were made by sales representatives.   _____

_____

_____

12. Addressing an audience for the first time, my knees shook and my voice wobbled.   _____

_____

NAME _____

Write the correct comparative or superlative form of the adjective shown in parentheses.

LEVEL I

Example: Carmen is (neat) than her sister.   _____neater_____

1. We hope that the new procedures prove to be (effective) than previous procedures. _____

2. Of all the suggestions made, Mr. Bradley's suggestion is the (bad). _____

3. Mrs. Schrillo's daughter is certainly (friendly) than she is. _____

4. Of the three individuals who volunteered, Ted is the one about whom I am (less) certain. _____

5. I don't believe I've ever seen a (beautiful) sunset than this one. _____

6. We make many printers, but the Model SX6 is the (fast). _____

7. No restaurant makes (good) hamburgers than Tommy's. _____

8. Located next to the airport, Malton is probably the (noisy) area in the city. _____

9. Living in the suburbs provides (quiet) surroundings than in the city. _____

10. Of all the letters we have received, this one sounds the (sincere). _____

11. For this job we need the (skilled) employee in the department. _____

12. I'm afraid Andrea has the (less) chance of being selected for the position. _____

13. No one at work is (slow) than Bob. _____

14. DataSource is (likely) to be awarded the contract than CompuPro. _____

15. This is probably the (unusual) request I've ever received. _____

16. Pierre had had (few) citations than any other driver. _____

17. The office is certainly looking (good) today than yesterday. _____

18. Everyone watching the video thought that Yong looked (credible) than any other actor. _____

19. It was the (bad) accident I've ever seen. _____

20. Sharon's report had the (few) errors of all those submitted. _____

If the underlined word or words in the sentences below are correctly expressed, write C. If they are incorrect, write a corrected form in the space provided.

LEVEL II

Example: Because <u>less</u> people made contributions, we failed to reach our goal. ___*fewer*___

1. He played his Internet music so <u>loud</u> that we couldn't work. _____

2. We have decided to increase our <u>point-of-purchase</u> advertising. _____

3. How much <u>further</u> will we proceed in our study of office automation? _____

4. <u>Less</u> opportunities exist in that field; therefore, I'm transferring to computer science. _____

5. The machine is running <u>quieter</u> since we installed a hood. _____

6. Gerald and I felt very <u>badly</u> about Ken's accident. _____

7. The general manager should not become involved in this <u>conflict of interest</u> issue. _____

8. Ms. Edelstein was dressed <u>neatly</u> for the interview. _____

9. At present we're searching for a source of <u>inexpensive, accessible raw</u> materials. _____

10. My organization has selected the <u>later</u> of the two proposals you submitted. _____

11. Kurt said he was sure he did <u>good</u> on his examination. _____

12. Most candidates completed the examinations <u>satisfactory</u>. _____

13. We are conducting the campaign from <u>house-to-house</u>. _____

14. Mrs. Wharton appeared to be looking quite <u>well</u> despite her recent illness. _____

15. You can <u>sure</u> depend on my help whenever you need it. _____

16. The children were playing <u>quiet</u> when the guests arrived. _____

17. We employees are <u>real</u> concerned about the new parking fee. _____

18. You are a preferred <u>charge-account</u> customer at our store. _____

19. We expect a signed contract in the <u>not too distant</u> future. _____

20. Unfortunately, we've had <u>less</u> applications this year than ever before. _____

In the following sentences, select the correct word(s).

LEVEL III

1. Only the (a) two last, (b) last two speakers made relevant comments. _____

2. No one could be more (a) perfect, (b) nearly perfect for the job. _____

3. Don is more stubborn than (a) anyone else, (b) anyone I know. _____

4. He is the most (a) nearly stubborn, (b) stubborn of all my friends. _____

5. (a) Mrs. Karim reports that she has only one volunteer.
   (b) Mrs. Karim only reports that she has one volunteer. _____

6. Applications will be given to the (a) first five, (b) five first job candidates. _____

7. Los Angeles is larger than (a) any other city, (b) any city in Calfornia. _____

8. I recommend this reference manual because it is (a) more nearly complete, (b) more complete than other reference manuals. _____

For each of the following sentences, underline any errors in the use of adjectives and adverbs. Then write the correct form. Mark *C* if the sentence is correct as written.

9. He can be counted on to paint the room as neat as a professional would do the job. _____

10. The uniform you are required to wear certainly fits you good. _____

11. Because we have less work to do this week, we should finish soon. _____

12. The recently-enacted law has received great support. _____

13. Apparently we have picked the worse time of the year to list an office for rent. _____

14. Although it is a honorary position, the chairmanship is important. _____

15. We hadn't hardly reached shelter when it began to rain. _____

16. The Andersons made a round the world tour last year. _____

17. Because of their many kindnesses to us, I feel badly that we cannot reciprocate in some way. _____

18. If less people were involved, the new procedures could have been implemented earlier. _____

19. He only said that he would work hard to complete the contract. _____

20. Festival promoters rented a 840 acre farm in Ulster County. _____

NAME _____

Underline any errors in the following sentences. Then write the correct form. If the sentence is correct as written, write *C*.

1. You should of seen the looks on their faces! _____

2. No one except Mr. Levine and he had access to supplies. _____

3. We plan to attend the lecture too. _____

4. Just between you and I, this engine has never run more smoothly. _____

5. Some of the magazines we borrowed off of Mrs. Kelsey. _____

6. If you will address your inquiry too our Customer Relations Department, you will surely receive a response. _____

7. The personnel director, along with the office manager and she, is planning to improve our hiring procedures. _____

8. You could of done something about the error. _____

9. Because we have to many machines, we are planning a sale. _____

10. All salespeople except Ms. Berk and he were reassigned. _____

11. Did you obtain your copy of the newspaper off him? _____

12. Please get your passes from either Mrs. Bowman or he. _____

13. See if you can get some change for the machine off of her. _____

14. Both the project coordinator and he should have verified the totals before submitting the bid. _____

15. The commission for the sale has to be divided between Ms. Carpenter and he. _____

16. Because to few spaces are available, additional parking must be found on nearby streets. _____

17. If you and he could of come yesterday, we might have been able to help you. _____

18. So that we may better evaluate your application, please supply references too. _____

19. You could of had complimentary tickets if you had called her. _____

20. The marketing manager assigned too many customers to Anwar and I. _____

For each of the following sentences, underline any errors in the use of prepositions. Then write a correct form. Mark *C* if the sentence is correct as written.

LEVEL II

1. We think that beside salary the major issue is working conditions. _____

2. Your support and participation in this new Web program will be greatly appreciated. _____

3. The warranty period was over with two months ago. _____

4. Please come into see me when you are ready for employment. _____

5. Just inside of the office entrance is the receptionist. _____

6. Old Mr. Wiggins left $3 million to be divided between three heirs. _____

7. Will you be able to deliver the goods like you said you would? _____

8. For most of us very few opportunities like this ever arise. _____

9. Exactly what type shingles did you have in mind? _____

10. Some of the trucks were moved in to the garage at dusk. _____

11. When can we accept delivery of the electrical components ordered from Hellman Ltd.? _____

12. Because of your concern and involvement in our community action campaign, we have received thousands of dollars in contributions. _____

13. I know the time and date of our next committee meeting, but I do not know where it is at. _____

14. If you were willing to accept further responsibility, I would assign you the committee chairmanship. _____

15. Joanna could not help from laughing when she saw her e-mail. _____

16. Please hurry up so that we may submit our proposal quickly. _____

17. What style furniture is most functional for the waiting room? _____

18. After going into meet the supervisor, Carla was hired. _____

19. All parking lots opposite to the corporate headquarters will be cleaned. _____

20. Immediately after Kathy graduated high school, she started college. _____

LEVEL III

In the following sentences, select the correct word.

1. Mrs. Shelton found that her voice was rising as she became angrier and angrier (a) at, (b) with the caller. _____

2. We know of no one who is more expert (a) in, (b) with cellphone technology than Dr. France. _____

3. If you concur (a) with, (b) in this action, please notify your representative. _____

4. After corresponding (a) to, (b) with their home office, I was able to clear up the error in my account. _____

5. The houses in that subdivision are identical (a) to, (b) with each other. _____

6. If you (a) plan to attend, (b) plan on attending the summer session, you'd better register immediately. _____

7. A few of the provisions are retroactive (a) for, (b) to January 1. _____

8. Jeff talked (a) to, (b) with his dog in a stern voice. _____

9. Standing (a) on, (b) in line is not my favourite activity. _____

10. She made every effort to reason (a) to, (b) with the unhappy customer. _____

11. Apparently the letters on the screen do not sufficiently contrast (a) with, (b) to the background. _____

12. The courses, facility, and students in this school are certainly different (a) from, (b) than those at other schools. _____

13. Do you dare to disagree (a) to, (b) with him? _____

14. We want a bond paper similar (a) with, (b) to this 20-pound paper. _____

15. I am angry (a) at, (b) with the proposal that we share the equipment. _____

16. Mr. Reese insisted that he was completely independent (a) of, (b) from his campaign contributors. _____

17. He went on working oblivious (a) from, (b) to the surrounding chaos. _____

18. The figures on the balance sheet could not be reconciled (a) to, (b) with the actual account totals. _____

19. A number of individuals agreed (a) to, (b) with the plan. _____

20. If you are desirous (a) about, (b) of taking a June vacation, you had better speak to the office manager soon. _____

NAME _____

LEVEL I

Name four coordinating conjunctions:

1. _____   2. _____

3. _____   4. _____

When coordinating conjunctions connect independent clauses (groups of words that could stand alone as sentences), the conjunctions are preceded by commas. The two independent clauses form a compound sentence.

> COMPOUND SENTENCE: We hope to increase sales in the East, *but* we need additional sales personnel.

Use a comma only if the sentence is compound. When the words preceding or following the coordinating conjunction do not form an independent clause, no comma is used.

> SIMPLE SENTENCE: The bank will include the cheque with your monthly statement *or* will send the cheque to you immediately.

In the following sentences, selected coordinating conjunctions are in italics. Mark (a) or (b) for each sentence.

> a = No punctuation needed   b = Insert a comma before the underlined conjunction.

5. Mr. Green is a specialist in information systems *and* he will be responsible for advising and assisting all our divisions. _____

6. Mr. Green is a specialist in information systems *and* will be responsible for advising and assisting all our divisions. _____

7. This is a sales meeting *but* other topics of interest may also be discussed. _____

8. I have studied the plan you are developing *and* feel that it has real merit. _____

9. We seek the reaction of the council *and* of others who have studied the plan. _____

10. Our executive vice-president will make the presentation in Toronto *or* he will unveil the plan in London. _____

11. I think that the plan will be effective *and* that it will save us time and money. _____

12. This new benefit plan will cost the employee more money *but* the expanded benefits will more than offset the increased costs. _____

13. We are taking over a portion of the fourteenth floor *but* we will not be moving into that area until March. _____

14. Send me your latest price list for all camera equipment *and* place my name on your mailing list for future mailings. _____

15. Our international telephone costs are very high *and* may become even more exorbitant if we don't use e-mail more extensively. _____

1. Name six conjunctive adverbs:

(a) _____ (c) _____ (e) _____

(b) _____ (d) _____ (f) _____

2. When a conjunctive adverb joins independent clauses, what punctuation mark precedes the conjunctive adverb? _____

3. Many words that serve as conjunctive adverbs can also function as parenthetical adverbs. When used parenthetically, adverbs are set off by what punctuation marks? _____

In the following sentences, words acting as conjunctive or parenthetical adverbs are underlined. Add necessary commas and semicolons to punctuate the sentences.

4. The company is planning <u>nevertheless</u> to proceed with its expansion.

5. The price of the tour is contingent upon double occupancy <u>that is</u> two people must share accommodations.

6. This organization <u>on the other hand</u> is quite small in the industry.

7. Our bank is extending its teller service until 6 p.m. <u>hence</u> we are better able to accommodate your banking needs.

8. Stationery and supplies are stored on open shelves <u>however</u> printed forms are kept in filing cabinets.

9. Our group will travel first to New York <u>then</u> we will proceed to Paris.

10. The manager has <u>consequently</u> requested a leave of absence.

11. We have few summer jobs available in our organization <u>consequently</u> we have to tell young people to look elsewhere.

12. When they graduate <u>on the other hand</u> these same young people will find a different employment picture with our organization.

13. We are <u>nevertheless</u> sending you samples of our principal products.

14. Profits were poor last year <u>on the other hand</u> profits this year are much better.

15. Today's job market is very competitive <u>however</u> recent graduates can find jobs if they are well trained and persistent.

16. Job candidates <u>consequently</u> often prepare different résumés for each opening.

17. Most recruiters prefer chronological résumés <u>consequently</u> we advise our graduates to follow the traditional résumé format.

18. Personnel professionals spend little time reading a cover letter <u>hence</u> keep your letter short.

19. A résumé emphasizes what you have done <u>however</u> a cover letter stresses what you can do for an employer.

20. During an employment interview recruiters try to uncover negative information <u>however</u> job candidates try to minimize faults and weaknesses.

LEVEL III

The correlative conjunctions *both ... and, either ... or, neither ... nor,* and *not only ... but (also)* should be used in parallel constructions. That is, the words these conjunctions join should be similarly patterned. Compare the words that *follow* the conjunctions. For example, if a verb follows *either,* a verb should follow *or.* If the active voice is used with *neither,* then the active voice should be used with *nor.* Study the following examples.

Parallel:	Suk Ying is *either* keying the Collins report *or* proofreading it. (Both conjunctions are followed by verbs.)
Not Parallel:	*Either* Suk Ying is keying the Collins report *or* proofreading it. (The subject follows *either* but a verb follows *or.*)
Parallel:	I have *neither* pumped the gas *nor* checked the oil.
Not Parallel:	*Neither* have I pumped the gas, *nor* was the oil checked. (An active voice construction follows *neither* while a passive voice construction follows *nor.*)

In the following, write the letters of the sentences that are constructed in parallel form.

1. (a) We have neither the energy to pursue this litigation, nor do we have the finances. _____
   (b) To pursue this litigation, we have neither the energy nor the finances.

2. (a) You may either write a research report, or a book report can be made. _____
   (b) You may either write a research report or make a book report.

3. (a) He is not only clever but also witty. _____
   (b) Not only is he clever, but he is also witty.

4. (a) The booklet contains both information, and it has an application blank. _____
   (b) The booklet contains both information and an application blank.

Revise the following sentences so that the correlative conjunctions are used in efficient parallel constructions.

5. You can either fax him your response, or you can send him an e-mail message. _____

_____

_____

6. Our goals are both to educate motorists, and also lives may be saved. _____

_____

7. Neither does Tony have a job offer, nor does he even have an interview lined up. _____

_____

_____

8. We knew either that we had to raise more money or begin selling stock. _____

_____

_____

NAME _____

Use *T* or *F* to indicate whether the following statements are true or false.

LEVEL I

1. A phrase is a group of related words without a subject and a verb. _____

2. A clause is a group of related words containing a subject and a verb. _____

3. An independent clause has a subject and a verb and makes sense by itself. _____

4. A dependent clause contains a subject and a verb but depends for its meaning on another clause. _____

5. Words such as *after, if,* and *when* are used preceding independent clauses. _____

Indicate whether the following groups of words are phrases (*P*), independent clauses (*I*), or dependent clauses (*D*). If you indicate that a group of words is an independent clause, capitalize the first word (use ⹀) and place a period at the end of the group of words.

    Example: he stood in a very long line⊙ _____ I

6. in the past year _____

7. although she came to every meeting _____

8. she came to every meeting _____

9. during the period from April to October _____

10. if sales continue to climb as they have for the past four months _____

11. the director asked for additional personnel _____

12. as soon as we can increase our production _____

13. we can increase our production _____

14. because your organization has financial strength _____

15. in the future _____

16. faster telephone service is now available _____

17. in order that we may improve service to our customers _____

18. we will compute your average monthly gas consumption _____

19. when he returns to the office _____

20. fill out and mail the enclosed card _____

21. by next fall _____

22. we are reworking our original plans _____

23. since a good résumé has five essential parts   _____

24. because your old résumé listed your work history and then went on to describe
previous jobs in grim and boring detail disregarding their current relevance   _____

25. A good résumé is a breath of fresh air to an employer   _____

Add necessary commas to the following sentences. If a sentence requires no punctuation, write *C* next to it.

LEVEL II

1. If you follow my suggestions you will help to improve the efficiency of our department.   _____

2. You will if you follow my suggestions help to improve the efficiency of our department.   _____

3. You will help to improve the efficiency of our department if you follow my suggestions.   _____

4. When completed the renovation should make the seventh floor much more attractive.   _____

5. Let's discuss the problem when Mrs. Gardner returns.   _____

6. The motorist who parked his car in the restricted area is in danger of being ticketed.   _____

7. Our latest company safety booklet which was submitted over six weeks ago is finally ready for
distribution.   _____

8. As you may know we have paid dividends regularly for over seventy years.   _____

9. These payments provided there is no interruption in profits should continue for many years
to come.   _____

10. If necessary you may charge this purchase to your credit card.   _____

11. Any employee who wishes to participate may contact our Human Resources Department.   _____

12. James Gilroy who volunteered to head the program will be organizing our campaign.   _____

13. I assure you that you will hear from Ms. Habib as soon as she returns.   _____

14. Before you send in the order may I see the catalogue?   _____

15. May I see the catalogue before you send in the order?   _____

16. The additional premium you were charged which amounted to $175.12 was issued because of
your recent accident.   _____

17. As expected the proposal should help us more clearly define long-term objectives.   _____

18. We will submit the proposal within four working days if that schedule meets with your approval. _____

19. Before we sign any contract we must make site visits and verify all information.   _____

20. In this proposal I have outlined a seven-step purchasing program that meets all the objectives
you indicated were important to you.   _____

LEVEL III

Use the information provided within parentheses to construct dependent clauses for the following sentences. Add subordinators such as *who, which, although,* and *since.*

Example: Dr. Cushman recently moved his practice to Victoria. (Dr. Cushman specializes in pediatrics.)
Dr. Cushman, who specializes in pediatrics, recently moved his practice to Victoria.

1. The original agreement was drawn between Mr. Hightower and Columbia Communications. (The agreement was never properly signed.) _____

_____

_____

2. Atlantic Insurance Company services not only individuals but also communities. (Atlantic Insurance Company is a company of people rather than statistics.) _____

_____

_____

3. Thank you for informing us that your credit card is missing. (This credit has an expiration date of April 30.)

_____

_____

Combine the following clauses into single sentences.

4. (Your account is four months past due.) We will be forced to take legal action. We must hear from you within seven days. _____

_____

_____

5. Sally Horton won an award as this month's outstanding employee. (She works in the Quality Control Department.) Ms. Horton is secretary to the manager in that department. _____

_____

_____

6. Pam Eichorn recently received her business diploma. Now she is looking for a job near Calgary. (Calgary is Pam's hometown.) _____

_____

_____

7. We are sending you four poster advertisements. They will appear in magazines in April. (April marks the beginning of a national campaign featuring our sports clothes.) _____

_____

_____

8. Mr. Girard plans to retire at the end of this year. (Mr. Girard has worked at Rocketwell for 37 years.) After he retires, Mr. Girard plans to devote more time to his orchid collection. _____

_____

_____

NAME _____

Add necessary commas to the following sentences. For each sentence indicate the number of commas that you added. If a sentence is correct, write *C*.

LEVEL I

1. Your present insurance Mr. Isaq does not cover the care and custody of property belonging to others. _____

2. By the way have you updated the fire insurance coverage on your home and its contents? _____

3. When the matter is resolved however we hope to continue our mutually profitable business relationship. _____

4. Debbie is from Calgary Alberta and is now working in Edmonton. _____

5. I believe that John's sister Doreen will be accompanying us. _____

6. The alternative plan on the other hand will not improve employee profit-sharing benefits. _____

7. Send the shipment to Data Products 750 Grant Road Burnaby British Columbia V5E 4B2 as soon as possible. _____

8. It appears sir that an error has been made in your billing. _____

9. You have until Friday April 30 to make complete payment on your past-due account. _____

10. Mr. Franklin T. Molloy who is an advertising executive has been elected chairman of the council. _____

11. Anyone who is interested in applying for the job should see Mrs. Isfahani. _____

12. I hope that your brother Gary will be able to join us. _____

13. You will in addition receive a free brochure outlining our software program. _____

14. Our new line of umbrellas pens and attaché cases will be available soon. _____

15. All things considered the company will be obligated to pay only those expenses directly related to the conference. _____

16. Only Mr. Hudson who is a specialist in information systems is qualified to write that report. _____

17. You can avoid patent trademark and copyright problems by working with a lawyer. _____

18. We are convinced incidentally that our lawyer's fees are most reasonable. _____

19. Mr. Van Alstyne developed the policy Ms. Thorson worked on the budget and Mr. Seibert handled compensation issues. _____

20. With your help our team can meet its goal by December of this year. _____

Add necessary commas to the following sentences. For each sentence indicate the number of commas that you added. If a sentence is correct, write *C*.

LEVEL II

1. There must be a practical permanent solution to our Internet access problems. _____

2. For a period of about six months it will be necessary to reduce all expenditures. _____

3. Melissa Meyer speaking on behalf of all classified employees gave a welcoming address. _____

4. We held a marketing meeting last week and we included representatives from all divisions. _____

5. I am looking forward to getting together with you when you are again in Halifax. _____

6. We do appreciate as I have told you often your continuing efforts to increase our sales. _____

7. Consumer patterns for the past five years are being studied carefully by our marketing experts. _____

8. For some time we have been studying the growth in the number of working women. _____

9. After you have examined my calculations please send the report to Bill Thompson. _____

10. Please send the report to Bill Thompson after you have examined my calculations. _____

11. Would you please after examining my calculations send the report to Bill Thompson. _____

12. Our personnel director is looking for intelligent articulate young people who desire an opportunity to grow with a young company. _____

13. Call me as soon as you return or drop me a card within the next week. _____

14. Beginning on the 15th of June Delco is slashing prices on house paints. _____

15. I mentioned to him at that time that we could not locate the monitor. _____

16. As soon as I can check the inventory we will place an order. _____

17. On October 25 the president and I visited Sandra Goodell who is president of Sandra Goodell Public Relations. _____

18. You may at your convenience submit a report describing when where and how we should proceed. _____

19. To begin the purchase process we will need your request by Thursday June 1 at the latest. _____

20. Any student who has not signed up for a team by this time must see the instructor. _____

Add necessary commas to the following sentences. For each sentence indicate the number of commas that you added. If a sentence is correct, write *C*.

LEVEL III

1. Michael Ferrari Ph.D. has written another book on consumer buying.   _____

2. In 1998 our company expanded its marketing to include the United Kingdom.   _____

3. By 2001 12 of our competitors were also selling in Great Britain.   _____

4. In 1998 our staff numbered 87; in 2001 103.   _____

5. It was a large manila envelope not a white folder in which the contract was placed.   _____

6. Long before our president conducted his own research into marketing trends among youthful consumers. (Tricky!)   _____

7. "We prefer not to include your name" said the auditor "when we publish the list of inactive accounts."   _____

8. You may sign your name at the bottom of this sheet and return it to us as acknowledgment of the enclosed letter.   _____

9. The provisions of your Policy No. 85000611 should be reviewed every five years.   _____

10. Irving Feinstein M.D. will be the speaker at our next meeting.   _____

11. Dr. Feinstein received both an M.D. and a Ph.D. from the University of Toronto.   _____

12. Ever since we have been very careful to count the number of boxes in each shipment.   _____

13. Mrs. Birdsall said "Charges are payable whether or not we installed the instrument."   _____

14. Did you say it was Mr. Chong not Mrs. Lambert who made the sale?   _____

15. Ten computers were sold in January; nine in February.   _____

16. Our figures show that 17365000 separate rental units were occupied in September.   _____

17. "The function of a supervisor" remarked Sid Stern "is to analyze results not to try to control how the job is done."   _____

18. By the way it was the president not the vice-president who ordered the cutback.   _____

19. "A diamond" said the therapist "is a chunk of coal that made good under pressure."   _____

20. Whoever signs signs at her own risk.   _____

NAME _____

Punctuate the following groups of words as single sentences. Add commas and semicolons. Do not add words or periods to create new sentences.

LEVEL I

Example: Come in to see our new branch office‸ meet our friendly tellers and manager.
                                      ;

1. Our principal function is to help management make profits however we can offer advice on personnel problems as well.

2. Delegates came from as far away as Charlottetown Prince Edward Island Mount Pearl Newfoundland and Fort McMurray Alberta.

3. Jerry looked up names Andrea addressed envelopes and Janelle stuffed the envelopes.

4. Thank you for your order it will be filled immediately.

5. Employees often complain about lack of parking space on the other hand little interest was shown in a proposed carpooling program.

6. Computers are remarkable however they are only as accurate as the people who program them.

7. This sale is not open to the general public we are opening the store to preferred customers only.

8. Some of the employees being promoted are Jill Roberts secretary Legal Department Lea Lim clerk Human Resources and Mark Cameron dispatcher Transportation Department.

9. We will be happy to co-operate with you and your lawyers in settling the estate however several matters must be reviewed.

10. In the morning I am free at 10 a.m. in the afternoon I have already scheduled an appointment.

11. The book was recently selected for a national award thus its sales are soaring.

12. Look over our catalogue fill out your order and send it in the enclosed envelope.

13. We hope that we will not have to sell the property but that may be our only option.

14. The film that you requested is now being shown to law students in Ontario it will be shown during June in Manitoba and it will be used during July and August in the provinces of Alberta and British Columbia.

15. We do not sell airline seats we sell customer service.

16. Our convention committee is considering the Hyatt Regency Vancouver British Columbia the Hotel Halifax Halifax Nova Scotia and The Valhalla Inn Toronto Ontario.

17. As requested the committee will meet Thursday May 4 however it is unable to meet Friday May 5.

18. Market research involves the systematic gathering recording and analyzing of data about consumer and product problems.

Add colons, semicolons, or commas to the following sentences. Do not add words or periods. Write *C* after the sentence if it is correct.

1. Three phases of our business operation must be scrutinized purchasing, production, and shipping.

2. The candidates being considered for supervisor are Ned Bingham, Sean Davis, and Anna Donato.

3. Senator Zoubek was quoted as saying "The economy can continue its recovery only if prices are controlled. In addition, inflation must remain below 7 per cent."

4. Following are four dates reserved for counselling. Sign up soon.

   September 28   January 4

   September 30   January 6

5. At this next meeting the board of directors must make a critical decision should the chief executive officer be retained or replaced?

6. This year's seminar has been organized to give delegates an opportunity to exchange ideas, plans, techniques, and goals.

7. The three Cs of credit are the following character, capacity, and capital.

8. Our Boston Massachusetts tour package included visits to these interesting historical sites the House of Seven Gables, Bunker Hill, the Boston Tea Party Ship and Museum, and Paul Revere's home.

9. I recommend that you take at least three courses to develop your language arts skills Business English 31, Business Communication 32, and Report Writing 35.

10. The speaker said that "membership is voluntary" but that contributions would be greatly appreciated.

11. Several of the tax specialists on the panel were concerned with the same thought government spending continues to rise while taxes are being reduced.

12. For each individual the credit bureau keeps the following information on file income, housing status, employment record, and estimate of character.

13. Scholarships will be awarded to Jill Hofer Jeremy Stone and Carolena Garay.

14. Our favourite Alberta resort is noted for fly fishing, mountain biking, tennis, and hiking.

15. Our favourite Alberta resort is noted for the following fly fishing, mountain biking, and hiking.

Add colons, semicolons, dashes, or commas as needed. If a word following a colon should not be capitalized, use a proofreading mark (/) to indicate lower case. Show words to be capitalized with a capitalization mark (_). Mark *C* if a sentence is correct as it stands.

LEVEL III

1. There are three ways to make a credit check namely in person, by mail, or by telephone.

2. Please order the following supplies Cartridges, paper, and staples.

3. Although we are expanding our services we continue to do business according to our original philosophy that is we want to provide you with flexible and professional investment services on a highly personal basis.

4. Word processing specialists are taught this rule Never turn the power off at a workstation unless a document has been stored.

5. Dr. Ruglio's plane departed at 2 15 and should arrive at 6 45.

6. We invited Damon, Kevin, Tony, and Tom but Tony was unable to come.

7. Three of our top executives namely Mr. Gabereau, Mr. Wright, and Mrs. Stranahan are being transferred to the Winnipeg office.

8. On our list of recommended reading is *Investment an Introduction to Analysis*.

9. The library, as you are already aware, needs space for additional books, particularly in the non-fiction field and even greater space will be required within the next five years.

10. Our airline is improving service in several vital areas for example baggage handling, food service, and weather forecasts.

11. Julie Schumacher was hired by a brokerage house and given the title of "registered representative" that is she is able to buy and sell securities.

12. Professor Wilson listed five types of advertising Product, institutional, national, local, and corrective.

13. We considered only one location for our fall convention namely Montreal.

14. Many important questions are yet to be asked concerning our program for instance how can we meet our competitor's low prices on the West Coast?

15. If possible, call him as soon as you return to the office but I doubt that he is still at his desk.

NAME _____

Add any necessary punctuation to the following sentences.

1. Will you please send this c o d shipment as soon as possible

2. You did say the meeting is at 10 a m didn't you

3. Mrs. Kephart is a C A working for Berman Ltd

4. Do you know if Donald L Cullens, Jr. applied for the job

5. Help The door is jammed

6. Will you please Miss Juarez send your card today for your free gift

7. What a day this has been

8. Although most candidates had B A degrees two applicants had M A degrees

9. Our C E O and C F O normally make all budget decisions

10. Cynthia asked if invitations had been sent to Miss Tan Mr Roe and Ms Rich

11. All calls made before 9 a m E S T are billed at a reduced rate

12. Alan Bennett M D and Gina Hawtin Ph D were our keynote speakers

13. Because Susanne typed 80 w p m she was hired as a word processing specialist for C I D A

14. We're expanding marketing efforts in Germany France and the U K

15. The C P U of this computer is made entirely of parts from the U S A

16. The sales representative did say that the price of the car was f o b Windsor didn't he

17. Would you please check Policy Nos 44657001 and 44657002 to see if each includes $50 000 comprehensive coverage

18. Did you say the order was received at 5 p m P S T

19. Wow How much was the lottery prize

20. Do we need postal codes for packages sent to S A

Write *T* (true) or *F* (false) after the following statements.

1. In typewritten or simple word processing–generated material, a dash is formed by typing two successive underscores.   _____

2. Parentheses are often used to enclose explanations, references, and directions.   _____

3. Dashes must be avoided in business writing since they have no legitimate uses. _____

4. Question marks and exclamation points may be used to punctuate parenthetical statements (enclosed within parentheses) within other sentences. _____

5. If a comma falls at the same point where words enclosed by parentheses appear, the comma should follow the final parenthesis. _____

Circle the letter of the correctly punctuated sentence.

6. (a) I am busy on all those dates—oh, perhaps October 18 is free.
  (b) I am busy on all those dates: oh, perhaps October 18 is free.
  (c) I am busy on all those dates, oh, perhaps October 18 is free.

7. (De-emphasize)
  (a) Directions for assembly, see page 15, are quite simple.
  (b) Directions for assembly—see page 15—are quite simple.
  (c) Directions for assembly (see page 15) are quite simple.

8. (a) Eat, sleep, and read: that's what I plan to do on my vacation.
  (b) Eat, sleep, and read—that's what I plan to do on my vacation.
  (c) Eat, sleep, and read, that's what I plan to do on my vacation.

9. (a) If the others can attend (May 21), could you make your report?
  (b) If the others can attend, (May 21) could you make your report?
  (c) If the others can attend (May 21) could you make your report?

10. (Normal emphasis)
  (a) Mrs. Hemphill (who is an excellent manager) may be promoted.
  (b) Mrs. Hemphill, who is an excellent manager, may be promoted.
  (c) Mrs. Hemphill—who is an excellent manager—may be promoted.

11. (a) "What is needed for learning is a humble mind." (Confucius)
  (b) "What is needed for learning is a humble mind.": Confucius
  (c) "What is needed for learning is a humble mind." —Confucius

12. (a) The due date is past (July 1;) however, your payment is welcome.
  (b) The due date is past; (July 1) however, your payment is welcome.
  (c) The due date is past (July 1); however, your payment is welcome.

13. (a) Only one person knows my password—Denise Powell, and I have confidence in her.
  (b) Only one person knows my password (Denise Powell), and I have confidence in her.
  (c) Only one person knows my password; Denise Powell, and I have confidence in her.

14. (Emphasize)
  (a) Our current mortgage rates: see page 10 of the enclosed booklet—are the lowest in years.
  (b) Our current mortgage rates (see page 10 of the enclosed booklet) are the lowest in years.
  (c) Our current mortgage rates—see page 10 of the enclosed booklet—are the lowest in years.

LEVEL III

Write *T* (true) or *F* (false) for each of the following statements.

1. When the exact words of a speaker are repeated, double quotation marks are used to enclose the words.   _____

2. To indicate a quotation within another quotation, single quotation marks (apostrophes on most keyboards) are used.   _____

3. When a word is defined, its definition should be underscored.   _____

4. The titles of books, magazines, newspapers, and other complete works published separately may be underscored or italicized.   _____

5. The titles of chapters of books and magazine articles may be underscored or enclosed in quotation marks.   _____

6. Periods and commas are always placed inside closing quotation marks.   _____

7. Brackets are used when a writer inserts his or her own remarks inside a quotation.   _____

8. The Latin world *sic* may be used to call attention to an error in quoted material.   _____

9. Semicolons and colons are always placed outside closing quotation marks.   _____

10. Question marks and exclamation points may be placed inside or outside closing quotation marks.   _____

Write the letter of the correctly punctuated statement.

11. (a) "Jobs," said Mr. Steele, "will be plentiful this summer."
    (b) "Jobs, said Mr. Steele, will be plentiful this summer."
    (c) "Jobs", said Mr. Steele, "will be plentiful this summer."   _____

12. (a) The manager said, "This memo is clearly marked Confidential."
    (b) The manager said, "This memo is clearly marked 'Confidential'."
    (c) The manager said, "This memo is clealy marked 'Confidential.' "   _____

13. (a) A *chattel* is defined as a "piece of movable property."
    (b) A "chattel" is defined as a *piece of movable property*.
    (c) A "chattel" is defined as a "piece of movable property."   _____

14. (a) Do you know who it was who said, "Forewarned is forearmed."
    (b) Do you know who it was who said, "Forewarned is forearmed"?
    (c) Do you know who it was who said, "Forewarned is forearmed."?   _____

15. (a) "We warn all e-mail users to avoid messages that are 'flaming,'" said the CEO.
    (b) "We warn all e-mail users to avoid messages that are "flaming," said the CEO.
    (c) "We warn all e-mail users to avoid messages that are 'flaming'", said the CEO.   _____

COMPLETE PUNCTUATION REVIEW

Insert all necessary punctuation in the following sentences. Correct any incorrect punctuation. Do not break any sentences into two sentences.

1. Did you see the article entitled Soaring Salaries of C E O s that appeared in The New York Times

2. This years budget costs are much higher than last years, therefore I will approve overtime only on a case by case basis.

3. The board has three new members Dr. Carla Chang Professor Mark Rousso and Robert Price Esq

4. Needless to say all contract bids must be received before 5 pm E S T

5. We formerly depended on fixed-rate not variable rate mortgages.

6. The following representatives have been invited Christine Lenski DataCom Industries, Mark Grant LaserPro Inc., and Ivan Weiner Image Builders.

7. Last year they moved corporate headquarters to Orlando Florida but maintained production facilities in Atlanta Georgia.

8. (Quotation) Did Dr. Tran say We will have no class Friday.

9. Graduation ceremonies for BA candidates are at 11 am, graduation ceremonies for MBA candidates are at 2 pm.

10. As we previously discussed the reorganization will take effect on Monday August 8.

11. We feel however that the cars electrical system should be fully warranted for five years.

12. Will you please send copies of our annual report to Anna Golan and D A Rusterholz?

13. Although he had prepared carefully Mitchell feared that his presentation would bomb.

14. In the event of inclement weather we will close the base and notify the following radio stations CFRB CHIN and CHUM.

15. (Emphasize) Three excellent employees Gregorio Morales, Dawna Capps, and DaVonne Williams will be honoured at a ceremony Friday June 5.

16. (Quotation) "Your attitude not your aptitude will determine your altitude, said Zig Ziglar.

17. By May 15 our goal is to sell 15 cars, by June 15 20 additional cars.

18. The full impact of the C R T C ruling is being studied you will receive information as it becomes available.

19. If the fax comes before 9 pm we can still meet our June 1 deadline.

20. Send the contract to Ms Courtney Worthy Administrative Assistant Globex Industries 7600 Normandale Boulevard Scarborough ON M1K 5G4 as soon as possible.

21. (De-emphasize) Please return the amended budget proposal see page 2 for a summary of the report to the presidents office by Friday March 4.

22. Prospective entrepreneurs were told to read a Success magazine article entitled A Venture Expert's Advice.

23. Larry Zuckerman our former manager now has a similar position with I B M.

24. Employees are concerned primarily with three job issues namely wages, security, and working conditions.

25. As expected this years expenses have been heavy, consequently we may have to freeze hiring for the next six months.

NAME _____

Write the letter of the group of words that is correctly capitalized.

LEVEL I

1. (a) a case of german measles   (b) a case of German measles   _____
2. (a) in the field of marketing   (b) in the field of Marketing   _____
3. (a) the Richardson Building   (b) the Richardson building   _____
4. (a) for all Catholics and Protestants   (b) for all catholics and protestants   _____
5. (a) an order for china and crystal   (b) an order for China and crystal   _____
6. (a) both Master's and Doctor's degrees   (b) both master's and doctor's degrees   _____
7. (a) Welland Canal   (b) Welland canal   _____
8. (a) a class in conversational French   (b) a class in Conversational French   _____
9. (a) a memo from our Edmonton Office   (b) a memo from our Edmonton office   _____
10. (a) a salad with French dressing   (b) a salad with french dressing   _____
11. (a) an irish setter   (b) an Irish setter   _____
12. (a) traffic in the big apple   (b) traffic in the Big Apple   _____
13. (a) the King Edward room   (b) the King Edward Room   _____
14. (a) the Remembrance Day holiday   (b) the Remembrance day holiday   _____
15. (a) the waters of the bay of Fundy   (b) the waters of the Bay of Fundy   _____

Use proofreading marks to capitalize (_) or to show lower-case (/) letters in the following sentences.

16. Bob's Esso Station is located on Speedway Avenue in the next County.

17. Many employees of the Meredith Corporation plan to participate in the Company's profit-sharing plan.

18. Over 3600 supporters attended a gala benefit for the AIDS committee of Toronto at the metro toronto convention centre.

19. During the Winter I will enroll in management, business english, and accounting.

20. The American Association Of Nurses will open its annual meeting in the Pacific ballroom of the Regency hotel in San Francisco.

21. Our persian cat and russian wolfhound cohabit quite peacefully.

22. Last Summer my family and I visited epcot center in orlando, florida.

23. The two companies signed a stipulation of interest agreement last april.

24. Interior designers recommended italian marble for the entry and spanish tiles for the patio.

25. A limousine will take guests from pearson international airport directly to the royal york hotel.

Write the letter of the group of words that is correctly capitalized.

LEVEL II

1. (a) my uncle and my aunt   (b) my Uncle and my Aunt   _____

2. (a) Very sincerely yours,   (b) Very Sincerely Yours,   _____

3. (a) Send it to Vice-President Lee   (b) Send it to vice-president Lee   _____

4. (a) Volume II, Page 37   (b) Volume II, page 37   _____

5. (a) located in northern Saskatchewan   (b) located in Northern Saskatchewan   _____

6. (a) stored in building 44   (b) stored in Building 44   _____

7. (a) within our Human Resouces Department   (b) within our human resouces department   _____

8. (a) the World Wildlife Federation   (b) the world wildlife federation   _____

9. (a) in appendix III   (b) in Appendix III   _____

10. (a) heading South on Highway 5   (b) heading south on Highway 5   _____

11. (a) the book *Love and Will*   (b) the book *Love And Will*   _____

12. (a) both federal and provincial laws   (b) both Federal and Provincial laws   _____

13. (a) Q-tips and kleenexes   (b) Q-tips and Kleenexes   _____

14. (a) orders from Sales Director Ali   (b) orders from sales director Ali   _____

15. (a) a trip to the east coast   (b) a trip to the East Coast   _____

Use proofreading marks to capitalize (_) or to show lower-case letters (/) in the following sentences.

16. We have a directive from Ruth MacVean, Supervisor, Administrative Services Division.

17. The President of our Company gave an address entitled "Leadership: What Effective Managers do and how They do it."

18. Gina Schmidt, customer service representative, attended a convention in the Eastern part of the province.

19. To reach my home, proceed north on highway 10 until you reach exit 7.

20. Major Bruno visited the Capital in an attempt to increase the city's share of Provincial funding.

21. The best article is "Does your training measure up?" by Leslie Brokaw.

22. John placed his ray-ban sunglasses on the formica counter.

23. Sue's Mother and Father were scheduled to leave on flight 37 from gate 6 at phoenix sky harbor international airport.

24. In April our data entry and data verification departments will be merged into the technical services division.

25. Taxicab, Bus, and Limousine service are available from the Airport to the ritz-carlton hotel.

Write the letter of the group of words that is correctly capitalized.

LEVEL III

1. (a) photographs sent from Venus to Earth   (b) photographs sent from Venus to earth   _____

2. (a) a room marked "private"   (b) a room marked "Private"   _____

3. (a) the Egyptian Room and the Sahara Room   (b) the Egyptian room and the Sahara room   _____

4. (a) the finest production on earth   (b) the finest production on Earth   _____

5. (a) from President-Elect Ross   (b) from President-elect Ross   _____

6. (a) When, sir, are you free?   (b) When, Sir, are you free?   _____

7. (a) some asian cultures   (b) some Asian cultures   _____

8. (a) an envelope stamped "confidential"   (b) an envelope stamped "Confidential"   _____

9. (a) our sales director, Joe Hines   (b) our Sales Director, Joe Hines   _____

10. (a) to ex-Premier Davis   (b) to Ex-Premier Davis   _____

Use proofreading marks to capitalize (_) or to show lower-case letters (/) in the following sentences.

11. The cheque that was returned was stamped "Insufficient funds."

12. A paddleboat travelled south down the Mississippi river.

13. No one recognized ex-minister Thurston when he toured the Okanagan valley.

14. We wonder, professor, if the gravity of Mars might be similar to that of earth.

15. The Organization's bylaws state: "On the third Monday of every month the Club's Treasurer will prepare the financial report."

16. The President of our Company has travelled to Pacific Rim Countries to expand foreign markets.

17. The Minister of foreign affairs met with the prime minister to discuss this country's National policy toward african nations.

18. Have you any sheets of bond paper left? only a few.

19. In malaysia we soon learned that muslims do not eat pork and that buddhists and hindus do not eat beef.

20. Although he was known as a "banker's banker," Mr. Wong specialized in Mortgage Financing.

NAME _____

In the space provided, write the letter of the correctly expressed group of words.

1. (a) for 24 employees   (b) for twenty-four employees   _____

2. (a) only 9 pens left   (b) only nine pens left   _____

3. (a) twenty-five dollars   (b) $25   _____

4. (a) on the thirtieth of May   (b) on the 30th of May   _____

5. (a) it cost 20 cents   (b) it cost twenty cents   _____

6. (a) (military style) 5 April 1995   (b) April 5, 1995   _____

7. (a) $2.05, 85¢, and $5.00   (b) $2.05, $.85, and $5   _____

8. (a) we started at 9 a.m.   (b) we started at nine a.m.   _____

9. (a) 2 Highland Avenue   (b) Two Highland Avenue   _____

10. (a) 226 Sixth Street   (b) 226 6th Street   _____

Underline any errors in the expression of numbers in the following sentences. Write the correct forms.

11. 194 representatives were sent the price lists December 1st.   _____

12. 2 companies have moved their corporate offices to twenty-fifth Avenue.   _____

13. Three of the least expensive items were priced at $5.00, $3.29, and 99 cents.   _____

14. If your payment of $100.00 is received before the 2 of the month, you will receive a discount.   _____

15. On February 1st the guidelines for all fifteen departments went into effect.   _____

16. Our office, formerly located at Two Ford Place, is now located at One Kent Avenue.   _____

17. Please call me at 815-611-9292, Ext. Three, before 4 p.m.   _____

18. On May 15th 2 performances will be given: two p.m. and eight p.m.   _____

19. 3 of our employees start at 8:00 a.m., and 5 start at 8:30 a.m.   _____

20. If reservations are made before the fifteenth of the month, the fare will be 204 dollars.   _____

21. Grossmont College offers a fifteen-hour training course that costs one hundred twenty-five dollars.   _____

22. Classes meet Monday through Thursday from 11:45 a.m. until one p.m.   _____

23. The Werners moved from 1762 Milburn Avenue to 140 East 14th Street.   _____

24. Lisa had only $.25 left after she purchased supplies for forty-four dollars.   _____

25. On the third of January and again on the 18th, our machine needed service.   _____

LEVEL II

Write the letter of the correctly expressed group of words.

1. (a) for 82 students in 3 classes   (b) for 82 students in three classes   _____

2. (a) an interest period of ninety days   (b) an interest period of 90 days   _____

3. (a) over the past thirty years   (b) over the past 30 years   _____

4. (a) two 35-day contracts   (b) 2 thirty-five-day contracts   _____

5. (a) he is 45 years old   (b) he is forty-five years old   _____

6. (a) line three   (b) line 3   _____

7. (a) nearly 2.6 billion   (b) nearly 2,600,000,000   _____

8. (a) 26 ten-page pamphlets   (b) twenty-six 10-page pamphlets   _____

9. (a) Lois Lamb, 65, and John   (b) Lois Lamb, sixty-five, and
        Lamb, 66   John Lamb, sixty-six   _____

10. (a) exactly two years and seven months ago (b) exactly 2 years and 7 months ago   _____

Underline any errors in the expression of numbers in the following sentences. Write the corrected forms.

11. We have received 50 reservations over the past 14 days.   _____

12. Please order twenty-five two-ring binders large enough to hold 100 pages each.   _____

13. 33 of the corporations had operating budgets that exceeded one million dollars.   _____

14. Only 10 telephones are available for the forty-eight employees in 5 offices.   _____

15. Chapter eight in Volume two provides at least three references to pumps.   _____

16. About 100 chairs are stored in Room Four, and another eight chairs are in Room 14.   _____

17. We ordered two thirty-inch desks and three chairs.   _____

18. Of the twenty requests we received, five were acted on immediately and three had to
    be tabled.   _____

19. The 2 loans must be repaid within 90 days.   _____

20. When she was 24 years old, Mrs. Ibrahim supervised over 120 employees.   _____

21. Only two of the 125 letters in the mass mailing were undeliverable.   _____

22. Frank Morris, sixty-four, plans to retire in one year.   _____

23. Linda Hannan and her fifteen-person company signed a four million dollar contract.   _____

24. She purchased new equipment to beam fifty-two World Cup games from nine
    locations to forty million avid soccer fans in Pacific Rim countries.   _____

25. The thirty-year mortgage carries an interest rate of eight per cent.   _____

Assume all the following phrases appear in complete sentences. Write the letter of the phrase that is appropriately expressed.

1. (a) the tank holds just 9 gallons   (b) the tank holds just nine gallons   _____

2. (a) only a three per cent gain   (b) only a 3 per cent gain   _____

3. (a) 4/5 of the voters   (b) four-fifths of the voters   _____

4. (a) a 50% markup   (b) a 50 per cent markup   _____

5. (a) a one-half share   (b) a one half share   _____

6. (a) a decline of .5 percent   (b) a decline of 0.5 percent   _____

7. (a) he placed 3rd in the state   (b) he placed third in the state   _____

8. (a) in the nineteenth century   (b) in the 19th century   _____

9. (a) a 5-pound box of candy   (b) a five-pound box of candy   _____

10. (a) at least 95% of the stockholders   (b) at least 95 per cent of the stockholders   _____

Underline any errors in the expression of numbers. Write the corrected form.

11. A No. Ten envelope actually measures four and a half by nine and a half inches.   _____

12. All the drivers in the 33rd Grand Prix finished the race.   _____

13. Tests show that the driver responded in less than seven two hundredths of a second.   _____

14. Great strides in communication technology have been made in the 20th century.   _____

15. The desk top measured thirty and three-fourths inches by sixty and a half inches.   _____

16. Payment must be received by the thirtieth to qualify for a three per cent discount.   _____

17. The office was moved about fifty blocks on the tenth of December.   _____

18. Place the date of a business letter on line 13, which is two inches from the top edge of the paper.   _____

19. The computer weights thirty-one pounds and is seventeen and a half inches wide.   _____

20. Appropriation measures must be passed by a 2/3 majority.   _____

21. She ordered a nine by twelve rug to cover two thirds of the floor.   _____

22. After completing Form Ten Forty, the accountant submitted his bill for 800 dollars.   _____

23. By the year 2,005, women will represent forty-eight per cent of the work force.   _____

24. Nine different airlines carry over one hundred thousand passengers daily.   _____

25. The company car was filled with twenty-five litres of gasoline and one litre of oil.   _____

NAME _____

Revise the following sentences to eliminate wordy phrases and needless repetition.

1. In the event that the shares rise, please sell my holdings. _____

_____

2. In a summary at the end of her report, Catherine Perkins reported increased service costs. _____

_____

3. At this point in time, please sign your name in the space provided for your signature. _____

_____

4. In spite of the fact that a tall fence surrounded the parking lot on all sides, security was a problem.

_____

_____

5. As a rule in the contemporary workplace of today, we generally expect all employees to have good computer skills.

_____

_____

Revise the following sentences to avoid passive voice verbs.

6. Apparently this letter was written by an employee from your office. _____

_____

7. The lights were left on by the last person who used the room. _____

_____

8. We were informed by your electronics division that your prices will be raised. _____

_____

9. Credit cannot be extended because your bills have not been paid. _____

_____

10. A nine-person intervention team was trained by Canada Post. _____

_____

Revise the following sentences to make them more unified.

11. Phil will be taking a two-week vacation, and your work assignment has been changed. _____

_____

12. We need to land some new accounts, and each of us must do what we can to save funds. _____

_____

Revise the following sentences to avoid faulty parallel construction. **LEVEL II**

1. Figures were checked, corrections were made, and we sent the report. _____

_____

2. Mrs. Ralston had to supervise office workers, order supplies, and all salespeople were contacted daily by her.

_____

_____

3. Our administrative assistant should be proficient in keyboarding, computer applications, and writing reports is also required.

_____

_____

4. Consumer activists seek to ensure that products perform as advertised, they are safe, and the physical environment is not harmed.

_____

_____

5. The policy affected all vendors, suppliers, and those involved with consulting. _____

_____

Revise the following sentences to avoid misplaced modifiers.

6. The busy personnel director interviewed only candidates who had excellent computer skills in the morning.

_____

_____

7. You and your staff will have no trouble in any of the 21 countries you visit with exchange rates and red tape.

_____

_____

8. Our placement service is in constant touch with industry in placing our graduates located on the eighteenth floor.

_____

_____

Revise the following sentences to avoid unclear pronoun references. Be particularly careful with the pronouns *this, that, which,* and *it.* Be sure they refer to clear antecedents.

9. Computers and new software helped us reduce personnel costs, increase productivity, and improve quality. That justifies the cost of this investment.

_____

_____

10. An initial registration fee is required of all new members, which is due on the 1st of the month. _____

_____

11. Both data and word processing functions are performed with the new software; therefore, this should reduce overall costs.

_____

_____

Use subordinate conjunctions (such as *if, because, although,* and *since*) or relative pronouns (such as *who, that,* and *which*) to create one sentence from the two ideas shown below.

LEVEL III

Primary Idea	**Secondary Idea**
1. The Time Book Club will send you a free bestseller if you join now.	We have given over $30 million worth of books to our members.
2. Electricity is the most powerful servant ever made available to man.	Electricity can be dangerous if used carelessly.
3. Business executives have difficulty forecasting future sales and profits.	Complex variables such as income, unemployment, and taxes influence buying power.
4. The RCMP has more than 20,000 members and handles problems of national significance.	The force began as the North-West Mounted Police in 1873.

Improve the coherence of the following sentences by adding appropriate transitional expressions (such as *therefore, however, for example,* and other expressions discussed in the chapter).

5. Our bank has experienced unprecedented growth in the past five years. _____, we plan to expand our facilities to meet the growing demand for our services.

6. You could be enjoying the many conveniences that Imperial Credit Card holders enjoy. _____, to do so, you must first complete the enclosed application to receive one of our cards.

7. We are sending you a new Imperial Credit Card Directory. _____, we are sending you a handy form for ordering other directories for your use.

8. Only a few of our salespeople have made reservations for the April 10 seminar. _____, we are sending this reminder of the seminar.

9. Our college savings plan will help you finance more than your children's tuition costs. _____, fees for room, board, books, and other expenses may be included.

Chapter 1 Self-Help Answers

1. c 2. b 3. c 4. a 5. a 6. c 7. a 8. b 9. d 10. b

Chapter 2 Self-Help Answers

Worksheet 1

A. *Answers will vary.* 2. substitutes for a noun he she it
3. shows action or joins words that describe the subject
jumps works is 4. describes nouns or pronouns tall soft
five 5. modifies verbs, adjectives, or other adverbs
hurriedly very nicely 6. joins nouns and pronouns to the
sentence to for at 7. connects words or groups of words
and but or 8. shows strong feelings Wow! Gosh! No!
B. 1. pronoun 2. adv 3. verb 4. noun 5. conj
6. pronoun 7. verb 8. prep 9. adj. 10. noun 11. prep
12. pronoun 13. interj 14. adj 15. noun 16. conj
17. noun 18. verb 19. adj 20. adj 21. noun 22. prep
23. adj 24. noun 25. pronoun 26. verb 27. adverb
28. conj 29. adj 30. adj 31. noun 32. verb 33. adv

Worksheet 2

1. pronoun 2. verb 3. noun 4. prep 5. noun 6. conj
7. adj 8. noun 9. verb 10. adv 11. adv 12. adj 13. interj
14. verb 15. noun 16. adv 17. verb 18. pronoun 19. verb
20. verb 21. adj 22. noun 23. prep 24. noun 25. adj
26. adj 27. adj 28. noun 29. verb 30. conj 31. adj 32 conj
33. adj 34. conj 35. adj 36. noun 37. verb 38. verb
39. pronoun 40. adv 41. prep 42. adj 43. adj 44. adj
45. noun 46. noun 47. adv 48. verb 49. prep 50. adj
51. adj 52. noun 53. prep 54. adj 55. adj 56. adj 57. noun

Chapter 3 Self-Help Answers

Worksheet 1

1. (S) one (V) sold 2. (S) speaker (V) made 3. (S) telephones
(V) rang 4. (S) we (V) will hire 5. (S) team (V) built
6. (S) salespeople (V) received 7. (S) manager (V) will send
8. (S) we (V) released 9. (S) one (V) was given
10. (S) computers (V) require 11. (S) Mr. Thomas (V) is
12. (S) copiers (V) are 13. (S) Mrs. Seymour (V) is
14. (S) Dul Youn Hu (V) has been 15. (S) offices (V) are

Worksheet 2

Answers will vary. 1. applauded 2. fell 3. honked 4. rang
5. ended 6. dropped 7. policy 8. letter 9. letter 10. him
11. the door 12. letters 13. good 14. manager 15. Mr. Jones
16. Mary 17. Mr. Smith 18. John 19–23. *Answers will vary.*

Worksheet 3

1. a 2. c(.) 3. d(?) 4. b(.) 5. e(!) 6. a 7. c(.) 8. b(.) 9. a
10. c 11. b 12. d 13. a 14. a 15. c 16. d 17. b 18. a 19. c
20. b

Chapter 4 Self-Help Answers

LEVEL I

1. giraffes 2. feet 3. switches 4. Bushes 5. boxes
6. languages 7. faxes 8. sandwiches 9. income taxes
10. children 11. successes 12. conveyers 13. dresses
14. branches 15. recommendations 16. women
17. mismatches 18. taxis 19. loaves 20. annexes 21. beliefs
22. Rosses 23. storms 24. ranches 25. Joneses 26. Chavezes
27. letters 28. businesses 29. computers 30. wishes

LEVEL II

1. wharves 2. chiefs of police 3. 1980s 4. Wolfs
5. embargoes 6. cm 7. size 10s 8. amts. 9. faculties
10. by-products 11. entries 12. lookers-on 13. companies
14. knives 15. courts-martial 16. A's 17. Shermans
18. memos 19. valleys 20. zeros 21. lives 22. yrs.
23. Murphys 24. runners-up 25. oz. 26. journeys
27. M.B.A.s 28. wolves 29. Kellys 30. minorities

LEVEL III

1. data 2. theses 3. bacteria 4. Chinese 5. parentheses
6. the Miss Soltans 7. alumnae 8. Messrs. West and Turner
9. genera 10. news 11. pp. 12. ff. 13. larvae 14. Mmes.
Smythe and Webb 15. criteria or criterions 16. are 17. is or
are 18. formulas 19. analyses 20. is

Chapter 5 Self-Help Answers

LEVEL I

Worksheet 1

1. students' books 2. company's office 3. children's toys
4. two months' rent 5. movie star's mansion 6. neighbours'
feelings 7. pilot's landing 8. partners' agreement 9. Jeffrey's
notebook 10. department's strengths 11. two years' time
12. people's customs 13. week's merger 14. bank's credit
15. citizens' savings 16. Canada's mountains 17. employer's
requirements 18. all candidates' résumés 19. government's
policies 20. both lawyers' fees

Worksheet 2

1. year's 2. drivers' 3. carpenter's 4. thief's 5. day's
6. employees' 7. CEO's 8. readers' 9. caller's 10. authors'

11. secretaries' 12. C 13. country's 14. months'
15. organization's 16. vice-president's 17. family's 18. C
19. years' 20. farmer's 21. citizens' 22. year's
23. customer's 24. Children's 25. supervisor's

LEVEL II

1. public's 2. company's 3. stationer's 4. The suggestions of
my uncle's lawyer 5. desk top or top of the desk 6. aunt and
uncle's 7. C 8. last month's 9. C 10. telephone number of
the president's secretary 11. sales 12. beards of my two
brothers-in-law 13. birds' 14. Rick's 15. England's 16. C
17. Anderson and Clark's 18. Angeles 19. architects'
20. last year's 21. C 22. Diana and Graham's 23. reporters'
24. day's day's 25. C

LEVEL III

1. someone else's 2. Ross' or Ross's 3. classes' 4. Saunders'
or Saunders's 5. Rodriguezes' 6. Les' or Les's 7. boss's
8. bosses' 9. Abramoviches 10. actresses' 11. Harris' or
Harris's 12. Burns' or Burns's 13. James' or James's
14. waitress's 15. Garveys' 16. Morrises' 17. Betz' or Betz's
18. Walkers' 19. Simons' or Simons's 20. Jones' or Jones's
21. White's 22. Williamses' 23. Kimballs

Chapter 6 Self-Help Answers

LEVEL I

Worksheet 1

1–14. *Order of answers may vary.* 1–7. I, you, he, she, it, we,
they 8–14. me, you, him, her, it, us, them 15. I 16. she
17. he 18. they 19. she 20. we 21. she 22. he 23. she
24. he 25. I

Worksheet 2

1. me. 2. him 3. them 4. me 5. her 6. him 7. her 8. them
9. us 10. me 11. it's 12. theirs 13. its 14. There's 15. hers
16. it's 17. yours 18. Whose 19. ours 20. You're

LEVEL II

1. them 2. I 3. her 4. We 5. me 6. me 7. her 8. he 9. him
10. I 11. himself 12. her 13. her 14. she 15. me 16. us
17. she 18. him 19. I 20. me 21. me 22. She and I 23. her

LEVEL III

Worksheet 1

1. she 2. he 3. they 4. she 5. him 6. she 7. she 8. he
9. me 10. they 11. he 12. him 13. her 14. I 15. she
16. she 17. I 18. him 19. I 20. she 21. he 22. him 23. she
24. she 25. he

Worksheet 2

1. he 2. me 3. its 4. she 5. us 6. there's 7. he 8. I 9. me
10. her 11. us 12. you're 13. her 14. him 15. yours 16. me
17. he 18. its 19. him or me 20. There's 21. him 22. me
23. I 24. their 25. she 26. I 27. me 28. us 29. she
30. there's

Chapter 7 Self-Help Answers

LEVEL I

1. her 2. his or her 3. his or her 4. their 5. their 6. he or
she 7. his or her lunch 8. him or her 9. her 10. their
pictures 11. her 12. his 13. Every employee must obtain his
or her … 14. Every employee must obtain a parking permit
… 15. All employees must obtain their parking permits …

LEVEL II

1. use *her* instead of *their* 2. *its* instead of *it's* 3. *his or her*
instead of *their* 4. *his or her* for *his* 5. *his* for *their* 6. *her* for
their 7. C 8. *its* for *their* 9. *its* for *their* 10. *him or her* for
them 11. C 12. *his or her* for *their* 13. *his or her* for *their*
14. *his or her seat* for *their seats*. 15. *its* for *their* 16. *its* for
their 17. *them* for *it* 18. *his* for *their* 19. *her* for *their*
20. *they* for *she or he*

LEVEL III

Worksheet 1

1. Whom 2. whom 3. who 4. whom 5. whom 6. whom
7. Who 8. Whom 9. Who 10. who 11. who 12. who
13. whom 14. who 15. Who

Worksheet 2

1. whoever 2. whoever 3. whomever 4. whomever
5. whoever 6. whoever 7. whoever 8. Whoever 9. whoever
10. Whoever 11. Who 12. who 13. who 14. whoever
15. whom

Worksheet 3

1. Whom 2. who 3. whom 4. whoever 5. whom 6. whom
7. Whoever 8. who 9. who 10. who 11. whom 12. whom
13. Who 14. Whom 15. whomever 16. whom
17. Whoever 18. whom 19. whom 20. whom 21. whom
22. who 23. whoever 24. who

Chapter 8 Self-Help Answers

LEVEL I

1. transitive 2. intransitive 3. linking 4. complements 5. I
6. L—Fran 7. T—cards 8. I 9. L—lifeguard 10. T—pants
11. T—cheques 12. L—better 13. L—he 14. I
15. T—questions 16. T—gifts 17. L—best 18. I
19. L—justified 20. T—expectations

LEVEL II

Worksheet 1

1. <u>mail carrier</u> (Our mail carrier did not pick up the mail yesterday.)
2. <u>Mattel</u> (Mattel shipped our order last week.)
3. <u>Mrs. Bradford</u> (Mrs. Bradford must authorize withdrawals ...)
4. <u>Mr. Stern</u> (Mr. Stern asked Bill to be responsible ...)
5. <u>management</u> (Management forced employees who...)

Worksheet 2

Revised sentences will vary. 1. Clerks must complete ... 2. Mr. Smith wrote cheques ... 3. John programmed ... 4. Judges made decisions ... 5. When manufacturers first introduced ... 6. We give cash ... 7. Management warned employees ... 8. We limit the value ...

LEVEL III

1. were 2. be 3. was 4. be 5. would 6. be 7. were 8. be 9. rest 10. were 11. were 12. be 13. were 14. meet 15. were 16. be 17. were 18. was 19. were 20. be

Chapter 9 Self-Help Answers

LEVEL I

1. is 2. occurred 3. is 4. is 5. is 6. plan 7. will sell 8. supplied 9. studied 10. will analyze 11. applied 12. considered 13. varies 14. insists 15. will appeal 16. requires 17. will demand

LEVEL II

Worksheet 1

1. become 2. froze 3. hid 4. chosen 5. built 6. drunk 7. forgotten or forgot 8. given 9. gone 10. bitten 11. eaten 12. sang 13. C or struck (meaning?) 14. sprang 15. shaken 16. worn 17. written 18. stolen 19. taken 20. gone

Worksheet 2

1. laid 2. lie 3. lying 4. laid 5. laying 6. lie 7. lay 8. lay 9. lain 10. lie 11. lie 12. lying 13. lie 14. lay 15. lain 16. lay 17. lying 18. lie 19. laid 20. laying

LEVEL III

1. has opened 2. is planning 3. had called 4. has worked 5. were seeing 6. will be signing 7. had been broken 8. have seen 9. are considering 10. was being heard 11. rung 12. drank 13. choose 14. driven 15. saw 16. gone 17. saw 18. eaten 19. written 20. rose

Chapter 10 Self-Help Answers

LEVEL I

Worksheet 1

1. provide 2. is 3. comes 4. think 5. is 6. was 7. is 8. needs 9. has 10. are 11. is 12. are 13. have 14. are 15. sounds 16. was 17. is 18. are 19. have 20. was

Worksheet 2

1. travels 2. are 3. is 4. are 5. appear 6. are 7. was 8. is 9. are 10. is 11. has 12. provide 13. Has 14. is 15. is 16. has 17. appears

LEVEL II

1. is 2. has 3. deserves 4. is 5. is 6. is 7. were 8. mention 9. merits 10. every one 11. are 12. has 13. belongs 14. is 15. is 16. has 17. Were 18. has 19. have 20. is

LEVEL III

1. has 2. is 3. enjoy 4. was 5. was 6. is 7. favour 8. are 9. are 10. am 11. is 12. is 13. like 14. are 15. is 16. need 17. were 18. are 19. complain 20. has

Chapter 11 Self-Help Answers

LEVEL I

1. your 2. his 3. Mr. Cortina's 4. our 5. Mr. Frank's 6. C 7. your criticizing 8. your calling 9. Mr. Davidson's 10. our faxing 11. C 12. my working 13. C

LEVEL II

1. While preparing the report 2. Surrounded 3. seeing his opportunity 4. installed just two months ago 5. rereading the article several times 6. Opening a new account 7. Irritated 8. opening a new account 9. model, 10. Dallas, stockbroker, 11. C 12. transactions, 13. C 14. Sanderson, firm, 15. behalf,

LEVEL III

1. b 2. b 3. a 4. b 5. b 6. a 7. b
8. Completing the examination in only 20 minutes, Maria earned a perfect score.
9. To locate the members' names and addresses, we used a current directory.
10. Driving through the desert, we thought the highway seemed endless.
11. To stay in touch with customers, sales representatives made telephone contacts.
12. Addressing an audience for the first time, I felt my knees shake and my voice wobble.

Chapter 12 Self-Help Answers

LEVEL I

1. more effective 2. worst 3. friendlier 4. least certain
5. more beautiful 6. fastest 7. better 8. noisiest 9. quieter
10. most sincere 11. most skilled 12. least 13. slower
14. more likely 15. most unusual 16. fewer 17. better
18. more credible 19. worst 20. least

LEVEL II

1. loudly 2. C 3. C 4. Fewer 5. more quietly 6. bad
7. conflict-of-interest 8. C 9. C 10. latter 11. well
12. satisfactorily 13. house to house 14. C 15. surely
16. quietly 17. really 18. charge account 19. not-too-
distant 20. fewer

LEVEL III

1. b 2. b 3. a 4. b 5. a 6. a 7. a 8. a 9. neatly 10. well (for
good) 11. C 12. recently enacted 13. worst (for *worse*)
14. an (for *a*) 15. had hardly 16. round-the-world 17. bad
(for *badly*) 18. fewer people 19. said only 20. an 840-acre

Chapter 13 Self-Help Answers

LEVEL I

1. should have (for *should of*) 2. him (for *he*) 3. C 4. me (for
I) 5. from (for *off of*) 6. to (for *too*) 7. her (for *she*) 8. could
have (for *could of*) 9. too (for *to*) 10. him (for *he*) 11. from
(for *off*) 12. him (for *he*) 13. from (for *off of*) 14. C 15. him
(for *he*) 16. too (for *to*) 17. could have (for *could of*) 18. C
19. could have (for *could of*) 20. me (for *I*)

LEVEL II

1. besides (for *beside*) 2. support *of* 3. omit *with* 4. in to (for
into) 5. omit *of* 6. among (for *between*) 7. as (for *like*) 8. C
9. type *of* shingles 10. into (for *in to*) 11. C 12. concern *for*
13. omit *at* 14. C 15. omit *from* 16. omit *up* 17. style *of*
18. going *in to* meet 19. omit *to* 20. graduated *from*

LEVEL III

1. b 2. a 3. b 4. b 5. b 6. a 7. b 8. a 9. b 10. b 11. a 12. a
13. b 14. b 15. a 16. a 17. b 18. b 19. a 20. b

Chapter 14 Self-Help Answers

LEVEL I

The order of Answers 1–4 may vary. 1. and 2. or 3. nor 4. but
(also acceptable for 1–4: for, so, yet) 5. b 6. a 7. b 8. a 9. a
10. b 11. a 12. b 13. b 14. b 15. a

LEVEL II

Answers may vary. 1. therefore, however, consequently,

moreover, then, hence, thus 2. semicolon 3. commas
4. planning, nevertheless, 5. occupancy; that is,
6. organization, on the other hand, 7. 6 p.m.; hence
8. shelves; however, 9. York; then 10. has, consequently,
11. organization; consequently, 12. graduate, on the other
hand, 13. are, nevertheless, 14. year; on the other hand,
15. competitive; however, 16. candidates, consequently,
17. résumés; consequently, 18. letter; hence 19. done;
however, 20. information; however,

LEVEL III

1. b 2. b 3. a 4. b
5. You can either fax him your response or send him an
   e-mail message.
6. Our goals are both to educate motorists and also to save
   lives.
7. Tony has neither a job offer nor even an interview lined
   up.
8. We knew that we had to either raise more money or
   begin selling stock.

Chapter 15 Self-Help Answers

LEVEL I

1. T 2. T 3. T 4. T 5. F 6. P 7. D 8. I 9. P 10. D 11. I
12. D 13. I 14. D 15. P 16. I 17. D 18. I 19. D 20. I 21. P
22. I 23. D 24. D 25. I

LEVEL II

1. suggestions, 2. will, if you follow my suggestions, 3. C
4. completed, 5. C 6. C 7. booklet, which was submitted
over six weeks ago, 8. know, 9. payments, provided there is
no interruption in profits, 10. necessary, 11. C 12. Gilroy,
who volunteered to head the program, 13. C 14. order,
15. C 16. charged, which amounted to $176.12,
17. expected, 18. days, 19. contract, 20. C

LEVEL III

Answers may vary.
1. Although never properly signed, the original agreement
   was drawn between Mr. Hightower and Columbia
   Communications.
2. Atlantic Insurance Company, which is a company of
   people rather than statistics, serves not only individuals
   but also communities.
3. Thank you for informing us that your credit card, which
   has an expiration date of April 30, is missing.
4. Because your account is four months past due, we will
   be forced to take legal action unless we hear from you
   within seven days.
5. Sally Horton, who works as secretary to the manager in
   the Quality Control Department, won an award as this
   month's outstanding employee.

6. Pam Eichorn recently received her business diploma, and now she is looking for a job near Calgary, which is her hometown.

7. We are sending you four poster advertisements that will appear in magazines in April, which marks the beginning of a national campaign featuring our sports clothes.

8. Mr. Girard, who has worked at Rocketwell for 37 years, plans to retire at the end of this year and devote more time to his orchid collection.

Chapter 16 Self-Help Answers

LEVEL I

1. (2) insurance, Mr. Isaq, 2. (1) By the way, 3. (2) resolved, however, 4. (2) Calgary, Alberta, 5. C 6. (2) plan, on the other hand, 7. (4) Data Products, 750 Grant Road, Burnaby, British Columbia V5E 4B2, 8. (2) appears, sir, 9. (2) Friday, April 30, 10. (2) Molloy, who is an advertising executive, 11. C 12. C 13. (2) will, in addition, 14. (2) umbrellas, pens, 15. (1) considered, 16. (2) Hudson, who is a specialist in information systems, 17. (2) patent, trademark, 18. (2) convinced, incidentally, 19. (2) policy, budget, 20. C

LEVEL II

1. (1) practical, 2. (1) months, 3. (2) Meyer, employees, 4. (1) week, 5. C 6. (2) appreciate, often, 7. C 8. C 9. (1) calculations, 10. C 11. (2) please, calculations, 12. (1) intelligent, 13. (1) return, 14. (1) June, 15. C 16. (1) inventory, 17. (1) Goodell, 18. (2) when, where, 19. (3) process, Thursday, June 1, 20. C

LEVEL III

1. (2) Ferrari, Ph.D., 2. C 3. (1) 2001, 4. (1) 2001, 5. (2) envelope, not a white folder, 6. (1) before, 7. (2) name," said the auditor, 8. C 9. C 10. (2) Feinstein, M.D., 11. C 12. (1) since, 13. (1) said, 14. (2) Chong, not Mrs. Lambert, 15. (1) nine, 16. (2) 17,365,000 (or 17 365 000) 17. (3) supervisor," remarked Sid Stern, results, 18. (3) way, president, vice-president, 19. (2) diamond," said the therapist, 20 (1) signs, signs

Chapter 17 Self-Help Answers

LEVEL I

1. profits; however, 2. Charlottetown, Prince Edward Island; Mount Pearl, Newfoundland; and Fort McMurray, 3. names, envelopes, 4. order; 5. space; on the other hand, 6. remarkable; however, 7. public; 8. Roberts, secretary, Legal Department; Lea Lim, clerk, Human Resources; and Mark Cameron, dispatcher, 9. estate; however, 10. 10 a.m.; 11. award; 12. catalogue, order, 13. property, 14. Ontario; Manitoba; 15. seats; 16. Hyatt Regency, Vancouver, British

Columbia; the Hotel Halifax, Halifax, Nova Scotia; and the Valhalla Inn, Toronto, 17. requested, Thursday, May 4; however, Friday, 18. gathering, recording,

LEVEL II

1. scrutinized: 2. C 3. saying: 4. C 5. decision: 6. C 7. following: 8. Boston, Massachusetts, sites: 9. skills: 10. C 11. thought: 12. file: 13. Hofer, Stone, 14. C 15. following:

LEVEL III

1. check; namely, 2. supplies: cartridges, 3. services, philosophy; that is, 4. rule: 5. 2:15 6:45 6. Tom; 7. executives—namely, Mr. Gabereau, Mr. Wright, and Mrs. Stranahan— 8. *Investment: An* 9. field; 10. areas; for example, 11. representative"; that is, 12. advertising: product, 13. convention, namely, 14. program; for instance, 15. office;

Chapter 18 Self-Help Answers

LEVEL I

1. c.o.d. possible. 2. 10 a.m., didn't you? 3. C.A. Ltd. 4. Donald L. Cullens, Jr., job? 5. Help! jammed! 6. please, Miss Juarez, gift. 7. been! 8. B.A. degrees, M.A. degrees. 9. CEO CFO decisions. 10. Tan, Mr. Roe, and Ms. Rich. 11. 9 a.m. EST rate. 12. Bennett, M.D., Hawtin, Ph.D., speakers. 13. 80 wpm, CIDA. 14. Germany, France, and the U.K. 15. CPU U.S.A. 16. f.o.b. Windsor, didn't he? 17. Nos. $50,000 coverage. 18. 5 p.m. PST? 19. Wow! prize? 20. S.A.?

LEVEL II

1. F (use two hyphens) 2. T 3. F 4. T 5. T 6. a 7. c 8. b 9. a 10. b 11. c 12. c 13. b 14. c

LEVEL III

1. T 2. T 3. F 4. T 5. F 6. T 7. T 8. T 9. T 10. T 11. a 12. c 13. a 14. b 15. a

Chapter 18 Review

1. "Soaring Salaries of CEOs" The New York Times? 2. This year's last year's; therefore, case-by-case 3. members: Dr. Carla Chang, Professor Mark Rousso, and Robert Price, Esq. 4. say, 5 p.m. EST. 5. fixed-rate , not variable-rate, 6. invited: Christine Lenski, DataCom Industries; Mark Grant, LaserPro Inc.; and Ivan Weiner, 7. Orlando, Florida, Atlanta, 8. say, "We Friday"? 9. B.A. 11 a.m.; M.B.A. 2 p.m. 10. discussed, Monday, August 8. 11. feel, however, car's 12. D.A. Rusterholz. 13. carefully, "bomb." 14. weather, stations: CFRB, CHIN, and CHUM. 15. employees—Gregorio ... Williams—Friday, June 5. 16. attitude, aptitude, altitude," 17. cars; by June 15, 18. CRTC studied; 19. 9 p.m., 20. Ms.

Courtney Worthy, Administrative Assistant, Globex Industries, 7600 Normandale Boulevard, Scarborough, ON M1K 5G4, 21. (see page 2 for a summary of the report) to the president's Friday, 22. Success "A Venture Expert's Advice." 23. Zuckerman, our former manager, IBM. 24. issues; namely, 25. expected, this year's heavy; consequently,

Chapter 19 Self-Help Answers

LEVEL I

1. b 2. a 3. a 4. a 5. a 6. b 7. a 8. a 9. b 10. a 11. b 12. b 13. b 14. a 15. b 16. station county 17. company's 18. Committee Metro Toronto Convention Centre 19. winter English 20. of Ballroom Hotel 21. Persian Russian 22. summer Epcot Center Orlando, Florida 23. Stipulation of Interest Agreement April 24. Italian Spanish 25. Pearson International Airport Royal York Hotel

LEVEL II

1. a 2. a 3. a 4. b 5. a 6. b 7. a 8. a 9. b 10. b 11. a 12. a 13. b 14. a 15. b 16. supervisor 17. president company Do How Do It 18. eastern 19. Highway Exit 20. capital provincial 21. "Does Your Training Measure Up?" 22. Ray-Ban Formica 23. mother and father Flight 37 Gate 6 Phoenix Sky Harbor International Airport 24. Data Entry and Data Verification Departments Technical Services Division 25. bus limousine airport Ritz-Carlton Hotel

LEVEL III

1. a 2. b 3. a 4. a 5. b 6. a 7. b 8. b 9. a 10. a 11. Funds 12. River 13. Minister Valley 14. Professor Earth 15. organization's 16. president company countries 17. Foreign Affairs Prime Minister national African 18. Only 19. Malaysia Muslims Buddhists Hindus 20. mortgage financing

Chapter 20 Self-Help Answers

LEVEL I

1. a 2. b 3. b 4. b 5. a 6. a 7. b 8. a 9. a 10. a 11. A total of 194 December 1 12. Two 25th Avenue 13. $5 $.99 14. $100 2nd 15. February 1 15 departments 16. 2 Ford Place 17. (815) 611-9292, Ext. 3 18. May 15 two 2 p.m. 8 p.m. 19. Three 8 a.m. five 20. 15th $204 21. 15-hour $125 22. 1 p.m. 23. 14 24. 25 cents $44 25. 3rd

LEVEL II

1. b 2. b (preferred) 3. a 4. a 5. b 6. b 7. a 8. a 9. a 10. b 11. fourteen 12. 25 two-ring 13. Thirty-three $1 million 14. ten 48 five 15. Chapter 8 Volume 2 16. Room 4 8 chairs 17. 30-inch 18. 20 requests 5 3 19. two loans 20. twenty-four years 21. Only 2 22. 64 23. 15-person

$3 million 24. 52 40 million 25. thirty-year or 30-year 8 percent

LEVEL III

1. a 2. b 3. b 4. b 5. a 6. b 7. b 8. a 9. a 10. b 11. No. 10 4 1/2 by 9 1/2 inches 12. thirty-third 13. 7/200 14. twentieth 15. 30 3/4 inches by 60 1/2 inches 16. 30th 3 percent 17. 50 blocks 10th 18. 2 inches 19. 31 pounds 17 1/2 inches 20. two-thirds 21. 9 by 12 two-thirds 22. Form 1040 $800 23. 2005 48 percent 24. 100,000 or 100 000 25. 25 litres 1 litre

Chapter 21 Self-Help Answers

LEVEL I

Answers will vary.
1. If the shares rise, please sell my holdings.
2. In her summary, Catherine Perkins reported increased service costs.
3. Now please sign your name in the space provided.
4. Although a tall fence surrounded the parking lot, security was a problem.
5. In today's workplace we generally expect all employees to have good computer skills.
6. An employee from your office apparently wrote this letter.
7. The last person who used the room left the lights on.
8. Your electronics division informed us that you are going to raise your prices.
9. We cannot extend credit because you have not paid your bills.
10. Canada Post trained a nine-person intervention team.
11. Because Phil will be taking a two-week vacation, your work assignment has been changed.
12. Until we land some new accounts, each of us must do what we can to save funds.

LEVEL II

Answers will vary.
1. We checked figures, made corrections, and sent the report.
2. Mrs. Ralston had to supervise office workers, order supplies, and contact all salespeople daily.
3. Our administrative assistant should be proficient in keyboarding, computer applications, and report writing.
4. Consumer activists seek to ensure that products perform as advertised, are safe, and do not harm the environment.
5. The policy affected all vendors, suppliers, and consultants.
6. In the morning the busy personnel director interviewed only candidates ...
7. You and your staff will have no trouble with exchange rates and red tape in any of the ...

8. Our placement service, located on the eighteenth floor, is in constant touch with industry …

9. Computers and new software helped us reduce personnel costs, increase productivity, and improve quality. These results justify the cost of this investment.

10. An initial registration fee is required of all new members. That fee is due on the 1st of the month.

11. Both data and word processing functions are performed with the new software; therefore, this software should reduce overall costs.

LEVEL III

Answers will vary.

1. The Time Book Club, which has given over $30 million worth of books to members, will send you a free bestseller if you join now.

2. Although dangerous if used carelessly, electricity is the most powerful servant ever made available to man.

3. Because complex variables such as income, unemployment, and taxes influence buying power, business executives have difficulty forecasting future sales and profits.

4. The RCMP, which began as the North-West Mounted Police in 1873, has more than 20,000 members and handles problems of national significance.

5. Therefore (*or* Consequently) 6. However 7. In addition (*or* Moreover) 8. Consequently (*or* Therefore) 9. For example (*or* In fact)

Unit 1 Review Chapters 1-3

1. F   2. T   3. F   4. F   5. T   6. F   7. T   8. F   9. T   10. T
11. b   12. c   13. d   14. b   15. a   16. c   17. b   18. a   19. b
20. a   21. c   22. c   23. a   24. b   25. d   26. c   27. a   28. e
29. b   30. c   31. a   32. d   33. e   34. b   35. a   36. c   37. a
38. b   39. b   40. c

Unit 2 Review Chapters 4-7

LEVEL I

1. a   2. b   3. b   4. c   5. a   6. b   7. b   8. a   9. b   10. d
11. c

LEVEL II

12. a   13. c   14. b   15. a   16. b   17. a   18. b   19. a   20. b
21. c   22. b

LEVEL III

23. b   24. b   25. d   26. b   27. a or b   28. a   29. b   30. b
31. a   32. a   33. b   34. b   35. b

Hotline

36. b   37. a   38. a   39. b   40. b

Unit 3 Review Chapters 8-11

LEVEL I

1. c   2. c   3. a   4. b   5. a   6. a   7. b   8. a   9. a   10. a
11. b

LEVEL II

12. a   13. b   14. b   15. b   16. b   17. b   18. b   19. 2
20. 0   21. 1

LEVEL III

22. b   23. a   24. a   25. b   26. b   27. a   28. b   29. b
30. b   31. b

Hotline

32. a   33. b   34. a   35. b   36. b

Unit 4 Review Chapters 12-15

LEVEL I

1. a   2. b   3. b   4. a   5. b   6. a   7. b   8. c   9. e   10. a
11. e

LEVEL II

12. a   13. a   14. b   15. a   16. a   17. a   18. d   19. c   20. e
21. a   22. c

LEVEL III

23. a   24. b   25. a   26. b   27. a   28. c   29. e   30. d

Hotline

31. b   32. b   33. a   34. b   35. a

Unit 5 Review Chapters 16-18

LEVEL I

1. circumstances, Greenwood   2. C   3. financing, delivery,
4. C   5. feels, hand,   6. C   7. c   8. b   9. a   10. a

LEVEL II

11. b   12. a   13. c   14. a   15. a   16. b   17. a   18. b   19. a
20. c

LEVEL III

21. c   22. a   23. b   24. b   25. b   26. c   27. b   28. c   29. c
30. b

Hotline

31. a   32. b   33. a   34. a   35. a

Unit 6 Review Chapters 19-21

LEVEL I

1. b   2. b   3. b   4. a   5. b   6. a   7. b   8. a   9. b
10. b   11. a   12. b

LEVEL II

13. b   14. a   15. a   16. a   17. b   18. a   19. a   20. b
21. a   22. a   23. b   24. c

LEVEL III

25. a   26. b   27. b   28. b   29. a   30. a   31. b   32. b
33. b   34. a   35. b   36. a   37. b   38. a

Index